Time Series Analysis for the Social Sc

Time series or longitudinal data are ubiquitous in the
often treat the time series properties of their data as a
meaningful dynamic process to be modeled and in
Social Sciences provides accessible, up-to-date instruc........ ....p.... ...
in time series econometrics. Janet M. Box-Steffensmeier, John R. Freeman, Matthew P. Hitt,
and Jon C. W. Pevehouse cover a wide range of topics, including ARIMA models, time
series regression, unit root diagnosis, vector autoregressive models, error correction models,
intervention models, fractional integration, ARCH models, structural breaks, and forecasting. This book is aimed at researchers and graduate students who have taken at least one
course in multivariate regression. Examples are drawn from several areas of social science,
including political behavior, elections, international conflict, criminology, and comparative
political economy.

Janet M. Box-Steffensmeier is the Vernal Riffe Professor of Political Science and Professor of
Sociology at The Ohio State University (courtesy), where she is a University Distinguished
Scholar and directs the Program in Statistics and Methodology (PRISM). Box-Steffensmeier
served as president of the Midwest Political Science Association and the Political Methodology Society and as treasurer of the American Political Science Association. She has twice
received the Gosnell Prize for the best work in political methodology, and she received the
Emerging Scholar Award from the Elections, Public Opinion, and Voting Behavior Subsection of the American Political Science Association and the Career Achievement Award from
the Political Methodology Society. She was an inaugural Fellow of the Society for Political Methodology. The Box-Steffensmeier Graduate Student Award, given annually by the
Interuniversity Consortium for Political and Social Research (ICPSR), is named after her in
recognition of her contributions to political methodology and her support of women in this
field.

John R. Freeman is the John Black Johnston Distinguished Professor in the College of Liberal
Arts at the University of Minnesota and a Fellow of the American Academy of Arts and
Sciences. Among his honors are the Morse-Alumni, All-University, and College of Liberal
Arts Distinguished Teaching awards at the University of Minnesota. Freeman is the author
of *Democracy and Markets: The Politics of Mixed Economies*, which won the International
Studies Association's Quincy Wright Award, and the coauthor of *Three Way Street: Strategic
Reciprocity in World Politics*. Freeman also edited three volumes of *Political Analysis*. He has
(co)authored numerous research articles in academic journals. Freeman's research projects
have been supported by the National Science Foundation, as well as by the Bank Austria
Foundation and the Austrian Ministry of Science.

Matthew P. Hitt is an assistant professor of political science at Louisiana State University.
His interests include judicial politics, legislative politics, interest groups, the presidency, and
quantitative methodology. His research has been published in the *American Political Science
Review* and *Presidential Studies Quarterly*.

Jon C. W. Pevehouse is a professor of political science at the University of Wisconsin. His
work examines the relationship between domestic and international politics. Pevehouse is the
author of *Democracy from Above* (Cambridge University Press, 2005) and *While Dangers
Gather* (2007). He is the coauthor, with Joshua Goldstein, of *International Relations*, the
leading textbook on international politics. He is the recipient of the Karl Deutch Award,
given by the International Studies Association, and has received numerous teaching awards,
including the Chancellor's Distinguished Teaching Award at the University of Wisconsin.
Pevehouse is also the editor of the journal *International Organization*.

Analytical Methods for Social Research

Analytical Methods for Social Research presents texts on empirical and formal methods for the social sciences. Volumes in the series address both the theoretical underpinnings of analytical techniques as well as their application in social research. Some series volumes are broad in scope, cutting across a number of disciplines. Others focus mainly on methodological applications within specific fields such as political science, sociology, demography, and public health. The series serves a mix of students and researchers in the social sciences and statistics.

Series Editors:
R. Michael Alvarez, California Institute of Technology
Nathaniel L. Beck, New York University
Stephen L. Morgan, Johns Hopkins University
Lawrence L. Wu, New York University

Other Titles in the Series:

Time Series Analysis for the Social Sciences

JANET M. BOX-STEFFENSMEIER
The Ohio State University

JOHN R. FREEMAN
University of Minnesota

MATTHEW P. HITT
Louisiana State University

JON C. W. PEVEHOUSE
University of Wisconsin, Madison

CAMBRIDGE
UNIVERSITY PRESS

CAMBRIDGE
UNIVERSITY PRESS

32 Avenue of the Americas, New York, NY 10013-2473, USA

Cambridge University Press is part of the University of Cambridge.

It furthers the University's mission by disseminating knowledge in the pursuit of
education, learning, and research at the highest international levels of excellence.

www.cambridge.org
Information on this title: www.cambridge.org/9780521691550

First published 2014

Printed in the United States of America

A catalog record for this publication is available from the British Library.

Library of Congress Cataloging in Publication Data
Box-Steffensmeier, Janet M., 1965–
Time series analysis for the social sciences / Janet M. Box-Steffensmeier, The Ohio State University,
John R. Freeman, University of Minnesota, Matthew P. Hitt, Louisiana State University,
Jon C. W. Pevehouse, University of Wisconsin Madison.
    pages   cm. – (Analytical methods for social research)
Includes index.
ISBN 978-0-521-87116-7 (hardback) – ISBN 978-0-521-69155-0 (paperback)
1. Time-series analysis.   2. Time-series analysis – Mathematical models.   I. Title.
HA30.3.B69   2014
300.1′51955–dc23   2014010088

ISBN 978-0-521-87116-7 Hardback
ISBN 978-0-521-69155-0 Paperback

All that really belongs to us is time; even he who has nothing else has that.

Balthasar Gracian

This book is dedicated to our families, who make time so valuable.

To Mike, Andrew, Zach, Nate, and Lizzy from Jan
To Tom from John
To Jen, Theodore, Shelley, and Larry from Matt
To Jessica, Claire, Ava, and Carl from Jon

Contents

Preface

Our work has several motivations. We think that longitudinal analysis provides infinitely more insight than does examining any one slice of time. As we show throughout the book, longitudinal analysis is essential for the study of normatively important problems such as democratic accountability and international conflict. Given the importance of dynamic analysis in answering new questions and providing new answers to old questions, we want to get more social scientists thinking in dynamic terms. Time series is one of the most useful tools for dynamic analysis, and our goal is to provide a more accessible treatment for this approach. We are also motivated by the burgeoning supply of new social science time series data. Sometimes this causes the opposite problem of too much data and figuring out how to analyze it, but that is a problem we gladly embrace. The proliferation of new social science data requires techniques that are designed to handle complexity, and time series analysis is one of the most applicable tools. The incorporation of time series analysis into standard statistical packages such as STATA and R, as well as the existence of specialized packages such as RATS and Eviews, provides an additional motivation because it enables more scholars to easily use time series in their work.

We have found over our years of teaching time series that, although many social science students have the brain power to learn time series methods, they often lack the training and motivation to use the most well-known books on the topic. We specifically wanted to write an accessible book for social scientists so that they too could leverage the power of time series analysis from the introductory material to current innovations. That said, we are not able to offer complete coverage. We do not address dynamic panel data analysis, Bayesian time series analysis, spectral analysis, or the event history approach to temporal data. We hope the foundation and discussion of recent advances we do provide result in a useful reference book for scholars.

Chapter 1 provides an intuitive motivation for the study of time series and social dynamics. Important issues such as measurement, fit and scale, and structural change are introduced here. Chapter 2 focuses on univariate models, which are important because we argue that understanding the nature of the data-generating process should be the first step in the data analysis process. Chapter 3 provides a discussion of conventional time series regression methods, in particular the workhorse model in which a single lag of the endogenous variable is included on the right side of a single regression equation. In contrast, Chapter 4 explores the specification, estimation, and interpretation of familiar multiequation regression models with strong restrictions, simultaneous structural equation models, and also weakly restricted multiequation dynamic models – vector autoregressions – that allow uncertainty about the specification. The chapter highlights the differences between the approaches. Chapter 5 introduces the concept of stationarity and discusses its methodological and substantive importance. Chapter 6 discusses cointegration, which is a cornerstone of current time series analysis. Cointegration is especially useful for studying equilibrium relationships. Chapter 7 concludes with discussions of four critical concepts in current time series analysis: fractional integration, heterogeneity, unknown structural break(s), and forecasting. The Appendix covers difference equations. This is a foundational concept needed for understanding the mathematical foundation of common time series approaches, such as vector autoregression. Although readers interested in directly estimating models without mathematical preliminaries may skip the Appendix, we strongly encourage readers interested in working in time series methodology to read it closely.

We have had the privilege of team-teaching time series together for about 15 years. John, an award-winning teacher (we think he has won every teaching award possible), graciously offered to team-teach with Jan; this was made possible by the innovation pioneered by Phil Shively and Pete Nardulli, the cross-campus interactive television (I.T.V.) program. We welcomed Jon to the team shortly after he finished graduate school. Indeed, he had been a student in the first iteration of the course, and later, while still in graduate school, he wrapped up a time series course for Jan when her third child was seriously ill. Team-teaching time series for the three of us is a biennial occurrence that does not come frequently enough for us, but is thoroughly enjoyed each time the occasion arises. Matt Hitt was a student in the course who later became a valuable collaborator who pushed the book to completion.

We have a long list of thank you's to our home departments, the I.T.V. program, and our many students. Brandon Bartels, Quintin Beazer, Patrick Brandt, Harold Clarke, Dave Darmofal, Suzie DeBoef, Charles Franklin, Jeff Gill, Tobin Grant, Agnar Helgason, Mel Hinich, Tana Johnson, Ben Jones, Luke Keele, Paul Kellstedt, Matt Lebo, Tse-Min Lin, Eleonora Mattiacci, Sara Mitchell, Jason Morgan, Dave Ohls, Heather Ondercin, Erica Owen, Dave

Peterson, Eve Ringsmuth, Darrell Steffensmeier, Anand Sokhey, Jim Stimson, Mark Toukan, Felicity Vabulas, Eve Van Sice, Herb Weisberg, Dan Wood, and especially Ben Jones and Corwin Smidt. In addition, we are grateful for the guidance and encouragement of the series editors, Mike Alvarez and Neal Beck, and the Cambridge editors, Ed Parsons and Lew Bateman.

1

Modeling Social Dynamics

Many social processes are best understood in terms of changes over time. Current social conditions are outgrowths of people's memories of past conditions and, sometimes, also of people's expectations about future conditions. Social processes are rarely, if ever, at rest. Rather they are moving in time, trending in a regular way or exhibiting patterns that recur in time. Understanding the causal relationships between social variables across time and the forces that drive these variables through time is essential to explaining and forecasting social processes. We call these relationships and forces social dynamics. Time series methods are a powerful means by which to analyze these dynamics. In his essay on the history of time series, Tsay (2002, 121) emphasizes that studies of dynamic structures and dynamic relationships between variables have played a vital role in the development of the field, especially through applications in business and economics.

Many important social problems are conceived in terms of dynamics. Indeed, a broad array of questions across the social sciences cannot be addressed without utilizing data comprised of measurements of variables over time. The substantive bite of many empirical findings from the social world comes not from knowing the static level of an important variable at one frozen moment, but rather from understanding the dynamics of that variable. For instance: Is not is the phenomenon of interest rising? Falling? Repeating a pattern seasonally? Drifting randomly? Reverting to a stable value that we can forecast? And how do the dynamics in the phenomenon relate and react to the dynamics in other phenomena? Substantively meaningful answers to questions of this sort require that we conceive our data as a dynamic process and utilize techniques such as those we present in this book.

Moving beyond the abstract, what sorts of phenomena can be conceptualized and studied under the framework we promote here? Consider economic

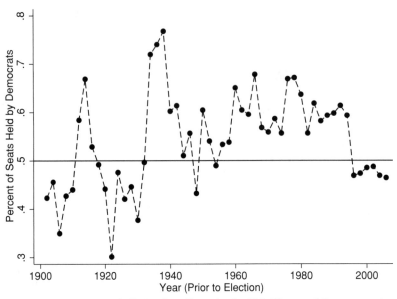

FIGURE 1.1. Democratic Party Seat Share in the U.S. House of Representatives, 1990–2004. Compiled by the authors from data supplied by the Clerk of the House of Representatives.

performance indicators such as unemployment, inflation, or gross domestic product. As both independent and dependent variables, they are integral to empirical analysis in many disciplines, including economics and political science. Measurements of aggregate fertility, obesity, smoking prevalence, and mortality over time are of keen interest in population studies and public health. In the field of education, fundamental data such as rates of literacy, graduation, and dropouts can all be well conceptualized as dynamic processes. A sophisticated understanding of the complex dynamic processes undergirding the rates of various crimes, incarceration, and recidivism is nothing short of foundational to the field of criminology. Adolescent fertility and drug use rates, along with rates of suicide and interpersonal violence across time, are all dynamic processes of great interest in sociology. These are, of course, but a few examples. The point is that, across the social sciences, some of our most interesting and fundamental empirical questions can be best addressed by properly understanding that our data are composed of dynamic processes and then modeling them as such.

What do data composed of dynamic processes look like in practice? We now turn to several illustrations of interesting time series data from a variety of fields. To begin, an important idea in political science is that of representation in democracies. Among other things, this concept implies a recurring alternation of power between contending groups. Consider, for example, Figure 1.1, which shows the balance of power in the U.S. House of Representatives over the

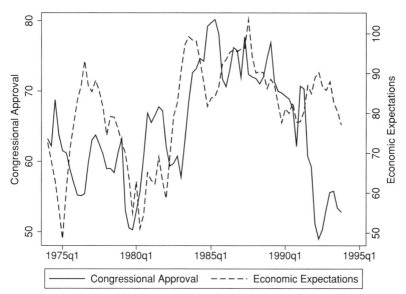

FIGURE 1.2. Congressional Approval and Economic Expectations in the U.S., 1974q1–1993q4. Compiled by the authors from replication data on website of Christina Wolbrecht (Durr, Gilmour, and Wolbrecht, 1997).

previous century.[1] The data are proportions of the seats held by the Democratic Party in the House ordered over time. Do the workings of our institutions produce regular shifts in the balance of power between the Republicans and Democrats? Is there a pattern of alternating control over time? The figure suggests that there might be, but the timing between changes in partisan control is not clear. There was a prolonged period of Democratic control in the middle of the century, but then power shifted to the Republicans. So conceivably there are recurring alterations of power between competing groups, but only over long periods of time. Time series methods help us characterize this process of representation and predict its behavior. We discuss methods for modeling and forecasting from a univariate time series like that in Figure 1.1 in Chapters 2, 5, and 7.

Patterns of political accountability, a concept closely related to representation, provide shorter term insights into this subject. Figure 1.2 shows time series for the proportion of citizens who approve of Congress in each quarter from the beginning of 1974 to the end of 1993. It also depicts the proportion of respondents who have positive expectations about the economy in the same time period. The two series appear to move together, suggesting that the public dispenses approval on the basis of how it evaluates economic policy. If so, the

---

[1] We denote annual time series by the first and last year of the series, for instance, 1985–1993. We denote quarterly data by the year and quarter, e.g., 1995q1 (see Figure 1.2 above). Monthly time series are denoted by the year and month of the observation, for example, 1997:5–2006:9. Data and STATA replication code for all figures and tables in this book are available at www.politicalscience.osu.edu/faculty/jbox/tsass.

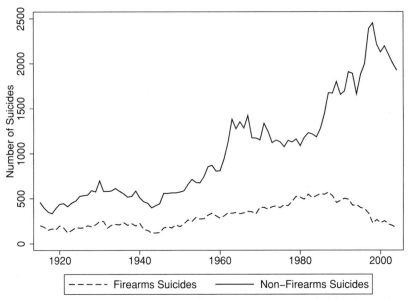

FIGURE 1.3. Suicide Deaths in Australia, 1914–2004. Compiled by the authors from replication data on website of Andrew Leigh (Neill and Leigh, 2008).

data indicates that Congress is held accountable for its policies. But what exactly is the nature of this relationship? Are the evaluations of the economy temporally prior to changes in representation? Is the effect immediate or lagged? Time series methods, such as those we discuss in Chapters 3, 4, and 6, enable us to describe exactly how these variables trend together.

Let us turn to a different field: since the pioneering work of one of the discipline's founding thinkers, Emile Durkheim, sociologists have studied the question of suicide. In very broad strokes, some sociologists study questions such as the following: What are the different types of suicidal behavior? What, if anything, can (or should) governments do to discourage people from committing suicide? Figure 1.3 shows deaths from firearms and non-firearms suicides in Australia from 1915–2004, first collected and analyzed by Neill and Leigh (2010). Non-firearms suicides seem to spike in the 1960s and again in the 1990s, whereas firearms suicides seem to decline in the mid-1990s. After several mass killings, the Australian government implemented a massive firearms buyback program in 1997 to reduce the number of guns in circulation in Australia. Did this program reduce the amount of suicides by firearms in Australia? Using time series intervention models (discussed in Chapter 2), and endogenous structural break models (discussed in Chapter 7), analysts can explore this and other similar questions.[2]

---

[2] For more on the sociology of suicide, Wray, Colen, and Pescosolido (2011) provide an excellent overview covering research predating Durkheim to modern times. Interested readers are

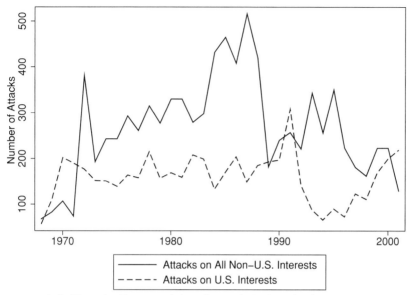

FIGURE 1.4. Terrorist Events and Attacks on the U.S. and other interests, 1968–2003. Reprinted with permission of Elsevier under STM guidelines (Sandler and Enders, 2004).

A different social problem stemming from the field of international relations is terrorism. Figure 1.4 charts the number of terrorist attacks on the United States and on other countries between 1968 and 2003.[3] The two series tend to move in opposite directions between the mid-1980s and mid-1990s. But, in the 1970s and early 1980s as well as in the late 1990s to 2003, the two series often move in the same direction. In addition, the surge in attacks on U.S. interests in 1991 (308) appears to be a precursor to the surge in attacks on other countries in 1993 (343) and 1995 (340). In contrast, the surge in attacks on other countries in 1999 (226) and 2000 (226) seems to foreshadow the surge in attacks on the United States in 2001 (219).[4] Are these series, in fact, related? If so what is the nature of this relationship? More importantly, if we can model this relationship could we use it to forecast and even prevent terrorist attacks? We discuss forecasting as used in the field of time series in Chapter 7.[5]

---

also referred to O'Brien and Stockard (2006), who utilize a technique (SUR) for time series data we cover in the online appendix to this book (available at www.politicalscience.osu.edu/faculty/jbox/tsass).

[3] Data taken from Sandler and Enders (2004).

[4] Time series data on terrorism now are published regularly by government agencies such as the State Department. See, for example, Sabasteanski (2005). An example of a website on terrorist activity is that of START, www.start.umd.edu/data/gtd/.

[5] For a review of the literature on forecasting in international relations see Brandt, Freeman, and Schrodt (2011).

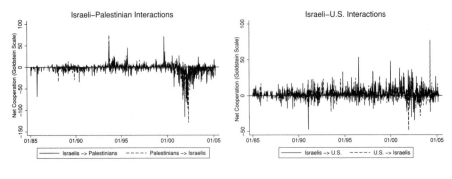

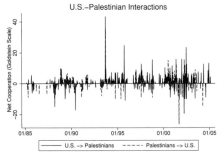

FIGURE 1.5. Israeli-Palestinian-American Relations. Compiled by authors from event data produced by Kansas Event Data System.

Finally, the top-left panel in Figure 1.5 is a representation of relations between the Israelis and Palestinians, which obviously have enormous implications for international politics. The data are based on events data coded to capture the day-to-day interactions of actors in the Levant. This panel shows that the amount of cooperation and conflict in the directed behavior of the two toward each other ordered in time. Events data such as these are based on content analysis and, in recent years, on automated text parsing. Events are extracted from newspaper text and then coded into particular kinds of directed behavior. Each such behavior is given a numerical value indicating the level of cooperation or hostility between the parties.[6]

The density of these data is much greater than that on which Figures 1.1–1.4 are based. This makes it difficult to discern trends and relationships. But, clearly there were short periods of cooperation between the Palestinians and Israelis in and around 1994, 1995, and 1999, as well as periods of marked conflict in 1985 and especially in 2001–2002. These two time series suggest that a complex social dynamic exists between the Israelis and Palestinians. For instance, at times they reciprocate each other's behavior, and at other times they do not: neither a stable relationship nor one that connotes a common

---

[6] For an overview of this kind of data see Monroe and Schrodt (2008). See also Schrodt (1994) and Merritt, Muncaster, and Zinnes (1993).

trend in behavior appears. Does this mean there is no basis for the evolution of cooperation between the Israelis and Palestinians? Despite the lack of a consistent pattern, like many international actors – ranging from the great powers, to international organizations, to peace organizations – we would like to be able to forecast Israeli-Palestinian relations and perhaps even design foreign policy interventions to help resolve areas of conflict. On the basis of the pattern in the top panel of Figure 1.5, what is the best forecast of relations between these two parties? With respect to an intervention, many observers think that the United States has a role to play. The middle and bottom panels in Figure 1.5 show how the United States acts toward and responds to the Israelis and Palestinians. How are the six time series in the figure related? Do the patterns in Figure 1.5 reveal the potential for mediation by the United States?

Studies of social dynamics such as those illustrated in Figures 1.1–1.5 involve a "process orientation" or an appreciation of how social variables both are composed of trends and cycles and are governed by relationships that evolve over time. Reconsider Figures 1.1 and 1.2. Someone who studied the period between the Great Depression and Reagan presidency might have warned of the capture of American institutions by the Democratic Party (Sprague 1981). But, in fact, the series shows that the Democrats eventually lost control of the House, so such a warning would have been premature.[7] Regarding Figure 1.2, suppose that one researcher studied the question of political accountability in the period between 1975 and 1979 while another analyzed the 1982–1984 period. The two scholars would reach very different conclusions. The former would infer there was no relationship between the two series, whereas the latter would conclude there was a positive relation between them. In all likelihood neither researcher would detect the possibility that the two series move together. Progress in the study of political accountability would suffer as a result.

A process orientation also is required for forecasting. Consider the Israeli-Palestinian conflict. As we will learn, forecasts based on simple extrapolations of time series such as those in the top-left panel of Figure 1.5 are unlikely to be accurate. Nor do such extrapolations provide meaningful ways to evaluate the possible effects of third party intervention. Even rigorous forecasts are often criticized for what is called the off-on-time problem. That is, these forecasts can only tell policy makers that a certain decision is likely to be made, *not when this decision will be made*.[8]

To make sound causal inferences and forecasts we require statistical tools of various kinds, which help us discover short, medium, and long term trends in

---

[7] Although he provides some data for the first seven decades of the 20th century, Sprague (1981) focuses on the period between 1930 and 1970. He suggests that in this particular era there is a stable level of Democratic control towards which the political system moves; he calls this level the "system telos."

[8] As an example of such forecasting, such as the expected utility model, see Bueno de Mesquita (1997, 264) and Organski (2000, 350).

our variables, as well as the causal relationships between them. We will learn
how to use these tools in this book.

1.1 TIME SERIES ANALYSIS

Time series analysis explains the temporal dependencies within and between
social processes. By temporal dependency *within* a social process, we mean
that the current value of a variable is in part a function of previous values of
that same variable. Temporal dependency *between* social processes, conversely,
means that the current value of a variable is in part a function of previous values
of both other variables and of that same variable. Time series analysis presumes
that univariate and multivariate social systems are composed of short, medium,
and long term processes of these dependencies, sometimes all at once.

Sorting out (decomposing) these different components of social processes is
one of the primary objectives of time series analysis. In this way, it emphasizes
the ordering of social behaviors over time. Because of its process orientation,
time series analysis resists methods that treat slices of time as independent from
one another especially within the same unit of study.[9] It traces the history of
variables over time. In doing so, various modeling goals of time series analysis
become clear. These include studying the dynamic structure of the series, investigating dynamic relationships, improving regression analysis when errors are
serially correlated, and producing forecasts (Tsay, 2002).

Time series analysts test theories about social dynamics. Competing causal
claims about the temporal composition of processes of representation, terrorism, suicide, crime, economic activity, and civil strife are some of what time
series analysts evaluate. Hypotheses about causal relationships between the
variables *in time* are what analysts test. Time series analysts eschew methods
that chop time into slices and treat the resulting observations as independent.
Instead, they consider that, for instance, we should be able to know more
about the economic activity of a country in 2012 if we account for its level
of economic activity in 2011, rather than treating economic activity in 2012
as an isolated data point. Time series analysis is a powerful approach in part
because it treats these dynamics inherent in social processes as phenomena to
be modeled and understood instead of as nuisances to be corrected or, worse,
ignored.[10]

---

[9] While they are closely related, time series analysis and event history analysis are different forms
of inquiry. In contrast to time series analysis, event history analyzes whether and how long it
takes for events to occur (if at all). Event history can be thought of as extending discrete time
models to consider time. That is, it is not only the study of whether or not an event occurs,
which could be modeled with a logit or probit model, but when those events occur as well. The
dependent variable in event history analysis is *duration* – how long until the event of interest
occurs (Box-Steffensmeier and Jones, 2004).

[10] Time series analysis is also related to, but is distinct from, panel methods. In panel data observations are cross sections of some units (e.g., individuals, countries, states, firms) over multiple

The idea of social equilibrium is at the heart of time series analysis. As we will learn, time series analysts have well-developed concepts of fixed and moving equilibria. When social systems are at rest or in stable equilibrium we say they are static. Mathematical modeling of social systems often produces results about comparative statics or contrasting features of systems at rest. The contributions of much of rational choice theory are illustrative in this regard. A system in equilibrium is in a "steady state." That is, it settles to a certain value in the long run (fixed equilibria), or oscillates between a set of values in the long run (moving equilibria). Using the tools in this book, we can identify the equilibria of social processes, capturing their long-term temporal dynamics.

In all branches of social science, knowing these equilibria allows us to predict how systems will behave. The case of the U.S. House of Representatives is illustrative. If we can find the moving equilibrium that characterizes the alternation of power in that body, we can predict long-term swings in Democratic (Republican) Party control.[11]

In addition, time series analysis gives us insights into social systems' behaviors when they are *not* in equilibrium or are in their *out-of-equilibrium* paths. With time series methods, we can derive the paths variables will take from their initial levels to equilibria and/or how variables will return to their equilibria after the respective social system experiences a surprise one-time or repeated series of increases or decreases ("shocks") in a particular variable. On this basis we then can evaluate theoretical counterfactuals of various kinds. An example with respect to political accountability, shown in Figure 1.2, would be modeling the effect that a hypothetical, surprise, one-time surge of positive economic expectations would have on the time path of U.S. Congressional approval.

1.1.1 Contending Approaches and the Quasi-Experimental Tradition

Generally speaking, time series analysts take three approaches to model building. When they are confident they know that some variables are exogenous to others and also how long the delays are in the effects of these independent variables on their dependent variables, time series analysts use extensions of familiar time series regression methods to analyze social processes. The regression equations they employ thus are "strongly restricted." Scholars who use

time periods. Panel data, in a broad sense, refer to any data spanning multiple dimensions, usually, but not necessarily, time and space. Typically the N's (number of units) are larger than the T's (time periods). If T is "short" (that is, less than 40–50), panel data methods are more likely to be used than time series methods. See, for instance, Wawro (2002).

[11] Political scientists, sociologists, and other scholars have well-developed ideas of equilibrium. But most of these ideas are static in nature. Evolutionary game theory offers more dynamic notions of equilibrium (Samuelson, 1997; Young, 1993), but this branch of game theory is only beginning to be applied in these disciplines. For applications in political science see (Mebane, 2000, 2005).

these models emphasize the magnitudes of the effects of changes in independent variables on dependent variables. On the basis of analysis of the time series data in Figure 1.2, for instance, they produce results about exactly how large an increase in congressional approval would be produced in the short and long term by a one percentage point increase in economic expectations.

When they are less certain about the specification of their equations, time series scholars employ reduced form or "weakly restricted" models. Theory always informs the choice of variables in this kind of model. The reduced form is treated as a representation of what is an unknown, structural model. These modelers are willing to trade off quantitative precision for sounder inferences about the existence and direction of relationships. They emphasize the results of what are called Granger causality tests and the pattern of responses of their equation systems to hypothetical shocks in selected variables (impulse response functions), a method we discuss in Chapter 4.

Last, there is a quasi-experimental tradition in time series analysis. Some scholars who study social dynamics induce the functional forms of their models from their data. They devote their energy to characterizing the data-generating process (DGP) that gave rise to their data and to illuminating facts about the temporal composition and dynamic responses of variables in social systems. These efforts are theoretically informed in their choice of variables and in scholars' interpretations of their results. These results provide empirical challenges for theorists because the results must be explained by contending theories.

Our own approach utilizes each of these schools of thought. Throughout this book, we give examples of each, discussing the tradeoffs found in adopting one approach over another.

1.1.2 The Architecture of the Book

The structure of the book is as follows: The Appendix explains the calculus of finite differences, the key branch of mathematics on which much of time series analysis is based. In it, we explain in detail the idea of social equilibration and the different forms that equilibration might take. We show how political representation and other ideas from the social sciences are captured by these conceptions of equilibrium. Readers interested in working in time series methodology or the mathematical foundations for the rest of the book are strongly encouraged to read the Appendix before beginning Chapter 2. Chapter 2 introduces a particular statistical model that decomposes single time series into certain types of social memory: the autoregressive, moving average (ARMA) model. We use this univariate model to analyze homicides in the United States and Middle East politics. We then proceed in Chapters 3 and 4 to study multivariate models. Chapter 3 reviews single equation time series regression models. Again, readers may wish to consult the Appendix to better comprehend both the nature of the error processes for regression models and the implications of the functional forms of these models. Chapter 4 studies multiequation time series regression models. It covers both strongly restricted, structural equation (time series regression) and weakly restricted vector autoregressive (VAR) models. We show how both strongly and weakly restricted models of several social processes, including European monetary policy, can be constructed and used.

Chapter 5 discusses testing for nonstationarity in univariate time series. Building on the framework of nonstationarity, models that capture stochastic trends in social data and also relationships between long-memoried series – random walk and error correction models (ECMs) – are the subject of Chapters 5 and 6. In Chapter 5, for example, we show how to model the political accountability suggested in Figure 1.2. In Chapter 6, we examine defense spending of India and Pakistan as an error correction process. Social forecasts based on univariate ARMA and weakly restricted multivariate, VAR models are discussed in Chapter 7. In it, we consider both how forecasting can be used to evaluate theories (ex post) and to make the kind of practical contribution that international peace organizations aspire to for the Middle East and other regions of the world (ex ante). Several other advanced topics are considered in Chapter 7 including a a brief introduction to incorporating heterogeneity, fractional integration, and testing for structural break(s).

In the remainder of this introduction, we briefly review some of the general challenges that confront the time series analyst. These challenges, which are related to the collection and measurement of time series data, along with some modeling concerns that are not specific to any particular model, are helpful to consider before estimating any of the models to follow in later chapters. Some of these problems are unique to the time series context, whereas others are more general, but all are helpful to review before engaging in any statistical modeling exercise.

1.2 CHALLENGES IN TIME SERIES MODELING

1.2.1 Time Series Measurement

The first thing an analyst requires is, of course, data to analyze. Lengthy time series increasingly are available for a host of social issues. This includes time series with high densities of coverage such as the events data for the Israeli-Palestinian conflict in Figure 1.5.[12]

---

[12] Historically, one of the oldest time series is the Beveridge Wheat Price Index. It covers the period from 1500 to 1869. An important source of historical time series is Playfair's *The Commercial and Political Atlas*. Playfair's book contains economic series for Britain in the 1700s. Also, Mitchell's *International Historical Statistics* series, contains data from 1750–2005 for many regions of the world. New sources of time series data appear regularly. An example is the Cambridge University Press's *Historical Statistics of the United States*; see http://www.cambrdge.org/us/americanhistory/hsus. Again, the website for this book contains the time series for the illustrations in the first part of this chapter as well as references to many other social time series and related websites.

As in all social science endeavors, periodically, measurement errors in data are found and corrected. Also, the definitions of variables change and therefore new series are published. Hence researchers must monitor the sources from which their data are gathered. For instance, in 1995 the Bureau of Economic Analysis (BEA) changed the definition of the U.S. real gross domestic product, a key variable in political and economic analyses. For a summary of the history of this and other key economic variables see Robertson and Tallman (1998).[13]

We next discuss other practical measurement issues that apply to time series analysis.

Data Vintaging

As Figure 1.2 suggests, many social scientists advance theories based, in part, on economic variables. Unfortunately, some economic variables are published in a way that presents serious conceptual challenges. In particular, at any given time, government agencies regularly publish what are only preliminary estimates of key variables such as real gross domestic product and industrial production and, simultaneously, update recent estimates of the same variables. In other words, recent vintages of these series are always in flux. The current values are only estimates, and for a while, these estimates are repeatedly updated. Robertson and Tallman (1998, fn. 1) write, "A data series vintage or 'age' is denoted by the month in which the entire series existed–when that specific set of numbers was available as data." These authors give numerous examples of how a whole set of recent estimates of variables such as real GDP change with each quarterly publication of the BEA's statistics.

For these reasons, a time series analyst who employs the most current estimates of economic variables needs to distinguish between "pseudo real time" and "real time." The former applies to final estimates of variables, estimates that are not available to either the analyst or human agents in real time. The final estimates are available only later. "Real time" connotes the estimates that are actually available on a given date; some of these may be only preliminary estimates. So, for instance, someone who today is studying the impact of unemployment on crime in the 1950–2005 period and uses the final estimates of the respective variables is working in pseudo real time. She might use ex post forecasting to evaluate the explanatory power of her model in the 2005–2010 period, employing the final estimates for those five additional years. In these cases, she is presuming that the human behavior is determined by the actual levels of variables, rather than by the published information about these levels at the respective times. Another analyst who uses real GDP growth to predict presidential approval in the post–World War II era must be sensitive to the fact that the most recent estimates in his economic series are preliminary and under revision. In his explanation he must address the status of these data of

---

[13] A useful review of real time data and related econometric issues for the United Kingdom is Garratt and Vahey (2006).

more recent vintage: whether citizens dispense approval on the basis of published *preliminary* estimates of real GDP or whether citizens somehow correct these preliminary estimates before dispensing their evaluation of the president. Similarly, if this second scholar wants to formulate a theory based on citizens' anticipation of future presidential performance, he must explain citizens' real-time expectations. He must describe how citizens use preliminary estimates of real GDP and other variables to make forecasts of how the president will perform in future years (and then also evaluate those forecasts with what will be in the preliminary estimates of relevant economic variables). Presumably, the president also cares about the real-time forecasts on which his approval ratings are based, and thus he must also take vintaging into account.

In sum, social scientists who use economic and other time series must be aware of their vintage and, concomitantly, of the conceptual challenges this vintaging creates for their theories and forecasts. We return to these points in Chapter 5.

Systematic Sampling and Temporal Aggregation

At any given instant, there are levels of civil conflict, terrorism, and governmental approval. In practice, however, we do not measure these variables continuously. Rather, we sample the levels – usually, but not always – at regular intervals. Even when variables such as the level of partisan control of the House of Representatives only exist at discrete intervals, we sometimes sample a subset of them. This practice is called systematic sampling.

Consider the data in the top panel of Figure 1.6. These data are drawn from the Uniform Crime Reports, which are well known to criminologists. The top panel shows the monthly estimates of total homicides, 1975–1993, and the bottom panel shows the annual total homicides per 100,000 persons in the United States in the 1960–2011 period. For the year 1991 the actual monthly values starting with January are 1,827, 1,592, 1,834, 1,785, 1,853, 2,035, 2,080, 2,111, 2,040, 1,939, 1,760, and 2,955. Say we depicted the quarterly homicide levels in 1991 and that we used the *last monthly value in each quarter* as our estimates (the levels in March, June, September, and December). Then our systematic sample would be 1,834, 2,035, 2,040, and 2,955. If we sampled annually and used the December value, our measure for the year 1991 would be simply 2,955. But clearly, by doing that we are losing information. The best illustration for this is that the yearly estimate of 2,955 the largest value in the entire sample. It therefore is unrepresentative both of 1991 and of the series as a whole.

The problem of data selection and measurement is also exemplified by comparing the top and bottom panels of Figure 1.6. Note that the top panel (where the data are cut off in 1993) would seem to suggest that violent crime is on a steady upward trend. But if we extend the series out to 2011 (the bottom panel), it becomes clear that the number of homicides then is nowhere near the peak of the early 1990s; our inferences about the trend in violent crime in

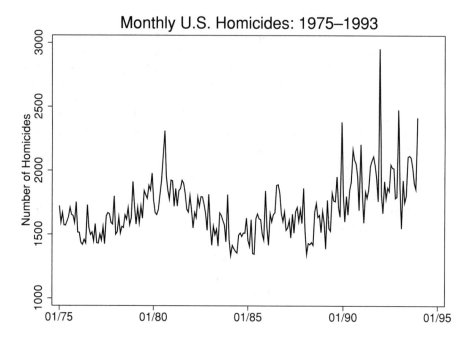

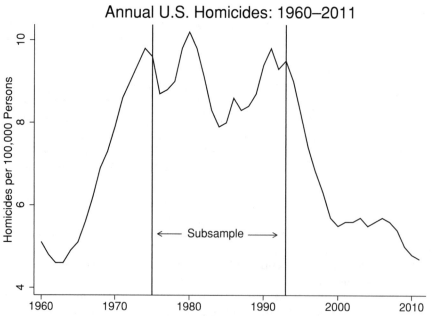

FIGURE 1.6. U.S. Homicide Data: Two Samples. Compiled by authors from FBI Uniform Crime Reports.

the United States change dramatically depending on which window of data we study.[14]

The Uniform Crime Reports are oriented toward an annual report. Some cities report their data monthly, others do so quarterly, and still others annually. For an annual analysis this issue is nonproblematic, but monthly disaggregation of the UCR series may be undesirable for many purposes.[15] Some cities "catch up" with their data by reporting everything in December, which may explain the outlier result, although increased social interaction around the holidays also may provide greater opportunities for violent interactions. The broader point is that many time series are aggregations of multiple official sources. As such, if the method of data collection/reporting/sampling varies among the sources that produce the aggregated series, these differences can have profound implications for our inferences. Even, when we do not have concerns about aggregation from many disparate sources, information losses in aggregating up from daily to monthly or yearly time series data can also be profound. We now turn to these challenges.

Systematic sampling is illustrated in Figure 1.7. This figure shows presidential approval levels in the second Clinton administration and in the presidency of George W. Bush. The point at which Bush succeeded Clinton is indicated by a vertical line in roughly the middle of each panel. The top left panel displays all the polls from the Gallup-CNN/USA Today in this period. The other panels represent different systematic samplings – the approval levels at the end of months, end of quarters, and end of years. Note that as the sampling interval becomes wider and wider, the original pattern in the top left panel of the figure is obscured. The wider sampling smooths the series and makes the unusual surge in approval of Bush in the fall of 2001 less and less evident. In this way, information loss is more severe in the bottom two panels.

"Temporal aggregation" is the practice of summing or averaging the values of series over a regular interval. Return to the homicide example in Figure 1.6. One way to aggregate temporally these data is to average the values for the three months in each quarter. This would produce the following quarterly estimates for 1991: 1,751, 1,891, 2,077, and 2,218. Notice that, in comparison with the quarterly estimates based on the systematic sampling in the last month of the quarter, these temporally aggregated estimates suggest a much smoother upward trend. The average of the twelve monthly levels is 1,984, which is very different from the systematically sampled estimate based on the December value alone of 2,955. Once more, the point is that time series measurement can discard information, thus leading to mistaken inference about the properties of a time series.

---

[14] Steffensmeier et al. (2011) discuss the trends (and lack thereof) in the homicide time series in detail.

[15] Our aim here in presenting the monthly series is pedagogical. Although the monthly data are imperfect, they do have pedagogically desirable properties that would be lost in using the annualized data.

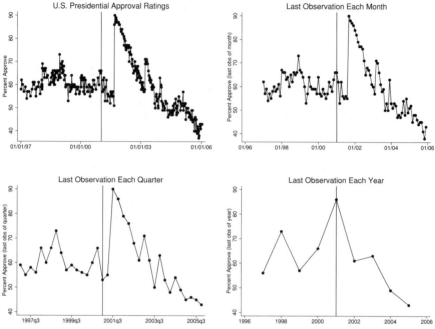

FIGURE 1.7. Presidents Clinton's and G.W. Bush's Approval Ratings, Systematically Sampled. Compiled by the authors from Gallup Polls and from CNN/USToday/Gallup.

The problem of temporal aggregation is illustrated again in bivariate analysis in Figure 1.8 where we sum the event scores (Goldstein weights) for conflict and cooperation for the United States and China by days, months, and years. As they become more temporally aggregated, the data become smoother and the original (daily) pattern is altered. In this case, the information loss produces what appears to be long swings in U.S.-Chinese relations.[16] Once more, the point is that time series measurement can discard information, thus leading to mistaken inferences about the properties of a time series.

Given that temporal aggregation can mask important dynamics in time series data through the discarding of information, the preceding discussion should make it clear that analysts must consider not only the length of their series but also the frequency. A series lasting 40 years can be far more informative if each year consists of 12 (in the case of monthly data) or even 52 (in the case of weekly data) observations, whereas a time series measured with annual frequency, of course, has but one observation per year. Ideally, an analyst's best choice is to use data that both cover a long time horizon in years and are measured with regular, high frequency, if such data are available.

---

[16] Sometimes temporal aggregation masks unsystematic sampling. Illustrative is the practice of averaging what are *irregular* series of polls of presidential approval into one monthly measure.

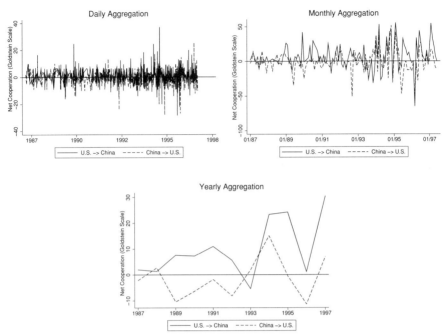

FIGURE 1.8. U.S.-Chinese Relations: Alternative Levels of Temporal Aggregation. Compiled by the authors from events data produced by the Kansas Event Data System.

Statistically, we learn in Chapters 3 and 4 that, for simple, strongly restricted regression models, systematic sampling and temporal aggregation can produce losses in precision of our coefficient estimates. If we are using regression models with lags on our independent variables, a more serious concern is that these measurement practices can bias the estimates of the respective coefficients. When using weakly restricted models, systematic sampling and temporal aggregation can produce mistaken inferences about the functional forms of our models and also about the existence and/or direction of causality between our variables. These measurement practices also can alter the frequency and amplitude of cycles in data. We demonstrate the first result in Chapter 3 and the second in the last half of Chapter 4.

Time series measurement thus challenges us to theorize a *natural time unit* for social relationships. Usually, this concept is based on arguments about the temporal frames in which humans think. And, it is not the case that the unit is always the same. For example, remarkably, we now have cases in which we can chart conflicts by the hour, if not by the minute. Figure 1.9 shows hourly behavior for all 598 hours in the 2008–2009 Gaza conflict measured in 15-minute increments, aggregated to the hour.[17] But we do not know whether the people making decisions in this and other conflicts find such information too

---

[17] Data in figure come from Zeitzoff (2011).

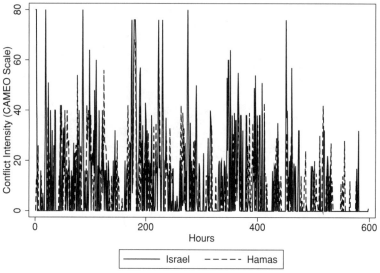

FIGURE 1.9. Gaza Conflict by the Hour. Reprinted with permission from Sage Publications.

noisy. Hence they may base their decisions on daily, weekly, or even monthly levels of conflict and cooperation. In contrast, legislators designing criminal justice statutes and fiscal policies usually think in annual terms. The point is that the problems of systematic sampling and temporal aggregation force social scientists to include in the conceptual scaffolding of their theories a temporal unit and to be sensitive to the problems that an error in this regard can create for their causal inferences.[18]

1.2.2 Fit: On the Use of Time Trends and Counters

Regardless of which time series model they use, analysts frequently want to control for generic *time trends* in the data, usually with some form of a time counter as an independent variable. Why? The levels of some time series increase (decrease) relatively smoothly. Economic growth series are illustrative, as are the data in Figure 1.1 on the balance of partisan control in the U.S. House of Representatives. When working with series of this kind, social scientists often attribute some of the variance of their series to *time trends*. To be more specific, analysts include among their independent (right-hand side) variables a *time counter* that is valued at 1 at the initial time of observation and then increases by one unit for new time point. Rarely is any meaningful justification offered for using this particular (linear deterministic) representation of trends. Indeed, many studies include a variable noting the year of observation.

---

[18] For an introduction to these concepts and problems with applications from political science, see Freeman (1989).

Although such a variable may be a more explicit measure of a time trend (perhaps even more theoretically justified), it still suffers from the problems discussed here.

The problem with such counters is that operationally, the effect is that the analyst's model applies to the *deviations* from this trend. And if the trend actually is of a different form (i.e., the trend does not increase in an orderly linear fashion), these deviations will be unrepresentative of the underlying data-generation process and causal inferences will be prone to error. For example, the use of a time counter for series that have stochastic trends can mask the existence of long-term social memory (nonstationarity), as discussed in Chapter 6.[19]

We discuss issues of fit in more detail in Chapter 4.

1.2.3 Discerning Structural Change

Underpinning most time series models is the assumption that the underlying structure of a data-generating process does not change for the entire sample period under study.[20] In time series analysis, *structure* often is equated with the (fixed) values of model coefficients. Structural change then is synonymous with a permanent shift in coefficient values. More complex conceptions treat the functional forms of the model as the structure and allow for time-varying parameters. That is, there is a fixed functional form that describes the way in which the coefficients change over time.[21]

In still other cases, a permanent change in the functional form that describes a univariate process or multivariate relationship is interpreted as a structural change. For example, a permanent change from an autoregressive process to a moving average process would be treated as a structural transformation of a social processes.

Failure to account for this kind of change can create mistaken inferences, such as concluding that a series has a long social memory and that it seeks a single moving equilibrium when, in fact, the series actually is produced by two different processes (parts) both with shorter or medium term memories, each of which, in fact, move toward (different) stable equilibria. In other

---

[19] Say that one is interested in the relationship between Y_t and X_t, which are both smooth series that seem to grow together over time. A common practice is to run a regression of the form $Y_t = \beta_0 + \beta_1 X_t + \beta_2 T$ where β_0, β_1, and β_2 are coefficients to be estimated and T is the time counter that is valued 1 at the first time point, 2 at the second time point, and so on. Again, this functional form says that it is the *deviations* from the time counter that are causally related. Social scientists who use such functional forms rarely explain the forces that produce T as distinct from those that produce the relationship between the deviations in Y_t and X_t. Nor do they interpret their coefficients in these terms.

[20] In the context of time series analysis, the term "sample period" does not refer to a randomly sampled subset of a population as might be inferred, but instead refers to the fact that our time series data are almost always a subset of a longer series for which we do not have all the data.

[21] See, for instance, Box-Steffensmeier and Lin (1995); see also Wood (2000).

cases what appears to be structural instability is not. Episodic volatility, as in public opinion series, may appear to indicate structural change. But such volatility actually is the result of temporal dependence in the variance of the shocks that the series experiences; the same (fixed) structure (functional form) – an autoregressive conditional heteroskedastic model – produces the respective observations.

To illustrate these issues, return to the top left panel of Figure 1.7. The unusually high levels of presidential approval in the aftermath of the 9/11 tragedy could indicate that the process by which citizens evaluate their presidents was altered structurally by virtue of that event; that is, after 9/11 a structurally distinct data-generating process is responsible for presidential approval compared to the process that produced the data in the second Clinton administration. On the other hand, the structure of the data-generating process that produces George W. Bush's approval ratings may be identical to that which produced the ratings for Clinton. The 9/11 tragedy may have amounted to a temporary, one- or maybe two-month positive surge or shock to presidential approval, the social memory of which gradually dissipated over time.

We will learn methods to test for each of these possibilities. At the end of Chapter 2, for example, we discuss a test for structural change in univariate processes. We study modeling volatility in series such as presidential approval ratings in Chapter 7 as well.[22]

There are even more complex models, called Markov switching models, that allow series to switch back and forth through time between models with distinct coefficients or with error terms with different variances.[23] We briefly cover some techniques for detecting single and multiple unknown structural breaks in Chapter 7.

1.3 THE FIRST STEP

Before we can meet these challenges we need to learn how to build and interpret time series models. The following chapters discuss common time series models in increasing order of complexity. Readers interested in applying an existing model, while skipping some important mathematical preliminaries, may proceed to the next chapter on univariate time series models.

However, for the discrete time framework we use in this book, difference equations, covered thoroughly in the Appendix, are an invaluable tool. Understanding the nature and solution of these equations is at the heart of time series analysis. Thus, any reader who is serious about conducting research in time

---

[22] On the idea that presidential approval experiences shocks that are themselves temporally dependent see Gronke and Brehm (2002).

[23] See Hamilton (1994, chapter 22); Krolzig (1997); Kim and Nelson (1999); and Frühwirth-Schnatter (2006). Social science applications of Markov switching models include Freeman, Hays, and Stix (2000); Hays, Freeman, and Nesseth (2003); and Brandt and Freeman (2009).

series methodology must understand difference equations to fully understand the models discussed in this book. This is because all discrete time models are expressed in this form. The solutions of difference equations hold the key to unlocking social dynamics, both out of and in equilibrium. Their solutions – time functions – tell us about the kinds of trends that social processes may follow, the path that variables take on the way to equilibria, and the values of these equilibria. If we know how to solve difference equations and interpret their solutions, we can make sound inferences about the dynamic implications of our estimates – what those estimates tell us about the deep properties of social processes.[24] Readers interested in these issues are encouraged to turn to the Appendix before moving on to Chapter 2.

1.4 FOR FURTHER READING

Croushore, Dean and Tom Stark. 2003. "A Real-Time Data Set for Macroeconomists: Does the Data Vintage Matter?" *Review of Economics and Statistics* 85 (3): 605–617.

Giuliodori, Massimo and Roel Beetsma. 2008. "On the Relationship between Fiscal Plans in the European Union: An Empirical Analysis Based on Real-Time Data." *Journal of Comparative Economics* 36 (2): 221–242.

Granger, Clive W. J. and P. R. Sikklos. 1995. "Systematic Sampling, Temporal Aggregation, Seasonal Adjustment, and Cointegration: Theory and Evidence." *Journal of Econometrics* 66: 357–369.

Mitchell, Sara McLaughlin, and Will H. Moore. 2002. "Presidential Uses of Force during the Cold War: Aggregation, Truncation, and Temporal Dynamics." *American Journal of Political Science* 46 (2): 438–452.

Shellman, Stephen M. 2004. "Time Series Intervals and Statistical Inference: The Effects of Temporal Aggregation on Event Data Analysis." *Political Analysis* 12 (1): 97–104.

Shellman, Stephen M., Clare Hatfield, and Maggie J. Mills. 2010. "Disaggregating Actors in Intranational Conflict." *Journal of Peace Research* 47 (1): 83–90.

---

[24] A continuous time framework would employ spectral methods that are based in the frequency domain. With few exceptions (Beck, 1991), most time series analyses in the social sciences – especially outside of economics – are in the discrete time domain, probably because in most social sciences measurement is in discrete intervals. As Tsay (2002) points out, the gulf between proponents of frequency versus time domain approaches no longer exists. Instead which approach is used now is due more to practicality than philosophy. A useful example is Dejong and Dave (2007, Chapter 3), which compares the value of both approaches to removing trends and analyzing cycles in economic data.

2

Univariate Time Series Models

2.1 UNDERSTANDING UNIVARIATE PROCESSES

The first class of time series models we investigate are univariate models called ARMA (autoregressive moving average) models.[1] In the Appendix, we show how to gain significant insights into the dynamics of difference equations – the basis of time series econometrics – by simply solving them and plotting solutions over time. By stipulating a model based on our verbal theory and deriving its solution, we can note the conditions under which the processes we model return to equilibrium.

In the series of models discussed in this chapter, we turn this procedure around. We begin by studying the generic forms of patterns that could be created by particular datasets. We then analyze the data to see what dynamics are present in the data-generating process, which induce the underlying structure of the data. As a modeling process, ARMA models were perfected by Box and Jenkins (1970), who were attempting to come up with a better way than extrapolation or smoothing to predict the behavior of systems. Indeed, their method of examining the structures in a time series, filtering them from the data, and leaving a pure stochastic series improved predictive (i.e., forecasting) ability. Box-Jenkins modeling became quite popular, and as Kennedy notes, "for years the Box-Jenkins methodology was synonymous with time series analysis" (Kennedy, 2008, 297).

The intuition behind Box-Jenkins modeling is straightforward. Time series data redundant can be composed of multiple temporal processes. Through a series of diagnostic tests, one can compare a realized series with the generic (or

---

[1] Many publications refer to this class of models as ARIMA (autoregressive integrated moving average). However, because the "integrated" portion indicates nonstationarity; we discuss those models in Chapter 5.

archetypical) forms to decide what processes occur in the data. The diagnosis of these properties alone tells us something about the data-generating process: how much more important are recent events than past events? Do perturbations to the system last a finite amount of time or indefinitely?

Knowing the answers to these questions tells us something substantive about what we are studying. Does a recession in a country permanently alter the path of economic growth, or does its influence subside in a matter of months or years? Are political party identifications ingrained long term, or do external events play a larger role in shifting the partisan balance? Will an increase in presidential popularity due to war last days, months, or years? Is there a cycle of international conflict so that conflict rises and falls over time? The seemingly simple univariate models reviewed in this chapter will help us uncover answers to these important questions.

2.1.1 Why Stochastic Models of Time Series?

Many researchers frequently deal with time series data. Whether as a part of a longitudinal study or as a part of a panel dataset, much of the data we use is measured over time. Often, this fact is ignored when modeling the data-generating processes that we hope to analyze. Sometimes, however, researchers realize that their time series data may have particular properties, such as a rising or declining trend over time. This realization may lead them to conclude that the data should be transformed or cleaned in some way to eliminate these trends in the data – after all, researchers often do not think they are substantively interested in secular rises or declines in a data series. One typical solution is to "detrend" the data, for example, by regressing the data on a linear time trend. Why not use this simple strategy to deal with time-related data issues instead of using alternative time series methodologies?

Take Figure 2.1, for example, which is a truncated graph of Figure 1.6 in Chapter 1.[2] One might examine this series and argue that a linear trend term should be a part of any econometric model:

$$\text{HOMICIDES} = \beta_o + \beta_1 \text{MONTH} + \cdots + a_t \tag{2.1}$$

The month variable will remove any trending from the dependent variable, allowing the other covariates to explain the remaining variance. Indeed, regressing a count of months on the dependent variable yields a statistically significant coefficient estimate for β_1 and fits a visually acceptable trend line to the data. But is such a linear transformation the best strategy for dealing with a time trend?

---

[2] As noted in Chapter 1, because not all cities report their crime data on a monthly basis, the Uniform Crime Reports are most reliable for analysis at the annualized level. We examine the monthly series here for pedagogical purposes only.

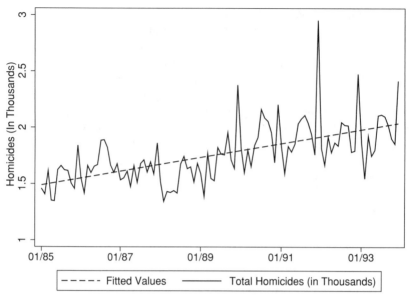

FIGURE 2.1. Homicides in the U.S. 1985–1993. Time series compiled by the authors from FBI Uniform Crime Reports. OLS trend line constructed by authors.

In reality, fitting these linear terms to data is not an optimal way to deal with trends. Three problems arise. First, the OLS parameter estimate (β_1 in equation 1) is sensitive to outliers.[3] In our homicide example, removing the large spike from the series in December 1991 (a value that is 4.5 standard deviations above the mean) reduces the parameter estimate of *Month* in Table 2.1 by nearly 7%.[4]

Second, OLS trend line estimates are sensitive to first and last observations (McLeary and Hay, 1980, 34). The independent variable used to detrend the data will increase monotonically over time. Recall that OLS attempts to minimize the sum of squares. Usually, in cases of a monotonic time series as an explanatory variable, the most important observations for minimizing the sum of squares (to fit the line) will be the first and the last. This essentially weights the time series in an unequal manner. Ideally, all observations of the series would have equal weight.

Finally, the estimate of our trend parameter in OLS will be static over time. In other words, our estimate will be deterministic (McLeary and Hay, 1980, 35). In fact, it can be useful to think about two types of trends: deterministic and

---

[3] McLeary and Hay (1980, 33–34) provide examples on this point.

[4] The early 1990s generally represented a peak period in homicides, partially because of the intensity of inner-city turf wars over the market for crack cocaine, and represent an outlier in the homicide time series. If we extend these data out until today, homicide rates regress to the mean, and the upward trend in Figure 2.1 would reverse direction. Steffensmeier et al. (2011) study these dynamics in greater detail, arguing that many crime time series are not trending.

TABLE 2.1. *Month Regressed on Homicides*

Variable	Coefficient	(Std. Err.)
Month	0.005	(0.001)
Intercept	−0.05	(0.23)

stochastic. A *deterministic trend* is a fixed function of time. A data-generating process that changes by the same amount every time period may be adequately described by a deterministic trend in the previous equation. In predicting the number of homicides, we expect the number to change by β_1 each month.

Yet, it is unlikely that most of our time series in the social sciences operate in this time-deterministic (i.e., nonstochastic) way. The prevalent practice of modeling time trends as deterministic was borrowed from economics where there was strong underlying theory arguing for something like constant, deterministic growth patterns in data. In a GDP time series, for example, inflation will drive the value of that series higher over time, but economists were not interested in the "normal" growth in the series, but in deviations from that growth. Thus, removing the time trend allowed the analysis of deviations from the series, which were deemed to be more interesting.[5]

In most social science applications, we lack the strong theory to suggest that a deterministic time trend is at work. Therefore, a better conceptualization of behavior of the series over time might be a *stochastic trend*, which we conceptualize as an outcome of a process operating over time. This process may drift upward or downward over finite (but perhaps long) periods, but most social science time series are more likely to behave stochastically rather than deterministically, thus necessitating the use of the stochastic models used by time series analysts and introduced in this chapter.

For an example of data that require a stochastic, rather than deterministic model, take measures of aggregate partisanship (also called macropartisanship), defined as the proportion of the electorate that identifies with one of the two major parties in the United States. A lively debate has emerged in political science as to whether swings in partisan identification have long-term electoral implications or whether they are simply short-term perturbations based on scandals, particular candidates, or macroeconomic conditions. What both of these views have in common, however, is the idea that shifts in partisan identification are stochastic (the debate is over the duration of the impact of exogenous shocks), rather than deterministic (moving mechanistically upward or downward over time).

The fact that many social science time series are likely to be stochastic rather than deterministic, plus the difficulties in accurately estimating the coefficients

---

[5] For historical examples, see Hooker (1905) and Yule (1921). For a further discussion of those historical examples, see Pevehouse and Brozek (2010).

using classical linear techniques, leads to the need to model time series processes stochastically.[6] Fortunately, we can use our knowledge of difference equations from the Appendix to get dynamic estimates of trends in our time series data. Recall the difference equation of a trend:

$$y_t = y_{t-1} + \theta_0, \tag{2.2}$$

where θ_0 is the estimated mean of the differenced time series. This difference equation describes the exact same trend as the OLS trend equation:

$$y = \beta_0 + \beta_1 t \tag{2.3}$$

when $\beta_1 = \theta_0$. Thus, it is better to use what we know about difference equations to test for trends in a stochastic manner. Later, we show how to test for the presence of a stochastic trend in a series. As we will show, some series do indeed trend up or down stochastically, yet others just give the appearance of trending due to the presence of other time series properties.

The remainder of this chapter presents modeling strategies and techniques to uncover the processes creating time-related issues in our data. Before turning to a closer examination of the two types of processes to be analyzed using the Box-Jenkins methodology, we discuss the driving force of ARMA models – the white noise process – followed by a discussion of how to diagnose the constituent parts of a time series. We also review several examples illustrating the Box-Jenkins technique.

2.1.2 White Noise

The white noise process is the "building block of discrete stochastic time series models" (Enders, 2004: 50). It is essentially the stochastic process left after filtering the time-based dynamics out of the data. By definition, the white noise process is normally distributed with mean zero and constant variance. There will also be no correlation in the white noise series over time. Thus, for a white noise process, a_t,

$$E(a_t) = E(a_{t-1}) = \cdots = 0 \tag{2.4}$$

$$E(a_t^2) = E(a_{t-1}^2) = \cdots = \sigma^2 \tag{2.5}$$

$$E(a_t a_{t-j}) = E(a_{t-k} a_{t-k-j}) = 0 \text{ for all } j \text{ and } k. \tag{2.6}$$

This a_t can be described as the "residual" from the Box-Jenkins filtering process. This does not mean that after removing the various time series elements

---

[6] Parenthetically, this is not just an issue of needing nonlinear parameter estimates. For example, even fitting a polynomial trend would suffer from similar critiques. As Box and Jenkins (1976) argued, there are important differences between fitting (deterministically) and forecasting (stochastically) a series.

(trends, autoregression, etc.) that there is nothing interesting left to analyze, as the name "white noise" might imply. Rather, for those performing multivariate analyses (such as multiple regression), this "residual" can then be used as a dependent variable, giving the analyst confidence that any time series properties in the data will not account for any observed correlation between the covariates and the dependent variable. In the univariate context (our focus in this chapter), the white noise process is important because it is what we would like to "recover" from our data – after stripping away the ways in which a univariate series can essentially explain itself. By removing the time series properties of our data, leaving only white noise, we have a series that can then be explained by other sources of variation.

Another way to conceptualize white noise is as the exogenous portion of the data-generating process. Each of our data series is a function of those forces that cause the series to rise or fall (the independent variables we normally include to test our hypotheses) and of time series properties that lead those forces to be more or less "sticky." After we filter away those time series properties, we are left with the forces driving the data higher or lower. We often refer to these forces as "shocks" – and these shocks then reverberate in our data, sometimes for a short spell or a long spell or even infinitely. The goal of time series analysis is to separately model the time series properties (the reverberations) so the shocks (i.e., the white noise) can be captured.

Indeed, the focus of much time series modeling is on discovering the underlying structure of the data, rather than determining what the covariates predicting the data-generating process may be. Most time series models emphasize the dynamics of the error structure rather than the functional form of the econometric model. Although some may consider these techniques to be overly inductive, we argue that modelers in the social sciences often move too far in the other direction – writing models based on loosely specified theory with little thought to what temporal dynamics may exist in the data.

2.1.3 A Note on Notation

Before getting much deeper into statistical notation and derivations, we should review some algebraic notations that are helpful in the study of time series. This section is also repeated in the Appendix, where we discuss the building blocks of time series models: difference equations. For those not reviewing the Appendix, it is still important to review some notation that will be used throughout the remainder of the book.

Anyone who has studied mathematics has encountered the idea of an operator. Operators transform variables and functions. A simple example is the operator of squaring. Denote this operator by S. If x is a variable, $S(x) = x^2$. Consider the function $f(x) = 2x$. Then $S(f(x)) = (2x)^2 = 4x^2$. Readers who have studied calculus are familiar with the derivative and integral operators. For instance, sometimes the former is written as D to mean $\frac{d}{dx}$. So, for our function, $f(x)$, we have $D(f(x)) = D(2x) = \frac{d}{dx}(2x) = 2$. An algebra of operators has been developed by mathematicians. For instance, operators such as D can be applied to sums. That is, if $f(x)$ and $g(x)$ are differentiable functions, $D(f+g) = D(f(x)) + D(g(x))$.

Among the operators that are used in time series analysis, three are especially important. The first is the backshift operator, B, also known as a lag operator. This operator simply takes the previous value of a time function or, for a time function $y(t)$, $B(y(t)) = y(t-1)$. Say, $y(t)$ is $.5^t$. Then $B(y(t)) = B(.5^t) = .5^{t-1}$. If the function is a constant, its lag stays the same (because y always has the same value in the past and future). Backshift operators also apply to sums. Here is an example that illustrates these two properties of this first operator: $B(.4t + .1) = B(.4t) + B(.1) = .4(t-1) + .1 = .4t - .3$. When B is raised to a power, such as B^i where i is a natural number, it means to take the ith lag of a time function. So $B^i(y(t))$ is equal to $y(t-i)$. An important property of the backshift operator that we use repeatedly in this book is the following: for a constant α such that $|\alpha| < 1$, the infinite sum $(1 + \alpha B + \alpha^2 B^2 + \cdots)y(t) = \frac{y(t)}{(1-\alpha B)}$.[7] We refer to this property later in this chapter and several times throughout the book.

The difference operator can be written in terms of the backshift operator. The difference operator, Δ, is simply $(1 - B)$. We write $\Delta y(t)$ to mean $(1 - B)y(t) = y(t) - y(t-1)$. Returning to our earlier examples, $\Delta(.5^t) = .5^t - .5^{t-1}$. And $\Delta(.4t + .1) = (.4t + .1) - (.4(t-1) + .1) = .4$. The difference operator also can be raised to a power. Its relation to the backshift operator helps interpret powers of Δ. Consider the square of the difference operator:

$$\Delta^2 y(t) = (1-B)^2 y(t) = (1 - 2B + B^2)y(t)$$
$$= y(t) - 2y(t-1) + y(t-2). \tag{2.7}$$

So, if $y(t)$ again is $.5^t$, we have

$$\Delta^2(.5^t) = .5^t - 2(.5^{t-1}) + .5^{t-2} = .5^t. \tag{2.8}$$

The third is called the expectations or lead operator. It is denoted either as E or as the inverse lag operator, B^{-1}. Simply put, $Ey(t) = y(t+1)$. For our second example, $E(.4t + .1) = B^{-1}y(t) = .4(t+1) + .1 = .4t + .5$. For a time function, $y(t)$, we can combine all three operators together in the following way:

$$E\Delta y(t) = E(1-B)y(t) = B^{-1}(1-B)y(t)$$
$$= (B^{-1} - 1)y(t) = y(t+1) - y(t). \tag{2.9}$$

---

[7] This fact is based on the properties of geometric series. A simple proof can be found in Enders (2010: section 9). In this section, Enders lists the properties of the backshift operator we discussed in the text plus a few additional ones.

In other words the lead of the difference between $y(t)$ and $y(t-1)$ is equal to the difference between $y(t+1)$ and $y(t)$.[8]

Again, readers interested in a deeper discussion of these operators and the difference equations that form the underlying machinery behind time series models should carefully review the Appendix. The use of especially the backshift operator (B), these three operators, is important later in this chapter. Now, armed with knowledge of some basic functions needed for time series, we begin our investigation of single-variable time series models.

2.2 UNIVARIATE PROCESSES

The basic approach of the Box-Jenkins methodology, as expanded to include step four by McCleary and Hay (1980, 91) is summarized as follows:

1. Study generic forms and properties.
2. Using this (generic) knowledge, study these realizations for an indication of which possibility applies to your data.
3. Assess your guess – diagnose and iterate.
4. Perform a meta-analysis at the end to determine which specification is best, using R^2, RMS, over-modeling, under-modeling, white noise tests, and information criteria.

Generically, we estimate various models referred to as ARMA(p,q) models, where p is the order of AR terms and q is the order of moving average terms, and compare our real data with the results of common archetypes. Each term of the ARMA model (AR or MA) may or may not be present in the real data. In addition, each constituent part of the ARMA model may be of a different *order*. That is, the autoregressive portion of a time series may be a second-order process – an AR(2), with no other constituent parts present. We denote a series such as this an ARMA(2,0) model. This model would mean that, in our data series, the current period's value is influenced by the shock in the previous two periods. Our modeling approach then, is to develop an idea of the properties of a series with these constituent parts and then see how those ideal-type properties match up against the data we have. We continue with an examination of the first term of the ARMA model, which is likely to be familiar to any social scientist: autoregression.

2.2.1 The Autoregressive (AR) Process

Many people who have experience in statistics are familiar with the idea of an autoregressive process. The idea is that the best predictor of behavior at time t

---

[8] Some mathematicians develop difference equations in terms of the E operator rather than the B operator. They define Δ as E-1 rather than 1-B. We use both conventions here, but emphasize the latter. The reason for this will become apparent later in the book.

will be behavior at $t - 1$. Of course, influence could extend farther back than one period:

$$y_t = \phi_1 y_{t-1} + \phi_2 y_{t-2} + \cdots + \phi_p y_{t-p} + a_t, \tag{2.10}$$

where a_t is our white noise process. Expressing the same idea with the backshift operator (see the Appendix),

$$(1 - \phi_1 B - \phi_2 B^2 - \cdots - \phi_p B^p) y_t = a_t. \tag{2.11}$$

These equations both describe an AR(p) process where the value of p is the order of autoregression.

ARMA models allow for a much richer structure of dynamic processes. Indeed, a basic ARMA(1,0) model looks quite similar to a traditional regression model:

$$y_t = \phi_1 y_{t-1} + a_t. \tag{2.12}$$

Unlike traditional regression, we place an additional stipulation that $-1 < \phi < 1$. This condition is referred to as the bounds of stationarity, discussed later. First, however, note what the specification of an AR(1) process says about the data. Tracking a shock over time will tell us about the behavior of our model in response to deviations from equilibrium. Examining the first few observations of our data and substituting the previous values of observations, we obtain

$$y_0 = a_0 \tag{2.13}$$

$$y_1 = \phi_1 y_0 + a_1$$
$$\quad = \phi_1 a_0 + a_1$$

$$y_2 = \phi_1 y_1 + a_2$$
$$\quad = \phi_1(\phi_1 a_0 + a_1) + a_2$$
$$\quad = \phi_1^2 a_0 + \phi_1 a_1 + a_2$$

$$y_3 = \phi_1 y_2 + a_3$$
$$\quad = \phi_1(\phi_1^2 a_0 + \phi_1 a_1 + a_2) + a_3$$
$$\quad = \phi_1^3 a_0 + \phi_1^2 a_1 + \phi_1 a_2 + a_3$$

$$\vdots$$

$$y_t = \phi_1 y_{t-1} + a_t$$
$$\quad = \phi_1^t a_0 + \phi_1^{t-1} a_1 + \phi_1^{t-2} a_2 + \cdots + a_t.$$

This suggests that in an ARMA(1,0) process, random shocks affect all future observations but at an exponentially decreasing rate. This fits with our notion of autoregressive behavior: it is the most recent values that influence behavior the most. An ARMA(1,0) is essentially an *infinite sum of exponentially weighted random shocks*. Expressed more concisely,

$$y_t = \sum_{i=0}^{\infty} \phi_1^i a_{t-i}. \tag{2.14}$$

Thus, with each passing observation, an increasing amount of the shock "leaks" out of the system, but the shock never completely disappears. So although previous observations are important to predicting the current observation, the power of those previous observations diminishes over time as one moves more temporally distant from them. For example, if $\phi = 0.5$, then by the fifth period, the impact of a one-unit shock will be $\phi^5 = 0.03125$.

Another way to understand the dynamics implied by equation 2.9 is to think of it as a special case of a first-order stochastic difference equation. In the Appendix we show that the general form of this kind of equation is

$$y_t = b + a y_{t-1} + \epsilon_t. \tag{2.15}$$

For a known initial condition, y_0, we showed that this equation has the solution

$$y_t = b \sum_{i=0}^{t-1} a^i + a^t y_0 + \sum_{i=0}^{t-1} a^i \epsilon_{t-1}. \tag{2.16}$$

And we noted that as t goes to infinity, we have

$$\lim y_t = \frac{b}{1-a} + \sum_{i=0}^{\infty} a^i \epsilon_{t-1}. \tag{2.17}$$

Under the assumption that $|a| < 1$, a^i will get smaller and smaller. Hence the initial condition eventually will disappear from the solution, and distant shocks will produce less and less influence on the current value of y_t.

Equation 2.9 is simply a case in which $b = 0$ and $\phi = a$. The "leakage" result for $|\phi| < 1$ is the same as the result we show in the Appendix for $|a| < 1$.

Returning to the issue of why $-1 < \phi_1 < 1$, imagine that $|\phi_1| \geq 1$. In this case, ϕ_1 raised to a power will grow *larger* over time – thus the impact of previous shocks will grow. If this were the case, the best predictor of today's value of y_t would be the first value, y_0, which does not correspond to our conceptualization of autoregression. Moreover, it suggests that shocks accumulate (or *integrate*) over time. If $\phi = 1$ then there is accumulation, whereas if $\phi > 1$, both an accumulation and a growth process occur. In either case, the ARMA(1,0) specification will be incorrect. It also suggests that the mean of our series is not stationary; that is, because the impact of shocks accumulates over time (versus dissipating as new ones arise), the mean of a nonstationary time series is time dependent. Taking the mean of a nonstationary series' first 20 observations will yield a different mean from the mean of the last 20 observations, for example.

If ϕ_1 lies outside the bounds of stationarity, one has uncovered a stochastic trend or integrative process, which we confront in Chapter 5.

Traditionally, it was thought that most social science time series could be well represented by an AR(1) or an AR(2) process and that, if $p \geq 3$, the process would be more parsimoniously represented by a lower order moving average process. As the social sciences have developed longer and higher frequency time series, however, increasing numbers of series appear to be AR(3) and higher. Later, after we present the moving average process, we discuss how the AR and MA processes are related mathematically. This relationship means that our models can often stay parsimonious, but it does create a challenge in identification.

2.2.2 The Moving Average (MA) Process

The second component of the ARMA model is the moving average process. Recall that, for both the integrated and the autoregressive process, shocks persist for long periods of time. In the case of the autoregressive process, they diminish exponentially, whereas in the integrated process they accumulate over time and never leave the system. In the moving average process, noted as MA(q), shocks persist exactly q periods and then disappear from the system. We represent the MA process as lagged shocks to our variable, y_t. For example, an MA(1) would be represented as

$$y_t = a_t - \theta_1 a_{t-1} \tag{2.18}$$

or

$$y_t = (1 - \theta_1 B) a_t.$$

We can evaluate realizations of an MA process over time to examine its behavior. For our first observation, take the value of y_t as given in equation 2.15. Then, take the second observation of y_{t-1}:

$$y_{t-1} = a_{t-1} - \theta_1 a_{t-2}. \tag{2.19}$$

Now, solving for a_{t-1} and substituting into equation 2.15,

$$y_t = a_t - \theta_1(y_{t-1} + \theta_1 a_{t-2}) \tag{2.20}$$

$$= a_t - \theta_1 y_{t-1} - \theta_1^2 a_{t-2}. \tag{2.21}$$

Expressing y_{t-2} in terms of a_{t-2} and then substituting back into the equation for y_t would yield

$$y_t = a_t - \theta_1 y_{t-1} - \theta_1^2 y_{t-2} - \theta_1^3 a_{t-3}. \tag{2.22}$$

Continuing this process infinitely yields

$$y_t = a_t - \sum_{i=1}^{\infty} \theta_i^i y_{t-i}. \tag{2.23}$$

Consequently, an ARMA$(0, q)$ process can be expressed as an *infinite sum of exponentially weighted past observations*.

Again, as with the AR term, the requirement that $-1 < \theta_1 < 1$ is imposed. This is done to prevent "explosions," cases where shocks' influence on the value of y_t grows with importance over time. Estimated values of θ (or of ϕ in the case of an autoregressive process) outside these bounds may indicate the need for differencing, because such high values may be indicative of a stochastic trend or integrative process at work (again, Chapter 5 discusses diagnostic methods for these processes). If the data have already been differenced several times, then an estimated value of θ or $\phi \geq 1$ can also imply that there has been too much differencing.

2.2.3 The Equivalence of AR and MA Processes

We have shown that AR processes can be expressed in terms of the sum of shocks, whereas MA processes can be expressed in terms of sums of past observations. The ability to do so is called *invertibility*. Invertibility means that if certain conditions are met, a *finite* order MA process has an equivalent AR process of *infinite* order. Similarly, for a stationary AR process of *any* order there exists an equivalent MA process of *infinite* order.[9] We have expressed our MA and AR process so far by examining the first few observations of a series of each type.

To show this in a more general form, first consider an AR(1):

$$y_t = \phi_1 y_{t-1} + a_t \tag{2.24}$$

$$y_t = \phi_1 B y_t + a_t$$

$$a_t = y_t - \phi_1 B y_t$$

$$a_t = (1 - \phi_1 B) y_t$$

$$y_t = \left(\frac{1}{(1 - \phi_1 B)} \right) a_t.$$

In this instance the AR process is written in terms of shocks, but the y_{t-1} term has been eliminated. Recall from our definition of the backshift operator that an infinite number of backshifts operating on a term is equivalent to $\frac{1}{(1-B)}$.

---

[9] This assumes that the boundary requirements for ϕ and θ are met.

Using this equivalence, $(1 - \phi_1 B)^{-1} a_t = (1 + \phi B + \phi^2 B^2 + \phi^3 B^3 + \cdots) a_t$. This implies that any AR(1) process is an infinite MA process.

Consider an MA(1):

$$y_t = a_t - \theta_1 a_{t-1} \tag{2.25}$$

$$y_t = (1 - \theta_1 B) a_t$$

$$a_t = \left(\frac{1}{(1 - \theta_1 B)} \right) y_t.$$

Thus, any MA(1) process is an infinite AR process. Taken together, these results illustrate the equivalence of AR and MA processes, which has two important implications. First, from an identification perspective, in finite samples (especially short ones), AR processes could mimic an MA process. One must always be sure to check for correct identification of the ARMA model by over-fitting, under-fitting, and checking model residuals (all of which we discuss later).

Second, because of the relationship between the MA and the AR process, one is unlikely (although it is not impossible) to find "mixed" ARMA processes with both p and q terms. Indeed, McCleary and Hay (1980, 46–47) show that a mixed ARMA(1,1) process can be written strictly in terms of random shocks. In brief, they show how

$$y_t = \phi_1 y_{t-1} + a_t - \theta_1 a_{t-1} \tag{2.26}$$

can be rewritten, using a similar equivalence process as earlier, as

$$y_t = a_t + (\phi_1 - \theta_1) \sum_{i=1}^{\infty} (\phi_1^i a_{t-i}). \tag{2.27}$$

Now, if $\phi_1 = \theta_1$, then equation X reduces to $y_t = a_t$, or white noise. Similarly, for a host of potential values of ϕ and θ, it can be shown that an ARMA(1,1) reduces to white noise or a more parsimonious model, such as an ARMA(1,0). Thus, although it may be possible to uncover a time series that is ARMA(1,1), other models are more likely to offer superior fit of the data. For other examples, see McCleary and Hay (1980), as well as McLeary and Hay (1980).

2.3 DIAGNOSING STATIONARY UNIVARIATE PROCESSES

How does one determine what processes are in the data? Recall our discussion of the steps in the Box-Jenkins modeling process.[10]

| Identification | ⇒ | Estimation | ⇒ | Diagnosis | ⇒ | Metadiagnosis | ⇒ | Analysis |

---

[10] The schematic is taken from McLeary and Hay (1980, 92).

We begin by discussing the identification phase using two important tools in the identification process: the autocorrelation function and the partial autocorrelation function.

2.3.1 The Autocorrelation Function (ACF)

The most important set of tools for diagnosing the time series properties of data is the *correlogram*. The correlogram is a graph that presents one of two statistics: the autocorrelation function (ACF) and the partial autocorrelation function (PACF). We begin with the ACF.

$$ACF(k) = \frac{cov(y_t, y_{t+k})}{var(y_t)}$$

$$= \frac{\sum\limits_{t=1}^{N-k}(y_t - \overline{y})(y_{t+k} - \overline{y})}{\sum\limits_{t=1}^{N}(y_t - \overline{y})^2} \left[\frac{N}{N-k}\right]. \tag{2.28}$$

The ACF statistic measures the correlation between y_t and y_{t+k} where k is the number of lead periods into the future. It is not strictly equivalent to the Pearson product moment correlation. Note that the denominator (the variance) is measured over all N observations of the series, yet the numerator (the covariance) is calculated over $N - k$ observations. Thus, as the length of series grows (i.e, as k increases), confidence in $ACF(k)$ decreases. In addition, $ACF(0) = 1$. That is, any data point in a time series is perfectly correlated with itself.[11] The final property of the ACF statistic to note is that $ACF(k) = ACF(-k)$. That is, whether one computes the statistic from leads or lags, one should arrive at identical estimates.

The ACF statistic is a powerful tool in time series analysis. In theory, every time series has a unique ACF. This means that one can match that unique ACF to an archetype that is known to represent a particular data-generating process. Let us examine what we expect for the values of the ACF statistic for an AR(1) process. Recall our AR(1) process:

$$y_t = \phi_1 y_{t-1} + a_t. \tag{2.29}$$

$$y_{t+1} = \phi_1 y_t + a_{t+1}.$$

---

[11] Statistical packages vary in whether they report ACF(0). RATS and R, for example, show ACF(0), whereas STATA does not.

Now, consider the expected values of the first two k's for the AR(1), beginning with the numerator of ACF(1):

$$cov(y_t, y_{t+1}) = E[(y_t)(y_{t+1})] \qquad (2.30)$$
$$= E[y_t(\phi_1 y_t + a_{t+1})]$$
$$= E[\phi_1 y_t^2 + y_t a_{t+1}]$$
$$= E[\phi_1 y_t^2] + E[y_t a_{t+1}].$$

Recall that because our white noise process is a series of independent random shocks, it is uncorrelated with y_{t-k} and y_{t+k} (e.g., $E[y_t a_{t-k}] = 0$). This reduces the previous expression to

$$= E[\phi_1 y_t^2] \qquad (2.31)$$
$$= \phi_1 E[y_t^2]$$
$$= \phi_1 \sigma_y^2.$$

Substituting this into the numerator of the ACF formula gives us

$$ACF(1) = \frac{\phi_1 \sigma_y^2}{\sigma_y^2} = \phi_1. \qquad (2.32)$$

Computing the value of ACF(2) for our AR(1) series, the expected value of the covariance is

$$cov(y_t, y_{t+2}) = E[(y_t)(y_{t+2})] \qquad (2.33)$$
$$= E[y_t(\phi_1 y_{t+1} + a_{t+2})]$$
$$= E[y_t(\phi_1(\phi_1 y_t + a_{t+1}) + a_{t+2})]$$
$$= E[y_t(\phi_1^2 y_t + \phi_1 a_{t+1} + a_{t+2})]$$
$$= E[\phi_1^2 y_t^2 + \phi_1 y_t a_{t+1} + y_t a_{t+2}]$$
$$= E[\phi_1^2 y_t^2]$$
$$= \phi_1^2 E[y_t^2]$$
$$= \phi_1^2 \sigma_y^2.$$

Again, substituting this into the numerator of the ACF formula yields

$$ACF(2) = \frac{\phi_1^2 \sigma_y^2}{\sigma_y^2} = \phi_1^2. \qquad (2.34)$$

Ultimately the pattern that emerges is that the ACF of an AR(1) process is

$$ACF(k) = \phi_1^k, \qquad (2.35)$$

which represents an exponential decay of ϕ_1 as the ACF is computed over increasing periods of k. Knowing that this pattern is the expected ACF of an AR(1) series, we can turn to our own data to see if this general pattern is matched by estimating a series of ACFs. This example assumes that the value of $\phi > 0$, which need not be the case. If $\phi < 0$, the ACF will still decay exponentially, but will oscillate between positive and negative values.

In a similar fashion, we can develop expectations of how an ACF would appear if we are working with an MA(1) process. Recall the MA(1) equation as

$$y_t = a_t - \theta_1 a_{t-1}. \tag{2.36}$$

Computing the numerator of the ACF for $k = 1$,

$$
\begin{aligned}
cov(y_t, y_{t+1}) &= E\left[(a_t - \theta_1 a_{t-1})(a_{t+1} - \theta_1 a_t)\right] \\
&= E\left[a_t a_{t+1} - \theta_1 a_{t-1} a_{t+1} - \theta_1 a_t^2 + \theta_1^2 a_{t-1} a_t\right] \\
&= E\left[-\theta_1 a_t^2\right] \\
&= -\theta_1 E\left[a_t^2\right] \\
&= -\theta_1 \sigma_a^2.
\end{aligned}
\tag{2.37}
$$

Again recall that a property of white noise is that each random shock is independent of every other random shock (e.g., $E[a_t a_{t+k}] = 0$).

The variance (denominator) of y_t is given by

$$
\begin{aligned}
E\left[y_t^2\right] &= E\left[(a_t - \theta_1 a_{t-1})^2\right] \\
&= E\left[a_t^2 - 2\theta_1 a_t a_{t-1} + \theta_1^2 a_{t-1}^2\right] \\
&= \sigma_a^2 + \theta_1^2 \sigma_a^2 \\
&= \sigma_a^2(1 + \theta_1^2).
\end{aligned}
\tag{2.38}
$$

Substituting into our ACF formula, we obtain

$$ACF(1) = \frac{-\theta_1 \sigma_a^2}{\sigma_a^2(1 + \theta_1^2)} = \frac{-\theta_1}{1 + \theta_1^2}. \tag{2.39}$$

Now, computing the ACF(2) for our MA(1) process, we obtain

$$
\begin{aligned}
cov(y_t, y_{t+2}) &= E\left[(a_t - \theta_1 a_{t-1})(a_{t+2} - \theta_1 a_{t+1})\right] \\
&= E\left[a_t a_{t+2} - \theta_1 a_{t-1} a_{t+2} - \theta_1 a_t a_{t+1} + \theta_1^2 a_{t-1} a_{t+1})\right] \\
&= 0.
\end{aligned}
$$

This implies $ACF(2) = 0$.

For an MA(1) process, for every $k > 1$, the ACF will yield a value of zero. Why? Recall that an MA(q) process stipulates that shocks disappear completely from the system after q periods. As such, the ACF of an MA(1) process should show no significant associations after one period has passed. Again, this assumes $\theta > 0$. If $\theta < 0$ in our MA(1) process, then the value of any ACF beyond $k = 1$ will be zero, but the value of the ACF itself will be negative. Already, then, we have a big difference in the theoretical values of our ACFs between an AR(1) process and an MA(1) process. An AR(1) will yield values that slowly dampen as k grows, whereas an MA(1) process will yield a nonzero ACF value only at $k = 1$. What if, however, we suspect that higher order processes might be at work? For example, that there might be an AR(2) process?

By undertaking the same procedures as earlier, we can develop an expectation about the values of our ACFs at higher orders. For higher order AR(p) processes, as p grows larger, the ACF will still decay toward zero, possibly in an oscillating manner, depending on the values of ϕ_1 and ϕ_2. For a higher order MA process (e.g., MA(2)), we would expect to see nonzero values of ACF(k), where $k \leq q$, where q is the order of the MA process. All other values of the ACF where $k > q$ will be equal to zero.

Of course, we will rarely encounter ACFs with our data whose values truly are equal to zero. Rather, we can compute confidence intervals of our ACFs. Should the value of our ACF lie outside the confidence interval, we functionally treat those values as zero for purposes of diagnosing our time series.[12]

Most scholars examine the value of a number of ACF(k)'s on one graph, creating what is known as a *correlogram*. Figures 2.2 and 2.3 are a series of correlograms showing ideal-type ACF graphs (and PACFs, see the later discussion). The correlograms show the value of various lags of the ACF statistic as well as the accompanying standard errors, so one may visually inspect the series. These graphs are essential to the identification stage of Box-Jenkins modeling. At the end of this chapter, we demonstrate with two datasets how to use the correlograms and their ACF and PACF statistics to diagnose what dynamic processes occur in data.

2.3.2 The Partial Autocorrelation Function (PACF)

Although the ACF is a powerful identification tool, there may be instances where it is difficult to determine the components of a series based only on the correlogram of an ACF. McLeary and Hay (1980, 75), note that higher order AR(p) and MA(q) models yield such similar ACFs that "it is nearly impossible to distinguish between these two processes on the basis of an estimated ACF

---

[12] The standard error of the ACF is computed as $ACF_{se} = \sqrt{N^{-1}(1 + 2\sum_{i=1}^{k} [ACF(i)]^2)}$.

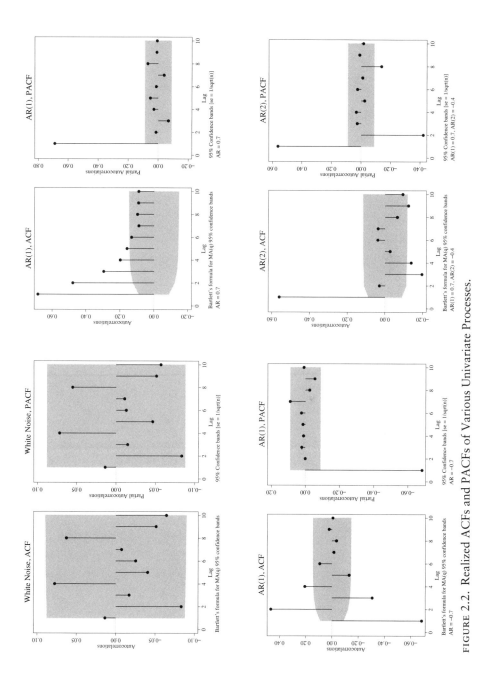

FIGURE 2.2. Realized ACFs and PACFs of Various Univariate Processes.

39

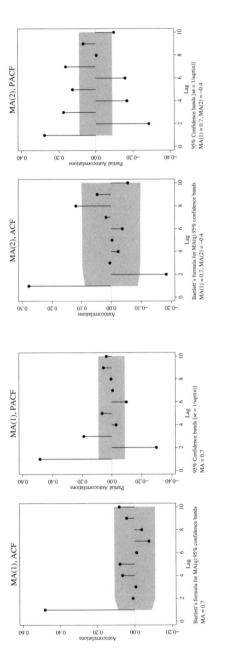
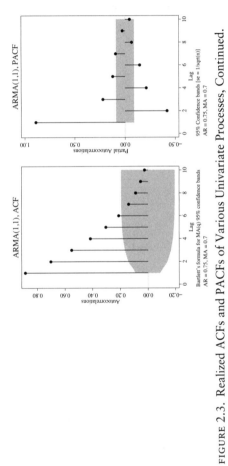

FIGURE 2.3. Realized ACFs and PACFs of Various Univariate Processes, Continued.

alone." Fortunately, another tool can help us in the identification process: the partial autocorrelation function.

The PACF(k) is a measure of correlation between times series observations that are k units apart, after the correlation at intermediate lags has been controlled for or "partialed" out. In other words, the PACF(k) is the correlation between y_t and y_{t+k} after removing the effect of the intermediate y's.

**Unfortunately, the computation of the PACF is complex, requiring a solution to the Yule-Walker equation system to estimate PACF(k). One can, however, use the values of estimated ACFs to get a feel for how the value of a PACF is computed.

$$PACF(1) = ACF(1) \tag{2.40}$$

$$PACF(2) = \frac{ACF(2) - [ACF(1)]^2}{1 - [ACF(1)]^2} \tag{2.41}$$

$$PACF(3) = \frac{ACF(3) + ACF(1)[ACF(2)]^2 + [ACF(1)]^3 - 2ACF(1)ACF(2) - [ACF(1)]^2 ACF(3)}{1 + 2[ACF(1)]^2 ACF(2) - [ACF(2)]^2 - [ACF(1)]^2} \tag{2.42}$$

Notice that the value of the PACF is based on having the previous values of the ACF removed or partialed out of the current value. As in the ACF case, we can develop expected values for the PACF based on our knowledge of the values of the ACFs. Recall that for an ARMA(1,0) the expected value of the ACF(k) is ϕ_1^k. Based on this, we can substitute into the previous equations

$$PACF(1) = \phi_1^1 \tag{2.43}$$

$$PACF(2) = \frac{\phi_1^2 - \phi_1^2}{1 - \phi_1^2} = \frac{0}{1 - \phi_1^2} = 0 \tag{2.44}$$

It can be shown that substituting into higher values of PACF(k) the expectations will continue to be zero. Thus, whereas the ACF of an ARMA(1,0) process will exponentially decay, the PACF of that same process will be nonzero for $k = 1$ but zero for all $k > 1$. Additionally, for the ARMA(2,0) process, we can use the same method of substitution to conclude that the PACF(1) and PACF(2) will be nonzero, but all $k > 2$ will again be zero. This pattern continues as the order of P increases, although as we have suggested, higher order AR processes are more likely to be more parsimoniously represented by a lower order MA process.

Turning to our expectations of the PACF for an ARMA(0,1), recall that our expectation of the ACF $= \frac{-\theta_1}{1+\theta_1^2}$, and that for all $k > 1$, our expected ACF value is zero. Substituting to find out expectations of the PACF, however, yields the following:

$$PACF(1) = \frac{-\theta_1}{1 + \theta_1^2} \tag{2.45}$$

$$PACF(2) = \frac{-\theta_1^2}{1 + \theta_1^2 + \theta_1^4} \tag{2.46}$$

$$PACF(3) = \frac{-\theta_1^3}{1 + \theta_1^2 + \theta_1^4 + \theta_1^6} \tag{2.47}$$

Note that the value of the denominator continues to grow as k grows, suggesting a dampening of the PACF. In the case of an ARMA(0,2), we would expect similar dampening behavior with the first two values of PACF(k) to be statistically significant.

Return to Figures 2.2 and 2.3. Now, with the knowledge of the ACF and PACF statistics, one can begin to unravel the processes present in a time series. These figures present ideal-type graphs generated from simulated data. Thus, correlograms from actual data may not appear so clean, yet as we discuss later in the chapter, post-estimation tools exist to help us decide between what could be two compelling models should ACFs and PACFs prove indeterminate.

Note that the expected patterns of ACFs and PACFs are mirror images of each other, whether one is working with an ARMA(1,0) or an ARMA(0,1). That is, for an AR(1) process, the PACF has one statistically significant spike, while the ACF of the MA(1) has the same. This "mirroring" highlights the fact that there is a strong link between the two models, but also reminds us to be careful in our diagnosis of our time series.

We should also note that the first two correlograms in Figure 2.2 depict white noise. It is possible that one's time series has little in the way of temporal dynamics. Thus, a correlogram with no statistically significant spikes in any lags is likely white noise. Later, we discuss a formal test for white noise that, in combination with a "quiet" correlogram, can be used to confirm a white noise series, either before or after estimating an ARMA model.

Let us make two more parts on ACFs and PACFs. First, the direction and patterns of the estimates of the ACFs and PACFs help predict the value of the actual parameter estimates. That is, depending on the sign of ϕ or θ, the ACF or PACF may be positive and dampening, negative and dampening, or oscillating. For example, a positive value of θ (and $\phi = 0$ will produce a *negative* ACF and PACF. A positive value of ϕ (and $\theta = 0$) will lead to *positive* ACF and PACF values. A negative value of ϕ (along with a $\theta = 0$) will lead to a single, negative PACF estimate and oscillating values on the ACF. Substantively, positive values of ϕ or θ mean that larger proportions of previous shocks continue to reverberate in the system for that particular lag.

Second, your own time series ACF and PACF will never be quite as clean as the idealized ones presented here. There will often be some noise in these diagnostic graphs. It is not unusual, for example, to see a random spike at a longer lag after most previous lags are statistically insignificant. In these cases, one can estimate competing models to see which is superior in terms of explanatory power or information criteria. Thus, these graphs, combined with model-fitting estimates, will help diagnose the underlying time series structure of your data.

2.3.3 Seasonality

So far, we have discussed the possibility that our series could have one of two parts: an autoregressive component or a moving average component. Now, we add a final possibility: seasonality. Seasonality can be defined as any cyclical or periodic fluctuation in a time series that recurs or repeats itself at the same phase of the cycle or period. There are numerous examples of seasonality in the social sciences. Many economic time series contain seasonal elements (e.g., boosts in employment in the workforce over the summer months, sales data for holiday shopping). Some have hypothesized that the outbreak of interstate war follows a cyclical pattern (Goldstein, 1988). Many crime patterns appear to follow seasonal patterns, with violent crimes often reaching their apex in the summer months. As social science data become increasingly temporally disaggregated (moving from yearly to monthly, weekly, or even daily), the possibilities of finding cyclical or seasonal patterns increase.

Both seasonal and nonseasonal cases use the same diagnostic and modeling processes with only a slight difference in notation. We usually refer to the seasonal components of a time series in the Box-Jenkins context as an ARMA $(p, q)_s$ model, where s is the period over which the process repeats itself. For example, if one is using monthly data and there is a strong autoregressive component that repeats itself every year, one would denote this as an ARMA $(1,0)_{12}$. Such a model would be represented as

$$y_t = \phi_{12} y_{t-12} + a_t. \tag{2.48}$$

A seasonal MA model (for example, an ARMA $(0,1)_4$ for a quarterly MA process using monthly data) would be represented as

$$y_t = \theta_1 a_t + \theta_4 a_{t-4}. \tag{2.49}$$

The ACFs and PACFs for each of these types of models are similar to those discussed for nonseasonal data, except that the statistically significant spikes will occur with the appropriate cycle – in equation 2.45, that means a noticeable spike every 12, 24, 36, ... months in the PACF, whereas for equation 2.46, it would mean a noticeable spike every 4, 8, 12, ... months in the ACF. Of course, one may have mixed seasonal and nonseasonal processes as well, where cyclical AR processes reside in the data along with a nonseasonal AR(1) process, for

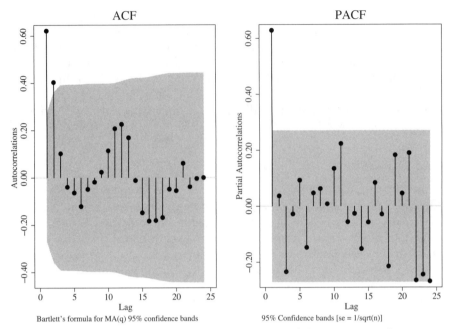

FIGURE 2.4. ACF and PACF of Democratic Proportion of the U.S. House of Representatives, 1902–2006.

example.[13] Such a model, for a joint nonseasonal and seasonal AR process (say, monthly), would be noted as an ARMA $(1,0)(1,0)_{12}$.

Later, we present an example of a time series with strong seasonality, so we do not develop an example here. In the example to come, the data are homicide rates, and past research and theory suggest the strong likelihood of a seasonal component, which we subsequently model.

2.4 MODEL ESTIMATION, INTERPRETATION, AND DIAGNOSIS

Once the data have been diagnosed using the appropriate processes it is time to estimate the model. Of course, one initially fits the model closest to that diagnosed using the previously discussed techniques. Most statistical packages easily estimate ARMA models.

As an example, take a simple ARMA(1,0) model of the proportion of Democrats in the U.S. House of Representatives from 1902–2006 (see Figure 1.1 from Chapter 1). We begin with this model because the ACF of the series appears to be slowly decaying, whereas the PACF shows one statistically significant spike at $k = 1$ (see Figure 2.4). Sprague (1981) examined this very

---

[13] We discuss seasonal unit roots in Chapter 5.

TABLE 2.2. *AR(1) Estimates of the Democratic Proportion of House notes: Standard errors in parentheses*

Variable	Coefficient
intercept	0.54
	(0.03)
ϕ_1	0.64
	(0.11)
σ	0.08
	(0.01)

Note: Standard errors in parentheses.

series and investigated whether, given the institutionalization of incumbency effects, a telos existed in the proportion of seats controlled by Democrats. By "telos," Sprague (1981, 265) referred to a particular proportion that could be estimated to which the electoral system would converge over time. Although particular events could push that proportion higher or lower, the system would self-correct and move "much like a thermostat" back to that "telos" or what could be labeled an equilibrium. To determine this underlying equilibrium, however, one needs to uncover the structure of the data-generating process in the time series.

Table 2.2 shows the estimates of this model. Note that this series shows a strong autoregressive component, with a statistically significant estimate of ϕ_1. This result suggests that the proportion of Democrats in year t is highly related to the proportion of Democrats in $t - 1$. Substantively, this makes sense, given the advantages of incumbency for House members (Cox and Katz, 1996; Gelman and King, 1990). When an autoregressive component is present in the model, the constant can be interpreted as an intercept. Note that the value of the constant suggests that the natural equilibrium proportion is above 50%, suggesting that a Democratic majority is the equilibrium state of the House of Representatives. Throughout the 20th century (and as is indeed evident from inspecting the time plot, Figure 1.1), such a result is not surprising.

After estimating an initial model, however, it is important to both over- and under-fit the model to ensure its proper specification. In this case, under-fitting would be a simple white noise model, which we could reject based on the ACFs and PACFs of the series in Figure 2.4. We can quickly estimate an ARMA(2,0) model to check for the possibility of additional AR terms. Although we do not show the estimates of the over-fit model, the estimate of ϕ_1 remains positive and statistically significant, but the estimate of ϕ_2 is close to zero (0.04) and is not statistically significant ($z = 0.27$). One could also consider an MA (1) or ARMA (1,1) model, but given the correlograms, such a model is highly unlikely.

Thus, we can be fairly certain that we have the correct model specification based on over- and under-fitting, yet to be more confident of this fact, we turn to two additional steps: residual analysis and metadiagnosis.

2.4.1 Residual Analysis

How can one be sure that one has the correct specification other than by over- and under-fitting the model? One of the easiest ways to check is to analyze the residuals from the ARMA estimation. Two important analyses can be quickly performed to check model specification. First, ACFs and PACFs can be estimated from the residuals of the ARMA estimation. Recall that if each "filter" of the data has been removed, one should be left with white noise. If one has white noise residuals, the ACFs and PACFs of the residuals should be zero at all k lags.

Second, a summary statistic can test for the presence of white noise residuals. The Q statistic is a helpful diagnostic instrument that is straightforward to estimate. We define Q as

$$Q = T(T+2)\sum_{k=1}^{s} r_k^2/(T-k), \tag{2.50}$$

where T is the number of observations in the time series, s is the total number of lags being tested, and r_k is the autocorrelation of the series at lag k.[14] The null hypothesis is that all values of $r_k = 0$. The Q statistic is asymptotically distributed χ^2 with s degrees of freedom. Thus, a significant Q statistic suggests that there is at least one or more lags that are distinguishable from zero, indicating that the series is *not* white noise.

In our example of Democratic control of the U.S. House, the Q test on the residuals of the ARMA(1,0) models yields an estimate of $Q = 23.98$, $p > \chi^2$ (24 df) $= 0.46$, suggesting that the residuals are white noise. This result, in combination with our over- and under-modeling, can give us confidence that our model selection is adequate.

2.4.2 Metadiagnosis

What if one's results are not quite as "clean" as in our previous example? How does one decide between an ARMA(2,0) or an ARMA(1,1) or an ARMA(0,2), if all parameters are significant and all residuals are white noise? There are a number of ways to compare specifications across various nested and non-nested ARMA models. We begin with a discussion of two information criteria that

---

[14] The test is often referred to as the Ljung and Box (1978) Q or the Portmanteau test. An earlier version of the Q test, from Box and Pierce (1970), had poor small sample qualities, which the Ljung-Box Q improves on. Bartlett's periodogram-based test for white noise is also appropriate for these purposes. For more on the Bartlett test, see Bartlett (1955) and Newton (1988).

are commonly used to compare non-nested model specifications: the Akaike information criteria (AIC) and the Schwartz Baysesian criteria (BIC).[15]

$$\text{AIC} = \text{T} \, ln(\text{SUM OF SQUARED RESIDUALS}) + 2n \qquad (2.51)$$

$$\text{BIC} = \text{T} \, ln(\text{SUM OF SQUARED RESIDUALS}) + n \ln(\text{T}) \qquad (2.52)$$

where T is the number of observations (which should be kept constant across models with different numbers of lags) and n is the number of parameters estimated (AR terms, MA terms, constants).

One uses information criteria by selecting the model with the *smallest* value of the statistic (even when the statistic is negative). The general intent of these criteria is to reward explanatory power, but not at the expense of parsimony. That is, although one could always add additional terms to gain better fit, doing so would come at a loss of degrees of freedom. In particular, growth in n will lead to higher values, unless these values are offset by gains in the residual sum of squares.

Comparing the two statistics, it should be noted that the BIC will almost always favor the more parsimonious model, because $\ln(T)$ will always be greater than 2 in time series models (Enders, 2004, 69). This property is important because occasionally, the information criteria will disagree on which is the preferred model. It should also be noted that the AIC has better small sample properties, even though it may favor over-parameterized models (Enders, 2004, 70).

Traditional regression measures of goodness of fit could also serve as a basis for comparison. The R^2 or adjusted R^2 may also be used as a criteria for model selection. Of course, many criticize an over-reliance on the R^2, but as one piece of the toolkit of model diagnosis, the statistic has its place. Recall that unlike our information criteria, however, there are no penalties for over-modeling in the R^2 measure as there are in the adjusted R^2.

A heretofore unstated principle in our discussion of ARMA modeling generally, and of model selection specifically, is that one should select the most *parsimonious* model possible. One can always attempt to add additional covariates to fit additional data points, but time series analysis generally relies on the Occam's razor, principle and favors the simplest explanation.

Finally, it is worth noting that one criterion for model selection and diagnosis is the requirement that our ϕ's and our θ's are invertible (i.e., both are less than 1). Recall that parameter estimates greater than 1 indicate an explosive growth process – a process that does not diminish over time, but instead grows in importance. Occasionally, however, one sees an estimate outside of these bounds of invertibility early in the model-building process. In these cases, often the process is not stationary and the data require differencing. We return to this discussion in Chapter 5.

---

[15] Recall that nested models can be tested using an F or chi-squared statistic for the inclusion of new explanatory terms.

Now that we have discussed the Box-Jenkins modeling process, we turn to two examples of real data to illustrate the process from beginning to end. Both examples deal with stationary time series; we defer the discussion of nonstationary models until Chapter 5. The following examples, one drawn from political science and the other from criminology, should serve as a guide to those who wish to put their new-found knowledge into practice.

2.5 APPLICATION: U.S. HOMICIDE RATES

With many of the social phenomena we study, it is hoped that a better understanding of their causes can lead to more effective policies. Time series analysis has been a common methodology to study crime. Here, we analyze a monthly time series of homicides in the United States from 1975–1993,[16] using Box-Jenkins methodology to understand the underlying data structure of the series; this approach is quite common in the study of crime rates.

Although our example here is simple and pedagogical, criminologists analyzing homicide time series data have explored its nonlinearity (McDowall, 2002; McDowall and Loftin, 2005), error correction mechanisms (Cantor and Land, 2001; Greenberg, 2001), the added value of nationally aggregated data over disaggregated sources (Levitt, 2001), the effect of capital punishment on local homicide rates (Land, Teske, and Zheng, 2009), and spatial dependencies in its seasonal patterns (McDowall, Loftin, and Pate, 2012).

Recall Figure 2.1, which presents a portion of the raw data that we analyze here.[17] Notice two features in the plot of the raw data. First, there appears to be an increasing number of homicides over time (as show by the OLS trend line). Such an upward trend could indicate nonstationarity if shocks over time integrate into the system. Second, there appear to be periodic but consistent spikes in the data over time, suggesting a possible seasonal component to the data. Indeed, other studies of homicide rates have also noted seasonal components in time series of homicide rates.[18]

To begin our diagnosis, we turn to Figure 2.5, which depicts the ACF and PACF of our homicide series. Note the large spikes in both graphs that appear to be seasonal: at 12 and 24 months, the values of the ACF and PACF are quite large. Moreover, these seasonal spikes do not appear to die out more quickly in the ACF than in the PACF. Normally, if one dampened more slowly than the

---

[16] As noted earlier and in Chapter 1, some cities report their homicide data on an annual rather than monthly basis. There are interesting dynamics in the monthly series for pedagogical purposes, but for many analytic endeavors the monthly series is not recommended. Our purpose here is pedagogical.

[17] Although Figure 2.1 plots only 8 years of the data, we use all 18 years of the monthly data for this analysis.

[18] For a recent analysis of seasonality in the homicide time series, see McDowall, Loftin, and Pate (2012).

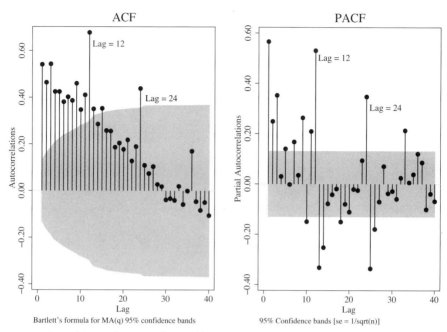

FIGURE 2.5. ACF and PACF of Monthly Homicide Data.

other, one would suspect a seasonal autoregressive (moving average) process at work. Because of the ambiguity present here, we test for both.

Substantively, why would one expect seasonality? Past empirical work, in particular those papers using the Box-Jenkins methodology, has reached this conclusion. Work by Tennenbaum and Fink (1994) found a strong seasonal component to a monthly homicides crime series running from 1976–1989. In addition, scholars working with other crime-related time series consistently find seasonal AR terms present in data. For example, D'Alessio and Stolzenberg (1995) found a strong seasonal AR(1) component to both misdemeanors and felonies. Chamlin (1988) observed moving average seasonal components to several violent crime time series.

The cause of the seasonality is debated, but there are several possibilities. First, some studies have uncovered relationships between temperature and violent crimes, which could lead to spikes of violent behavior due to "short fuses" over summer months (cf. Dagum, Huot, and Morry, 1988; DeFronzo, 1984; McDowall, Loftin, and Pate, 2012; McLeod, MacNeill, and Bhattacharyya, 1985). Warm temperatures also encourage greater social interaction among individuals. As social interactions (particularly accompanied by alcohol and drug use) increase, so do opportunities for conflict and ultimately violence. Thus motivated, scholars have used seasonal ARMA models with high frequency in this area.

TABLE 2.3. *Modeling Monthly Homicide Rates*

	Model 1	Model 2	Model 3	Model 4
intercept	1.73	1.71	1.73	1.72
	(0.10)	(0.05)	(0.12)	(0.07)
AR(p)				
ϕ_1	0.37	0.39	0.32	0.33
	(0.05)	(0.05)	(0.05)	(0.05)
ϕ_2	0.26	0.23	0.17	0.12
	(0.06)	(0.05)	(0.07)	(0.06)
ϕ_3			0.21	0.28
			(0.06)	(0.06)
$AR(p)_{12}$				
ϕ_1	0.71		0.68	
	(0.05)		(0.05)	
MA(q)				
θ_1		0.42		0.39
		(0.06)		(0.06)
σ	0.13	0.15	0.13	0.15
	0.004	0.004	0.003	0.004
AIC	−269.31	−193.73†	−277.66	−209.67
BIC	−252.16	−176.58†	−257.09	−189.09
R^2	0.66	0.53	0.68†	0.56
Q test	68.20	158.77	69.20	37.97
p of χ^2	0.00	0.00	0.00	0.56

Notes: Standard errors in parentheses; † = model favored by this criterion.

As previously discussed, seasonality may well exist alongside other temporal dynamics. In these correlograms, there are several large values in the PACF that dampen quickly and corresponding large values in the ACF that die out more slowly. These values indicate the presence of an autoregressive process in the data.[19] Given what appears to be a seasonal component in a 12-month interval and some order of autoregressiveness, we begin by fitting an ARMA(2,0)(1,0)$_{12}$ model.

Table 2.3 shows the estimates of our initial model in the first column. Each parameter estimate, including the seasonal component, is statistically significant. Unfortunately, the Q test for white noise residuals fails to reject the hypothesis that at least one autocorrelation in the residuals is statistically significant. Because we could not deduce whether the seasonal pattern was of the autoregressive or moving average variety, we move to another model that is

---

[19] The slow decay of the ACF could indicate an integrative process as well. Tests for an I(1) process can confidently reject the hypothesis that the series contains a unit root. See Chapter 5 for a discussion of these tests.

identical in its nonseasonal components, but its seasonal component is adjusted to include a moving average term. As shown in column 2 of Table 2.3, each estimate is statistically significant, and the information criteria values are much lower in this new model, although the overall explanatory power (as measured by the R^2) falls. As before, the Q test for white noise residuals cannot reject the hypothesis that meaningful temporal dynamics still exist in the residuals.

In an attempt to obtain white noise residuals, we add an autoregressive term to the nonseasonal component of the model. These estimates, appearing in column 3, are quite similar to those in column 1. Although the R^2 of this new model is higher than the more parsimonious version, the Q test still does not give us confidence that the residuals are white noise. Next, returning to our model with the seasonal MA component, we add a third nonseasonal autoregressive term. All estimates (found in the final column) are statistically significant (although ϕ_2 only at the $p < 0.10$ level), and the Q test can reject the hypothesis that there is meaningful variation left in the residuals of this model. Although the information criteria would point to the second model as the preferred model, the addition of the third-order AR term (Model 4) is necessary to create white noise residuals. As is evident in this example, one will sometimes find that different modeling favors different models. How does one choose which modeling approach to use when the criteria differ? Our approach prioritizes the Q test because the overall point of this exercise is to model the time series elements in the series, leaving white noise. Frequently, multiple models will reject the null hypothesis under the Q test, and at that point, it is often best to rely on information criteria.

Figure 2.6 plots the correlograms of the residuals of the final model. No significant values of the ACF or PACF can be found until one examines very large lags in the PACF. Given the lack of statistical significance at lower ACF and PACF lags, it would likely be difficult to capture these long lag dynamics. In these cases, the analyst often accepts the model even with statistically significant ACFs or PACFs at large lags, especially if the Q statistic suggests white noise residuals.

Our Box-Jenkins model confirms past research on the strong seasonal component to the homicide rate. Why have some studies found autoregressive processes while we find a moving average process? Although it is difficult to be certain, many of the studies we reviewed in this area did not report their model specification procedures. That is, it is impossible to know if the models were specified a priori or were specified using an iterative Box-Jenkins approach. It is possible that a systematic effort at model identification could change some of the extant findings. On the other hand, the relatively short length of our series may have precluded findings of nonstationarity, which might have necessitated the use of cointegration analysis (which we cover generally in Chapter 6), as argued by Greenberg (2001). Because we present this example for pedagogical purposes, readers are referred to the sophisticated recent work of McDowall, Loftin, and Pate (2012); Greenberg (2001); Cantor and Land

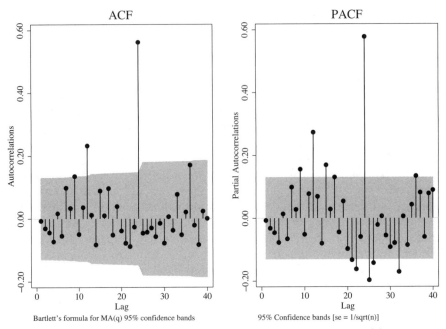

FIGURE 2.6. ACF and PACF of Residuals from ARMA(2,0)(0,1) 12 Model.

(2001); Steffensmeier et al. (2011), and Land, Teske, and Zheng (2009) on the analysis of homicide time series data.

2.6 APPLICATION: U.S. RELATIONS WITH THE MIDDLE EAST

Perhaps no region of the world has received more attention from scholars and policy makers alike in the past four decades than the Middle East. Numerous religious, ethnic, and civil conflicts have wracked the region for decades, and American strategic interests in the area remain high. Perhaps the central conflict of the region is the struggle between the state of Israel and the Palestinian people. The conflict has deep implications for various security and economic issues involving the United States, which has played various roles in the conflict: mediator, broker, supporter, and enforcer.

Of course, America has done a better or worse job at these roles depending on who is at the receiving end of U.S. foreign policy. Those in government throughout the past decades would perhaps object to this characterization, because U.S. foreign policy explicitly attempts to stay even-handed in response to behavior emanating from the region. Government officials would argue that consistency has been and should be the hallmark of American foreign policy, at least since the signing of the Oslo Accords in the early 1990s. But a basic empirical question remains: does U.S. behavior toward each side vary over time and, if so, in what ways?

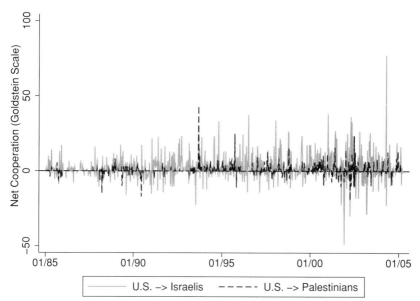

FIGURE 2.7. U.S. Behavior Toward Israelis and Palestinians, 1985–2005. Compiled by the authors from event data produced by the Kansas Events Data System.

Using our knowledge of time series processes, we can develop a simple model of American behavior toward the Middle East to begin to unravel this question. We begin by plotting the time series of directed action of the United States to Israel and to the Palestinians, shown in Figure 2.7. As Chatfield (2003, 13) has famously noted, "The first, and most important, step in any time-series analysis is to plot the observations against time."

The first property to note about the series is its high frequency. The low-aggregation weekly data provide a rich source of information, which can be used to estimate our models accurately. Second, note that there appears to be no trend in the series: the mean of each appears to stay relatively stable over time. This suggests little possibility of a unit root.[20] Finally, substantively, there appears to be far more interactions concerning the U.S.-Israel dyad than the U.S.-Palestinian one, suggesting (not surprisingly) that the data-generating process for each of these series may be different.

As our next step, we estimate the ACFs and PACFs of each series. Figure 2.8 shows the correlograms for each series. Note that neither the ACF nor PACF of either series nicely matches one of the ideal-type correlograms of Figures 2.2 and 2.3. In fact, for both sets of correlograms the ACFs and PACFs look

---

[20] In this example, we do not conduct tests for unit roots or fractional integration because we want to keep the example simple. Estimates of d suggest that there is a very minor fractional integration $d \sim 0.1$. Fractionally differencing the two series presented here, and repeating the diagnosis and estimation, yields extremely similar models. We discuss unit roots and fractional integration in Chapter 5.

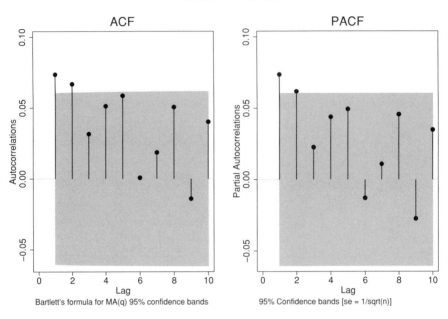

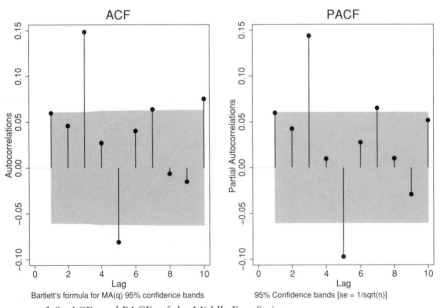

FIGURE 2.8. ACFs and PACFs of the Middle East Series.

TABLE 2.4. *U.S. Behavior to Israel*

	AR[1]	AR[2]	AR[3]	MA[1]	MA[2]
constant	2.49	2.49	2.49	2.49	2.49
	(0.27)	(0.29)	(0.30)	(0.27)	(0.29)
AR(p)					
ϕ_1	0.07	0.07	0.07		
	(0.02)	(0.02)	(0.02)		
ϕ_2		0.06	0.06		
		(0.03)	(0.03)		
ϕ_3			0.02		
			(0.03)		
MA(q)					
θ_1				0.07	0.07
				(0.02)	(0.02)
θ_2					0.06
					(0.03)
σ	7.89	7.88	7.88	7.90	7.88
	(0.07)	(0.07)	(0.08)	(0.07)	(0.07)
AIC	7366.32	7364.29†	7365.74	7366.96	7364.99
BIC	7381.21†	7384.13	7390.55	7381.85	7384.84
R^2	0.005	0.009	0.01†	0.005	0.009
Q test	41.78	36.79	35.33	42.68	37.81
p of χ^2	0.39	0.62	0.68	0.36	0.57

Notes: Standard errors in parentheses; † = model favored by this criteria.

remarkably similar. The second issue to note is the small estimated values of the ACFs and PACFs. Even if AR or MA processes are present, they appear to be muted, even if statistically significant. Finally, although it may appear at first that there could be seasonality in the U.S.-Palestinian series, note that the spikes at $k = 3$ do not repeat at normal intervals (e.g., 3, 6, 9). This suggests that although there could be a longer term AR or MA process, it is unlikely to be seasonal.

Given that there appear to be some low-order AR or MA processes occurring in the data, but we cannot diagnose the structure of the model with much confidence based on the correlograms, we move to the estimation part of the exercise. We begin by proposing some simple models of each process, and then move to over-modeling to assess model fit and adequacy. Tables 2.4 and 2.5 present estimated models of the U.S.-Israel and U.S.-Palestinian series, respectively.

Table 2.4 presents the coefficient estimates of five U.S-Israel Box-Jenkins models, as well as several measures of model fit and adequacy. Note that the estimates of the AR(1) and MA(1), as well as the AR(2) and the MA(2), are

TABLE 2.5. *U.S. Behavior to Palestinians*

	AR[1]	AR[2]	AR[3]	MA[1]	MA[2]	MA[3]
constant	0.50	0.50	0.50	0.50	0.50	0.50
	(0.12)	(0.12)	(0.14)	(0.12)	(0.12)	(0.14)
AR(p)						
ϕ_1	0.06	0.06	0.05			
	(0.02)	(0.02)	(0.02)			
ϕ_2		0.04	0.03			
		(0.02)	(0.03)			
ϕ_3			0.14			
			(0.02)			
MA(q)						
θ_1				0.06	0.05	0.05
				(0.02)	(0.02)	(0.02)
θ_2					0.03	0.06
					(0.02)	(0.03)
θ_3						0.15
						(0.02)
σ	3.16	3.16	3.13	3.16	3.16	3.13
	(0.02)	(0.02)	(0.02)	(0.02)	(0.02)	(0.02)
AIC	5434.48	5434.57	5414.51	5434.74	5435.82	5413.54†
BIC	5449.37	5454.42	5439.33	5449.62	5455.66	5438.36†
R^2	0.004	0.005	0.026	0.003	0.004	0.027†
Q test	73.22	75.27	51.39	73.25	75.10	47.70
p of χ^2	0.00	0.00	0.11	0.00	0.00	0.19

Notes: Standard errors in parentheses; † = model favored by this criteria.

identical in their coefficient and standard errors. The ϕ's and θ's are clearly within the bounds of invertibility and are statistically significant in all columns except column 3. Indeed, in column 3 (the AR(3) model), the ϕ_3 coefficient does not achieve statistical significance, suggesting the point of over-fitting has been reached.[21]

Given the similarity of these models, how is one to decide which one is the most appropriate? Here, relying on our information criteria and/or model fit criteria is helpful. The bottom lines of Table 2.4 present two information criteria plus an R^2 measure. The first thing to notice is that the information criteria prefer the AR to the MA specifications. Unfortunately, within the AR models, the AIC and BIC reach different conclusions as to which is the superior model. This is not surprising, given our earlier discussion that the BIC often prefers

---

[21] The MA(3) estimation is similar to the AR(3) in that the final θ term does not achieve statistical significance. The estimates of this model are omitted.

the more parsimonious model. Yet, given the increase in overall explanatory power and the statistically significant ϕ_2 term, we settle on the AR(2) model as the preferred choice.

Substantively, the AR(2) suggests that U.S. behavior toward Israel has a two-week "look-back" period, where the best predictors of today's behavior is the behavior last week and two weeks earlier. Also recall that the AR process suggests that previous behavior matters over a long period of time – shocks affect all future observations at a decreasing rate – unlike the MA process where there is a finite persistence. It is worth noting that when we posit any lag structure in our models, it is usually an AR(1) by default. Yet in this example, the AR(1) by default would not adequately capture the time series dynamics in the series. Of course, this longer-than-usual memory could be the result of the long and deep political ties between the United States and Israel.

Moving to Table 2.5, we follow the same strategy of beginning with a simple model and then moving to more complex, higher order models. Note that, like the estimates in Table 2.4, these coefficient estimates are also similar across AR and MA processes. Again, we turn to information criteria to adjudicate between these models. Although the information criteria generally favor the AR specifications, this ceases to be the case once a third term is introduced into the model. The MA(3) model is favored by each information criteria, as well as for its overall explanatory power. The fact that a third-order model is chosen is not surprising: the large spike at ACF(3) and PACF(3) suggested that a third-order dynamic of some type was present in the data.

Yet, interpreting what this third-order term means substantively could prove more challenging. Of course, one possible explanation could lie in the nature of the data-coding process: are reports of actor behavior taken on a three-period basis, or could there be a three-week lag in reporting similar events? This is unlikely given the density of media coverage in the Middle East (Schrodt and Gerner, 1997). A more straightforward explanation is that shocks that occur in American behavior toward the Palestinians are relatively short-lived (i.e., approximately three weeks). Shocks enter the system and do not persist for longer than three periods. This is a plausible interpretation given the brief history of U.S.-Palestinian relations (recall that the United States did not recognize the PLO as the representative of the Palestinian people until the late 1980s, preferring to work through other intermediaries). In other words, there are no long-term relationships guiding interactions, but rather newly formed and highly variant interactions. This is in contract to the U.S.-Israeli relationship, which is more than six decades old and more established and stable.

Finally, we draw your attention to the last line of each table. The Q statistic is computed on the residuals from each estimated model to ensure that a white noise process was recovered from the data. In all cases for the U.S.-Israel series, the Q statistic is not significant, indicating the presence of no statistically significant autocorrelations. This suggests that the residuals of each of these models are indeed white noise. For the U.S.-Palestinian series, however, it is not until the third-order AR or MA term enters the model that the Q statistic shows white noise residuals. Thus, in addition to the information criteria, the white noise test suggests that the more parsimonious models are inadequate to model this series.

Figure 2.9 plots the residuals of the two models selected for the U.S.-Israel series and the U.S.-Palestinian series. Although a small number of values exceed the confidence intervals, these graphs, along with the Q statistics from the estimated residuals give us confidence that our models are quite plausible. Not only do few ACF and PACF values appear to be statistically significant but those that do appear also show no pattern and would likely be difficult to model explicitly.

Overall, what are the methodological and substantive lessons we take from this exercise? First, using these series showed the benefits of over-fitting, especially in cases where the correlograms may be inadequate to completely diagnose the data-generating process. Second, this example highlighted the importance of the information criteria and the fact that different criteria may yield different preferred models. Thus, although these criteria are not the only way to evaluate a model, they are quite useful.

Substantively, it is clear that different data-generating processes produced each of these series, providing evidence for the argument that the United States does not treat each side in the conflict the same. Of course, a more fully developed model would include the reciprocal behavior (e.g., Israeli and Palestinian behavior to the United States), which would help us understand the context of the series being modeled here. But this goes to the issue of multiple time series analysis, which we begin to tackle in Chapter 3. Still, that an AR process best represents American behavior to Israel and an MA process best reflects American behavior toward the Palestinians suggests fundamentally different rates of persistence in behavior.

2.7 INTERVENTION MODELS

So far, we have only examined univariate models of our time series. Yet, even when examining a single series, we may want to ask whether the patterns we discover in our ARMA modeling are constant over the length of the series. In other words, armed with our knowledge of the underlying data-generating process, might we test for events that influence the series? Did a crime bill influence the rate of robberies or homicides? Did third-party intervention in a conflict lessen or increase violence between the warring parties? Did a change in campaign finance law effectively limit campaign contributions? Or as summarized by Box and Tiao (1975, 70), "Given a known intervention, is there evidence that change in the series of the kind expected actually occurred, and, if so, what can be said of the nature and magnitude of the change?"

U.S. –> Israel

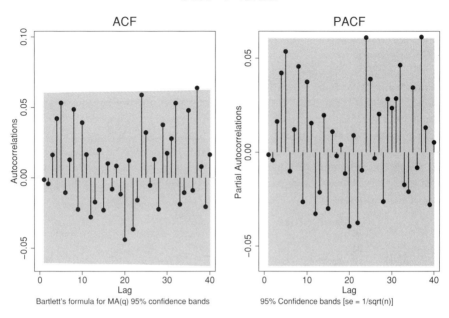

U.S. –> Palestinians

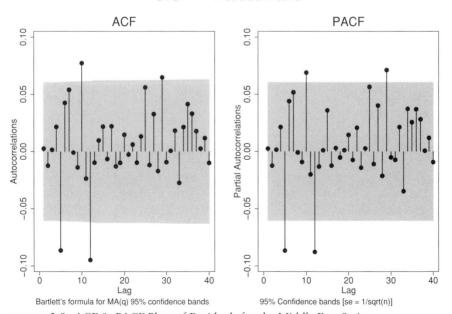

FIGURE 2.9. ACF & PACF Plots of Residuals for the Middle East Series.

The types of models that answer such questions are often referred to as having a *quasi-experimental design.*[22]

Using a method that is part and parcel of ARMA modeling, known as intervention analysis or impact assessment, we can answer these questions in a relatively simple way. There are numerous studies using this method in many social science literatures. Campbell and Ross (1968) famously asked whether changes in traffic laws led to fewer accidents on Connecticut roadways. Box and Tiao's (1975) article outlining the intervention model reported on the impact of air pollution control laws. In political science, Caporaso and Pelowski (1971) examined the progress of European integration and Lewis-Beck (1979) examined the economic effects of revolutions, to cite two examples.

To conduct an intervention analysis, one initially postulates an event (defined as a qualitative change in state), which may be represented as a dummy variable in the following form:

$$I_t = \begin{cases} 0, & \text{prior to the event} \\ 1, & \text{thereafter} \end{cases}.$$

Note that this method requires that the analyst know the event a priori to the analysis. The full impact assessment model can be written as

$$Y_t = f(I_t) + N_t, \tag{2.53}$$

where, I_t denotes the intervention variable and N_t denotes the white noise component of the ARMA model. If one then subtracts the white noise component from the series, this yields

$$Y_t^* = Y_t - N_t = f(I_t) \tag{2.54}$$

or

$$Y_t^* = \omega_0 I_t. \tag{2.55}$$

Recall that I_t takes on a value of 1 after the event in question takes place. Thus, in equation 2.52,

$$Y_t^* = \begin{cases} 0, & \text{prior to the event} \\ \omega_0, & \text{thereafter} \end{cases}.$$

This defines what is known as an abrupt intervention, depicted graphically in Figure 2.10 in the upper left quadrant. We may hypothesize that our event permanently shifts the underlying data-generating process and that adding this new intervention variable to our ARMA model will allow us to assess the impact of that event.

**As shown in Figure 2.10, however, our intervention could take other potential patterns. Each of these are tested by developing a different functional form of the intervention model, with the abrupt, permanent change

---

[22] For a more advanced treatment, see Lütkepohl (2005, 606–608).

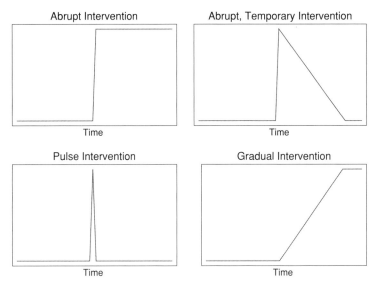

FIGURE 2.10. Types of Interventions.

(equation 18) being the simplest model. If we suspect a more gradual yet permanent intervention process (lower right quadrant of Figure 2.10), we would estimate the following:

$$Y_t^* = f(I_t) = \frac{\omega_0}{1 - \delta B} I_t, \tag{2.56}$$

where ω_0 and δ are both parameters to be estimated. Moreover, it is required that δ be within the bounds of system stability (i.e., $-1 < \delta < 1$. I_t remains defined as above).

The previous equation can easily be rewritten as

$$Y_t^* = \delta Y_{t-1}^* + \omega_0 I_t. \tag{2.57}$$

Now, recall that I_t equals 1 after the occurrence of the event, so that beginning in the period immediately after the event observations take on a value of 1, whereas before the event observations have a value of 0. Now let us derive some of the values of Y_t^* through implied recursions.

Before the event, Y_t^* has a zero level:

$$Y_t^* = \delta Y_{t-1}^* + \omega_0 I_t \tag{2.58}$$
$$Y_t^* = \delta(0) + \omega_0(0)$$
$$Y_t^* = 0.$$

At the time of the event, we have

$$Y_{t+1}^* = \delta Y_t^* + \omega_0 I_{t+1} \tag{2.59}$$

$$Y_{t+1}^* = \delta(0) + \omega_0(1)$$

$$Y_{t+1}^* = \omega_0.$$

In the first period after the event, we have

$$Y_{t+2}^* = \delta Y_{t+1}^* + \omega_0 I_{t+2} \tag{2.60}$$

$$Y_{t+2}^* = \delta(\omega_0) + \omega_0(1)$$

$$Y_{t+2}^* = \delta\omega_0 + \omega_0.$$

In the second period after the event, we have

$$Y_{t+3}^* = \delta Y_{t+2}^* + \omega_0 I_{t+3} \tag{2.61}$$

$$Y_{t+3}^* = \delta(\delta\omega_0 + \omega_0) + \omega_0(1)$$

$$Y_{t+3}^* = \delta^2\omega_0 + \delta\omega_0 + \omega_0.$$

Finally, the value of Y_{t+n}^* at the nth post-intervention observation is given by

$$Y_{t+n}^* = \delta Y_{t+n-1}^* + \omega_0 I_{t+n} \tag{2.62}$$

$$Y_{t+n}^* = \delta(\delta^{n-1}\omega_0 + \cdots + \delta\omega_0 + \omega_0) + \omega_0(1)$$

$$Y_{t+n}^* = \sum_{k=0}^{n} \delta^k \omega_0.$$

Recall that δ must be between -1 and 1, thus ensuring that as the time from the event grows, the increase due to ω_0 will lessen over time. The result will be a function that increases quickly at first and then "levels off" as the time from the event grows.[23]

A third type of intervention functional form is shown in the bottom left quadrant of Figure 2.10; it is known as a pulse function. The pulse function is specified when a short, temporary change is expected in the series caused by an event. Recall our previous specification of I_t as a dummy variable coded as 1 beginning in the period after the specified event occurs (e.g., 0,0,0,0,1,1,1,1). Thus, differencing I_t would leave a single value of 1 at the onset of the event. We thus build on the previous intervention model by differencing I_t, which yields

$$Y_t^* = \frac{\omega_0}{1 - \delta B}(1 - B)I_t. \tag{2.63}$$

---

[23] Also note the similarities between this final equation and the solution to the first-order difference equations presented in the Appendix.

Multiplying both sides by $(1 - \delta B)$ and rearranging terms yields

$$Y_t^* = \delta Y_{t-1}^* + \omega_0(1 - B)I_t. \tag{2.64}$$

Again, we evaluate the values of Y_t^* using recursion applied to equation 2.61. Before the event, Y_t^* will have a zero level. Recall that 1 minus the backshift operator is the same as a first difference and that before the event, I_t is coded 0. Thus, $(1 - B)I_t$ will be zero at any t before the event:

$$Y_t^* = \delta Y_{t-1}^* + \omega_0(1 - B)I_t \tag{2.65}$$
$$Y_t^* = \delta(0) + \omega_0(0)$$
$$Y_t^* = 0.$$

At the first period after the event, I_{t+1} is differenced such that $I_{t+1} - I_t$, which is equivalent to $1 - 0$ or 1. Thus, the value of Y_{t+1}^* is

$$Y_{t+1}^* = \delta Y_t^* + \omega_0(1 - B)I_{t+1} \tag{2.66}$$
$$Y_{t+1}^* = \delta(0) + \omega_0(1)$$
$$Y_{t+1}^* = \omega_0.$$

Continuing, at time I_{t+2}, when $I_{t+2} - I_{t+1} = 1 - 1$ or 0,[24]

$$Y_{t+2}^* = \delta Y_{t+1}^* + \omega_0(1 - B)I_{t+2} \tag{2.67}$$
$$Y_{t+2}^* = \delta(\omega_0) + \omega_0(0)$$
$$Y_{t+2}^* = \delta\omega_0.$$

Finally, the value of the nth post-intervention observation is

$$Y_{t+n}^* = \delta Y_{t+n-1}^* + \omega_0(1 - B)I_{t+n} \tag{2.68}$$
$$Y_{t+2}^* = \delta(\delta^{n-2}\omega_0) + \omega_0(0)$$
$$Y_{t+n}^* = \delta^{n-1}\omega_0.$$

When δ is zero, one is left with simply the value of ω_0 at the time of the event, leading to the pulse function. When δ is nonzero (and less than one), it will weight the estimate of ω_0, thereby lowering its effect as n increases and yielding a functional form similar to that shown in the upper right quadrant of Figure 2.10.

How one estimates impact assessment models depends on the software used. STATA does not implement the full impact assessment framework as SAS or RATS does. In SAS or RATS, one may specify an abrupt and permanent intervention and then estimate the immediate impact (ω_0) and the decay (δ) term.

---

[24] Recall that we do not recode our intervention variable, but instead difference the original I_t coded 0 before the event and 1 after the event.

Should the estimate of δ be statistically insignificant, one can then respecify the model to only estimate the ω_0 term. The estimate of ω_0 can help differentiate between the pulse or decay functions and the abrupt or gradual functions because the two are nested within one another.

In STATA, however, one must specify the functional form of the event's impact as a part of the I_t variable. Thus, for a pulse function ($I_t = \cdots 0,0,0,1,0,0,0\ldots$); for an abrupt, permanent change ($I_t = \cdots 0,0,0,1,1,1,1\ldots$); for a gradual, permanent change ($I_t = \cdots 0,0.3,0.6,1,0,0,0\ldots$); and for a decay function ($I_t = \cdots 0,0,0,1,0.6,0.3,0\ldots$). Each of these can then be added as an independent variable to assess the impact of the event on the variable at hand. The choice of the exact functional form is up to the analyst and depends on the hypothesized nature of the event. That is, does the event take 10 periods to reach sustained impact? Or five periods? Or two periods? Keep in mind that one could use information criteria to test various alternate specifications of the intervention variable.

2.7.1 Impact Assessment: Continuing the Middle East Example

As an example of this methodology, we return to our example of Middle East politics, in particular relations between the United States and Israel. We are interested in figuring out if the signing of the Oslo Accords in 1993 led to increased cooperation between the United States and Israel. Although we suspect that the Oslo Accords led to increased cooperation of the United States with Israel (to reward that country for completing the first round of the peace process with Palestinians), we do not have a strong prior belief as to the exact functional form of the intervention event. However, we do know the exact signing date of the Oslo Accords, and we expect relations to change in the period immediately following that date.

Table 2.6 presents the estimates of this model. Note for all the models, our estimates of both AR terms continue to be statistically significant, at least at the $p < .10$ level. Three of the four estimates of ω_0 achieve statistical significance, with only the pulse specification performing poorly. Our information criteria and R^2 all point to the abrupt specification as the most appropriate model, although the gradual specification is not much less appropriate. As shown in column 1, the estimate of ω_0 achieves statistical significance and suggests an increase in the mean of the series of more than 2 points. Given that the mean of the entire series is 2.5, this represents a significant increase in the series mean. Thus, we would conclude that the United States engaged in significantly more positive behavior toward the Israelis post-Oslo.

A final note on intervention models. Although the timing of the intervention point is out of the control of the analyst, it is difficult to estimate these quasi-experimental models when that point is at the very beginning or end of the series. It is difficult to determine both the long-run shift in mean if there are little data before or after the intervention. Likewise, it is difficult to discern

TABLE 2.6. *U.S. Behavior to Israel: Assessing Oslo*

	Abrupt	Decay	Pulse	Gradual
constant	1.23	2.44	2.48	1.27
	(0.60)	(0.29)	(0.29)	(0.60)
AR(p)				
ϕ_1	0.05	0.06	0.07	0.05
	(0.02)	(0.02)	(0.02)	(0.02)
ϕ_2	0.05	0.06	0.06	0.05
	(0.03)	(0.03)	(0.03)	(0.03)
Intervention				
ω_0	2.19	11.95	8.96	2.12
	(0.67)	(4.02)	(22.31)	(0.67)
σ	7.82	7.86	7.87	7.82
	(0.07)	(0.07)	(0.07)	(0.07)
AIC	7350.46†	7360.14	7365.00	7351.55
BIC	7375.27†	7384.95	7389.81	7376.36
R^2	0.024†	0.015	0.010	0.022

Notes: Standard errors in brackets; † = model favored by this criteria.

whether that shift is abrupt or gradual if the intervention comes toward the end of the series. As is our mantra throughout the book, more data are better, and, a good amount of data (an $N \approx 20$) both before and after an event are ideal.

2.7.2 Structural Breaks

Although the preceding discussion is quite useful for identifying situations in which there is a clear intervention and a subsequent, likely temporary, change in the mean of a given series, real-life situations may not always be so clear-cut. It may be straightforward to think about the effect of a new crime bill on monthly homicide rates, or the effect of signing the Oslo Accords on U.S. policy toward Israel, but identifying clear, discrete interventions may not always be possible. Indeed, it may be the case that over the duration of a series there are slower moving or less clear cut changes that occur that nevertheless result in *structural breaks*. A structural break occurs when an entire series is no longer characterized by the same underlying process; instead, there are two (or more) distinct subsamples of the observations, each of which is characterized by a unique underlying process. Such breaks may either be the result of an observed event or an unknown process. Such a situation is distinct from the interventions described earlier, because the break results in a permanent change in the underlying series, and because the precise timing of the break may be unknown. In such situations, testing for the presence of a structural break is considerably more complicated.

When the timing of a structural break is known, a Chow test may be used to test for the presence of a structural break. Chow tests should be familiar to those who have experience working with linear regression models, because such tests are commonly used to examine whether coefficients remain constant across subsamples of the data. In time series analysis, Chow tests essentially determine whether or not two subsamples of the series, corresponding to observations before and after the hypothesized break, are characterized by the same underlying process. For example, a Chow test might be employed to test the null hypothesis that, in both subsamples of the data, the underlying process may be characterized as an ARMA(0,1). If the null hypothesis is rejected, this would provide evidence of a structural break, because there is a change in the underlying process before and after the break, such that both could not be characterized by the same ARMA(0,1) process. The Chow test is structured around comparing the sum of squared residuals from a pooled model to the sum of squared residuals from two models estimated on subsamples of the data. Because this test is based on the residuals of each of these models, one of its important underlying as assumptions is that the residuals from the two subsample models are independent. However, as Box and Tiao (1975) argue, this is potentially problematic in a time series framework in which residuals frequently display serial dependence. Thus, when using Chow tests with time series data, it is important to make sure that all trends are filtered out of the data, so that what remains are independent, white noise residuals. As mentioned earlier, Chow tests of this sort are only applicable when the timing of a break is known, which allows for a straightforward division of the observations into two subsample. When the timing of a break is unknown, the Chow test is no longer applicable because it is impossible to separate the series a priori. In such instances, it is necessary to use a more advanced testing procedure.[25] In Chapter 7 we present a short discussion of techniques for estimating structural breaks when the timing of the break is unknown.

2.8 CONCLUSION

In this chapter, we began our work with real time series data. Although all of the models and techniques reviewed in this chapter are univariate, they are powerful tools of analysis for the social scientist. Understanding the nature of the data-generating process at work in a time series of interest is, in our view, the first step in data analysis – before choosing covariates and before concerning oneself with hypothesis testing and the interrelationships among multiple variables. That said, time series techniques may also help us understand that process as well. It is to those techniques that we now turn.

---

[25] For a general overview of these tests, see Greene (2003), and for a more detailed discussion, see Andrews (1993).

2.9 FOR FURTHER READING

Corporale, Tony and Kevin Greier. 2005. "How Smart is My Dummy? Time Series Tests for the Influence of Politics." *Political Analysis* 13: 77–94.

Haynie, Stacia. 1992. "Leadership and Consensus on the U.S. Supreme Court." *Journal of Politics* 54 (4): 1158–1169.

John, Peter and Will Jennings. 2010. "Punctuations and Turning Points in British Politics: The Policy Agenda of the Queen's Speech, 1940–2005." *British Journal of Political Science* 40 (3): 561–586.

Lebo, Matthew J. and Helmut Norpoth. 2007. "The PM and the Pendulum: Dynamic Forecasting of British Elections." *British Journal of Political Science* 37 (1): 71–87.

Li, R.P. 1976. "A Dynamic Comparative Analysis of Presidential and House Elections." *American Journal of Political Science* 20: 670–691.

Quinn, Dennis P. and R. Jacobson. 1989. "Industrial Polity through Restrictions on Capital Flows." *American Journal of Political Science* 33 (3): 700–736.

Rasler, Karen. 1986. "War, Accommodation, and Violence in the United States, 1890–1970." *American Political Science Review* 80: 921–945.

Rasler, Karen and William R. Thompson. 1985. "War and the Economic Growth of the Major Powers." *American Journal of Political Science* 29 (3): 513–538.

Wood, B. Dan and Han Soo Lee. 2009. "Explaining the President's Issue-Based Liberalism: Pandering, Partisanship, or Pragmatism." *Journal of Politics* 71 (4): 1577–1592.

Wood, B. Dan and R.W. Waterman. 1991. "The Dynamics of Political Control of the Bureaucracy." *American Political Science Review* 85 (3): 801–828.

3

Dynamic Regression Models

In Chapter 1 we discussed the distinction between strongly and weakly restricted time series models. A weakly restricted model uses techniques such as those we studied in Chapter 2, where one primarily infers from the data the structure of the data-generating process by assessing the AR and MA components of an observed univariate series. Extending the weakly restricted approach to multivariate models, which we do in subsequent chapters, leads to the use of vector autoregression (VAR) and error correction models (ECMs). Important modeling choices, such as how many lags of a variable to include, are inferred from the data rather than specified before the analysis. Recall as well that the quasi-experimental approach uses weakly restricted models, highlighting the problem of specification uncertainty.

In this chapter we discuss strongly restricted time series modeling, which assumes that we know much more about the functional forms of our data-generating process. Making these strong assumptions about a time series' functional form and proceeding directly to testing hypotheses about the relationships between variables encompass what we term the "time series regression tradition."[1] This approach is popular and widely used. It is appropriate whenever an analyst can comfortably and ably make the strong assumptions required for the technique.

We provide an overview of the basic components of time series regression models and explore tests for serial correlation in the residuals, which provide guidance to analysts regarding various types of serial correlation. We then discuss two methods for estimating regression models when the standard solution (including lags of the dependent variable) fail to sufficiently correct for serial correlation, concluding with an illustration of one of these methods. We begin

---

[1] Another name for the time series regression approach is the theory-as-equations approach, first presented in Kydland and Prescott (1991).

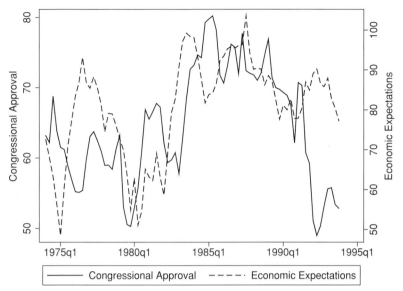

FIGURE 3.1. U.S. Congressional Approval and Economic Expectations, 1974q1–1993q4. Compiled by the authors from replication data on website of Christina Wolbrecht (Durr, Gilmour, and Wolbrecht, 1997).

our exposition of the workhorse time series regression model with a short example. Note the strong functional form assumptions we make in order to estimate the models in the following example and throughout this chapter.

We first estimate a time series regression model using the political accountability example from Chapter 1 and the Appendix. How do economic expectations relate to congressional approval levels in the United States? Figure 3.1 again shows the quarterly time series for the proportion of citizens who approve of the Congress from 1974 through 1993. This figure also depicts the proportion of respondents who have positive expectations about the economy in the same time period. The two series appear to move together. Visual inspection suggests that the public dispenses approval in part on the basis of how it evaluates economic policies. If so, then Congress is held accountable these policies. Although it is natural to expect that economic perceptions influence congressional approval, it is less intuitive to suggest that the causality goes in the other direction. We have good reason to assume one-way causality from economic expectations to congressional approval. Further, we also assume that we are sure about how long it takes for this impact to be manifest in evaluations of Congress, so we therefore also assume the number of lags in economic expectations (and approval) to include in the model. We then specify the following model:

$$CA_t = \alpha_0 + \alpha_1 CA_{t-1} + \beta_1 E_{t-1} + \epsilon_{1t}.$$
$$E_t = \gamma_0 + \gamma_3 E_{t-3} + \epsilon_{2t}.$$

(3.1)

where CA_t and E_t are the levels of congressional approval and economic expectations, respectively; the α's, β, and γ's are constant coefficients; and the ϵ's are error terms. This equation is strongly restricted in several ways. First, we stipulated the number of lags in both variables, rather than discovering the lag length by using tools like the ACF and PACF as we did in Chapter 2. Equally important, the E_t variable depends solely on prior values of economic expectations, and not an any values of congressional approval. We stipulated that CA_t has *no* causal impact on E_t; the causality runs only from E_t to CA_t. This stipulation amounts to assuming exogeneity; see Granato and Smith (1994a, 1994b) for a discussion of weak and strong exogeneity in the cases of stationarity and nonstationarity.

Proper estimation of models such as our congressional approval example requires an above-average level of diligence, but these models also offer a frequently overlooked but exciting opportunity for in-depth inference about social dynamics. To illuminate these challenges and opportunities, consider this very simple, strongly restricted time series regression model:

$$Y_t = \alpha + \beta X_t + \epsilon_t. \tag{3.2}$$

This equation stipulates that X_t and the error term instantaneously cause Y_t at all points in time. The parameters of interest, α and β, and their standard errors are easily estimated via ordinary least squares. Of course, if the error term ϵ is positively serially correlated, these standard errors will be underestimated, and any statistical inferences may be in error. When analysts have dynamic data, the standard approach is to use with tools such as the Durbin-Watson, Q, or LM statistics (discussed later) to diagnose serial correlation. Then, the degree of serial correlation, for the case of AR(1) errors, is estimated using, say, the Cochrane-Orcutt procedure, which is presented later. Finally, the serial correlation is corrected with such methods as generalized differencing.[2]

---

[2] Generalized differencing is a method used to transform a regression model with serially correlated errors into a model with errors that are not serially correlated. Pindyck and Rubinfeld (1998, section 6.2.1) give the following example. Suppose we have a model with AR(1) errors:

$$Y_t = \beta_1 + \beta_2 X_{2t} + \cdots + b_k X_{kt} + \epsilon_t$$
$$\epsilon_t = \rho \epsilon_{t-1} + v_t \quad 0 \le |\rho| \le 1.$$

Suppose further that we have data for the time period $t = 1, 2, \ldots, N$. Then the desired (transformed) equation becomes

$$Y_t^* = \beta(1 - \rho) + \beta_2 X_{2t}^* + \cdots + \beta_k X_{kt}^* + v_t$$

where each variable is a generalized difference in terms of the correlation coefficient, ρ. For instance, $Y_t^* = Y_t - \rho Y_{t-1}$, $X_{2t}^* = X_{2t} - \rho X_{2,t-1}$, and so on. This transformation only uses the data for $t = 2, \ldots, N$. To include the first observation of all the variables, one uses the transformations $Y_1^* = \sqrt{1 - \rho^2} Y_1$, $X_{21}^* = \sqrt{1 - \rho^2} X_{21}, \ldots$. Higher order differencing is required if the error process is not AR(1). For the development of generalized differencing in matrix form and a summary of how one handles higher order autoregressive processes, see Hibbs (1973–1974, 266–269, 282 fn. 30).

Estimating a regression on time series data in this manner views serial correlation as a "nuisance" to be corrected so that estimation of equation 3.2 via ordinary least squares may proceed.[3] In addition to the case of (1) deterministic regressors, i.i.d. Gaussian errors with zero mean and constant variance, Hamilton also considers the cases of (2) stochastic regressors, i.i.d. Gaussian errors that are independent of the regressors, and (3) stochastic regressors with i.i.d. non-Gaussian errors that are independent of the regressors (see also Greene, 2003, chapters 4, 5, and 12).

This method, however, has two notable drawbacks in application: first, analysts using it typically assume and test only for AR(1) errors, but now we know that the errors could be AR(2), MA(1), ARMA(2,2), or other combinations of AR and MA processes. Second, this approach seeks only to correct for temporal dependence in the errors, rather than to analyze any social dynamics embodied in equation 3.2, thereby obscuring potentially interesting patterns in the data.

What do we mean by social dynamics embodied in equation 3.2? Suppose that the ϵ_t in equation 3.2 is an AR(1) process. Then in parallel to our model for congressional approval and economic expectations, we can write equation 3.2 as

$$
\begin{aligned}
Y_t &= \alpha + \beta X_t + \epsilon_t \\
\epsilon_t &= \rho \epsilon_{t-1} + v_t,
\end{aligned}
\tag{3.3}
$$

where v_t is a white noise error term and hence not serially correlated. Substitute the identity for ϵ_t in the first equation:

$$
Y_t = \alpha + \beta X_t + \rho \epsilon_{t-1} + v_t.
\tag{3.4}
$$

Notice that, as we discuss in the Appendix, we can use the backshift operator to rewrite the first equation in 3.3 as

$$
Y_{t-1} = \alpha + \beta X_{t-1} + \epsilon_{t-1}.
\tag{3.5}
$$

Equation 3.5 implies that

$$
Y_{t-1} - \alpha - \beta X_{t-1} = \epsilon_{t-1}.
\tag{3.6}
$$

Finally, using equation 3.6, substitute for ϵ_{t-1} in (3.4). After collecting terms, we obtain

$$
Y_t = (1 - \rho)\alpha + \rho Y_{t-1} + \beta X_t - \rho\beta X_{t-1} + v_t.
\tag{3.7}
$$

Equation 3.7 is a stochastic difference equation such as those analyzed in the Appendix. It also resembles the intervention model we analyzed at the end of Chapter 2. Hence equation 3.7 implies social dynamics. For example, its solution tells us about the qualitative behavior of Y_t as it approaches a long-term equilibrium level (if X is at rest) and how Y_t moves in response to

---

[3] For an in-depth treatment of the small sample and asymptotic properties of OLS and GLS estimators for equation 3.2, see Hamilton (1994, chapter 8).

changes in X_t. Equation 3.7 is still "strongly restricted" because it is based on the functional forms that are stipulated in equation 3.3. As we just showed, it is the particular functional forms in equation 3.3 that produce a single lag of Y_t and one lag of X_t on the right-hand side of equation 3.7. Greene (2003, section 12.10) provides a similar derivation for the relationship in deviations form, but he calls his final equation a "reduced form." We return to a discussion of this term in the next chapter in the context of multiequation models.

The point is that even the most simple models such as equation 3.3 imply social dynamics as represented in equation 3.7. Treating temporal dependence as a nuisance ignores this possibility. Beck and Katz (1996) made this point some years ago. Generally, whenever data exhibit some form of dependence – whether temporal, spatial, or some other form of natural clustering – analysts should resort to standard error "fixes" only as a last resort. An analysis that models these dependencies directly has the potential to generated additional insights about social dynamics and processes. Conversely, any method that treats these dependencies as a nuisance to be fixed misses out on these insights by design (Beck, 2012).

This chapter studies the dynamics implicit in some widely used, single equation, strongly restricted, time series regression models. We also study the challenges of estimating models that directly account for temporal dependence. In particular, the equations for them include on their right-hand sides one lag of dependent variable (Y_{t-1}), and/or a large number of lags of a single right-hand-side causal variable (X_t). We assume throughout this chapter that all our variables are stationary.

In Chapter 5 we introduce the idea of nonstationary data and some statistical tests for diagnosing the presence of stochastic trends. Diagnosing nonstationarity is essential econometrically and substantively. Chapter 6 shows that nonstationarity is more than just a problem to be fixed before proceeding. Rather, through the use of error correction models it is possible to theorize about nonstationarity and to model it in a theoretically justified fashion. Finally, Chapter 7 shows that more nuanced tests of fractional integration are likely to be useful in addressing the question of whether the data are stationary. For the present discussion, however, we bypass these issues and simply assume that all variables are stationary.

3.1 VARIATIONS OF THE GENERAL DYNAMIC REGRESSION MODEL

We begin by walking through several variations of the following general dynamic regression model, following the notation of Keele and Kelly (2006):

$$Y_t = \alpha Y_{t-1} + \beta X_t + u_t \qquad (3.8)$$

$$X_t = \rho X_{t-1} + e_{1t}$$

$$u_t = \phi u_{t-1} + e_{2t}.$$

The general dynamic regression model is often called the "incremental model" because the observed value of Y_t is, in part, the result of an incremental change in its previous value, Y_{t-1}. Estimating even this simple model can be a challenge. For instance, take the case in which $\alpha = 0$, $\rho = 0$, and only the errors are serially correlated, $\phi \neq 0$. Keele and Kelly (2006, 190–91) refer to this case as the "common factor model." If, in attempting to correct for the serial correlation, an analyst incorrectly includes a lagged endogenous variable on the right side of the equation, then the estimates of both α and β will be biased (Achen, 2000). As we walk through the variants of the dynamic regression model, we note how best to deal with underlying modeling and estimation issues.

3.1.1 Building Blocks

In its most simple form, the time series regression model is

$$Y_t = \alpha Y_{t-1} + \epsilon_t, \tag{3.9}$$

where α is a constant coefficient such that $|\alpha| \leq 1$ and ϵ_t is an error term that, for now, is i.i.d with Gaussian properties. Because the errors in equation 3.9 are i.i.d., the ϕ term in equation 3.8 is now 0, unlike in the common factor model, but $\alpha \neq 0$. Note that equation 3.9 is a stochastic difference equation. In the Appendix, we show that there are multiple realization of Y_t depending on the sequences of errors, ϵ_t. Interested readers are encouraged to refer to Examples A.5 and A.6 on this point. You also might recognize equation 3.9 as a simple AR(1) model without a constant. We learned how to infer such functional forms from our data in the previous chapter.

Because it begins by specifying equation 3.9, the time series regression approach focuses on the problem of estimating the coefficient α. Estimating equation 3.9 is a challenge. Even if the error term in equation 3.9 is not serially correlated, for finite (small) samples the ordinary least squares estimator of α is biased downward, and the t and F statistics are not valid.

Asymptotically, OLS estimates are unbiased and consistent, and the t and F are valid (this is Hamilton's case 4; see Hamilton, 1994, 215–216). But if the errors in equation 3.9 are serially correlated, the OLS estimate of the coefficient α is not only inefficient but it is also biased and inconsistent *regardless of the sample size*. Moreover, in this case the common tool from the standard regression approach, the Durbin-Watson statistic, cannot be used to detect this serial correlation. A special form of the Durbin-Watson statistic must be used instead. The LM and Q statistics still can be used in this case, however (see Greene, 2003, 270).

Thus, even for the simplest possible dynamic model, with the strong assumption that the errors of this AR(1) model are not serially correlated, the standard OLS approach produces invalid estimates in small samples. Although appealing to asymptotic properties rescues the usefulness of the OLS estimates when the errors are i.i.d., even an arbitrarily large sample size will not result in useful OLS estimates if there is any serial correlation in the error structure.

3.1.2 Autoregressive Models/Lagged Endogenous Variables

We now introduce serial correlation in the error term as in equation 3.3 into the dynamic regression model. The following presentation is condensed from Hibbs' (1973–1974, 290–292) article.

$$y_t = \beta y_{t-1} + \epsilon_t,$$ (3.10)

where

$$\epsilon_t = \rho \epsilon_{t-1} + v_t$$ (3.11)

and v_t is i.i.d. Gausian errors. Assume both β and ρ are bounded, $-1 < \beta < +1$ and $-1 < \rho < +1$, and that ϵ_t and v_t are random white noise:

$$E[\epsilon_t] = E[v_t]$$ (3.12)

$$E[\epsilon_{t-\theta} v_t] = E[\epsilon_t v_{t-\theta}] = 0 \quad \theta > 0 \forall t.$$

Using the backshift operator, which is presented in the Appendix, we can analyze the structure of the model in equation 3.10. Lag both sides of equation 3.10 and then multiply both sides by ρ. This yields the expression

$$\rho y_{t-1} = \beta \rho y_{t-2} + \rho \epsilon_{t-1}.$$ (3.13)

Collecting terms gives

$$\rho y_{t-1} - \beta \rho y_{t-2} = \rho \epsilon_{t-1}.$$ (3.14)

Equation 3.10 can be reexpressed in terms of equations 3.11 and 3.13:

$$
\begin{aligned}
y_t &= \beta y_{t-1} + \rho \epsilon_{t-1} + v_t \\
&= \beta y_{t-1} + \rho y_{t-1} - \beta \rho y_{t-2} + v_t \\
&= (\beta + \rho) y_{t-1} - \beta \rho y_{t-2} + v_t.
\end{aligned}
$$ (3.15)

Comparing equations 3.10 and 3.15 illustrates the shortcomings of estimating equation 3.10 via OLS:

- The coefficient on y_{t-1} will contain ρ, not just β.
- The variable y_{t-2} has been left out of equation 3.10.

Therefore, OLS estimation of equation 3.10 suffers *both* from omitted variable bias and the fact that the coefficient on y_{t-1} contains ρ. In addition, it can be shown that[4]

$$\text{plim}(\hat{\beta}) = \left[\frac{\beta + \rho}{1 + \rho\beta}\right] \tag{3.16}$$

$$\text{plim}(\hat{\beta} - \beta) = \left[\frac{\rho(1 - \beta^2)}{1 + \rho\beta}\right]. \tag{3.17}$$

If $\rho = 0$, then no serial correlation exists. In this case, the estimated beta converges in probability to the actual β. That is,

$$\text{plim}(\hat{\beta}) = \beta \tag{3.18}$$

$$\text{plim}(\hat{\beta} - \beta) = 0. \tag{3.19}$$

Otherwise, $\hat{\beta}$ will be biased. If $\beta > 0$ and $\rho > 0$, the bias will be positively valued, overestimating the effect of y_{t-1} on y_t. Thus, estimating an incremental OLS model is clearly fraught with issues. If a model with a lagged endogenous variable such as that in equation 3.10 is estimated with OLS, the coefficient on the lagged endogenous term will be incorrect, even asymptotically. In addition, the standard error estimate for this coefficient will be in error.

In short, the pitfalls of estimation of incremental models (via OLS) include the following:

- The variance estimate will be incorrect (inefficiency).
- The coefficient estimate will be biased (bias).
- Estimated residuals cannot be used to correct the problems (as in conventional regression models with AR errors) because the estimated residuals for (3.10) are inherently biased (misestimated).
- One cannot use the Durbin-Watson statistic to diagnose the problem because the residuals are not correctly estimated. The Durbin-H statistic can be used, although it also assumes that the errors have an AR(1) structure.

Given these pitfalls, we now turn to methods for estimating dynamic regression models that avoid the pathologies of standard OLS estimation. To illustrate these preferable options, we introduce a variant of the dynamic regression model frequently used by researchers.

3.1.3 The Workhorse Model

By introducing a constant and an exogenous causal variable with instantaneous influence, X_t, to equation 3.10 we obtain the following equation that is commonly seen in social science research:

$$Y_t = \alpha + \beta_1 Y_{t-1} + \beta_2 X_t + \epsilon_t, \tag{3.20}$$

---

[4] Recall that the probability limit, plim, is used to define the consistency of statistical estimators. To be more specific, plim is the limit, as N goes to infinity, of the probability that $|\hat{\beta} - \beta| < \delta = 1$ where δ is an arbitrarily small quantity.

where α, β_1, and β_2 are all constant coefficients and ϵ_t again is an error term. This equation is one of the most, if not the most, commonly used dynamic regression model. It captures the self-reinforcing, persistent nature, and incremental changes in Y_t variable for one lag. Further, it includes a "forcing" or causal variable X_t. Equation 3.20 resembles the intervention model we encountered in the last chapter, but now X_t is not just a pulse or step function, but can take on a great variety of values. For example, equation 3.20 might be a model of presidential approval (Y_t), economic expectations (X_t), or approval shocks (ϵ_t). A researcher might use equation 3.20 to estimate the immediate effect of economic expectations on presidential approval, while controlling for the autonomous movement in presidential approval (such as the varying levels of support for the presidency as an institution independent of the identity of the current office holder), and the immediate impact of shocks to approval caused by, for instance, unexpected events such as terrorist acts.

3.1.4 Serial Correlation: Tests and Solutions

Keele and Kelly (2006) examine this workhorse model, focusing on the consequences of serial correlation for estimating α, β_1, and β_2 and on the extent to which the familiar Breusch-Godfrey Lagrange Multiplier (LM) test detects serial correlation in this equation.

   They recommend that analysts not use GLS or OLS with corrected standard errors if the process is dynamic, but that using OLS with a lagged dependent variable is acceptable (even though, due to serial correlation, it consistently misestimates the estimates of the coefficients and hence the residuals). The latter model becomes unacceptable, however, if the model residuals are strongly autocorrelated and/or the dependent variable is not stationary. Given the importance of serial correlation for the choices that analysts must make when using these models, we present the widely used Breusch-Godfrey LM test and offer advice to analysts about three of its potential outcomes.

Breusch-Godfrey Lagrange Multiplier Test
When used to diagnose serial correlation, the Breusch-Godfrey LM test offers three advantages over a commonly used alternative, the Durbin-Watson d or h statistic; thus we recommend that analysts use the Breusch-Godfrey LM test to detect serial correlation in dynamic regression models. The first advantage is that the logic of the Breusch-Godfrey test allows researchers to explicitly test the null hypothesis of serial correlation against alternative hypotheses of serial correlation of some order. Second, the Breusch-Godfrey test does not require the potentially dubious assumption that the error term is i.i.d., as is as required by the Durbin-Watson procedures. Third, the Durbin-Watson procedure only allows analysts to test the possibility that the dependencies in the error are AR(1), though we know from Chapter 2 that these errors can be AR(2), AR(3), or some other order. The Breusch-Godfrey LM test enables analysts to specify

a number of lags for testing higher orders of dependency in the error structure, allowing them to avoid assuming AR(1) errors.

Greene (2003, 269) provides a detailed discussion of the Breusch-Godfrey LM test for interested readers.

The Breusch-Godfrey LM test uses the following simple procedure[5]:

1. Estimate the model via OLS, and obtain estimates of the residuals $\hat{\epsilon}_t$.
2. Regress these estimated residuals $\hat{\epsilon}_t$ onto all the independent variables and a specified number of lags of $\hat{\epsilon}_t$. If, for instance, you are testing the null of no serial correlation against the alternative hypothesis of AR(2) errors, include $\hat{\epsilon}_{t-1}$ and $\hat{\epsilon}_{t-2}$ in this second regression.
3. For large sample sizes, the R^2 from the regression of $\hat{\epsilon}_t$ on the independent variables and the lags of $\hat{\epsilon}_t$ can be used to obtain a test statistic – $(n - p)R^2$ – which will follow a χ^2 distribution with p degrees of freedom, where p is the specified number of lags and n is the number of data points. If the test statistic exceeds the χ^2_p critical value, reject the null hypothesis of no serial correlation.

There are three possible outcomes from the Breusch-Godfrey LM test; for each outcome, we present a recommendation to analysts.

Outcome 1: No Serial Correlation
In this happy situation, where no serial correlation is detected by the Breusch-Godfrey test, OLS may be used as normal.

Outcome 2: Serial Correlation without a Lagged Dependent Variable
If the Breusch-Godfrey test shows serial correlation, but the model in question does not include a lagged dependent variable, analysts may proceed with the relatively straightforward Cochrane-Orcutt procedure. In the presence of serial correlation in models without a lagged dependent variable, the Cochrane-Orcutt procedure produces consistent results. The Cochrane-Orcutt procedure is as follows:

1. Estimate the model via OLS, and save the residuals $\hat{\epsilon}_t$.
2. Regress these residuals on the lagged residuals: $\hat{\epsilon}_t = \hat{\rho}\hat{\epsilon}_{t-1} + \nu_t$. $\hat{\rho}$ is thus our estimate of serial correlation.
3. Using our estimate of serial correlation, transform the data to generate $Y_t^* = Y_t - \hat{\rho}Y_{t-1}$ and $X_t^* = X_t - \hat{\rho}X_{t-1}$. In so doing, we eliminate the first observation from our data.
4. Regress Y_t^* on X_t^* and save the residuals to produce an updated estimate of $\hat{\rho}$.
5. Repeat until convergence in the estimate of $\hat{\rho}$ is achieved (usually automated by statistical packages).

---

[5] This presentation of the test and of the Cochrane-Orcutt procedure follows the excellent presentation of Golder (N.d.; see https://files.nyu.edu/mrg217/public/timeseries.pdf).

Hamilton (1994, 226) notes that this procedure will converge to a local maximum, though Golder (N.d.) mentions that under asymptotic theory, the estimates from the first iteration are just as accurate. Most statistical software packages readily implement the Cochrane-Orcutt procedure.

Outcome 3: Serial Correlation with a Lagged Dependent Variable

The Cochrane-Orcutt process requires that estimates of β are consistent. Including a lagged dependent variable in our model and using the Cochrane-Orcutt procedure violates this assumption. If our model includes a lagged dependent variable and the Breusch-Godfrey LM test shows serial correlation, our estimation problem is more complicated. Keele and Kelly (2006) do not provide an analysis of the methods an analyst might employ to estimate the workhorse model (which includes a lagged dependent variable) when there is a high degree of serial correlation. We now turn to estimation in this situation. We review two methods for properly estimating α, β_1, and β_2, along with their standard errors, in the workhorse model. These methods should be used to estimate equation 3.20 when the errors exhibit a substantial degree of serial correlation (that is, the Breusch-Godfrey LM test returns a significant result). Recall that the Durbin-Watson d statistic is invalid for detecting serial correlation when estimating equation 3.20, because the model includes lags of Y_t on the right-hand side, which biases that test. We, along with Keele and Kelly (2006, 203), advocate using the Breusch-Godfrey LM test instead.

3.2 OBTAINING CONSISTENT ESTIMATES

Both methods reviewed in this section focus on obtaining consistent estimates of the residuals in equation 3.20, $\hat{\epsilon}_t$. The consistent residuals then are used to estimate the degree of autocorrelation, which is in turn used to construct generalized differences (see fn. 4). Analysts can then perform feasible GLS estimation on these generalized differences, obtaining valid estimates of the quantities of interest in equation 3.20: α, β_1, and β_2.

3.2.1 Approach Number One: Pseudo-GLS Estimation

The standard approach that has been in use since the late 1960s is pseudo-IV GLS (Wallis, 1967). This approach was introduced to political science by Hibbs (1973–1974). Although Hibbs refers to this method as pseudo-GLS, Hatanaka (1974) calls this approach the "two-step Aitken" method.

To simplify the presentation, assume that the model, in mean deviates, has only one independent variable with contemporaneous impact:

$$y_t = \beta y_{t-1} + \gamma x_t + \mu_t. \tag{3.21}$$

The following steps comprise this first method:

1. "Purify" the lagged endogenous variable. Estimate a regression of y_{t-1} on x_t and x_{t-1}. Save the fitted (predicted) values of the left-hand-side variable in the regression in this first step, $\hat{y}_{t-1}$.
2. Reestimate the model in equation 3.21 replacing the y_{t-1} with these fitted ("purified") values: $y_t = b_1\hat{y}_{t-1} + b_2 x_t + \omega_t$ where ω is the error term in this auxiliary regression. The coefficients from this auxiliary regression are consistently estimated. However, they may suffer from imprecision and so may not be efficiently estimated. Therefore a third step is performed.
3. Use these coefficients, b_1, b_2, with the *original data* to generate a new set of residuals. These residuals then will be consistently estimated.[6] Analyze these residuals for serial correlation using the methods we learned in Chapter 2.[7]
4. If the residuals in step 3 are found to be serially correlated, use the results from that step to form generalized differences from the *original data*. Reestimate the model in terms of these generalized differences, which are reviewed in fn. 4. In other words, use the estimate of ϕ as a ρ and adjust the variance-covariance matrix, in this case, generalized differences formed with the coefficients from the model of the residuals from step 3. Note that the fit statistics for GLS and OLS results cannot be directly compared because the former are based on transformed data using the consistently estimated residuals. For another illustration of these methods see Freeman, Williams, and Lin (1989).

Why bother with these extra steps? In his illustration, Hibbs reanalyzed a study of pre–World War I arms spending. He found that application of the pseudo-GLS method produced estimates implying a considerably smaller impact of past spending on current spending than that reported in the original study (which used OLS). The difference between pseudo-IV GLS and OLS was dramatic: the pseudo-IV GLS estimates implied a coefficient on lagged military spending that was 44% smaller than that reported in the original investigation. At the same time, the magnitude of the pseudo-IV GLS coefficients on some independent variables, such as the size of Britain's colonial domain, was larger than the corresponding OLS estimates. By failing to account for serial

---

[6] These are the residuals:

$$\hat{\mu}_t = y_t - \hat{b}_1 y_{t-1} - \hat{b}_2 x_t.$$

[7] In his illustration, Hibbs (1973–1974) seems to produce the ACF for his estimated $\hat{\mu}_t$. But the caption for his Figure 6 actually refers to the residuals from the original OLS estimation of Choucri and North. For his final step he infers an AR(2) structure for his error process.

correlation, the original analysts biased their results considerably, both over- and under-estimating parameters in their specification of the workhorse model.

3.2.2 Approach Number Two: Hatanaka's Method

An alternative to the first method has been developed by Hatanaka (1974). Both methods perform "roughly equally" on short time series data in Monte Carlo experiments. Hatanaka (1974, 200) advocates for his method because of its simpler formula for the asymptotic covariance matrix. Greene (2003, 277) explains the residual adjusted Aitken method as a form of instrumental variable estimation. We use Greene's notation here.

Consider a workhorse model in mean deviates form with an AR(1) error term, in particular, of the form

$$y_t = \gamma y_{t-1} + \mathbf{x_t}'\beta + \epsilon_t$$
$$\epsilon_t = \rho \epsilon_{t-1} + \mu_t \tag{3.22}$$

The steps in this second procedure are as follows.

1. First, estimate the auxiliary regression using y_t as the left-hand-side variable and the contemporaneous and lagged values of the independent variables as right-hand-side variables. The fitted values of y_t are consistently estimated because $\mathbf{x_t}$ and its lag $\mathbf{x_{t-1}}$ are, by construction, exogenous. In practice, analysts should take care to choose an instrumental variable that strongly influences the dependent variable and, more importantly, is exogenous from the dependent variable.

2. Next run the regression,

$$y_t = \mathbf{b}'_{IV}\mathbf{x_t} - c_{IV}y_{t-1} + \epsilon_t, \tag{3.23}$$

   where the IV subscript denotes the fact that this regression is run with the lagged, instrument of y on the right-hand side of the equation.[8] This equation produces consistent estimates of the errors, $\hat{\epsilon}_t$. From these estimates a first estimate of the serial correlation coefficient is obtained, $\hat{\rho}$.[9]

3. But one is not done estimating serial correlation yet. Run another auxiliary regression using a set of differences defined in terms of the estimate

---

[8] This is the notation Greene (2003, chapter 5) uses to denote an instrumental estimator.
[9] These consistently estimated errors are obtained from the expression

$$\hat{\epsilon}_t = y_t - \mathbf{b}'_{IV}\mathbf{x_t} - c_{IV}y_{t-1}.$$

The formulas for calculating $\hat{\rho}$ is the standard one for first-order serial correlation. For reasons that are not clear, Greene uses the same symbol, ϵ_t for the error term in the model and in this auxiliary regression.

of ρ from step 2:

$$y_{*t} = y_t - \hat{\rho}y_{t-1} \tag{3.24}$$

$$\mathbf{x}_{*t} = \mathbf{x_t} - \hat{\rho}\mathbf{x_{t-1}} \tag{3.25}$$

$$y_{*t-1} = y_{t-1} - \hat{\rho}y_{t-2} \tag{3.26}$$

$$\hat{\epsilon_{t-1}} = y_{t-1} - \mathbf{b}'_{IV}\mathbf{x}_{t-1} - c_{IV}y_{t-2}. \tag{3.27}$$

To be more specific, one runs the following regression:

$$y_{*t} = d_1 x_{*t} + d_2 y_{*t-1} + d_3 \hat{\epsilon_{t-1}} + \zeta_t, \tag{3.28}$$

where the $d_{1,2,3}$ all are constant coefficients and ζ_t is another error term.

4. The final, most efficient estimate of the degree of serial correlation then is

$$\hat{\hat{\rho}} = \hat{\rho} + d_3. \tag{3.29}$$

This estimate of serial correlation is used in the final GLS estimation – (an additional, final regression on generalized differences using $\hat{\hat{\rho}}$).

Hatanaka (1974) explains the asymptotic properties of these estimators. Greene (2003, 277, fn. 31) points out that additional lags of $\mathbf{x}$ can be added in the first step of this method to improve its small sample performance.

We now walk through a concrete example of pseudo-IV GLS estimation using data on economic voting in the United Kingdom.

3.3 ILLUSTRATION: EXPLAINING VOTING INTENTIONS IN THE UNITED KINGDOM

Suppose a scholar set out to build, for a subperiod of a recent Labor government, 1997:5–2006:9, simple workhorse models for voting intentions; that is, the proportion of British citizens who intend to vote for the incumbent in a given month.[10] The techniques reviewed earlier allow us to investigate how specific economic factors relate to support for the incumbent government, controlling for the lagged voting intentions in the previous month. Denote intent to vote for the incumbent (Labor) government V_t.

Here we examine how two economic factors relate to voter intentions. First, students of political economy commonly accepted that British citizens base their evaluations of government in part on the strength of the pound sterling (e.g., Hibbs, 1982). Is this still true? To find out, we will estimate a variant of the workhorse model (equation 3.20) with the pound per dollar exchange rate,

---

[10] In this book, we denote annual time series by the first and last year of the series, for instance, 1985–1993. We denote quarterly data by the year and quarter, e.g., 1995q1 (see Figure A.1 below). Monthly time series are denoted, as here, by the year and month of the observation, 1997:5–2006:9.

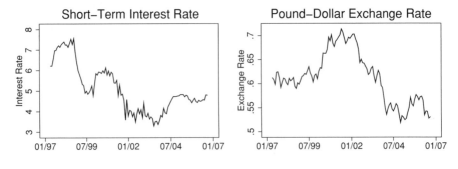

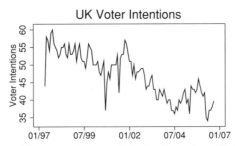

FIGURE 3.2. Two Possible Determinants of Voting Intentions Under the British Labor Government of 1997:5–2006:9. Compiled by the authors from the replication data set for Sattler, Brandt and Freeman (2010).

denoted XR_t, taking the role of the exogenous causal variable. The XR variable is defined as how much of a British pound one U.S. dollar will buy. So, as indicated in the top right panel of Figure 3.2, dollar appreciation – a weakening of the pound against the dollar – occurred around 2001 when a dollar rose to almost .7 pounds. For more details on the measurement of this variable see Sattler, Brandt, and Freeman (2010). Here, XR_t is hypothesized to have a negative relationship with V_t; that is, the more of a pound that a dollar can buy, the less voters will support the incumbent party. As the pound per dollar rate rises, V_t is predicted to fall. Specifically, the model we are interested is[11]

$$V_t = \lambda_0 + \lambda_1 V_{t-1} + \lambda_2 XR_t + \zeta_t. \tag{3.30}$$

The second economic factor we investigate is short-term interest rates, denoted IR_t. As interest rates fall, indicating a government is trying to stimulate a flagging economy, V_t is also predicted to fall, and vice versa.

The workhorse version of this model, with IR_t as the exogenous causal variable, is

$$V_t = \alpha_0 + \alpha_1 V_{t-1} + \alpha_2 IR_t + e_t. \tag{3.31}$$

[11] In our illustrations, we use the workhorse model in levels, not deviations form.

Figure 3.2 depicts these series. It shows that for this period support for the Labor government declined but also displayed a cyclical pattern. The pound depreciated and then appreciated against the dollar. Short-term interest rates exhibited a cyclical pattern, but also generally declined during the Labor government.

To test our hypotheses, we begin by estimating the separate bivariate workhorse models above in equations 3.30 and 3.31. The errors in both models exhibit serial correlation, as indicated by the alternative Durbin-Watson (h; hereafter DW) and Breusch-Godfrey (LM), (hereafter BG), statistics. Keele and Kelly's (2006) results confirm that serial correlation can produce biased and inconsistent coefficients. Application of pseudo-IV GLS estimation therefore is the appropriate method.[12]

3.3.1 Voting Intentions and Exchange Rates: Results

Table 3.1 reports the results from OLS estimation from one intermediate step, and from the final step (of pseudo-IV GLS estimation) for the effect of the pound per dollar exchange rate on voter intentions. The OLS results, reported in column two of Table 3.1, indicate that voting intentions are highly incremental and that the exchange rate may have an impact on voting intentions. But, surprisingly, the OLS results suggest that the appreciation of the dollar (weakening of the pound) *increases* the proportion of the British electorate intending to vote for their (Labor) government. Using OLS alone, analysts might conclude that voters in the UK reward the incumbent party for weakening the pound against the dollar, contradicting established theory on economic voting.

However, as noted, there is evidence of serial correlation; both the alternative DW (h) and BG (1) statistics are statistically significant. Hibbs (1973–1974) and more recently, Keele and Kelly (2006) showed that OLS estimation of the workhorse model (equation 3.20) in the presence of substantial serial correlation can suffer from considerable bias. Thus, the results from OLS in column two of Table 3.1 may be faulty. Will correction for bias and inconsistency reduce the estimated incrementalism in British voting behavior? Will this correction show that the coefficient on the XR_t variable is indeed positive and statistically significant?

---

[12] The data for this illustration are taken from Sattler, Brandt, and Freeman (2010). Voting intentions are from MORI polls. The short-term interest rate data and exchange rate data are from the UK. Office for National Statistics and International Monetary Funds International Financial Statistics, respectively. For example, the simple bivariate regression of voting intentions on one lag of voting intentions and the contemporaneous level of short-term interest rates ($N = 112$) yields residuals that, according to the alternative Durbin-Watson (h) statistic are serially correlated ($\chi^2(1) = 5.183$, $p < .0228$). The BG(1) value for these residuals is also statistically significant ($\chi^2(1) = 5.129$, $p < .0235$). For a useful discussion of the nature and relations between these statistics, see the STATA 9 Reference Guide, Regression Postestimation Time Series, pp. 101–102.

TABLE 3.1. *Application of the Pseudo IV GLS (Two Step Aitken) Approach to a Workhorse Model of Voting Intention in the UK; Exchange Rate version, 1997:5–2006:9*

Intercept/ Independent Variables	OLS	Step 2 Regression	Step 4 Pseudo-IV GLS, AR(1)	Step 4 Pseudo-IV GLS, AR(2)
intercept	2.13	10.15		
	(3.65)	(13.69)		
intercept (gd)			6.33	5.41
			(1.61)**	(1.36)**
V_{t-1}	0.82			
	(.06)**			
$\hat{V}_{t-1}$		−0.32		
		(1.74)		
V_{t-1} (gd)			−0.24	−0.26
			(.09)**	(.09)**
XR_t	10.42	85.46		
	(7.0)	(115.0)		
XR_t (gd)			3.74	1.45
			(22.41)	(22.66)
DW		0.35	2.16	2.06
Alt DW	5.94**			
BG(1)	5.84**	75.29**	4.07**	2.97
$\overline{R}^2$	0.74	0.26	0.05	0.05
F	159.7	20.78	3.80	3.72
(df)	(2109)**	(2109)**	(2108)	(2107)

Notes: Standard errors in parentheses. gd and df denote generalized difference and degrees of freedom, respectively. ** and * denote statistical significant at the .01 and .05 levels, respectively. Columns four and five of the table assume that the consistently estimated residuals are an AR(1) and AR(2) process, respectively.

To find out, we apply the pseudo-IV GLS method. For demonstrative purposes, column three of Table 3.1 shows the results of the intermediate regression step: the reestimation of the model using the "purified" instrument for the lagged endogenous term, $y_{t-1}^{\hat{}}$. Recall that the coefficients from this step are consistently estimated, but these estimates may still be inefficient. In fact, step 3 of the two-step Aitken approach – analysis of the residuals of a regression with these coefficients with the original data – produces an ACF and PACF that suggest an AR(1) or AR(2) process. Therefore, generalized differencing is called for.[13] The results for generalized differencing based on both AR(1) and AR(2) errors are reported in the last two columns of Table 3.1.

---

[13] We do not include the (transformation for) the first observation in either of our illustrations. Cf. fn. 4.

The final results are much more intuitive. First, because the degree of first-order autocorrelation in the errors from step 3 is positive, the coefficient on the lagged endogenous variable is much smaller than we would expect. In fact, these coefficients are negative, indicative of the fact that while intentions generally declined in the sample period, there is a cyclical character to voting intentions as well. More importantly, the coefficients on the exchange rate variable are much smaller and are clearly not statistically significant. Hence the seemingly anomalous result about British citizens rewarding incumbents for undermining the value of the pound against the dollar disappears.[14]

The estimation results for the relationship of voter intentions and short-term interest rates are reported in Table 3.2. The uncorrected OLS results indicate that short-term interest rates have an impact on voting intentions. The statistically significant, positive coefficient on IR_t suggests that an increase in short-term interest rates produces an increase in the number of British citizens intending to vote for the incumbent, as if they hold the government accountable for monetary policy.[15] But both the alternative DW(h) and BG statistics indicate that errors are serially correlated. Therefore the OLS estimates are biased and inconsistent. Again, we reestimate the model using the "purified" or "systematic" instrument for the lagged endogenous term, $\hat{y}_{t-1}$, and present the results of this intermediate step in column three of Table 3.2. These results produce consistent estimates of the coefficients. However, again, because the residuals from step 2 of the two-step Aitken approach are serially correlated, these estimates may not be efficient. Identification of the error process from the ACF and PACF for these residuals (step 4) turns out to be more difficult than in the first illustration (see the online appendix at www.politicalscience.osu.edu/jbox/tsass). The last column in Table 3.2 produces pseudo-IV GLS results for an AR(1) process. Because the first-order autocorrelation in this example actually is negative ($-.294$), these results are, qualitatively, the reverse of those in the exchange rate illustration. The pseudo-IV GLS results increase the magnitude of the impact of the lagged dependent variable on voting intentions and reduce, by nearly 50%, the impact of short-term

---

[14] The Q statistics for the residuals from the AR(1) model in step 3 were statistically significant at lags 9–12. And note that in the fourth column of Table 3.1, the BG(1) statistic is statistically significant. Therefore we also fit AR(2) and AR(3) models in step 3. But the coefficients for the second lag in the former and both the second and third lag of the latter were statistically insignificant. We nonetheless used generalized differencing based on the AR(2) model. These are the results in the last column of Table 3.1. As noted in the text, the substantive implications are the same as for the generalized differencing based on an AR(1) process. When generalized differencing is based on an AR(2) process, both the DW and BG (lags 1–6) statistics are statistically insignificant. The fit of the pseudo-IV GLS estimation should not be compared to that of the OLS estimation.

[15] Note that the tenure of the Labor government corresponded to the period in which the Bank of England was made nominally independent. So these OLS results suggest that British citizens still believed that the Labor government wielded some influence over the bank and that these citizens were inflation averse.

TABLE 3.2. *Application of the Pseudo IV GLS (Two Step Aitken) Approach to a Workhorse Model of Voting Intention in the UK; Short-Term Interest Rate Version, 1997:5–2006:9*

Intercept/ Independent Variables	OLS	Step 2 Regression	Step 4 Pseudo-IV GLS
intercept	6.03 (2.26)**	−3.09 (15.34)	
intercept (gd)			3.84 (2.09)
V_{t-1}	0.77 (.06)**		
$\hat{V}_{t-1}$		1.06 (.48)	
V_{t-1} (gd)			0.88 (.04)**
IR_t	0.87 (.32)**	−0.04 (1.58)	
IR_t (gd)			0.46 (.23)*
DW		0.42**	2.17
Alt DW	5.18**		
BG(1)	5.13*	168.71**	1.14
$\bar{R}^2$	0.75	0.36	0.87
F	169.6**	32.53**	3.80
df	(2109)	(2109)	(2108)

Notes: Standard errors in parentheses. gd and df denote generalized difference and degrees of freedom, respectively. ** and * denote statistical significance at the .01 and .05 levels, respectively.

interest rates.[16] The broader point from both illustrations is that incorrectly using OLS to estimate the workhorse model when errors exhibit serial correlation can results in seriously misguided inferences – inferences that can be corrected by estimating the workhorse model via pseudo-IV GLS.

[16] Note from equation 3.16 above, that pseudo-IV GLS estimation reduces the incremental effect of the lagged dependent variable when there is *positive* autocorrelation; it has the opposite effect when there is negative autocorrelation. The nature of the error process for the consistently estimated residuals is not entirely clear. AR(1), AR(2), AR(3), and MA(1) models of these residuals are all unsatisfactory in some way. For purposes of illustration, we use an AR(1) process in Table 3.2. As regards the residuals from the pseudo-IV GLS estimation in the last column, the DW statistic indicates no serial correlation (at the first lag) and the BG statistic indicates no serial correlation at lags 1–4. However, there is indication of some remaining serial correlation at lags 5 and 6 (according to the BG statistics for these lags).

3.4 DYNAMIC REGRESSION MODELS WITH MULTIPLE CAUSAL VARIABLE LAGS

Although the workhorse model discussed in detail in the preceding sections specifies an instantaneous effect of X_t on Y_t, an important class of time series models is made up of regressions with lagged variables. The lags may come in either the explanatory variables or the dependent variables or in both. We first discuss models with lags in only the independent variables and then models with lags in both independent and dependent variables. Finally, we show how these latter models have direct links to error correction models, which we discuss later in the book.

3.4.1 Distributed Lag Models

Distributed lag (DL) models include lags (and contemporaneous effects) of key independent variables, but not the dependent variable, on the right-hand side of a traditional regression model.

The simplest, most general form of a distributed lag model can be given as

$$Y_t = \beta_0 + \beta_1 X_t + \beta_2 X_{t-1} + \epsilon_t. \tag{3.32}$$

The model in equation 3.32 is known as a finite lag model. In finite lag models, the influence of a change in an independent variable persists only a small number of periods. In equation 3.32, the short-run or impact (multiplier) of X is the effect (at β_1). The long-run effect (also known as the equilibrium multiplier) is the sum of the individual period effects (given as $\sum_{i=0}^{\infty} \beta_i$).

DL models can take a variety of forms. DeBoef and Keele (2008) provide a typology of DL models (and of autoregressive distributed lag (ADL) models, discussed in the next section). A DL model must have some number of lags of a key independent variable. The choice of how many lags to include, however, is both the strength and weakness of the model. As we have emphasized, social scientists are too quick to restrict their models, assuming that one (or no) lag of key variables is the correct answer on an hoc basis. The DL (and ADL) frameworks force the researcher to make explicit their assumption of lags.

Yet theory is often weakly specified or silent as to the appropriate number of lags. One can use any of the information criteria discussed in Chapter 2 (as in the ARMA-building process) to determine the appropriate number of lags. But a short time series obviously limits the number of lags that can be used. Penalties for an overabundance of parameters can easily outweigh gains in variance explained when applying information criteria to select a lag length in short time series datasets. Moreover, multicollinearity can create problems in estimation because various lags of X are likely to be collinear.

To deal with the potentially large number of lags and the resulting collinearity, scholars sometimes use a common variant of the DL model, known as the Almon lag model. More formally, it is called a polynomial distributed lag model. In these models, each β_i can be expressed as a polynomial as such:

$$\beta_i = \alpha_0 + \alpha_1 i + \alpha_2 i^2 + \alpha_3 i^3 + \cdots + \alpha_q i^q. \tag{3.33}$$

Generally, the number of polynomials (q) is limited (usually to four or less; see Greene, 2003, 718), where q is strictly less than the number of lags in the model. See McDowell (2004) for a how-to guide to estimate these models in STATA.

Almon lag models have had a significant presence in political science research, but that presence has waned in the last decade. The models were often used to understand the relationship between presidential popularity and economic conditions (Monroe, 1978, 1979; Norpoth and Yantek, 1983). They have also been used in work on repression in comparative politics (Davenport, 1996).

Of course, if an analyst has dynamic data that are suited for a DL model, a natural consideration is whether lagging the dependent variable is also warranted, and it is to these models we now turn.

3.4.2 Autoregressive Distributed Lag Models

Autoregressive distributed lag (ADL) models are similar to DL models, but contain lagged values of the dependent variable as well. As noted by Greene (2003, 712), substance and theory set ADL models apart from classical regression models with lagged dependent variable (LDVs): "lagged values of the dependent variable appear as a consequence of the theoretical basis of the model rather than as a computational means of removing autocorrelation." Indeed, as Beck and Katz (2011) note, there is nothing inherently atheoretical or pernicious about the inclusion of a lagged dependent variable. If anything, including an LDV can cause what Beck and Katz term "correct" harm by helping analysts avoid reaching the incorrect conclusion that X has a significant effect on Y when in reality it does not.

These models are also referred to as infinite distributed lag models. Recall our finite lag model described earlier. Based on the same logic in Chapter 2, Section 2.3, one can express an infinite number of β_i's as a general ADL model[17]:

$$Y_t = \alpha_0 + \alpha_1 Y_{t-1} + \beta_0 X_t + \beta_1 X_{t-1} + \epsilon_t. \tag{3.34}$$

---

[17] Recall that in Chapter 2, we showed that a finite MA model could be expressed as an infinite AR model and vice versa. The same can be shown in this context: a distributed lag model can be reexpressed as an autoregressive distributed lag model.

Note that if we restrict this ADL model, setting $\beta_1 = 0$, we obtain the workhorse regression model discussed in the previous sections of this chapter.[18]

As with the DL model, analysts must specify the lag length for both lagged dependent and lagged independent variables, although theories are usually not well developed enough to provide useful guidance on this point. Greene (2003, 717) and Stock and Watson (2007, 549) suggest the use of information criteria for lag length selection, though this solution is not perfect for short time series.

It should be noted that, with DL and ADL models, OLS will generally be a consistent estimator, assuming the error term is independent and identically distributed (Greene, 2003, 725–726). If ϵ_t is not i.i.d., then one must move to a GLS-type framework, such as that discussed previously in this chapter. However, inclusion of the lagged variables frequently corrects any serial correlation in the errors, allowing for the use of OLS. Why? The error term at time t is simply all the omitted variables that influence Y_t. If (as often seems probable) a similar constellation of omitted variables variables existed at time $t - 1$ and exerted a similar effect on Y_{t-1}, then the lagged term carries with it the effect of the omitted variables (along with the true lagged effect of Y_{t-1}) that would otherwise generate serial correlation in the error term (Beck and Katz, 2011, 339). Of course, this point does not obviate the need for regression diagnostics on these models or the need to move away from OLS if serial correlation in the errors persists.

ADL models have become rare in political science in the past 15 years, though they still appear in studies of spending (e.g., Heo, 1996; Hetherington and Rudolph, 2008; Knopf, 1998) and of elections (Sanders, Marsh, and Ward, 1993). As DeBoef and Keele (2008) point out, however, autoregressive distributed lag models have a direct tie to another model that has become quite popular in contemporary research: the error correction model, discussed in Chapter 6.

Begin with the general ADL model in equation 3.34. Subtracting Y_{t-1} from both sides of this equation yields a first-differenced dependent variable and a right-hand-side transformation:

$$\Delta Y_t = \alpha_0 + (\alpha_1 - 1)Y_{t-1} + \beta_0 X_t + \beta_1 X_{t-1} + \epsilon_t. \tag{3.35}$$

Now, add and subtract $\beta_0 X_{t-1}$ from the right-hand side[19]:

$$\Delta Y_t = \alpha_0 + (\alpha_1 - 1)Y_{t-1} + \beta_0 \Delta X_t + (\beta_0 + \beta_1)X_{t-1}. \tag{3.36}$$

---

[18] Also note that if we restrict the model such that there are no contemporaneous effects of X_t (i.e., only lagged values of explanatory variables and lagged values of the dependent variable are allowed to affect the dependent variable), equation 3.34 is a one-lag vector autoregression (VAR). We discuss this model in Chapter 4.

[19] This process is known as the Bardsen transformation, and the resulting model as the Bardsen error correction model. See Davidson and MacKinnon (1993) or Banerjee et al. (1993, chapter 2).

Regrouping equation (3.34) yields

$$\Delta Y_t = \alpha_0 + \alpha_1^* Y_{t-1} + \beta_0^* \Delta X_t + \beta_1^* X_{t-1} + \epsilon_t. \tag{3.37}$$

This new equation is a form of an error correction model (for further discussion of this derivation, see DeBoef and Keele, 2008, 190). The predicted changes in Y_t are thus a function not only of past values of Y_t but also of past changes and levels in X_t. As we discuss in Chapter 6, error correction models (ECMs) are a very important class of models in understanding dynamic behavior. They are often used in the context of nonstationary data. But as DeBoef and Keele (2008), as well as the previous derivation, suggests, ECMs can be used with stationary data as well. Beck (1992) makes a similar argument concerning the applicability of ECMs with stationary data.

Thus, although ADL models have fallen out of favor, especially in political science, they serve as a foundation for models that are currently popular. They also serve to remind social scientists that we too often restrict our model specifications with little theoretical or empirical justification.

3.5 CONCLUSION

In this chapter we reviewed variants of the dynamic linear regression model and the violations of OLS assumptions that result from various dynamic specifications. In addition, we discussed estimation strategies in the presence of serially correlated error terms, focusing on the complex problems that result when a model with a lagged dependent variable exhibits serially correlated errors. We concluded the chapter with a discussion of models that contain multiple lags of key independent variables, tying them to the broader methodology of error correction models, which we take up fully in Chapter 6.

With the time series regression approach, we assume certainty about the specification of the relationships that interest us. Hence we restrict the functional form of our equations. These functional form restrictions might include assuming a priori that one variable causes another, but not vice versa. In fact, such an assumption was implicit in the previous chapter on ARMA modeling. We assumed from the outset that white noise has causal impacts on our dependent variable. Analysts differ on their comfort level with these functional form restrictions. Additionally, they often assume that this causal relationship is instantaneous; that is, changes in variable X at time t affect variable Y immediately at time t. Alternately, analysts may assume that the causal effect of X on Y occurs with a certain number of lags in X, where changes in X 1, 2, or more periods before time t affect Y at time t. The number of lags is also usually assumed in dynamic regression models. By making these assumptions, analysts may write down and then estimate strongly restricted models. We recommend instead that analysts test for the number of lags and the model structure.

The next topic we explore features models that contain multiple equations composed of lags of independent variables and the dependent variables. These models relax the strict exogeneity assumption of this chapter and allow for feedback within systems of equations. That is, X is not a priori assumed to be totally uninfluenced by lagged values of Y. Such models are the focus of structural equation and vector autoregressive approaches. The next chapter explores the specification, estimation, and interpretation of this approach to time series modeling.

3.6 FOR FURTHER READING

Beck, Nathaniel. 1991. "Comparing Dynamic Specifications: The Case of Presidential Approval." *Political Analysis* 3: 51–88.

Beck, Nathaniel and Jonathan N. Katz. 2011. "Modeling Dyanmics in Time-Series-Cross-Section Political Economy Data." *Annual Review of Political Science* 14: 331–352.

Grier, Kevin B. 1989. "On the Existence of a Political Monetary Cycle." *American Journal of Political Science* 33 (2): 376–389.

Krause, George A. 2000. "Testing for the Strong Form of Rational Expectations with Heterogenously Informed Agents." *Political Analysis* 8 (3): 285–305.

Rucker, C. Johnson and Steve Raphael. 2009. "The Effects of Male Incarceration Dynamics on Acquired Immune Deficiency Syndrome Infection Rates among African-American Women and Men." *Journal of Law and Economics* 52 (2): 251–293.

Skaggs, Sheryl. 2009. "Legal-Political Pressures and African-American Access to Managerial Jobs." *American Sociological Review* 74 (2): 225–244.

Stecklov, Guy and Joshua R. Goldstein. 2004. "Terror Attacks Influence Driving Behavior in Israel." *Proceedings of the National Academy of Sciences of the United States of America* 101 (40): 14551–14556.

4

Modeling the Dynamics of Social Systems

The study of social dynamics often entails the analysis of *systems of equations*. When we move from univariate to multivariate models, we usually work with a single equation that describes how one variable, say X_t, affects the behavior of another variable, call it Y_t. As we learned in the preceding chapter, these models are appealing because they are relatively easy to use. But implicit in such a single equation model is the assumption that there is no feedback between the variables (see the Appendix for details on this point). That is, we assume that the variables on the right-hand side of our equation are not affected by changes in the variables on the left-hand side. Substantively, this assumption often is problematic. Our theories and policy debates emphasize the existence and implications of feedback between variables.

Consider the conflict in the Middle East, referred to Figure 4.1.[1] Clearly the behavior of the Israelis directed toward the Palestinians depends on recent and past behaviors of the Palestinian directed towards the Israelis and vice versa. And the behavior of the United States toward the belligerents depends on the Israelis and Palestinians directed behaviors it has observed in the Middle East. But this conflict is even more complicated. For example, Palestinian behavior toward the Israelis also depends on American behavior directed toward both parties. Students of intrastate and international rivalry conceive of this case as a conflict *system* in which one belligerent's directed behaviors are both responses to and a provocation toward other belligerents. No single equation model could capture this action-reaction process.

---

[1] Figure 4.1 here is the same as Figure 1.5 in Chapter 1.

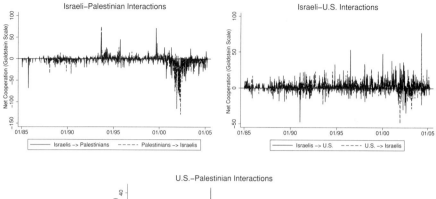

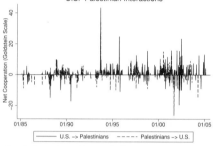

FIGURE 4.1. Israeli-Palestinian-American Relations, 1985–2005. Compiled by the authors from event data produced by the Kansas Event Data System.

Another way to grasp the importance of analyzing systems of equations is to think about how we test theories. Schematically, we usually employ the following logic:

Summarize the essential causal claims of a theory or theories → formulate a model (equation) in which the causal claims of the theory (theories) are represented → fit the model to data → assess goodness of fit and quality of our estimates → if necessary, revise the estimation to conform better to the assumptions our estimator → interpret the results (whether and which claims are falsified)

The second step is a challenge. We must formulate models that capture the causal claims of our theory, and our equations must accurately represent these claims. Many such claims imply feedback between our variables: the behavior of X_t causes Y_t but Y_t also causes X_t. Theories of democratic accountability are another good example of this feedback. These theories are based on the idea that changes in public opinion have impacts on the policies that elected representatives enact. These policies then affect macroeconomic and other kinds of outcomes. But these outcomes are then evaluated by members of the public, who may change their opinions (and voting intentions) again, provoking new changes in policy, outcomes, and opinions in a recurring process. The implication is that to produce meaningful tests of the respective theories we must build models that are multiequation systems, systems that allow for feedback between our variables.

Intervention models and transfer function models are two examples of models that do not allow for such feedback. The former type of model, which we studied in Chapter 2, helps us understand such issues as the impact of one-time changes (pulse) or permanent increases (steps) on a single variable of interest. The impact of the complete time path of a right-hand-side variable on the series is studied using transfer function models. Enders (2004, section 5.2) provides an useful introduction to transfer function models, but he is quick to point out that neither intervention nor transfer function models are appropriate for studying feedback in social systems (section 5.3).

In the introduction to the Appendix, we present several multiequation models of social systems as systems of difference equations. Later in the Appendix we study a system describing a hypothetical naval arms race between the United States and China (Example A.7) as an example of the linear, dynamic simultaneous equation model. Here is the two-variable version of this model:

$$Y_t = \alpha_0 + \alpha_1 Y_{t-1} + \cdots + \alpha_p Y_{t-2} + \gamma_0 X_t + \gamma_1 X_{t-1} + \cdots + \gamma_p X_{t-p} + \epsilon_{1t}$$
$$X_t = \beta_0 + \beta_1 X_{t-1} + \cdots + \beta_p X_{t-2} + \psi_0 Y_t + \psi_1 Y_{t-1} + \cdots + \psi_p Y_{t-p} + \epsilon_{2t},$$

$$(4.1)$$

where Y_t and X_t are the time series of interest; the α_i, β_i, γ_i, and ψ_i, $i = 0, \ldots, p$, are parameters to be estimated; p is the length of the lags on the indicated variables (assumed here to be the same for all the variables); and $\epsilon_{1t,2t}$ are stochastic disturbances. Notice that the contemporaneous values of X_t and Y_t appear on the right sides of both equations. This inclusion captures the contemporaneous feedback between the two variables.[2] Single equation models are special cases of this system in which one or more of the variables are determined solely by their own past behavior. For instance, if we posited as our model for the two variables only the first equation in equation system 4.1, we, in effect, would be saying that all the ψ coefficients are exactly zero. We then would say (imply) that X_t is "exogenous" to Y_t.[3]

---

[2] Technically, this is a system of linear stochastic difference equations with constant coefficients of dimension two. The example in equation A.14 of the Appendix shows a system of nonlinear stochastic difference equations with some time-varying coefficients. The more general expression for the linear dynamic simultaneous equation model is

$$A_0 Y_t = a + A_1 Y_{t-1} + \cdots + A_p Y_{t-p} + A_z Z_t + e_t$$

where Y_t is a $K \times 1$ vector of variables; Z_t is an $M \times 1$ vector of exogenous variables; each A_i, $i = 0, \ldots, p$ and A_z are $K \times K$ matrices of parameters; and e_t is a $K \times 1$ disturbance vector.

[3] The word exogenous is defined more precisely later. Also, note that, in this case, if we try to forecast Y_t, we need a forecast of X_t. And for this forecast of X_t we would use a univariate model that describes $X_t's$ behavior as a function of itself.

4.1 TWO APPROACHES TO MULTIVARIATE TIME SERIES ANALYSIS

Most social scientists employ one of two general approaches in using the linear, dynamic simultaneous equation model (SEQ) in equation 4.1. The first is called the structural equation or theory-as-equations approach. On the basis of "non-sample information" (Greene, 2003, 388), analysts using this approach make strong, a priori restrictions on the coefficients in the system. Causal inferences are based on the same ideas that are used in conventional time series regression analysis, which we studied in the preceding chapter.[4]

The alternative approach, vector autoregression (VAR), employs fewer such restrictions. It tests for some restrictions rather than imposes them a priori. The VAR restrictions include an assumption about the contemporaneous causal ordering of the variables. A certain kind of causality test and a tool called "innovation accounting" are used by VAR modelers.

The structural equation approach was popular in macroeconomics in the post–World War II period and is still popular in most social sciences today. The VAR approach grew out of the critique of the structural equation approach in empirical macroeconomics (Sims, 1980). One branch of modern macroeconomics now uses a third kind of formalism: the dynamic stochastic general equilibrium (DSGE) models (Ljungqvist and Sargent, 2000; Lucas, Stokey, and Prescott, 1989). Applications of DSGE models outside of economics are rare.[5] Some macroeconomists consider DSGE and VAR models to be complementary. See, for instance, Ingram and Whiteman (1994) for an explanation of how the Bayesian version of VAR models can be used to estimate the implications of DSGE models.

To begin our comparison of the two approaches, suppose that two social scientists set out to study the connection between public opinion, economic policy, and economic outcomes in Britain. The focus of their work is the debate about the prevalence (existence) of politically motivated economic policy. Suppose further that the variables of interest are consumer prices, CPI_t; interest rates, IR_t; the U.S. dollar–pound sterling exchange rate, XR_t; and the public's approval of the prime minister, PM_t. Figure 4.2 depicts these time series for May 1997 to September 2006, the period after the creation of a substantially more independent Bank of England. Both scholars allow for feedback between variables. The analyst using the structural equation approach might *posit* that this feedback exists solely between interest rates and consumer prices; this feedback might be indicative of the Bank of England's reaction function and of the impact of interest rates on citizens' consumption decisions. He assumes that there is no feedback to exchange rates from the other three variables and that exchange rates are determined "outside the system" by global markets.[6]

---

[4] See Kydland and Prescott (1991); see also Cooley and Leroy (1985).

[5] But see Freeman and Houser (1998, 2001).

[6] The term "outside the system" is common in this literature. See, for instance, Greene (2003, 379).

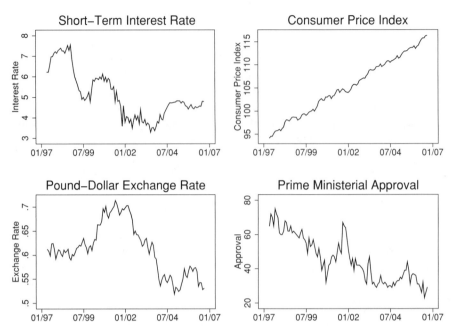

FIGURE 4.2. Macroeconomic Time Series for Four Variable Model of the British Political Economy Under an Independent Central Bank and Labour Party Prime Minister,
1997:5–2006:9. Compiled by the authors from the replication data set for Sattler,
Brandt, and Freeman (2010).

He also assumes there is no feedback to prime ministerial approval from prices,
interest rates, or exchange rates. The SEQ modeler thus assumes that PM_t is
not influenced by any of the other variables in the model. He therefore might
posit a system of equations such as the following:

$$CPI_t = \alpha_0 + \alpha_1 IR_t + \alpha_3 XR_{t-1} + \epsilon_{1t}.$$

$$IR_t = \beta_0 + \beta_1 CPI_t + \beta_2 PM_{t-1} + \epsilon_{2t}.$$

(4.2)

Thus, his model provides for contemporaneous feedback between interest
rates and consumer prices and specifies that the impacts of exchange rates on
prices and of prime ministerial approval on interest rates occur with one lag.
This model does not specify the forces that determine exchange rates and prime
ministerial approval, but it does assume that these forces do not include interest
rates and consumer prices. He proceeds to test the competing claims about the
statistical significance of β_2.

In contrast, the social scientist using the second approach, VAR, would *test*
for the appropriate lag length and *posit* the contemporaneous relationships
work through the relationships between (variance-covariance matrix for) the
stochastic disturbances. Say that she found that the data indicate four lags of

the variables are needed. Then her VAR would be

$$XR_t = \alpha_0 + \sum_{i=1}^{4} \alpha_{1i} XR_{t-i} + \sum_{i=1}^{4} \alpha_{2i} CPI_{t-i} + \sum_{i=1}^{4} \alpha_{3i} IR_{t-i} + \sum_{i=1}^{4} \alpha_{4i} PM_{t-i} + \mu_{1t}.$$

$$CPI_t = \beta_0 + \sum_{i=1}^{4} \beta_{1i} CPI_{t-i} + \sum_{i=1}^{4} \beta_{2i} XR_{t-i} \sum_{i=1}^{4} \beta_{3i} IR_{t-i} + \sum_{i=1}^{4} \beta_{4i} PM_{t-1} + \mu_{2t}.$$

$$IR_t = \gamma_0 + \sum_{i=1}^{4} \gamma_{1i} IR_{t-i} + \sum_{i=1}^{4} \gamma_{2i} XR_{t-1} + \sum_{i=1}^{4} \gamma_{3i} CPI_{t-1} + \sum_{i=1}^{4} \gamma_{4i} PM_{t-1} + \mu_{3t}.$$

$$PM_t = \psi_0 + \sum_{i=1}^{4} \psi_{1i} PM_{t-1} + \sum_{i=1}^{4} \psi_{2i} XR_{t-1} \sum_{i=1}^{4} \psi_{3i} CPI_{t-i} + \sum_{i=1}^{4} \psi_{4i} IR_{t-i} + \mu_{4t}.$$

$$(4.3)$$

And she would assume a particular ordering of the variables which, as we explain below, would imply the way in which contemporaneous shocks in the variables are related to each other.

Clearly the VAR model imposes fewer restrictions than the structural equation model. Most important, in addition to allowing the data to specify more lag lengths of the variables on the right-hand side of the equations, the VAR model allows for potential feedback between *all* the variables. Tests of the competing theories about politically motivated economic policy now would be based on the *joint* statistical significance of the γ_{4i} and the response of the system to a shock in the μ_{3t}.

Table 4.1 summarizes these and other key features of the two approaches. This chapter describes both in more detail, comparing in particular their conceptions of model identification and their treatments of public policy. We illustrate their strengths and weaknesses in an analysis of the political economy of monetary policy making in the United Kingdom, concluding with a summary of the tradeoffs inherent in the two approaches.[7]

4.2 THE STRUCTURAL EQUATION APPROACH

In essence, this first approach assumes that social science theory is relatively well developed and that on the basis of theory we can specify the functional form (structure) of our regression equations; for example, theory tells us which variables appear on the right side of our equations and how many lags of those variables we need to capture key causal relationships. Hypothesis testing then is usually based on assessments of the statistical significance of coefficients on the variables in question. For example, works such as Pindyck and Rubinfeld (1998, 340) and Greene (2003, 379) both note that the term

---

[7] To keep our illustrative example simple, we assume throughout that our time series are stationary and our relationships are linear.

TABLE 4.1. *Application of the Pseudo IV GLS (Two Step Aitken) Approach to a Workhorse Model of Voting Intention in the UK; Short-Term Interest Rate Version, 1997:5–2006:9.1997*

Features	Structural Equation Approach	Vector Autoregression Approach
Model Building		
Model Formulation	Reliance on a single theory for deciding which variables to include in the model, which variables to treat as exogenous, and sometimes which functional forms to use (strong restrictions imposed). Competing theories nested in a single structural formulation	Recognition of the statistical implications of several theories in deciding which variables to include in the model only and, in essence, for specifying the order of the causal chain of contemporaneous effects that is used in innovation accounting (weak restrictions imposed)
Model Estimation	Higher order least squares and maximum likelihood techniques; corrections for heteroskedasticity and serial correlation; tests of over-identification and of orthogonality	Ordinary least squares and tests of the order of the VAR process
Methodological Conventions		
Hypothesis Testing	Analyses of individual coefficients (tests of significance, t-tests, and examination of relative magnitude), of the goodness of fit of equations in the model, and sometimes of the forecasting accuracy of the model	Analyses of the statistical significance of sets of blocks of coefficients only; tests for econometric exogeneity – F-tests and modified likelihood ratio tests
Dynamic Analysis	Simulation; deterministic and stochastic; deduction of model's dynamic properties	Stochastic simulation; innovation accounting: analysis of the response of the recursive moving average representation of the model to orthogonalized shocks in individual and sets of variables

Features	Structural Equation Approach	Vector Autoregression Approach
Forecasting	Within and outside of sample forecasts; decomposition of forecast error variance with respect to error, coefficient, and exogenous variable variance via stochastic simulation	Within and outside of sample forecasts, model projection; decomposition of forecast error variance with respect to orthogonalized shocks in policy variables as indicative of the effects of policy innovation; the sum of such responses to a sequence of such shocks as indicative of the outcome of a policy alternative
Example – Policy Analysis	Policy as exogenous variable: sign and relative magnitude of respective coefficient as indicative of real and potential policy impact; deterministic and stochastic simulation of SEQ model under alternative trajectories or shocks in exogenous policy variable as revealing political effects of alternative policies. Policy as endogenous variable: signs and relative magnitudes of right-hand-side variables in policy equation as indicative of relative importance of respective policy targets; government as a classical (adaptive) controller. Policy as both endogenous and exogenous variables: in some cases government as an optimal controller; selected policy trajectories chosen to yield socially preferred time path of certain other variables in SEQ model	Policy as endogenous and also as unpredictable: the recursive moving average response of the model to shocks in policy variables as indicative of the effects of policy innovation; the sum of such responses to a sequence of such shocks as indicative of a policy alternative. Control of social reality as the derivation of socially best sequence on policy innovations or of best sequence of policy shocks; policy as control of environment is a sequence of corrections or deviations from predicted path of endogenous variables

"structural equation" is synonymous with "derived from theory." Theory also provides "non-sample information" that can be used in identifying and estimating these models, as we explain later.

Because students in fields other than economics often do not study simple simultaneous equation models in their courses on regression, we refer readers who have not yet been introduced to these models to our online appendix (http://politicalscience.osu.edu/faculty/jbox/tsass) on this topic. We continue now with a discussion of the counterpart to the workhorse model of Chapter 3: simultaneous equation models with a single lag of the dependent (left-hand-side) variable on the right side of the equations. We now turn to a illustration of SEQ estimation within the framework of the commonly used workhorse model discussed in the previous chapter.

4.2.1 The Workhorse Model of Time Series Regression Revisited

Recall from the last chapter that one of the most common time series regression models in social science is a single equation in which there is a single lag of the dependent variable on the right side of the equal sign along with some variables that are assumed to be exogenous to that variable. We called this the workhorse model of social science. The multiequation, simultaneous equation version of such a model also has single lags of the endogenous variables and exogenous variables on the right side of each equation. In addition, however contemporaneous values of other endogenous variables also appear on the right side.

In the previous chapter, we showed that if the errors are serially correlated in the workhorse model, the OLS estimates are biased and inconsistent. We therefore need a modified two-stage least squares (2SLS) procedure. This modified 2SLS procedure uses additional lags of the right-hand-side variables in the first stage of the data analysis. The first stage instruments should include the lagged dependent variable and lagged (one-period) values of all the included endogenous and exogenous variables (which means that the lagged dependent variable will be lagged twice). Under certain assumptions, this procedure will produce consistent estimates of the coefficients (Fair, 1970). We now summarize Pindyck and Rubinfeld's (1998, section 12.5) restatement of Fair's approach.[8]

To illustrate this procedure, consider the following supply and demand model:

$$q_t = \alpha_2 p_t + \alpha_3 q_{t-1} + \epsilon_t$$

$$\epsilon_t = \rho \epsilon_{t-1} + v_t$$

$$q_t = \beta_2 p_t + \beta_3 y_t + u_t, \tag{4.4}$$

[8] See also Greene (2003, section 16.5.2.e) and Lütkepohl (2005, chapter 10).

where q_t, p_t, and y_t denote quantity, price, and output respectively, in deviations form, and v_t and ϵ_t are independent disturbance terms that are uncorrelated with each other. We assume the market clears; that is, supply = demand.[9] In the first stage we estimate the following reduced form:

$$p_t = \gamma_2 y_t + \gamma_3 q_{t-1} + \gamma_4 p_{t-1} + \gamma_5 q_{t-2} + w_t. \tag{4.5}$$

Using this equation, we calculate the predicted values of prices, $\hat{p}_t$. In the second stage, we estimate the modified "structural equation":

$$q_t - r q_{t-1} = \alpha_2(\hat{p}_t - r p_{t-1}) + [v_t + (\rho - r)\epsilon_{t-1} + \alpha_2 \hat{w}_t], \tag{4.6}$$

where r is the estimate of the serial correlation coefficient and $\hat{w}_t = p_t - \hat{p}_t$ is the residual series from the first stage regression. The error term $(v_t + \alpha_2 \hat{w}_t)$ will be uncorrelated with other terms on the right-hand-side of equation 4.6, thus yielding consistent estimates. This procedure is similar to the generalized difference estimation strategy discussed in Chapter 3. However, note that the $\hat{p}_t$ on the right side of equation 4.6 is a special instrument created by regressing p_t on the exogenous variable excluded from the respective equation, a lag of itself, and *two* lags of the variable q_t. The reason $\hat{w}_t$ appears on the right side of equation 4.6 is that in the second stage we use the identity $\hat{w}_t = p_t - \hat{p}_t$. This identity implies $\hat{p}_t + \hat{w}_t = p_t$. So when we substitute for p_t in the generalized difference setup, α_2 multiplies both terms: $\hat{p}_t$ and $\hat{w}_t$. The second product term simply is moved to the far right of equation 4.6 and replaced with the error term.

4.2.2 The Structural Equation Approach in Practice

SEQ modelers face a number of practical challenges. First, identification is often a problem. Greene (2003, 388) and others stress the usefulness of "non-sample information" (e.g., assuming supply = demand, as in our earlier example) in addressing the identification issue. This means incorporating what we supposedly know about the relationships between the variables, what variables are excluded from each equation, the linear restrictions on the coefficients, and the restrictions on the disturbance covariance matrix. The assumption in the earlier economic model that markets always clear and hence that the quantity supplied equals the quantity demanded is illustrative. Whether this assumption is applicable to all goods at a given time is debatable. The assumption of market clearing is less common in other social sciences, but it can be found in some political studies.[10]

---

[9] To see simultaneous equation models of supply and demand and further exposition of the assumptions underpinning them, readers are referred to our online appendix at www.politicalscience.osu.edu/faculty/jbox/tsass.

[10] An illustration is Freeman and Snidal's (1983) analysis of the demand for and supply of legitimacy deriving from voting rights extensions in 19th- and 20th-century Europe.

Second, identification poses other problems in addition to the plausibility of non-sample information. For one, it is common to add and delete variables from equations to achieve particular kinds of identification. This practice can cause a variety of problems. For instance, it can encourage the use of variables with limited variability, which then undermines our ability to discover structural parameters (Pindyck and Rubinfeld, 1998, 346). The deeper question is whether theory is sufficiently well developed to provide this information, especially in the form of exact restrictions. For instance, is theory strong enough to exclude a variable from an equation, thereby making a priori all the coefficients on that variables and its lags exactly zero?

Third, pretesting before estimation is possible, but its role in practical analysis is unclear. There exist, for example, tests for simultaneity bias (Greene, 2003, section 15.3; Pindyck and Rubinfeld, 1998, section 12.4.2). These tests are rarely used in social science, however, despite the fact that some now are programmed into statistical software packages.

Fourth, although systems methods of estimation such as the three-stage least squares (3SLS) procedure are relatively efficient, they can exacerbate problems such as specification error and finite sample variation. This is because, unlike single equation methods, they allow these problems to propogate through the entire estimation procedure.[11]

Finally, there also are issues specific to 2SLS and 3SLS such as the fact that they can produce negative R^2 values. This is because 2SLS and 3SLS estimates are not nested within a constant-only model. In addition, for these two estimators, the residual sum of squares is not constrained to be smaller than the total sum of squares. This complicates the choice of models for theory testing and(or) prediction.

We now turn to a practical illustration of SEQ modeling.

4.2.3 Application: The Political Economy of Monetary Policy in the United Kingdom

One of the stylized facts in the field of comparative political economy is that central bank independence causes comparatively lower inflation than central bank dependence. *How* central bank dependence causes inflation is less well understood. One claim is that, when central banks are not insulated from political pressures, prime ministers and their parties manipulate monetary policy in response to changes in public opinion, especially in response to the public's evaluations of party leaders and of their expression of vote intentions. If this claim is true, then monetary variables should have no relationship with public opinion when central banks are independent. Britain is a good case in which to test this claim because the Bank of England became independent when Labor

---

[11] However, as we show, 2SLS and 3SLS also can be superfluous if every equation is exactly identified.

took power in mid-1997, the country's form of democracy is known for its clarity of responsibility, and it was not constrained by the European monetary system.

We assembled monthly data on four key variables for the relevant period, 1997–2006. What follows is a simplified, frequentist version of a much more complex, Bayesian analysis of the British case (Sattler, Freeman, and Brandt, 2008, 2010).

The British electoral system, by its majoritarian nature, produces single-party governments that are relatively independent of other political parties. The absence of a separation of power and a unicameral legislature affords political opponents comparatively few opportunities to alter government policies.[12] Political data analyzed in this simplified model are taken from the Gallup Organization (King and Wybrow, 2001). The variable PM_t measures the percent of respondents in each month who are satisfied with the performance of the prime minister; VI_t is the percentage of respondents who say they intend to vote for the incumbent (Tory) party each month. The economic series data are taken from the *International Financial Statistics (IFS)* of the International Monetary Fund (various years). To account for the international forces that operate on the British economy, we use the monthly average dollar/pound nominal exchange rate (IFS line rf). We denote this variable by XR_t; it corresponds to the number of U.S. dollars per British pound. For prices we use the British consumer price index (ISF line 64); this is denoted CPI_t. Finally, the monthly average short-term interest rate (IFS line 60b) is used for domestic monetary policy, IR_t. These time series are depicted in Figure 4.2.

We begin with the simple model presented in the introduction to this chapter, equation system 4.2. This posits that the impact of prime ministerial approval on interest rates occurs with a one-month lag due to the time needed to analyze polling data. Notice that in this case each equation has its own predetermined variable, and both equations are exactly identified. For reasons explained elsewhere (Pindyck and Rubinfeld, 1998, 351; Greene, 2003, 411), this means that 2SLS and 3SLS results will be identical, as shown in Table 4.2. But both estimators change the substantive conclusion from OLS. Both show that the coefficient on PM_t is positive and statistically significant, indicating that prime ministerial approval serves as a mandate, even under central bank independence, for raising interest rates; in contrast the OLS results indicate that there is no relationship between PM_t and IR_t. Indeed, the idea that public approval serves as a mandate for electoral officials is not new (Freeman, Williams, and Lin, 1989). These differences in substantive inferences underscore the importance of avoiding simultaneous equation bias, which was discussed earlier in this chapter. Note that the R^2 values for the interest rate equation for 2SLS and 3SLS are both negative. Although a negative R^2 value may seem peculiar

---

[12] See, for instance, Powell and Whitten (1993).

TABLE 4.2. *Estimates for An Identified Simultaneous Equation Model of the Politics of British Monetary Policy Making, 1981–1997*

Equation	Variable	OLS	2SLS	3SLS
CPI	IR_t	−3.72	−5.49	−5.49
		(.27)	(.46)	(.46)
	XR_{t-1}	−51.9	−50.50	−50.50
		(6.06)	(7.12)	(7.03)
	constant	156.02	164.17	164.17
		(3.94)	(4.86)	(4.80)
	R^2	0.71	0.60	0.60
	RMSE	3.35	3.94	3.89
	$F(p)[\chi^2]$	132.58	101.31	208.15
		(.00)	(.00)	(.00)
IR	CPI_t	−0.102	0.28	0.28
		(.27)	(.15)	(.15)
	PM_{t-1}	0.02	0.17	0.17
		(.01)	(.06)	(.06)
	constant	15.09	−32.63	−32.63
		(2.90)	(18.35)	(18.11)
	R^2	0.52	−0.66	−0.66
	RMSE	0.81	1.50	1.48
	$F(p)[\chi^2]$	60.17	16.38	33.64
		(.00)	(.00)	(.00)

Notes: Standard errors are in parentheses. STATA reports a χ^2 statistic for the equations for 3SLS. N = 113.

for any reader familiar with OLS, it is not a cause for alarm. In these applications, some of our regressors are used as instruments for endogenous variables. However, because we are fitting a structural model, the actual values of these endogenous variables are used to compute R^2, not the fitted instruments. The 2SLS and 3SLS models are not nested within a constant-only regression (as OLS is), so the R^2 value is not constrained to be between 0 and 1 as in OLS. Analysts should be more concerned with overall model significance, parameter estimates, and standard errors when evaluating the results from a 2SLS or 3SLS model.

Now suppose we had non-sample information about the polling process in the United Kingdom. Say we knew that under the Labor government, polling technology became sophisticated enough that the prime minister's staff could poll continuously and make a preliminary analysis of the results every 30 days. And suppose we assume that exchange rate fluctuations also had a more immediate impact on consumer prices. This non-sample information would lead us to add contemporaneous values XR_t and PM_t to the right side of the

TABLE 4.3. *Estimates for An Overidentified Simultaneous Equation Models of the Politics of British Monetary Policy Making, 1981–1997*

Equation	Variable	OLS	2SLS	3SLS
CPI	IR_t	−3.7	−5.56	−5.55
		(.28)	(.45)	(.44)
	XR_t	−8.36	23.68	13.85
		(28.15)	(33.80)	(31.56)
	XR_{t-1}	−43.67	−73.81	−63.76
		(28.41)	(34.05)	(31.75)
	constant	156.02	164.35	164.16
		(3.95)	(4.89)	(4.80)
	R^2	0.71	0.59	0.59
	RMSE	3.37	3.99	3.92
	$F(p)[\chi^2]$	87.68	71.17	221.44
		(.00)	(.00)	(.00)
IR	CPI_t	−0.09	0.32	0.32
		(.03)	(.15)	(.15)
	PM_t	0.02	0.14	0.14
		(.02)	(.05)	(.05)
	PM_{t-1}	0.01	0.06	0.05
		(.01)	(.03)	(.03)
	constant	13.03	−36.99	−36.93
		(3.35)	(19.25)	(18.91)
	R^2	0.53	−0.44	−0.44
	RMSE	0.80	1.41	1.38
	$F(p)[\chi^2]$	40.79	13.57	42.22
		(.00)	(.00)	(.00)

Notes: Standard errors in parentheses. STATA reports a χ^2 statistic for the equations for 3SLS. $N = 113$.

CPI_t and IR_t equations:

$$CPI_t = \alpha_0 + \alpha_1 IR_t + \alpha_2 XR_t + \alpha_3 XR_{t-1} + \epsilon_{1t}.$$

$$IR_t = \beta_0 + \beta_1 CPI_t + \beta_2 PM_t + \beta_3 PM_{t-1} + \epsilon_{2t}. \tag{4.7}$$

This model is overidentified. Hence, as is shown in Table 4.3, the results of 2SLS and 3SLS differ, but substantively, the story is the same: increases in prime ministerial approval serve as a mandate to increase interest rates. The negative R^2 values are obtained again for the interest rate equation.

At this point, you may be asking yourself some questions. Where does this "non-sample information" come from? How systematic is the use of such information? Does each researcher simply choose the information that she or he thinks is reasonable? Are our theories sufficiently well developed that they provide us with such information? Proponents of the structural equation approach shown in Table 4.1 are confident that theory does provide us with guidance about which pieces of non-sample information we should use in formulating and testing models. Another group of scholars are less confident that theory provides such guidance. It is to their alternative approach that we now turn.

4.3 VECTOR AUTOREGRESSION

Proponents of vector autoregression, or VAR, eschew the strong restrictions used by SEQ modelers. VAR modelers do not think that social science theories justify assumptions about exogeneity, lag length, and so on. In their minds, such restrictions often are inaccurate, and the inaccuracies compound as the SEQ modeling proceeds. These restrictions can result in mistaken inferences about causal relationships and in poor forecasts.

The social scientist perhaps most associated with VAR is the economist Christopher Sims. His article, "Macroeconomics and Reality," is well known for its critique of structural equation modeling. As he argues, "To the extent that [structural equation] models end up with very different variables on the right-hand side of [their] equations, they do so not by invoking economic theory but . . . by invoking an intuitive econometrician's version of psychological or sociological theory" (1980, 3). We return to Sims' arguments when we compare the SEQ and VAR approaches in more detail.

Yet VAR modelers do rely on theory to make restrictions. For example, they rely on theory to choose the variables in their models and to specify the contemporaneous relationships between them. But they focus on the reduced form of what is, in essence, an unknown structural model, and they let the data decide the lag length of the equations in its reduced form. That is, after choosing which variables to include in the model, VAR modelers select the amount of lags of each variable based on which number best fits the data, as determined by a variety of criteria we discuss later. The result, they contend, is more accurate causal inference; because theory may be imprecise as to how many lags to include, VAR modelers contend that this approach more precisely models the real-world phenomenon of interest without making potentially implausible assumptions. The tradeoff is a loss of efficiency and precision – an inability to make precise statements about the values of individual structural coefficients. Additionally, when large numbers of lags best fit the data, degrees of freedom can become an issue for VAR modelers dealing with relatively short time series data.

As before, we begin with a brief discussion of the theory behind vector autoregression. Then we discuss the practical problems encountered in using them to model social systems science.

4.3.1 Terminology and Stationarity

For purposes of illustration, let us focus here on the political mechanism in our model of the British political economy; more specifically, on the relationship between prime ministerial approval, PM_t, and interest rates, IR_t. Suppose we agree that theory is just too weak to make strong restrictions about which of the two variables is exogenous to the other; there is evidence that many citizens pay attention to interest rates and dispense prime ministerial approval on the basis of this variable. Hence there may be feedback between the two. And, to keep things simple, say that we used the tests described later and found that the data are best described by one lag of each variable. Then we would formulate a model such as the following:

$$PM_t = b_{10} - b_{12}IR_t + \gamma_{11}PM_{t-1} + \gamma_{12}IR_{t-1} + \epsilon_{PMt}$$

$$IR_t = b_{20} - b_{21}PM_t + \gamma_{21}IR_{t-1} + \gamma_{22}PM_{t-1} + \epsilon_{IRt}. \qquad (4.8)$$

where the stochastic terms (ϵ_{PMt} and ϵ_{IRt}) are uncorrelated, white noise disturbances with variances σ_{PM}^2 and σ_{IR}^2, respectively. This system allows for both contemporaneous and lagged feedback between the variables. It is an example of a linear simultaneous equation model that we defined in the introduction to this chapter. This example is inspired by the 2×2 system studied by Enders (2010, section 5.5).

To write the reduced form of equation 4.8, we substitute the expression for IR_t in the first equation, collect terms, and rewrite it in terms of the predetermined variables. We do the same for the second equation by substituting for PM_t. Our reduced form then is

$$PM_t = a_{10} + a_{11}PM_{t-1} + a_{12}IR_{t-1} + e_{1t}$$

$$IR_t = a_{20} + a_{21}IR_{t-1} + a_{22}PM_{t-1} + e_{2t}, \qquad (4.9)$$

where, for example, the term $a_{11} = \frac{\gamma_{11} - b_{12}\gamma_{22}}{1 - b_{12}b_{21}}$. Notice that all the variables are written in terms of the lags of the other variables. Each equation thus has an autoregressive structure. For this reason equation 4.8 is called the the vector autoregression in standard form. Because we assume our data indicate that one lag of each variable is needed in equation 4.8, our reduced form actually is a VAR model of order 1. If we had more lags in equation 4.9, our VAR would be of a higher order. The key point is that the VAR is the reduced-form representation of a more general simultaneous equation model (4.8).

There is some variation in how these equations are described in the literature. Enders (2010, 298) calls equation 4.8 a vector autoregression, but he also calls equation 4.9 the vector autoregression in standard form. In fact, equation 4.8 is best described as a structural vector autoregression; here we call it a linear simultaneous equation model. The key point is that the vector autoregression in standard form is the reduced form of a more general linear simultaneous equation model.[13]

In VAR, for reasons we later explain more fully, the relationship between the error terms in equation 4.9 is important. The derivation of the reduced form gives us

$$e_{1t} = \frac{(\epsilon_{PMt} - b_{12}\epsilon_{IRt})}{(1 - b_{12}b_{21})}.$$

$$e_{2t} = \frac{(\epsilon_{IRt} - b_{21}\epsilon_{PMt})}{(1 - b_{12}b_{21})}. \tag{4.10}$$

Because, in the original system – equation 4.8 – ϵ_{PMt} and ϵ_{IRt} are white noise processes, it can be shown that the expected values of both e_{1t} and e_{2t} are zero, the variances of these error terms are time invariant, and, individually, both e_{1t} and e_{2t} are not serially correlated.[14] However, the errors in the VAR system are mutually correlated. Their covariance is

$$Ee_{1t}e_{2t} = \frac{E[(\epsilon_{PMt} - b_{12}\epsilon_{IRt})(\epsilon_{IRt} - b_{21}\epsilon_{PMt})]}{(1 - b_{12}b_{21})^2}$$

$$= \frac{-b_{21}\sigma_{PM}^2 - b_{12}\sigma_{IR}^2}{(1 - b_{12}b_{21})^2}. \tag{4.11}$$

When there are no contemporaneous relationships in the original system in equation 4.8 – that is, both b_{12} and b_{21} are zero – this covariance is zero. Otherwise the shocks in the VAR are correlated. This correlation of shocks in VAR models means that a shock in one of the contemporaneous variables will be associated with some movement in other contemporaneous variables. Understanding and plotting how one variable moves in response to a shock to another variable in a VAR model is the basis of innovation accounting, a primary tool used with VAR. We discuss innovation accounting in detail later.

We can write the matrix for the variance-covariance matrix of the errors for our example as

$$\Sigma = \begin{bmatrix} \sigma_1^2 & \sigma_{12} \\ \sigma_{21} & \sigma_2^2 \end{bmatrix}. \tag{4.12}$$

The entries on the diagonal contain the variances of e_{1t} and e_{2t}, and the off-diagonal cells contain the covariance between e_{1t} and e_{2t}. Again, this matrix is important when we use the fitted model to make causal inferences.

---

[13] For the development of the VAR model in matrix form, see Johansen (1995, chapter 1). For the matrix derivation the 2×2 system we are using, see Enders (2010, 297–299).

[14] For derivations of these simple facts about the errors in the VAR system, see Enders (2010).

The relationships between the coefficients on the lag terms of the VAR model determine whether or not it is stationary. The nature of these relationships is complex, and the intuition is as follows.

The Appendix presents in greater detail simple stochastic difference equations of the form

$$y_t = a_0 + a_1 y_{t-1} + \epsilon_t. \tag{4.13}$$

This equation is a first-order autoregression with a constant for a single variable. We showed how we could rewrite such an equation in the form of an MA process:

$$y_t = a_0 + a_1 y_{t-1} + e_t \tag{4.14}$$

$$y_t - a_1 y_{t-1} = a_0 + e_t$$

$$(1 - a_1 B) y_t = a_0 + e_t$$

$$\left(\frac{1}{1 - a_1 B} \right)(1 - a_1 B) y_t = \left(\frac{1}{1 - a_1 B} \right)(a_0 + e_t)$$

$$y_t = \frac{1}{1 - a_1 B}(a_0 + e_t)$$

$$y_t = (1 + a_1 B + a_1^2 B^2 + \cdots) a_0 + (1 + a_1 B + a_1^2 B^2 + \cdots) e_t$$

$$y_t = a_0 + a_0 a_1 + a_0 a_2^2 + \cdots + e_t - a_1 e_{t-1} + a_1^2 e_{t-2} + \cdots$$

where B is the backshift operator (defined in Chapter 2) and, $\frac{1}{1 - a_1 B}$ is the sum of the geometric series $(1 + a_1 B + a_1^2 B^2 + \cdots)$. Also, recall that we found that, for a known initial condition, y_0, the solution of equation 4.13 is

$$y_t = a_0 \sum_{i=0}^{t-1} a_1^i + a_1^t y_0 + \sum_{i=0}^{t-1} a_1^i \epsilon_{t-i}. \tag{4.15}$$

The magnitude of a_1 determines whether this solution converges. If $|a_1| < 1$ the series converges and it is stationary.

The same logic is used to assess the stability and stationarity of a VAR, but now the condition applies to the matrices of coefficients that multiply the lagged terms. To be more specific, the particular solution to the first-order VAR model in equation 4.9 can be written in the form

$$x_t = \mu + \sum_{i=0}^{\infty} A_1^i e_{t-i} \tag{4.16}$$

where the μ is a vector of the means of the variables in the system and A_1 is the 2×2 matrix of coefficients that multiplies the lagged variables. This is the vector moving average (VMA) version of the model. Convergence of the system depends on a property of the array, A_1. In the case of our 2×2, first-order VAR in equation 4.9, the array is

$$A_1 = \begin{bmatrix} a_{11} & a_{12} \\ a_{21} & a_{22} \end{bmatrix}. \tag{4.17}$$

As this matrix is raised to an ever increasing power, the entries in its cells must vanish. When this happens the variance-covariance matrix of the system will be finite and the system will be stationary. Fortunately, many software packages offer routines for performing these tests. The key property of the matrix (matrices) has to do with the roots of the polynomial that is associated with the determinant of matrix A_1. Enders (2010, section 5) derives these conditions for a 2×2 system like ours. He also provides illustrations of VARs that are and are not composed of stationary processes.[15]

4.3.2 Specification and Estimation

The first step in specifying a VAR is choosing the lag length for the right-hand-side variables. There are several approaches to specifying lag length. Scholars often talk of rules of thumb that can be used for this purpose. One such rule is to include enough lags to "capture the full cycle of the data" (Brandt and Williams, 2007, 25); see also Enders (2010, 316). For instance, when working with monthly data, analysts sometimes use 12 lags of the variables. Experience also shows that six lags often are needed for analyzing quarterly economic data. Formal statistical tests for lag length include the likelihood ratio test. However, despite attempts to correct for sample size, this test performs poorly. One reason for this poor performance is that the likelihood ratio test is based on asymptotic theory.[16]

Another approach uses a variety of information criteria such as those developed by Akaike (AIC), Schwartz (BIC), and Hannan and Quinn (HC). In essence, these are measures of the overall fit of the equation system. They are based on the variance-covariance matrix of residuals that one obtains from fitting the model equation by equation with OLS, $\hat{\Sigma}$. Each criterion penalizes the fit for the number of parameters in the model, thus emphasizing the virtue

---

[15] A full derivation of the solution and of the conditions for stability can be found in Johansen (1995, chapter 1). Johansen also explains that the initial conditions for the system must be chosen to have a certain invariant distribution. Statistical software packages typically have routines for estimating the system stability of a VAR.

[16] On the likelihood ratio test for lag length and the Sims correction for sample size, see Brandt and Williams (2007, 25–27), Enders (2010, 316–317), and Lütkepohl (2005, chapter 4).

of parsimony. The formulas for these criteria are

$$AIC(p) = T \log|\hat{\textstyle\sum}| + 2(m^2 p + m) \tag{4.18}$$

$$BIC(p) = T \log|\hat{\textstyle\sum}| + log(T)(m^2 p + m) \tag{4.19}$$

$$HQ(p) = T \log|\hat{\textstyle\sum}| + 2((log(log((T)))(m^2 p + m), \tag{4.20}$$

where, $log|\hat{\sum}|$ is the the log determinant of the variance-covariance matrix of the residuals from the OLS fitted model, T is the sample size, p is the number of lags for each variable in the VAR, and m is the number of variables (equations) in the VAR. The p that yields the smallest value of the criterion among the candidate p's is considered the best specification. Finally, it is important that specifications be compared to exactly the same set of observations. For instance, if one has a sample of monthly data that covers the period 1980:1–2000:12 and is comparing a VAR model with four versus six lags, the period used should be 1980:7–2000:12 (for the estimation for both the VAR model with four lags and the model with six lags). For further exposition of these criteria see Brandt and Williams (2007, section 2.5.2) and Enders (2010, section 5.8). Both sources explain the connection between the criteria and maximum likelihood estimation of the model.[17]

Which information criterion is most preferred? Although in an ideal world all tests will point toward a single answer, it is much more common for the different criteria to suggest different lag lengths. In practice, all the criteria are used in conjunction with the rules of thumb. Many software packages produce information criteria as a part of their VAR routines. The main challenge is to avoid omitting a causal variable while, at the same time, constructing the most parsimonious model.

Once the lag length has been specified, each equation in the VAR can be estimated separately with OLS.[18] Choice of the appropriate lag length usually ensures that the errors are serially uncorrelated. If we assume those errors have constant variance, the OLS then will be consistent and asymptotically efficient. Moreover, even though there may be some correlation between the errors in the different equations, techniques such as seemingly unrelated regression (SUR) will not improve efficiency because each equation contains exactly the same right-hand-side regressors. However, if the VAR contains exogenous variables, SUR will produce more efficient coefficient estimates.[19] Post-estimation options for checking for serial correlation of the residuals and normality of the

---

[17] More in-depth comparisons between the criteria along with Monte Carlo comparisons of their performance in selecting a known lag order can be found in Lütkepohl (2005, chapter 4).

[18] On the estimation of VARs see Hamilton (1994, chapters 4, 11) and Johansen (1995).

[19] We cover the use of SUR to estimate VAR models more fully in the online appendix, available at politicalscience.osu.edu/faculty/jbox/tsass.

residuals are programmed into most statistical software packages. We encourage analysts to run these diagnostics after any VAR estimation.

4.3.3 Tools for Inference in VAR Modeling

Granger Causality

One of the most common and easy to understand concepts used by VAR modelers is Granger causality. In words, a variable X_t is said to Granger cause another variable Y_t if Y_t can be better predicted from the past of X_t and Y_t together than from the past of Y_t alone (Pierce, 1977). Put another way, Granger causality asks whether X_t helps you predict Y_t over and above your ability to predict Y_t on only the basis of Y_t's past history. So, returning to our illustration in this section, if monetary policy is politically motivated, PM_t will help us predict IR_t in comparison to a forecast of IR_t based only on IR_t's own past history.

On the basis of Monte Carlo tests, researchers discovered that, for testing relationships between two variables, the approach with the greatest statistical power in Granger causality assessment is a simple F test. In particular, the F test has the greatest power to determine the *joint* statistical significance of the coefficients on the lags of the variable hypothesized to Granger cause another variable. The null of no Granger causality is equivalent to the hypothesis that all these coefficients are jointly zero.

To illustrate the use of this test, assume that rather than positing that one lag of each variable is needed to model monetary policy making, as we did earlier in equation 4.8, we used the information criteria described earlier and discovered that p lags are needed in our investigation. Then the test for politically motivated monetary policy would proceed as follows. Estimate the unrestricted equation for interest rates:

$$IR_t = a_{20} + \sum_{i=1}^{p} a_{21,i} IR_{t-i} + \sum_{i=1}^{p} a_{22,i} PM_{t-i} + \mu_{1t}. \tag{4.21}$$

Then fit the restricted model for interest rates, which is a model that assumes *all* p coefficients on the lags of prime ministerial approval are zero, thus excluding this variable from the model:

$$IR_t = a_{20} + \sum_{i=1}^{p} a_{21,i} IR_{t-i} + \mu_{2t} \tag{4.22}$$

Next we compute the residual sums of squares for each model:

$$RSS_{Unrestricted} = \sum_{t=1}^{T} \hat{\mu_{1t}}^2 \tag{4.23}$$

$$RSS_{Restricted} = \sum_{t=1}^{T} \hat{\mu_{2}t}^2, \tag{4.24}$$

where $\hat{\mu}_{1t}, \hat{\mu}_{2t}$ are the residuals from the two fitted models, respectively. The test statistic for PM_t Granger causing IR_t then is

$$F(p, T - 2p - 1) = \frac{RSS_{Restricted} - RSS_{Unrestricted}/p}{RSS_{Unrestricted}/(T - 2p - 1)} \tag{4.25}$$

where T is the number of usable time periods and p is the number of estimated parameters. If this F statistic exceeds the critical value for the chosen level of statistical significance, we reject the null hypothesis of no Granger causality between PM_t and IR_t. If this test statistic does not exceed the selected critical value, we fail to reject the null hypothesis of no Granger causality of PM_t on IR_t.[20]

Granger causality testing is not foolproof. Although it is a useful tool, analysts should not take a significant result of a Granger causality test, in isolation, as dispositive evidence that one variable *causes* another. Measurement practices, missing variables, and rational expectations are among the issues that can produce mistaken Granger causal inferences. In addition, Granger causality is not the same as an exogeneity test. It is possible for a variable to be exogenous to another but also not Granger cause it. Nonetheless, VAR proponents often use Granger causality tests. We illustrate the use of the Granger causality tests later when we return to the British political economy example.[21]

Innovation Accounting

The second tool for causal inference in VAR models is a bit more challenging to understand. It uses the impulse response function for the VAR system to make

---

[20] Some software packages switch to the use of a χ^2 statistics when the sample sizes are large. This χ^2 statistic is based on a likelihood ratio test. Our exposition of the F test for Granger causality follows Brandt and Williams (2007, section 2.5.4); the same source explains the rationale for the use of the large sample χ^2 test. Enders (2010, 315ff) explains how to use the likelihood ratio test to analyze cross-equation causality hypotheses. In this case, a small sample correction is used, a which adjusts for the number of parameters estimated in each equation in the unrestricted system. Technically, the concept of Granger causality is a bit more complicated than suggested in the text. Formally, consider the process $[X_t, Y_y]$, which we again assume will be jointly covariance stationary. Denote by $\overline{X_t}, \overline{Y_t}$ all past values of X and Y, respectively. Let all past and present values of the variable be represented as $\overline{X_t}$ and $\overline{Y_t}$. Define $\sigma^2(X|Z)$ as the minimum predictive error variance of X_t given Z, where Z is composed of the sets $[\overline{X_t}, \overline{Y_t}, \overline{X_t}, \overline{Y_t}]$. Then there are four possibilities:

(1) Y causes X: $\sigma^2(X_t|\overline{Y_t}, \overline{X_t}) < \sigma^2(X_t|\overline{X_t})$.
(2) Y causes X instantaneously: $\sigma^2(X_t|\overline{Y_t}, \overline{X_t}) < \sigma^2(X_t|\overline{Y_t}, \overline{X_t})$.
(3) Feedback: $\sigma^2(X_t|\overline{X_t}, \overline{Y_t}) < \sigma^2(X_t|\overline{X_t})$, and $\sigma^2(Y_t|\overline{Y_t}, \overline{X_t}) \leq \sigma^2(Y_t|\overline{Y_t})$.
(4) Independence: X and Y are not causally related: $\sigma_2(X_t|\overline{X_t}, \overline{Y_t}) = \sigma^2(X_t|\overline{X_t}, \overline{Y_t}) = \sigma^2(X_t|\overline{X_t})$, and $\sigma^2(Y_t|\overline{Y_t}, \overline{X_t}) = \sigma^2(Y_t|\overline{Y_t}, \overline{X_t}) = \sigma^2(Y_t|\overline{Y_t})$.

The concept at one time was called Granger-Weiner causality after the scholar Norbert Weiner.

[21] On the potential pitfalls of Granger causality testing, see Freeman (1983) and Brandt and Williams (2007, 34–36). For an example of how a variable may be exogenous but not Granger cause another variable, see Enders (2010, 318).

inferences, under a new assumption about the contemporaneous relationships between our variables. This assumption allows us to draw inferences about the direction and magnitudes of relationships between our variables. This analysis requires us to make an additional specification decision about the way contemporaneous shocks propagate through the system.[22]

Let us begin by writing our simple two-variable VAR model in equation 4.9 in matrix form:

$$\begin{bmatrix} PM_t \\ IR_t \end{bmatrix} = \begin{bmatrix} a_{10} \\ a_{20} \end{bmatrix} + \begin{bmatrix} a_{11} & a_{12} \\ a_{21} & a_{22} \end{bmatrix} \begin{bmatrix} PM_{t-1} \\ IR_{t-1} \end{bmatrix} + \begin{bmatrix} e_{1t} \\ e_{2t} \end{bmatrix}. \tag{4.26}$$

Recall that the equivalent moving average representation of the system is

$$\begin{bmatrix} PM_t \\ IR_t \end{bmatrix} = \begin{bmatrix} \overline{PM} \\ \overline{IR} \end{bmatrix} + \sum_{i=0}^{\infty} \begin{bmatrix} a_{11} & a_{12} \\ a_{21} & a_{22} \end{bmatrix}^i \begin{bmatrix} e_{1,t-i} \\ e_{2,t-i} \end{bmatrix}, \tag{4.27}$$

where $\overline{PM}$ and $\overline{IR}$ are the means of the prime ministerial approval and of interest rates, respectively. This equation expresses each variable in terms of the errors in the VAR model, $e_{1t,2t}$. There is a still deeper relationship between the variables and the shocks in the original model, $\epsilon_{1t,2t}$. To see this relationship remember that when we created the reduced form we expressed $e_{1t,2t}$ in terms of the $\epsilon_{1t,2t}$. This was equation array 4.10. In matrix form, for our simple 2×2 system, equation 4.26 implies

$$\begin{bmatrix} e_{1t} \\ e_{2t} \end{bmatrix} = \frac{1}{1 - b_{12}b_{21}} \begin{bmatrix} 1 & -b_{12} \\ -b_{21} & 1 \end{bmatrix} \begin{bmatrix} \epsilon_{PMt} \\ \epsilon_{IRt} \end{bmatrix}. \tag{4.28}$$

We therefore can substitute equation 4.28 into equation 4.27 to obtain

$$\begin{bmatrix} PM_t \\ IR_t \end{bmatrix} = \begin{bmatrix} \overline{PM} \\ \overline{IR} \end{bmatrix} + \frac{1}{1 - b_{12}b_{21}} \sum_{i=0}^{\infty} \begin{bmatrix} a_{11} & a_{12} \\ a_{21} & a_{22} \end{bmatrix}^i \begin{bmatrix} 1 & -b_{12} \\ -b_{21} & 1 \end{bmatrix} \begin{bmatrix} \epsilon_{PM,t-i} \\ \epsilon_{IR,t-1} \end{bmatrix}. \tag{4.29}$$

This expression can be simplified by defining a matrix, ϕ_i which has in its cells the entries $\phi_{jk}(i)$:

$$\phi_i = \frac{1}{1 - b_{12}b_{21}} A_1^i \begin{bmatrix} 1 & -b_{12} \\ -b_{21} & 1 \end{bmatrix}. \tag{4.30}$$

---

[22] The explanation of the impulse response function follows Enders (2004, section 5.7). However, because it is often presented as a causal chain that is ordered from the top to the bottom of the list of variables, we use a Choleski decomposition that is lower rather than upper triangular in form. Cf. Enders (2004, 75).

With this expression for the ϕ_i we can write the vector moving process as

$$x_t = \mu + \sum_{i=0}^{\infty} \phi_i \epsilon_{t-i}, \tag{4.31}$$

where x_t is the vector of the variables, PM_t and IR_t; μ is the vector of the respective means, $\overline{PM}$ and $\overline{IR}$; and ϵ_{t-i} is the vector of original errors at $t - i$, $\epsilon_{PM,t-i}$ and $\epsilon_{IR,t-i}$ or,

$$\begin{bmatrix} PM_t \\ IR_t \end{bmatrix} = \begin{bmatrix} \overline{PM} \\ \overline{IR} \end{bmatrix} + \sum_{i=0}^{\infty} \begin{bmatrix} \phi_{11}(i) & \phi_{12}(i) \\ \phi_{21}(i) & \phi_{22}(i) \end{bmatrix} \begin{bmatrix} \epsilon_{PM,t-i} \\ \epsilon_{IR,t-i} \end{bmatrix}. \tag{4.32}$$

Equation 4.32 is the tool used in innovation accounting. Note that for each lag, including $i = 0$, it tells us how a shock affects the respective left-hand-side variable. For instance, $\phi_{12}(0)$ tells us how a shock in $\epsilon_{IR,t}$ affects PM_t. The same cell of the matrix for $i = 1$, $\phi_{12}(1)$ tells us the impact on PM_t of the same shock one lag back in time, $\epsilon_{IR,t-1}$. These effects are called *impact multipliers*. Their accumulated effects are called *long-run multipliers*.[23] Note that each $\phi_{jk}(i)$ is a series of values, an impact multiplier for each value of i. For this reason they are called *impulse response functions*. If we shock one of the ϵ's one-time, we can use the impulse response functions to trace out the effect of this one-time shock on the respective variable. For example, suppose in a simulation we subjected our system to a one-time shock in $\epsilon_{PM,t}$. Then we could use $\phi_{21}(i)$ to chart the resulting effect on IR_t. This chart would be the corresponding *impulse response* of IR_t. It would tell us about the direction of a relationship between these variables; more specifically, if a positive shock in prime ministerial approval caused an increase (decrease) in interest rates and for how long this increase (decrease) is sustained.

The problem is that, as we saw earlier, the shocks in the variables can be correlated. This means that if we shock one variable, we shock the other but then it will impossible to discern the directions of relationships between our variables. Because the impulse responses for each variable will be combinations of two impulse response functions, we will not be able to tell what the impact of a shock in one variable alone has on another.

VAR modelers solve this problem by making an assumption about the contemporaneous relationships between the variables. In effect, they impose a causal ordering on these contemporaneous relationships. This assumption structures the system in a particular way. This, in turn, makes it possible to use the impulse responses to make inferences about the effect of individual shocks on each variable.

To illustrate how this is done, return to the linear simultaneous equation model, equation 4.8, with which we started our discussion of VAR. Assume

---

[23] For instance, the cumulated effect of a shock in ϵ_{IRt} on PM_t is $\sum_{i=0}^{n} \phi_{12}(i)$.

that $b_{12} = 0$. That is, although interest rates may affect prime ministerial approval with a lag, they have no contemporaneous impact on prime ministerial approval. Then examine the equations for the error terms in the VAR in standard form in equation 4.9. With $b_{12} = 0$ we have

$$e_{1t} = \epsilon_{PM,t}. \tag{4.33}$$

$$e_{2t} = \epsilon_{IR,t} - b_{21}\epsilon_{PM,t}.$$

This restriction imposes an ordering on the contemporaneous relationship in the system. It means that shocks in prime ministerial approval affect both prime ministerial approval and interest rates contemporaneously, but shocks in interest affect only interest rates contemporaneously. Both kinds of shocks affect the two variables with a lag. This causal ordering of the contemporaneous shocks is called a Choleski decomposition. It also amounts to orthogonalizing the VAR.

If the errors in the VAR in matrix form are the vector u_t, we have

$$E(u_t u_t') = \Sigma.$$

It can be shown that

$$\Sigma = H^{-1}(H')^{-1}$$

$$H\Sigma H' = I,$$

where H^{-1} is a lower triangular, as is H^{-1}. And, if Σ is a positive definite symmetric matrix, this H is unique for a given ordering of the variables in the VAR, y_t.

Now transform this VAR with this H:

$$Hy_t = HA(L)y_t + Hu_t$$

$$H[I - A(L)]y_t = Hu_t.$$

This is equivalent to

$$y_t = B(L)e_t,$$

which is a VMA where

$$B(L) = [I - A(L)]^{-1}H^{-1} = B(L)H^{-1} = H^{-1} - B_1L - B_2L^2 \dots$$

$$e_t = Hu_t.$$

But

$$E(e_t) = E(Hu_t) = HE(y_t) = 0.$$

$$E(e_t e_t') = E(Hu_t(Hu_t)') = E(H\Sigma H') = I.$$

And this result is convenient because the identity matrix has a diagonal of unity, meaning that variance e_t is unity. Moreover the covariance is between the e_ts and zero. The significance of orthogonalization is that we can study the impact of individual shocks as independent experimental treatments.[24]

Note that, if there is any correlation between the errors, changing the ordering of variables in the VAR will change the H matrix. This means that we are forced to assume an ordering of variables when using the innovation accounting technique. This amounts to an assumption about how shocks cascade contemporaneously through the entire system. Analysts need to consider the ordering and, if alternative orderings are plausible, then empirically investigate them.

With this additional specification – an ordering of the contemporaneous relationships between the variables – impulse response analysis may proceed. Each variable can be shocked individually, and the resulting impulse responses will reveal the direction of the relationship between the variable that is shocked and the other variables in the system. To make these responses indicative of the period in which the systems has been observed, the shocks themselves are usually one standard deviation value of the residuals from the fitted VAR model. In other words, they are typical, positive shocks that have been observed in the sample period. These impulse responses now are the main tool used in VAR interpretation.

Enders (2010) illustrates the impulse responses for Choleski decomposition in a system like ours, but note that he uses a different ordering. His impulse responses therefore are the reverse of what our system would produce.[25] To gauge the magnitude of the effect of the shocks on the variables in the system, analysts sometimes use another tool: forecast error decomposition.[26] However, impulse responses are the main tool used by VAR proponents.

How best to construct confidence intervals (error bands) for these responses is a matter of some debate. Most software packages provide frequentist methods, such as the delta method and bootstrapping, for this purpose. Enders (2010) describes an algorithm for constructing confidence intervals for a single equation, AR(1) model and explains briefly how it can be extended to a VAR model. There are several options for constructing these confidence intervals. One is based on Lütkepohl's analysis of the asymptotic distribution of the impulse responses (2005, section 3.7). Another option is use of a bootstrap algorithm. One such bootstrap algorithm is as follows:

1. Fit the VAR model and save the estimated parameters.
2. Use the estimated coefficients to calculate the residuals.
3. Repeat steps 3a to 3c R times.
   (a) Draw a simple random sample of size T with replacement from the residuals. The random samples are drawn of the $K \times 1$ vectors of residuals where K is the number of endogenous variables (equations)

---

[24] See Hamilton (1994, section 11.4) on the nature of impulse response and for more details on orthogonalization.

[25] Enders (2010, 310) acknowledges this ordering issue.

[26] See Enders (2010, 313ff) and Brandt and Williams (2007).

in the VAR. When the *t*th vector is drawn, all K residuals are selected. This preserves the contemporaneous correlation of residuals.

(b) Use the p initial observations, the sample residuals, and the estimated coefficients to construct a new sample dataset (p is the lag length of the variables in the VAR).

(c) Fit the model, calculate the different impulse response functions, and forecast error variance decompositions,

(d) Save these estimates as observation r in the bootstrapped dataset.

4. For each impulse response function and forecast error decomposition, the estimated standard deviation from the R bootstrapped estimates is the estimated standard error of that impulse response function or forecast error decomposition.

The debate about the construction of the error bands for impulse responses (and forecast error decomposition) is, in part, the motivation for the Bayesian approach to VAR (Brandt and Freeman, 2006, 2009; Sims and Zha, 1998, 1999).

4.3.4 VAR Modeling in Practice

As we have seen, VAR incorporates theory in the choice of variables and in the causal ordering imposed in the impulse response analysis. Beyond this, however, VAR does not emphasize the kind of identification issues that are central to SEQ modeling. VAR modelers are more concerned about including all the relevant predetermined (lagged) values of their variables than in obtaining estimates of any structural coefficients; hence their interest in the joint statistical significance of a set of coefficients in Granger causality testing and the impulse response produced by a collection of coefficients, rather than in the recovery of particular structural coefficients. In this sense, they work with the reduced form of what often is an unknown structural model.[27]

Pretesting is a key feature of VAR, and lag length tests are an essential part of the modeling processes. VAR models let the data choose the lag lengths, according to the best fit by a variety of criteria. Sometimes, these tests are used to delete blocks of coefficients from the final model and are useful for determining if a variable should be added to a VAR. A small sample correction is recommended for one of these tests, the likelihood ratio test. The test for incorporating a variable in a VAR is described by Enders (2010, section 5.8).

Ostensibly there are fewer estimation issues for VAR. If the lag length is chosen carefully, OLS estimation should be sufficient. In fact, although they

---

[27] There is a variant of the approach called SVAR that does put more emphasis on the underlying structural model. But in this case, structure applies mainly to the contemporaneous relationships between the variables only. See, for instance, Enders (2010, chapter 5).

are readily available, diagnostic checks for serial correlation and non-normality often are not performed on the residuals from fitted models. There is, however, no reason to skip these diagnostic tests.

Nonstationarity poses problems for VAR, because t- and/or F-tests are problematic when applied to nonstationary variables. In addition, differencing in order to create stationary variables can cause problems if variables are cointegrated. The inclusion of time trends in VARs can be problematic as well. These time trends essentially soak up too much of the variance in the series (Sims and Zha, 1998, 958).[28]

A difficulty associated with weakly restricted models such as VARs is the problem of scale. Analysts who are sensitive to specification uncertainty often include numerous lags of their variables in each equation. They also give each variable its own equation (allowing all the variables potentially to be endogenous). The number of parameters in such models increases at a rapid rate.[29] Such a large amount of parameters naturally makes it impossible to make any meaningful inferences about the magnitudes of individual coefficients. It also means that such models invariably fit well in-sample. Evaluations of such models therefore are based on their implied dynamics and out-of-sample forecasting performance. But even then their dynamics and forecasts are difficult to interpret because the model complexity produces uncertainty about the signs and magnitudes of the impulse responses and forecasts. Bayesian time series methods can be employed to address these problems.

4.4 THE POLITICAL ECONOMY OF MONETARY POLICY IN THE UNITED KINGDOM REVISITED

Recall that the question motivating our study of UK monetary policy making is whether, even after the Bank of England was made more independent under the Labor government, interest rates were affected by fluctuations in prime ministerial approval. Our SEQ illustration indicated this to be the case.

The parallel VAR model is equation 4.3. It includes all four variables in the system. Most important, unlike our SEQ models in equations 4.2 and 4.8, the VAR model allows for the possibility of feedback between all our variables; for example, that prime ministerial approval, PM_t, is affected not just by the

---

[28] If series are nonstationary, the time trend is well approximated by a unit root plus drift; no time trend is needed. The issues of fitting VARs to nonstationary data are discussed in passing in Enders (2010, chapter 5); see also Sims, Stock, and Watson (1990). For reviews of the literature and applications in political science see Freeman, Williams, and Lin (1989); Brandt and Williams (2007), and Brandt and Freeman (2006).

[29] For instance, suppose we have a four-variable, weakly restricted VAR model and that each equation has a constant and six lags of each variable. Then our model has $4 \times (1 + 4 \times 6) = 100$ parameters.

TABLE 4.4. *Lag Length Test Statistics for Four Variable Model of the British Political Economy. Sample for these tests 1998:5–2006:9*

lag	LR	FPE[†]	AIC	HQIC	SBIC
0		1310	11.61	11.66	11.72
1	1118.80	0.028	0.86	1.07*	1.38*
2	39.96	0.026*	0.78*	1.16	1.71
3	19.94	0.029	0.90	1.44	2.25
4	36.93	0.028	0.85	1.56	2.61
5	20.18	0.032	0.97	1.85	3.14
6	25.50	0.034	1.03	2.08	3.62
7	15.18	0.041	1.19	2.41	4.20
8	12.70	0.052	1.38	2.77	0.80
9	35.50	0.052	1.35	2.90	5.18
10	39.52	0.051	1.28	2.99	5.52
11	52.88	0.045	1.07	2.96	5.73
12	45.14*	0.043	0.94	2.99	6.01

Notes: * denotes lag length favored by respective test statistic; [†] In thousandths.

interest rate decisions of the Bank of England but also by prices and by exchange rates (CPI_t, XR_t).[30]

The first step in building our VAR model is to test for lag length. Table 4.4 reports the results of the likelihood ratio test and of various information criteria for our data on the British political economy. The data sample for this test was determined by the maximum lag of 12; this maximum lag dictates that we use the sample 1998:5–2006:9. As is usually the case in finite samples, the test statistics (criteria) do not agree. Models were fit with 1, 4, and 12 lags. Serial correlation tests and tests for stability indicated that a four-lag VAR model was most appropriate in this case. Not surprisingly the R^2 statistics for all the equations in it were at least .90. More important, the four-lag model passed all stability tests.[31]

The Granger causality results for the four-lag VAR model are reported in Table 4.5. They show a number of relationships that are out of step with the SEQ model formulated earlier; for example, evidence that the exchange

---

[30] For a discussion of the theoretical and empirical arguments linking macroeconomic outcomes in the United Kingdom to prime ministerial and others forms of political accountability, see Sattler, Freeman, and Brandt (2008); and Sattler, Brandt, and Freeman (2010).

[31] Tests for serial correlation for the residuals from the 1- and 12-lag models were statistically significant at the .05 level at several lags. The 12-lag model failed the test for stability. For the four-lag VAR model, only the 12th lag of the residuals showed any sign of serial correlation. And the four-lag model passed stability tests. The tests for the normality of the residuals from the four-lag model were not reassuring. Several of the equations had Jarque-Bera and kurtosis statistics that were statistically significant. The possibility that electoral forces, for example, caused switches in the values of the coefficients at times of elections should be investigated.

TABLE 4.5. *Granger Causality Tests for Four Variable VAR Model of the British Political Economy, 1997:5–2006:9*

Equation	Excluded	F	df	df-r	*Prob > F*
XR	IR	1.74	4	92	0.15
XR	CPI	0.18	4	92	0.95
XR	PM	1.15	4	92	0.34
XR	ALL	1.18	12	92	0.31
IR	XR	2.86	4	92	0.03
IR	CPI	3.23	4	92	0.02
IR	PM	0.36	4	92	0.84
IR	ALL	1.70	12	92	0.08
CPI	XR	0.67	4	96	0.61
CPI	IR	1.27	4	92	0.29
CPI	PM	0.97	4	92	0.43
CPI	ALL	1.32	12	92	0.22
PM	XR	0.49	4	92	0.75
PM	IR	2.09	4	92	0.09
PM	CPI	1.88	4	92	0.12
PM	ALL	1.75	12	92	0.07

Note: N = 109.

Granger causes interest rates; infact, exchange rates are omitted from our SEQ models in equations 4.2 and 4.8. Also, there is evidence in the third row from the bottom of Table 4.5 that interest rates have a Granger causal impact on prime ministerial approval. But, as regards the relationship that is indicative of political influence on monetary policy, the seventh row indicates, contrary to our results for the SEQ model, that prime ministerial approval does not Granger cause interest rates. The impulse response analysis uses the ordering XR, IR, CPI, and PM; it assumes that shocks in exchange rates have an immediate effect on all the variables, shocks in interest rates have an immediate impact only on consumer prices and prime ministerial approval, and shocks in consumer prices have an immediate impact only on prime ministerial approval. Shocks in all four variables affect all the other variables with a lag as shown in Figure 4.3: shocks in interest rates have a short-term impact on consumer prices, and shocks in consumer prices have a short-term effect on interest rates. Of most concern to us here is the effect on interest rates of a positive shock in PM_t. This impulse response addresses the idea that under the Labor party monetary policy still was influenced by fluctuations in public opinion; to be more specific, fluctuations in prime ministerial approval. The second response in the last row of each impulse response chart shows no such effect. A positive shock in PM_t has no impact on the behavior of IR_t; the confidence interval for this response always spans zero.

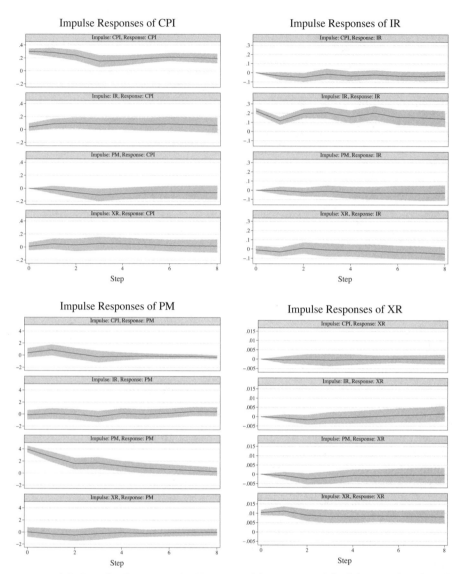

FIGURE 4.3. Impulse Responses for Four Variable, VAR Model of the British Political Economy, 95% Error Bands.

4.5 CONCLUSION: SEQ AND VAR MODELING COMPARED

As summarized in Table 4.1 in our introduction to this chapter, the two kinds of modeling clearly reflect different approaches to social science. SEQ modelers presume our theories are well developed and so justify strong restrictions on the coefficients in our equations, as well as assumptions about exogeneity.

Although SEQ models can be used for dynamic analysis, theory testing amounts to tests for the statistical significance of individual coefficients in these equations. The fit of these equations attests to the validity of the final model.[32] A few studies outside of economics attempt to report standard errors for long-run multipliers (DeBoef and Keele, 2008), but to our knowledge, dynamic analysis of SEQ models is rare outside of economics.

In contrast, VAR modelers are much more skeptical not just about the information provided by extant theories but also about our ability to arrive at a single, best model. VAR models stress the observational equivalence of competing structural models; being able to falsify one or two of what are several competing theories may be all we can accomplish. These modelers impose a weaker set of restrictions on their equations, pretesting for lag length, for example. The focus in theory testing is more on dynamics, especially on the direction and behavior of impulse responses. Fit is less important to VAR models because they have so many lags of the variables that, the VAR almost always fits the data well. But VAR models also incorporate theory. Based on theory, they make assumptions about which variables to include in the equation system, and as we have seen, they make a distinct assumption about the causal ordering of contemporaneous relationships.

These differences are reflected in the way the two modeling strategies approach policy analysis. The primary difference between VAR and SEQ approaches to policy analysis resides in the conception of policy choice. Consider the following SEQ model, with a policy variable X and an economic target Y:

$$Y_t = B X_t + C Z_{t-1} + e_t.$$
$$X_t = D Z_{t-1} + u_t.$$

(4.34)

The variable Z_{t-1} includes all past information on Y_t and X_t. The SEQ method of policy analysis entails setting e_t equal to zero and adjusting u_t to obtain the desired projection of Y_t. The structural approaches require that e_t not vary when u_t is manipulated. If these two error terms are not independent, then the policy variable cannot be treated as strictly exogenous, and policy analysis will fail to project the true response of Y_t when u_t is manipulated. In this sense the SEQ approach to policy analysis requires strict exogeneity of policy variables.

As regards causal inference, SEQ models have the potential for yielding information about the structure of relationships. If they are correctly specified and identified, SEQ models can produce efficient estimates of individual structural coefficients. The usually over-parameterized VAR models essentially can provide few, if any, insights about the values of individual structural coefficients. Again, VAR models purposely include additional lags of their variables

---

[32] See, for instance, Greene (2003, section 15.9) and Lütkepohl (2005, chapter 10).

so as to avoid omitted variable bias. They trade off efficiency for unbiasedness. In turn, they emphasize the overall response of variables – the response produced by the combination of coefficients in what is a weakly restricted system of equations – to shocks in orthogonalized variables.

4.6 FOR FURTHER READING

Christenson, Dino P. and Corwin D. Smidt. 2012. "Polls and Elections: Still Part of the Conversation: Iowa and New Hampshire's Say within the Invisible Primary." *Presidential Studies Quarterly* 42 (3): 597–621.

Enders, Walter, Todd Sandler, and Gaibulloev Khusrav. 2011. "Domestic versus Transnational Terrorism: Data, Decomposition, and Dynamics." *Journal of Peace Research* 48 (3): 319–337.

Evans, Geoffrey and Mark Pickup. 2010. "Reversing the Causal Arrow: The Political Conditioning of Economic Perceptions in the 2000–2004 U.S. Presidential Election Cycle." *Journal of Politics* 72 (4): 1236–1251.

Goble, Hannah and Peter M. Holm. 2009. "Breaking Bonds? The Iraq War and the Loss of Republican Dominance in National Security." *Political Research Quarterly* 62 (2): 215–229.

Green-Pederson, C. and R. Stubager. 2010. "The Political Conditionality of Mass Media Influence: When Do Parties Follow Mass Media Attention?" *British Journal of Political Science* 40: 663–677.

Habel, Philip D. 2012. "Following the Opinion Leaders? The Dynamics of Influence among Media Opinion, the Public, and Politicians." *Political Communication* 29 (3): 257–216.

Hansford, Thomas. 2011. "The Dynamics of Interest Representation at the U.S. Supreme Court." *Political Research Quarterly* 64 (4): 749–764.

Williams, John T. 1990. "The Political Manipulation of Macroeconomic Policy." *American Political Science Review* 84 (3): 767–795.

Wood, B. Dan. 2009. "Presidential Saber Rattling and the Economy." *American Journal of Political Science* 53 (3): 695–709.

5

Univariate, Nonstationary Processes: Tests and Modeling

5.1 STATIONARY DATA

Thus far, all of our models assumed that our data are stationary. A stationary series does not have statistical properties that depend on time. All shocks and past values in a stationary series eventually lose their influence on the value of the variable today. A stationary stochastic process is defined such that

- A stochastic process is stationary if the mean and variance are constant over time and covariance between two time points depends only on the distance of the lag between the two time periods and not on the actual time that the covariances are computed.
- In other words, if a time series is stationary, its mean, variance, and auto-covariance (at various lags) remain the same, no matter when we measure them.

Why should analysts care if variables are stationary? Econometric problems may occur when we run a regression with variables that are not stationary. For example, in the Box-Jenkins identification stage, because of nonstationarity, we may fail to diagnose a higher order AR process. We need to diagnose and correctly account for the characteristics of the data-generating process.

Several other issues arise with nonstationary data, which we discuss in this and the following chapters.[1] At a basic level, nonstationary data violate the invertibility condition for the value of ϕ (the AR process in our ARMA model) and bias our estimate of ϕ (that is, the extent to which past values of the dependent variable influence the current value). In addition, when dealing with multiple time series variables, the possibility of cointegration arises, which can

---

[1] We use the terms "integrated," "nonstationary," and "unit roots" interchangeably (i.e., to indicate a series that is not stationary).

lead to spurious results and false inferences when the data are nonstationary. For instance, if we regress one nonstationary series onto another, we may obtain statistically significant coefficient estimates, even if the relationship between the two series is nonsensical. That is, the t-statistics for the regression are statistically significant, and the R-squared is high, but the results have no meaning because the estimates are not consistent. We discuss the spurious regression problem and its solution (cointegration analysis) in the next chapter. For present purposes, it suffices to say that the failure to properly diagnose nonstationarity can lead to dire analytic errors. In this chapter, we review several tests for diagnosing nonstationarity, provide an applied example of these tests, and demonstrate with real data how dramatically our inferences can change if we fail to accurately diagnose nonstationarity.

Correctly diagnosing whether the series is stationary has important implications for our substantive understanding. Social scientists have long been interested in the ways political phenomena change over time. For example, there has been a long-standing interest in theories of incremental budgeting, dependent development, war cycles, political-business cycles, and periodicity in party systems. Implicit are hypotheses about the dynamic path each process follows and the response to shocks such as elections, social upheaval, war, international crises, or economic change. Theory may predict that the effects of a shock will diminish quickly or that the impact will endure for long periods. The common thread is that many social science hypotheses are concerned with the degree of persistence or memory, which refers to the rate at which a process moves toward an equilibrium level after being perturbed by a shock. Intuitively, social phenomena that move quickly toward equilibrium have short memory or low persistence. If they equilibrate slowly, they have long memory or high persistence. If they do not equilibrate at all, then they are integrated.

Because competing theories may have different implications for the persistence of effects of a shock, one way to test rival hypotheses is to investigate the degree of persistence and memory in a time series. For example, MacKuen, Erikson, and Stimson (1989) look at causes and dynamic consequences of shifts in macropartisanship. They conclude that the effect of presidential approval on aggregate partisanship quickly dissipated, whereas more elephantine memory exists for previous economic conditions. Conversely, realignment theory predicts that memories of political events will be more mid-range, in contrast to long periods of stable partisanship. These competing theories make predictions about the persistence of the series. The point is that the question of whether the dynamic behavior of a process is better represented by models for stationary or integrated series arises frequently for social scientists and needs to be taken seriously. It is essential to diagnose and correct for nonstationarity in our time series data.

To get a better sense of what stationarity and nonstationarity look like in practice, consider Figure 5.1, which depicts the level of macropartisanship from the first quarter of 1953 through the final quarter of 1992. As noted earlier, a

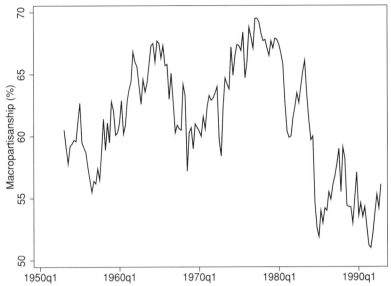

FIGURE 5.1. Quarterly Macropartisanship in the U.S., 1953:q1–1992:q4. Compiled by authors from ICPSR replication data set for Box-Steffensmeier and Smith (1996).

stationary series has a constant mean and variance over time. In other words, the effect of an exogenous shock on a stationary series is relatively short-lived, meaning that we would expect spikes in the series to be followed by the series quickly reverting back to an equilibrium value. Figure 5.1, however, does not appear to have a constant mean over time: the series seems to rise and fall without ever reverting back to an equilibrium value. If the exogenous shocks were short-lived, we would expect the series to move up or down, but to revert quickly to a mean value. However, because this is not the case we can see that shocks that enter the system tend to persist for a very long time, and as a result, we can begin to see that macropartisanship is likely to be a nonstationary series. By visually inspecting the series in this fashion, we can begin to diagnose it as being nonstationary, which has important implications for the substantive debate outlined earlier. Because Figure 5.1 seems to wander without reverting to a mean value, this provides some initial evidence in favor of the view of partisanship as being constantly shaped by exogenous shocks to the system, which seem to persist for a considerable period of time.

Recall from Chapter 2 our discussion of the ARMA model and the possibility of our data possessing either an autoregressive or moving average component (and, on rare occasions, both). We now add a third possible component – the integrative process – and use the more common label for these univariate models, ARIMA, where the "I" stands for the integrative process. We denote these models as ARIMA (p,d,q). Series that are integrated (that is, are nonstationary) are said to be ARIMA(0,d,0), where d, which refers to the number of times a series must be differenced to render it stationary, is typically equal to one.[2] Of course, a series may contain multiple components. For example, a nonstationary series with a first-order autoregressive component would be noted as ARIMA (1,1,0).

Schematically, one can now imagine the process of Box-Jenkins modeling as a series of filters that identify and remove each process, leaving only the underlying stochastic process (McLeary and Hay, 1980, 56). When we use the term "filtering," we refer to a traditional regression-based process. That is, regressing a dependent variable on an independent variable not only allows for substantive hypothesis testing but also, if one saves the residuals from the regression, the new variable represents what variation is left in the dependent variable after removing (or filtering) the influence of the independent variable. In the Box-Jenkins methodology that we review in this chapter, our independent variables are lags of the values of our dependent variable or lags of past error terms (which we refer to as shocks or disturbances). We are essentially asking, how much of the time series is explained by its past behavior or past shocks.

Partitioning a time series, we could find

$$y_t \longrightarrow \boxed{\text{Integration Filter}} \longrightarrow \boxed{\text{AR Filter}} \longrightarrow \boxed{\text{MA Filter}} \longrightarrow a_t$$

(Stochastic Trend)→(Long Term)→(Short Term)→(White Noise)

In this schematic, y_t is the data that we observe. After checking for and removing each type of dynamic process from the data, we are left with a_t. This residual is what is left unexplained by the filtering process: it is what the analyst really wants to analyze, because it represents everything that is not explained by the series itself. Unlike, many of our statistical models, which attempt to correct for the autoregressive process in the data – viewing it as a nuisance that gets in the way of statistical inference – time series analysis takes these dynamic processes as interesting substantively: they tell us important facts about the process that generated these observations. Moreover, the time series approach is a superior way to account for these temporal dynamics, even if the goal is to analyze the stochastic series that remains (see Chapter 2; also McLeary and Hay, 1980, 92).[3]

What occurs when exogenous shocks do not dissipate from the series? Some shocks may remain as a part of the series, integrating themselves into the data-generating process. Integrated series are also referred to as *unit root* or *random walks*, because they rise and fall, but never revert to a mean, similar to what

---

[2] Occasionally, time series analysts use *I* rather than *d* to denote the degree of nonstationarity in the data. These should be treated as equivalent notations.

[3] Analyses that treat time dependencies as a fixed effect (Jacobs and Carmichael, 2002) or level in a hierarchical model (Baumer, Messner, and Rosenfeld, 2003; Shor et al., 2007) generally also view these dependencies as a nuisance to be fixed.

was seen in Figure 5.1. Recall from Chapter 2 the discussion of deterministic versus stochastic trends (deterministic trends are a function of one variable such as time). If a series has a deterministic trend, it will likely appear to grow (or decline) steadily over time. That is, the increase (or decrease) in the value of the series will be a direct function of time, rather than the previous values of the variable itself. Although the presence of a deterministic trend will require work before proceeding to Box-Jenkins modeling (by regressing the series on a time trend), this procedure is straightforward. A series with a deterministic trend is said to be *trend stationary*.

Other trends, however, may be stochastic. That is, they "wander" up and down, yet never revert to a given mean. Recall our model of an autoregressive process:

$$y_t = \phi_1 y_{t-1} + a_t, \tag{5.1}$$

where a_t is our white noise error term. Also recall that we required ϕ_1 (and all ϕ) to be less than 1 (or greater than -1). When $\phi = 1$, equation 5.1 reduces to

$$y_t = y_{t-1} + a_t. \tag{5.2}$$

We can rewrite equation 5.2 (using Δ as a difference operator) so that

$$\Delta y = a_t. \tag{5.3}$$

We show in the Appendix that equation 5.3 is a first-order stochastic difference equation. The solution to this difference equation is

$$y_t = y_0 + \sum_{i=1}^{t} \epsilon_i. \tag{5.4}$$

The value of y_t is given by the initial condition, y_0, and the sum of all random shocks. Thus, shocks *integrate* into the system (McLeary and Hay, 1980, 43–45).

Integration in the univariate context is substantively interesting. In essence, the presence of a unit root suggests that a series has an extremely long (if not infinite) memory. Thus, any shock that enters the system persists over time. Imagine the relations between states being permanently influenced by a war or even by a highly cooperative overture (e.g., an arms control agreement). Another example is a major political program that shifts party allegiances for decades (e.g., the New Deal). One could also conceive of a social-political process, such as macropartisanship, which can be conceived of as a "running tally" where particular candidates may have an influence on whether people consider themselves Democrats or Republicans, but there is nonetheless an underlying persistence in political party affiliation once those exogenous shocks are controlled for (Box-Steffensmeier and Smith, 1996).

How long is a "long time"? Our answer involves another question: relative to what? Recall that in an AR(1) process, the impact of a previous observation dies out exponentially at the rate of ϕ. In a moving average process, the impact of a prior shock dies after a specified number of periods. There are tests for the hypothesis that $d = 1$, so that the question of whether a time series is a random walk does not have to be left only to theoretical interpretation. Using those tests, one can differentiate a long-lasting AR process from an integrated process.

At a basic level, dealing with an integrated series is straightforward. Differencing the series by subtracting the previous value of y_t (i.e., y_{t-1}) from the current value of y_t, we are left with our stochastic error term (a_t), which we know to be white noise (and indeed we can probe this fact with the white noise tests from Chapter 2). Thus, the appropriate technique for filtering a random walk is to do a simple difference to remove the stochastic trend. Because of this property, I(1) series are referred to as *difference stationary* series (versus trend stationary).

Of course, one should be careful to apply the correct detrending method. If one indeed has a simple time-invariant, deterministic trend, differencing is the incorrect solution. In this case, detrending (regressing the series on a variable such as time and saving the residuals) is the correct solution. Differencing when none is required (over-differencing) may induce dynamics into the series that are not part of the data-generating process. Usually, the result is the creation of a first-order moving average process (Maddala and Kim, 1998, 116–120).

In Chapter 2, we noted that an ACF with high initial values that die off very slowly could be a sign of a nonstationary series. Although that is often an analyst's first hint that a series may be integrated, there are statistical measures that can be applied to avoid relying only on tests of visual exploration. We turn now to those tests.

5.2 STATIONARITY AND UNIT ROOT TESTS

In contrast to stationary series, it is possible that some shocks permanently shift the series – that past shocks accumulate in our series. As previously discussed, in these cases, the use of AR or MA terms to represent this process is inappropriate. Yet, it may be difficult to tell from only a correlogram whether an autoregressive process with several AR terms is at work or whether integration is a problem in our series. If we conclude that the d term in our ARIMA(p,d,q) model equals 1 (meaning our series is integrated of order 1 or that it is I(1)), then our data must be differenced before attempting to diagnose any other ARIMA components.

An easy way to explain the use of unit root tests for determining if the series is stationary is to consider this equation, which is the random walk model when $\rho = 1$:

$$y_t = \rho y_{t-1} + a_t. \tag{5.5}$$

Ideally, we want to obtain an estimate of ρ to discern whether the data are indeed a random walk. In other words, is our statistical estimate of $\hat{\rho}$ different from 1 based on, for example, a t-test? Unfortunately, the value of t if $\rho = 1$ does not follow a traditional t distribution, even in large samples, because the test is over the residual term rather than the raw data. Thus, a new type of test must be devised to investigate the possibility of unit roots. Several candidates exist, and here we review the most common ones.

However, before diving into several examples of tests for unit roots, two points should be noted. First, some tests we review are of low power. That is, they have difficulty with type 1 errors in that they can accept the presence of a unit root when none is present. This is the case with the popular Dickey-Fuller (DF) test, where the null hypothesis is the presence of a unit root (Dickey and Fuller, 1979). The DF test only allows us to reject (or to fail to reject) the hypothesis that a variable is not a random walk. A failure to reject is only weak evidence in favor of the random walk hypothesis. The power of the test also depends more on the span of the data than on the number of observations. For example, if long business cycles are being studied, long spans of annual data are preferred to shorter spans of monthly data, even if the N is larger for monthly data (say daily for a year, which is 365 observations, or annually, which is 40 observations for 40 years).

Tests where the null hypothesis is that of a stationary series, such as the KPSS test from Kwiatkowski et al. (1992), have higher power. Nonetheless, scholarship on unit root testing is constantly changing as research continues in the area and as computational power increases. The section on fractional integration in Chapter 7 offers one such alternative test, which moves away from the assumption that d must either equal 0 or 1.

The presence (or absence) of a constant is a second important point in testing for a unit root. In most social science literature, analysts make the assumption (we would argue because of the commonality of working with OLS) that all our models will have a constant. Otherwise, our regression models would be forced to fit a line that crosses at the origin. We then traditionally interpret the constant (as we do in our Box-Jenkins models) as a sort of equilibrium condition: the value of the dependent variable absent the influence of covariates. Yet, consider the intuition behind the unit root – a series does not return to a mean value, but walks randomly over time. What does a constant mean in this context? Because of this issue, one should be careful when conducting unit root tests. Often times, especially in prewritten software routines, a constant is not specified in the model.

Yet this is not to say that we cannot have a constant in a series with a unit root. Rather than thinking of the constant as an equilibrium, however, we often refer to a constant term as *drift*. Thus, for the tests we review later, there is often a distinction made between a test for a pure unit root and a unit root with a drift. If one suspects some drift in a series or has a strong theoretical reason for expecting drift, one should adjust the choice of unit roots tests accordingly.

Some tests also allow for the presence of a deterministic (as well as stochastic) trend. As we soon discuss, one of the three versions of the Dickey-Fuller test for unit roots allows for the presence of a deterministic trend (see equation 5.9). However, some have found this test alone to be insufficient in testing for unit roots when a deterministic trend may be present. Schmidt and Phillips (1992), for example, have devised an alternative unit root test that provides several advantages over the DF test presented next.[4] In addition, Phillips and Perron (1988) have developed an alternative test for unit roots that is nonparametric in nature. Similar to the DF test, this test also allows for the presence of a drift, or a drift and a deterministic trend; for examples of the latter test, see Baillie and Bollerslev (1989) and Ferdere (1996). Some nonstationarity tests examine whether a series is trend stationary (regressing on a linear trend) versus level stationary (first differencing to remove nonstationarity). When using preprogrammed statistical routines, one should be particularly aware of the null hypothesis and model assumption in each test. In some cases, a "basic" test includes a linear trend unless otherwise specified. Although in some fields (economics and finance), this assumption may be justified, in other fields (political science), fewer scholars are likely to make this assumption. This difference arises from varying beliefs as to whether the data-generating process also includes a deterministic trend; that is, in addition to a stochastic trend, whether the series rises (or falls) over time in a predetermined fashion.

5.2.1 Dickey-Fuller and Augmented Dickey-Fuller Tests

Two of the most common tests for a unit root process are the Dickey-Fuller (DF) and augmented Dickey-Fuller (ADF) tests. To grasp the intuition behind these tests, we begin by rewriting the unit root equation (equation 5.5) by subtracting y_{t-1} from each side of the equation:

$$\Delta y_t = \gamma y_{t-1} + a_t, \tag{5.6}$$

where $\gamma = (\rho - 1)$. Now, testing ($\rho = 1$) is the same as testing for $\gamma = 0$. Note that the standard error for γ is identical to the standard error for ρ. The difference is that the t-statistic is computed by dividing that standard error into γ rather than ρ.[5]

The idea behind the test is that in a nonstationary series, the value of the series today does not help you predict the value of the series tomorrow, whereas the opposite is true for a stationary series. So if knowing the past value of the series helps predict the next period's change, there will be a negative coefficient in the equation. Still, there is an issue with the appropriate distribution of the t-statistic to assess statistical significance because the test is over the residual

---

[4] For an extension to this test and an empirical application of it to OECD income levels over time, see Strazicich, Lee, and Day (2004).

[5] Recall the estimate of ρ is equivalent to $(1 - \rho)$ in $y_t = \rho y_{t-1} + a_t$.

term rather than the raw data. This distribution is nonstandard. Dickey and Fuller (1979) conducted extensive Monte Carlo studies to generate critical values for a test of the statistical significance of γ. It is not possible to use a standard distribution to test for the statistical significance of γ, because under the null hypothesis of a unit root the test statistic that is produced by dividing the standard error into γ does not follow a t distribution, nor is it asymptotically normal, as is typically the case in calculating test statistics. Instead, such tests tend to produce type 1 errors in that they indicate that the null hypothesis of $\gamma = 1$ can be rejected when this may not, in fact, be the case. As a result, the standard critical values associated with a t distribution or a normal distribution are of little use in determining whether to reject the null hypothesis of stationarity, and instead it is necessary to rely on the critical values derived through Monte Carlo simulations.

There are three versions of the DF test, each with their own set of critical value t-test tables. The following regressions may be used to test for a unit root:

$$\Delta y_t = \gamma y_{t-1} + a_t. \tag{5.7}$$

$$\Delta y_t = c_0 + \gamma y_{t-1} + a_t. \tag{5.8}$$

$$\Delta y_t = c_0 + \gamma y_{t-1} + \beta_1 t + a_t. \tag{5.9}$$

The first of these equations is a pure random walk model, the second is a random walk with a drift, and the third is a random walk with a drift and a deterministic time trend. The distribution of the t-statistic for testing statistical significance of γ is different for each of the three versions and is often referred to as τ, τ_μ, and τ_τ, respectively. It may be found in most statistical textbooks and is reproduced here in Table 5.1 for ease of accessibility.

For the DF test, *failure to reject the null hypothesis indicates the presence of a unit root*. That is, only if the estimate of γ is statistically significant can we reject the possibility of a unit root in our series. In addition to selecting a model structure for the DF test, the analyst also chooses a confidence level (90%, 95%, or 99%). Finally, each of the critical values for the statistic also depends on sample size.

If one is unsure as to the presence of a drift or deterministic time trend, one may also conduct joint tests to assess whether the model is appropriately specified while diagnosing a unit root. Dickey and Fuller (1981) provide F-statistics based on their test to determine whether restricted specifications of the model are binding. The tests are conducted as are any nested model tests – specifying both a restricted and unrestricted model where a statistically significant F-statistic allows one to reject the restriction. The only difference is the critical values of the F distribution, which can be found in Dickey and Fuller (1981).

Finally, what if one's series is of a higher order autoregressive process, such as an AR(2)? In this case, one must turn to what is known as the augmented Dickey-Fuller test (ADF). This model is similar to the DF but allows for

TABLE 5.1. *Empirical Cumulative Distribution of* τ

Sample Size	Significance Level			
	99%	97.5%	95%	90%
The τ statistic ($c_0 = \beta_2 = 0$)				
25	−2.66	−2.26	−1.95	−1.60
50	−2.62	−2.25	−1.95	−1.61
100	−2.60	−2.24	−1.95	−1.61
250	−2.58	−2.23	−1.95	−1.62
300	−2.58	−2.23	−1.95	−1.62
∞	−2.58	−2.23	−1.95	−1.62
The τ_μ statistic ($\beta_2 = 0$)				
25	−3.75	−3.33	−3.00	−2.62
50	−3.58	−3.22	−2.93	−2.60
100	−3.51	−3.17	−2.89	−2.58
250	−3.46	−3.14	−2.88	−2.57
300	−3.44	−3.13	−2.87	−2.57
∞	−3.43	−3.12	−2.86	−2.57
The τ_τ statistic				
25	−4.38	−3.95	−3.60	−3.24
50	−4.15	−3.80	−3.50	−3.18
100	−4.04	−3.73	−3.45	−3.15
250	−3.99	−3.69	−3.43	−3.13
300	−3.98	−3.68	−3.42	−3.13
∞	−3.96	−3.66	−3.41	−3.12

additional AR terms, while taking those terms into consideration for unit root testing. After all, because the DF uses OLS to generate γ, it assumes a_t is independent and identically distributed, but if a higher order autoregressive process exists, autocorrelation will remain in the residuals and violate this OLS assumption, leading to poor estimates of γ.[6] The ADF test allows for heterogeneity and serial correlation in the errors. The ADF test for the general p-th order autoregressive process is

$$\Delta y_t = c_0 + \gamma y_{t-1} + \sum_{i=2}^{p} \zeta_i \Delta y_{t-i+1} + a_t, \tag{5.10}$$

where $\gamma = -(1 - \sum_{i=1}^{p} \beta_i)$ and $\zeta_i = -\sum_{j=1}^{p} \beta_j$.

---

[6] Indeed, one can check the residuals of the regression that generates the DF/ADF test to see if the residuals are white noise using any of the tests discussed in Chapter 2.

We show in the Appendix that in our difference equations, if the coefficients sum to one, then there is a least one characteristic root equal to unity. The same principle follows in the ADF test: if the sum of all β_i's is 1, then the value of γ will be 0, indicating a unit root. The same t-test tables are used with the ADF as with the DF test. However, because one needs to know the appropriate number of lags before conducting the ADF tests, there is a bit of a chicken and egg problem: how does one know whether to difference the data based only on the ACF and PACFs of a series? Empirically, the slowly decaying ACF is always an important signature of the presence of a unit root. If one finds this tell-tale sign, one should then difference the series and restart the lag selection process.

Why not err on the side of caution and include several AR terms in our ADF test to ensure proper specification? Again, the problem of low power arises. As the number of parameters estimated increases for the ADF test, the precision with which γ is estimated falls. Although normally we might not be so concerned with this eventuality, recall that for the DF and ADF tests, a null finding suggests the presence of a unit root. Thus, as our standard errors increase due to falling degrees of freedom, the probability that we incorrectly diagnose a unit root increases also.[7] In addition, as we discuss in Chapter 7, some fractional integration diagnosis methods do not depend on the number of lags present in the data and can thus avoid this potential conundrum.

5.2.2 Variance Ratio Test

Another test for the presence of a unit root utilizes information about the degree of persistence in the series. The test, proposed by Cochrane (1988), has a null hypothesis of a random walk, as does the Dickey-Fuller and augmented Dickey-Fuller tests. The variance ratio (VR) is the variance of the kth difference of a series, divided by k-times the variance of the first difference of the series. Thus,

$$V\hat{R}_k = \frac{k^{-1}var(y_t - y_{t-k})}{var(y_t - y_{t-1})} \left(\frac{T}{T - k + 1} \right). \tag{5.11}$$

The second term is a bias correction factor. The distribution of the test statistic is normal, with a mean of 1 and a variance of $2(2k - 1)(k - 1)/3kT$.[8]

The intuition behind the variance ratio test is as follows. When a time series contains a unit root, its variance grows linearly over time. Thus, for a unit root process, k periods multiplied by the variance from period 1 should be equal to the variance in the kth period. Deviations of the VR statistic from a ratio equal to one indicate departures from the unit root hypothesis. In other words, given

---

[7] Advances extending this literature include important work by Dolado, Gonzalo, and Maryoral (2002) on a fractional Dickey-Fuller test.

[8] For details on this distribution, see Lo and MacKinlay (1988).

that the variance of a unit root time series grows linearly over time, the ratio
of the variances, separated by k periods, should equal one. Deviations from
one provide evidence that the series is not a unit root. Diebold (1989) provides
critical values for the variance ratio statistic for 10 sample sizes when $k = 2$,
4, 8, 16, and 32. His simulations show that the variance ratio test has good
power in all cases, but is the most powerful when $k = 4$ or $k = 8$.

In implementing the VR test, it is usually prudent to choose several values of
k. In the words of Maddala and Kim (1998, 87), "it is customary to consider
VR_k for different values of k and consider a model rejected when at least some of
the VR statistics provide evidence against it." For an application of the VR test
in political science, see Box-Steffensmeier and Smith (1996, 573). Additional
applications of the VR test in political science include substantive questions of
dyadic foreign policy behavior (Lebo and Moore, 2003) and the growth and
institutionalization of the presidency (Dickinson and Lebo, 2007). There have
also been numerous applications outside of political science, in particular in
economics and finance, with substantive applications ranging from stock prices
(Choudhry, 1997), to foreign exchange rates (Liu and He, 1991), to commodity
prices (Cromwell, Labys, and Kouassi, 2000).

5.2.3 Modified Rescaled Range Test

Analysts also have at their disposal tests of the null hypothesis that a time series
is a strong mixing, stationary process. A time series is strong mixing if the rate
at which dependence between past and future observations goes to zero as the
distance between them grows is "fast enough" (Lo, 1991). Stationary series,
which decay at a geometric rate, are strong mixing processes, whereas unit root
processes, which do not decay, are not strong mixing. Because shocks persist
indefinitely or for an extremely long time in an integrated series, integrated
series do not exhibit this strong mixing property.

A number of tests of the null hypothesis of strong mixing have been developed. One of the first, developed by Lo (1991), is called the modified rescaled
range (R/S) statistic and is given as

$$\tilde{Q}_t = \frac{1}{\hat{\sigma}_T} \left[Max \sum_{t=1}^{k} (x_t - \bar{x}_T) - Min \sum_{t=1}^{k} (x_t - \bar{x}_T) \right] \qquad (5.12)$$

for $1 \leq k \leq T$, with $\bar{X}_T$ denoting the sample mean and where $\hat{\sigma}_T$ is the square
root of the variance of the partial sum process.

Lo's modification requires analysts to obtain a consistent estimate of the
"long-run" variance of the partial sum of deviations process. A consistent
estimate of this variance, denoted S2(Q), is calculated as

$$T^{-1} \left[\sum_{t=1}^{T} (X_t - \bar{X}_T)^2 + 2T^{-1} \sum_{s=1}^{l} \omega(s,l) \sum_{t=s+1}^{T} (X_t - \bar{X}_T) \right] \qquad (5.13)$$

where $\omega(s, \ell)$ is a weighting function that guarantees that estimates of the variance will be positive. The most commonly used weighting function is $\omega(s, \ell) = 1 - [s/(\ell + 1)]$, as suggested by Newey and West (1987). The modified R/S statistic is commonly computed for different values of ℓ, the truncation lag parameter.

The intuition behind Lo's test can be seen by examining its three components. The first term in the brackets in equation 5.12 represents the maximum value of the partial sum (over k) of the deviations process of the series, whereas the second term in the brackets is the minimum value of the partial sum (over k) of the deviations process. Thus, the entire quantity in brackets represents the "range" of the partial sum of the first k deviations. This range is then scaled by the square root of a consistent estimate of the variance of the partial sum of the deviations. Lo's modified R/S statistic has poor power in samples smaller than 250 observations.

5.2.4 KPSS Test

The Kwiatkowski, Perron, Schmidt, and Shin (1992) (KPSS) test adopts the absence of a unit root as the null hypothesis, the opposite of the tests reviewed so far. It is essentially a Lagrange multiplier test. The KPSS test begins by considering the following model:

$$y_t = \beta t + \eta_t + a_t, \tag{5.14}$$

where $\eta_t = \eta_{t-1} + \mu_t$, μ are *i.i.d.* with mean 0 and variance σ_μ^2, and a_t are *i.i.d.* with mean 0 and variance $\sigma_a^2 = 1$. We are concerned with σ_μ^2: if it is equal to zero, then we can reject the presence of a unit root and conclude that y_t is stationary around a deterministic trend (unless $\beta = 0$ – then it is stationary around its mean). If $\sigma_\mu^2 > 0$ then we cannot reject the hypothesis of stationarity.

The KPSS test is constructed as follows:

$$\eta_j = \frac{T^{-2} \sum_{t=1}^{T} S_t^2}{s_T^2(l)}, \tag{5.15}$$

where S_t is the partial sum of residuals (denoted e_t) from either a regression of y_t on an intercept or from a regression on an intercept and a trend, depending on whether one is testing for stationarity around the mean or for a deterministic trend. $s_T^2(l)$ is an estimate of the error variance from the appropriate regression. The estimator used for the error variance in the denominator is

$$s_T^2(l) = T^{-1} \sum_{t=1}^{T} e_t^2 + 2T^{-1} \sum_{s=1}^{l} w(s, l) \sum_{t=s+1}^{T} e_t e_{t-s} \tag{5.16}$$

where $w(s, l)$ is a weighting function that corresponds to the choice of a spectral window. Kwiatkowski et al. (1992), use the Bartlett window ($w(s, l) = 1 - s/(l + 1)$) where l is the lag truncation parameter. The Bartlett window is taken from Newey and West (1987). The choice of lag truncation parameter can have implications for the estimate of the KPSS statistic. For further discussion, see Maddala and Kim (1998, 107–109), who discuss modifications of the Bartlett window assumption to the Phillips-Perron test to increase power. Kwiatkowski et al. (1992) provide advice for choosing the optimal truncation lag for various sample sizes.

As discussed by Maddala and Kim (1998), none of these unit root tests are perfect diagnostic instruments. Therefore, is common for those concerned with unit roots to conduct multiple tests on the data and base their conclusions about a unit root (or stationarity) on the pattern of the tests conducted.

5.2.5 Double Unit Roots

Double unit roots are possible, though rare in most social science applications. There are two general approaches to testing for double unit roots. First, nonstationary is taken as the null. Then one tests I(2) versus I(1), and if the hypothesis of I(2) is rejected, then I(1) versus I(0) is tested. This is a top-down approach. Alternatively, a second approach treats stationarity as the null. Here one tests I(0) versus I(1), and then I(1) versus I(2) if the first hypothesis is rejected. This is a bottom-up approach. Both can be used in tandem as confirmatory analysis. See Maddala and Kim (1998, chapter 11) and Enders (2004, 194–195) for more information on double unit roots.

5.3 APPLICATION: MACROPARTISANSHIP

Proper diagnosis of unit roots is of the utmost importance for sound social scientific research. This is the case not only because a failure to detect and properly account for such properties may lead to biased statistical inferences but also because understanding such processes allows us to advance our theoretical knowledge of social processes. One example of the importance of such proper diagnosis pertains to a debate in the study of American politics over the nature of macropartisanship. Macropartisanship, as noted previously, refers to the aggregate level of identification with a political party. In *The American Voter*, Campbell et al. (1968) emphasized the psychological nature of an individual's attachment to a given party. They theorized that an individual's attachment to a particular party was expected to be quite stable over time, because it became a part of an individual's conception of self, making it slow to change and generally impervious to small shocks. However, in contrast to this view, MacKuen, Erikson, and Stimson (1989, 1992), Weisberg and Smith (1991), and Weisberg and Kimball (1995), among others, have argued that macropartisanship is actually far less stable – meaning that levels of aggregate partisanship may vary in response to exogenous shocks such as ratings of the economy, unemployment levels, and presidential approval. In turn, other time series analysts have suggested that macropartisan adjustments occur on a much smaller scale and at a much more gradual pace than suggested by Mackuen et al. (1989, 1992), a claim that is consistent with Campbell et al.'s earlier argument (Abramson and Ostrom, 1991; Green and Palmquist, 1990; Green, Palmquist, and Schickler, 1998; Whiteley, 1988). Thus, much of this debate centers around the degree to which exogenous shocks persist within the macropartisanship series. As a result, testing for unit roots plays an important role in this debate, because such tests can illuminate whether the series in question have low or high levels of memory.

Before proceeding to the formal tests for unit roots, it is always a good idea to begin with an informal evaluation of plots for each of the respective variables. Although examining plots alone does not provide strong enough evidence to conclude that a series contains a unit root or not, it can nevertheless prove instructive. We now consider plots for three univariate time series – macropartisanship, consumer sentiment, and presidential approval – because the latter two variables are important independent variables in the debate surrounding macropartisanship (see MacKuen, Erikson, and Stimson, 1989). The data for this example come from Box-Steffensmeier and Smith (1996).

5.3.1 Macropartisanship: Diagnostic Plots

Recall from the previous discussion that a stationary series has a constant mean and variance, regardless of when these parameters are measured. A nonstationary series, in contrast, does not have a constant mean and thus appears to wander without ever reverting back to a constant value. Moreover, the variance of a nonstationary series increases linearly over time. With these characteristics in mind, recall the time series plot for macropartisanship, presented in Figure 5.1, which seems to show some of the classic signs of a unit root. The series appears to wander in a stochastic fashion and shows no tendency to revert back to a constant mean value. This interpretation, although preliminary, certainly seems to be consistent with the view of macropartisanship that finds party identification to change based on a series of exogenous shocks, rather than being fundamentally realigned by large-scale, rare shocks. The time series plot for consumer sentiment (Figure 5.2) shows some of the same characteristics as does the plot of macropartisanship: it does not seem to have a constant mean, as the trend wanders in a stochastic fashion. Moreover, it appears as though, as time increases, the variance of the series also increases, which is what one would expect in a unit root process. Finally, Figure 5.3 presents the time series plot for presidential approval. Once again, this series seems to display some of the characteristics of a unit root, because there is no apparent mean value around which the series is centered. Thus, each of these figures provides some preliminary support for the notion that the data in question are nonstationary or, in other words, that in each of the three series, random shocks are integrated into the series and persist for an extended period of time. However, it is important to recognize that an analysis of this sort is inherently limited because

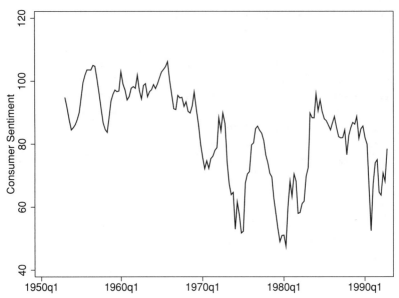

FIGURE 5.2. Consumer Sentiment in the U.S., 1953:q1–1992:q4. Compiled by authors, with permission, from Surveys of Consumers, University of Michigan.

of its subjective nature.[9] Thus, based on these figures alone it is not possible to discern whether shocks integrate into the system and then dissipate over time, or if shocks remain in the series indefinitely.

In addition to the time series plots, it is frequently instructive to consider the ACF plots for each of the series in question, because these plots allow us to observe the rate at which exogenous shocks decay from the series. Figure 5.4 shows the ACF for macropartisanship. Note the fact that the autoregressive component decays extremely slowly over time: there are statistically significant spikes through 10 lags. This indicates that macropartisanship is characterized by a relatively high degree of memory, or persistence, over time as shocks remain within the system and dissipate very slowly. Substantively, this plot suggests that aggregate levels of partisanship are unlikely to quickly return to an equilibrium level after being subjected to an exogenous shock. Although it provides further evidence that macropartisanship is not a stationary process, it does not provide conclusive evidence that there is a unit root. Figure 5.5 shows the ACF for consumer sentiment. As is the case with macropartisanship, the ACF for consumer sentiment is characterized by a slowly decaying autoregressive component. Although this decay is not as slow as that observed in the macropartisanship function, consumer sentiment contains a relatively high

[9] Moreover, for the purposes of detecting a unit root, visual inspection of plots is even more difficult because it is nearly impossible to differentiate between a unit root process and a fractionally integrated process (discussed in Chapter 7) with an estimate of *d* that is close to 1.

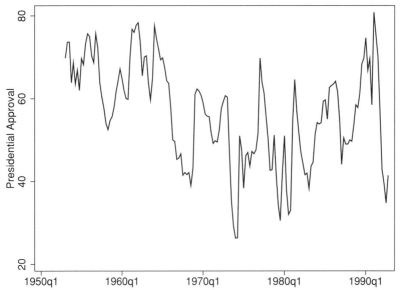

FIGURE 5.3. Presidential Approval in the U.S., 1953:q1–1992:q4. Compiled by the authors from Gallup polls.

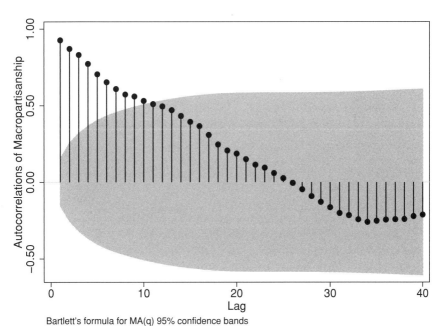

Bartlett's formula for MA(q) 95% confidence bands

FIGURE 5.4. Autocorrelations of Macropartisanship.

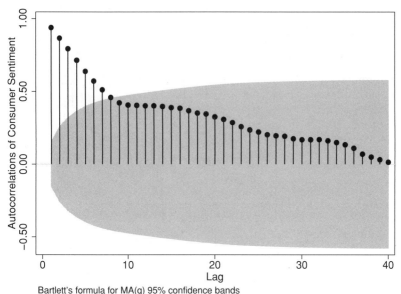

FIGURE 5.5. Autocorrelations of Consumer Sentiment.

degree of memory, which is consistent with nonstationarity. Finally, the ACF for presidential approval is shown in Figure 5.6. Once again, the ACF indicates that there is a fairly slowly decaying autoregressive component; however, this component decays more quickly than in both the macropartisanship and consumer sentiment plots. Thus, each ACF considered seems to indicate that there is nonstationarity in the data because they each display, albeit to varying degrees, slowly decaying autoregressive components.

5.3.2 Macropartisanship: Formal Statistical Tests

After having gained a basic intuition about the likely degree of memory in each of the series through visually inspecting the plots, it is necessary to turn to more formal tests for the presence of a unit root. We begin by considering the results of a Dickey-Fuller test for each of the three variables in question (see Table 5.2).[10] Recall from the previous discussion that the null hypothesis of this test is that the series in question has a unit root. Therefore, if we are unable to reject the null hypothesis, then this lends some support to the conclusion that there is a unit root present in the series. As Table 5.2 shows, the estimate of γ for presidential approval is equal to -3.361, which has a corresponding p-value of .0124. Thus, it is possible to reject the null hypothesis that a unit

---

[10] Some statistical programs, such as STATA, use McKinnon's p-values when the Dickey-Fuller test contains a trend or constant.

TABLE 5.2. *Dickey-Fuller Test for Unit Root*

Variables	Test Statistic	McKinnon approx. p Value
Presidential approval	−3.36	0.01
Consumer sentiment	−2.25	0.19
Macropartisanship	−2.25	0.19

root is present in the series with 99% confidence. As is the case for the ACF of presidential approval in Figure 5.6, this statistical finding means that the effect of exogenous shocks on presidential approval is likely to be relatively short-lived in the series. In contrast, the estimates of γ for both consumer sentiment and macropartisanship are not statistically significant, because they have corresponding p-values of .1903 and .1899, respectively. As a result, we fail to reject the null hypothesis, which provides some evidence that there may be a unit root present in these series. Substantively, this test provides additional evidence that shocks are likely to persist in levels of aggregate partisanship and in consumer sentiment, such that neither series is likely to revert quickly to an equilibrium level after experiencing such shocks. However, given the relatively low power of the Dickey-Fuller test, it is not uncommon for type 1 errors to occur; that is, it fails to reject the null hypothesis even though a unit root may not be present. Thus, it is necessary to turn to alternative tests with higher power to compensate for this shortcoming.

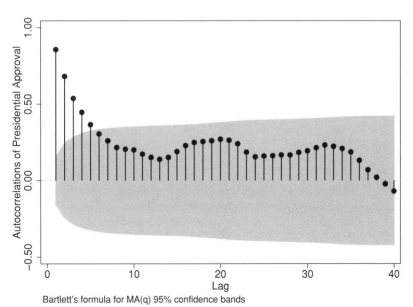

Bartlett's formula for MA(q) 95% confidence bands

FIGURE 5.6. Autocorrelations of Presidential Approval.

TABLE 5.3. *Lo-MacKinlay Variance Ratio Test*

Variables	VR(2)	VR(4)	VR(8)	VR(16)
Presidential approval	1.14[†]	1.02	0.76	0.40
Consumer sentiment	1.07	1.16	1.16	0.70
Macropartisanship	0.86[†]	0.76	0.72	0.58

[†] $= p < .10$.

The next formal test to be considered is the Lo-MacKinlay variance ratio test, the results of which are presented in Table 5.3. Recall that this test is constructed around the fact that a time series with a unit root will have a linearly increasing variance over time, and it relies on a ratio test such that deviations from 1 indicate that the variance of the series is not linearly increasing. Thus, the null hypothesis of the test is the presence of a unit root. Beginning with presidential approval, the ratio of the variance is significant at the 90% confidence level for the first lag ($k = 2$), because the variance ratio ($V\hat{R}_k$) is equal to 1.137 and has a corresponding p-value of .1001. Thus, we are able to reject the null hypothesis of a unit root with 90% confidence for the first lag. However, for each of the subsequent lags ($k = 4, 8, 16$), we fail to reject the null hypothesis that the variance is increasing linearly over time. Because of the relatively low level of statistical significance of the first variance ratio, and the fact that this test is most powerful when $k = 4$ or $k = 8$, there is a fair amount of evidence that the variance of the presidential approval series is increasing linearly over time, which suggests the presence of a unit root. Similarly, $V\hat{R}_k$ for the first lag of the macropartisanship series is equal to .855 and has a corresponding p-value of .0809, allowing us to reject the null hypothesis of a unit root at the 90% confidence level. However, as is the case with presidential approval, each of the subsequent variance ratios is not statistically significant. Therefore, this test result suggests that the variance of the macropartisanship series is increasing linearly over time, providing additional evidence for the conclusion of a unit root. Finally, none of the VR statistics is statistically significant in the consumer sentiment series, which means that we fail to reject the null hypothesis of a unit root in this series. This provides even more evidence for the conclusion that consumer sentiment is an integrated series, because the variance ratio test indicates that the variance of the series is likely increasing linearly over time, as was initially suggested after a visual inspection of Figure 5.2.

The next formal test to be considered is the modified rescaled range test, the results of which are presented in Table 5.4. The purpose of this test is to examine whether each of the series in question is characterized by strong mixing – which is to say whether shocks dissipate quickly from the series or not. In turn, the presence of strong mixing provides additional information as to whether a unit root is present in the series. Interestingly, none of the test statistics presented in Table 5.4 are statistically significant at any meaningful

TABLE 5.4. *Modified Rescaled Range Test*

Variables	Test Statistic
Presidential approval	1.54
Consumer sentiment	1.23
Macropartisanship	1.1

level. Even at the 90% confidence level, all of the test statistics are located within the confidence interval, which ranges from .861 to 1.747. As a result it is not possible to reject the null hypothesis that each of these series is strong mixing. In other words, this test indicates that exogenous shocks that affect aggregate presidential approval, consumer sentiment, and macropartisanship all decay very quickly, suggesting that there may not be a unit root in any of these series, because such a process would experience no decay at all. Of course, as noted earlier, this test has poor power in sample sizes smaller than 250, underscoring the need to conduct multiple unit root tests in any applied exercise.

The final formal test to be considered in this example is the KPSS test. One of the key insights of Kwiatkowski et al. (1992) in developing this test is that most existing tests for units roots assume the presence of a unit root as the null hypothesis, which means that the presence of unit roots may be accepted too frequently (type 1 errors). Therefore, they proposed testing for both the presence *and* the absence of unit roots in an attempt to triangulate the answer. Table 5.5 presents the results of the KPSS test with the null hypothesis of stationarity, and Table 5.6 presents the results of the KPSS test with the null hypothesis of level stationarity. With respect to presidential approval, it is possible to reject the null hypothesis of stationarity with 95% confidence for all lag truncation parameters. Similarly, it is possible to reject the null hypothesis

TABLE 5.5. *KPSS Test for Time Trend*

Variables	Lag Truncation Parameter (l)				
	0	2	4	6	8
Presidential approval	1.16	0.46	0.32	0.26	0.23
Consumer sentiment	1.08	0.39	0.25	0.20	0.17
Macropartisanship	2.33	0.83	0.52	0.39	0.32
Critical values					
0.01	0.22	0.22	0.22	0.22	0.21
0.05	0.15	0.15	0.15	0.15	0.15
0.10	0.12	0.12	0.12	0.12	0.12

TABLE 5.6. *KPSS Test for No Time Trend (Strong Mixing)*

Variables	Lag Truncation Parameter (l)				
	0	2	4	6	8
Presidential approval	3.54	1.37	0.93	0.75	0.65
Consumer sentiment	6.37	2.25	1.43	1.08	0.89
Macropartisanship	3.40	1.21	0.76	0.56	0.46
Critical values					
0.01	0.74	0.74	0.74	0.74	0.74
0.05	0.46	0.46	0.46	0.46	0.46
0.10	0.35	0.35	0.35	0.35	0.35

of a unit root for presidential approval at the 95% confidence level for all values of *l*. These two results combine to indicate that the series is likely neither stationary nor a unit root process.[11] The consumer sentiment series is quite similar, in that it is possible to reject the null hypothesis of stationarity and the null hypothesis of a unit root for all values of *l* with 95% certainty. Again, this suggests that consumer sentiment is neither fully integrated nor stationary. Finally, macropartisanship displays much the same tendency as the other two series, which is to say that in both KPSS tests, the null hypothesis is consistently rejected with 95% certainty for all values of *l*. Thus, it is possible to reject both the null hypothesis that macropartisanship in an integrated process and the null hypothesis that it is a stationary process. As a result, the KPSS tests suggest that exogenous shocks do persist in aggregate levels of partisanship, but not indefinitely, and that they will eventually decay.

As noted previously, none of these tests is perfect, and it would be unwise to consider the findings of one test in isolation. Instead, it is important to consider all of the plots and tests as a constellation and then rely on the general pattern that emerges. In this example, all of the plots and tests, with the exception of the modified rescaled range test, indicated that all of the series are nonstationary. Substantively, this finding implies that shocks are likely to integrate into each of the series over time and to decay slowly. As the KPSS test for unit roots showed, however, it is unlikely that any of the series is completely integrated either, meaning that shocks will eventually decay over time. This makes intuitive sense given the substantive issue area of macropartisanship, because it would be unreasonable to assume that all shocks that affected aggregate levels of party identification would remain integrated indefinitely. This finding, in

---

[11] As a result, it seems likely that the series is fractionally integrated, which means substantively that exogenous shocks affect the series and persist for a given period of time, but ultimately decay. This is explicitly explored in Chapter 7 for this series.

TABLE 5.7. *A Box-Jenkins Model of Macropartisanship*

	ARIMA[1,0,0]	ARIMA[1,1,0]
constant	60.85	−0.03
	(1.99)	(0.13)
AR(p)		
ϕ_1	0.93	−0.15
	(0.03)	(0.08)
σ	1.72	1.73
	(0.09)	(0.09)
AIC	634.92	631.62[†]
BIC	644.15	640.83[†]

Notes: Standard errors in parentheses. † = model selected by this criteria.

turn, suggests that it is important in this example, as well as in many other applications, to test for unit roots.

5.3.3 Macropartisanship: An ARIMA Model

The tests described in the previous section indicated a highly likelihood that the macropartisanship series is nonstationary. To show the practical impact of diagnosing nonstationarity, we return to our Box-Jenkins models of Chapter 2. We first estimate an ARIMA(1,0,0) model with the data in levels (as originally constructed). Next, we difference the data before estimating the same specification. That is, we estimate an ARIMA (1,1,0) model. The results are shown in Table 5.7.

Note that our initial estimate of ϕ_1 using the undifferenced data is very large and very near to 1. Not surprisingly, it is also highly statistically significant. Yet, when estimating the same model on the first difference of the macropartisanship data, a very different result emerges. While the estimate of ϕ_1 is significant at the $p < .10$ level, the size and sign of the coefficient are noticeably different.

Of course, this change in model estimates should not be surprising, because we are no longer modeling the level of partisanship in the American electorate, but rather the change in the level of partisanship. This represents a fundamentally different dependent variable in several ways. Yet, without differencing our nonstationary variables we risk committing costly econometric errors. The way out of this potential conundrum is presented in the next chapter, where we introduce multivariate models that can use the information about the long-run behavior of a time series (e.g., undifferenced variables containing a unit root) and the short-term dynamics also present in the data (e.g., differenced variables where the long-run behavior is removed by the differencing).

5.4 CONCLUSION

In this chapter, we introduced the concept of nonstationary data and some statistical tests for diagnosing the presence of stochastic trends. Diagnosing nonstationarity is not only essential econometrically but is also important substantively. Knowing that shocks to a data-generating process will integrate into the system is an interesting and potentially powerful finding. Evidence of this in a time series is itself an important substantive finding. Indeed, one need only consider the debate about the nature of macropartisanship to understand the substantive importance of identifying whether shocks persist in a series for an extended period of time or disappear rapidly.

From a statistical standpoint, dealing with nonstationarity is essential. In this chapter we discussed using a simple first difference as a corrective to the presence of nonstationarity. It removes the stochastic trend, leaving a series that can then be used in the context of a Box-Jenkins model or a traditional VAR. Removing that trend is of the utmost importance because the failure to diagnose nonstationarity and model it appropriately may result in what Granger and Newbold (1974) refer to as a spurious regression. A spurious regression is a model that produces an extremely high R-squared, value, large t-statistics, and corresponding low p-values, but such results are essentially hollow. As a result, if nonstationarity remains undiagnosed, it has the potential to lead to faulty inferences, because the p-values from a spurious regression are meaningless. This is the case because the presence of a unit root violates several of the core assumptions of OLS, resulting in inconsistent estimates and leading to the use of inappropriate tests for statistical significance. Thus, spurious regression resulting from unmodeled nonstationarity is a serious problem. However, as we discuss in the next chapter, it is not merely a problem to be fixed before proceeding. Rather, through the use of error correction models it is possible to theorize about nonstationarity and to model it in a theoretically justified fashion.

But as we emphasized in this chapter, diagnosis is not a matter of a single-shot statistic. Rather, because many of the diagnostic statistics needed to detect unit roots are of low power, it is best to rely on a battery of tests to investigate whether a time series contains a unit root, as in our example. Moreover, a preliminary visual analysis of the data series, in addition to ACF plots, can further help contextualize the results of the diagnostic tests and assist in determining whether there is a unit root present. In Chapter 7, we return to the topic of integration and suggest how the "all or nothing" approach in the tests presented here can be relaxed with a more advanced. In the next chapter, however, we examine further the problem encountered in our macropartisanship example: how to deal with nonstationary data while still investigating long-term dynamics that may be present in our data.

5.5 FOR FURTHER READING

Box-Steffensmeier, Janet M. and Renee M. Smith. 1996. "The Dynamics of Aggregate Partisanship." *American Political Science Review* 90 (3): 567–580.

Byers, David, James Davidson, and David Peel. 2000. "The Dynamics of Aggregate Political Popularity: Evidence from Eight Countries." *Electoral Studies* 19 (1): 49–62.

Freeman, John, Daniel Houser, Paul M. Kellstedt, and John T. Williams. 1998. "Long-Memoried Processes, Unit Roots, and Causal Inference in Political Science." *American Journal of Political Science* 42 (4): 1289–1327.

Hendershot, Marcus E., Mark S. Hurwitz, Drew N. Lanier, and Richard L. Pacelle. 2013. "Dissensual Decision Making: Revisiting the Demise of Consensus Norms within the U.S. Supreme Court." *Political Research Quarterly* 66 (2): 467–481.

Lebo, Matthew and Harold D. Clarke. 2000. "Modeling Memory and Volatility: Recent Advances in the Analysis of Political Time Series." *Electoral Studies* 19 (2): 1–7.

6

Cointegration and Error Correction Models

6.1 INTRODUCTION

The study of equilibrium relationships is at the heart of time series analysis. Because cointegration provides one way to study equilibrium relationships, it is a cornerstone of current time series analysis. The original idea behind cointegraton is that two series may be in equilibrium in the long run, but in the short run the two series deviate from that equilibrium. Clarke, Stewart, and Whiteley (1998, 562) explain that "cointegrated series are in a dynamic equilibrium in the sense that they tend to move together in the long run. Shocks that persist over a single period are 'reequilibrated' or adjusted by this cointegrating relationship." Thus cointegration suggests a long-run relationship between two or more series that may move in quite different ways in the short run. Put a bit more formally, cointegration says that a specific combination of two nonstationary series may be stationary. We then say these two series or variables are cointegrated, and the vector that defines the stationary linear combination is called the cointegrating vector.

Recall from the previous chapter that a time series is stationary when its mean and variance do not vary over or depend on time. Lin and Brannigan (2003, 153) point out that "many times series variables in the social sciences and historical studies are nonstationary since the variables typically measure the changing properties of social events over, for example, the last century or over the last x-number of months or days of observations. These variables display time varying means, variances, and sometimes autocovariances." The error correction model captures the joint dynamics of multiple nonstationary series. It is appealing not only because of its methodological properties but also because it eloquently captures substantive hypotheses about long- and short-run dynamics.

What exactly is a cointegrating relationship between multiple nonstationary series? Miller (1994) shares a humorous example. A drunkard might stumble about town randomly; charting her movements as she leaves a tavern would constitute a nonstationary series (that is, the best predictor of her current location is her immediately preceding location, plus a random shock). Similarly, an unleashed puppy's movements around town would also constitute a nonstationary series; the dog might chase after any number of random sights and smells. If there is no relationship between the drunk and the dog, there would be no reason for the drunkard's random walk to be influenced by the puppy's wanderings, and vice versa. But if the drunkard owns the puppy, that changes things. Imagine that the drunk leaves her dog outside the tavern while carousing one night. When she emerges, her dog has wandered off. As the drunkard stumbles randomly off into the night, she calls out for her lost puppy. Assuming that the dog is close enough to hear the drunkard's calls, the puppy responds by running toward the owner's call and barks in reply. As the dog barks, the owner moves closer to the noise. So, although both the drunkard's stumbles and the puppy's wandering are random walks, their relationship is not random. That is, each adjusts their movements in response to the action of the other. Thus, eventually, the drunkard and the dog will get closer and closer together. Although both of their movements are individually random, they approach a stationary equilibrium where they are near each other. Even though their individual movements are nonstationary random walks, their joint location is not random. Knowing something about where the dog is tells us something about where the drunkard is, and vice versa. The joint series of their movements is said to be cointegrated, and the process by which they hear each other in the dark and move closer together is an error correction mechanism.

The concept of cointegration caught on quickly because, among other things, it is intuitively appealing. Cointegration says that two nonstationary variables may be related in multiple ways. Specifically, it allows us to consider the possibility that two variables that are nonstationary can be related in the short term (which we could induce using any of the techniques discussed in Chapter 3 on differenced data), while also exhibiting correlation over the long term. Because many social science series are nonstationary, it is important to know methodologically how to handle such series to allow for correct substantive inferences about the processes and the temporal dynamics that we care about. As we discuss more fully, simple differencing of nonstationary series eliminates the possibility of capturing long term relationships, yet ignoring nonstationarity in a multiple time series model threatens that false relationships between variables will be found. The spurious regression problem is quite serious – analysts can easily falsely conclude that there are significant relationships between nonstationary variables, even when such relationships are clearly nonsense.

For example, in pioneering work, Yule (1926) showed a strong, significant relationship between the proportion of marriages performed in the Church of England from 1866–1911 and the standardized mortality per 1,000 persons for those same years. This relationship makes no sense and the two variables should have no relationship to each other: any theory positing that a decline in the proportion of marriages performed in the Anglican Church might lead to a decline in population mortality rate would be absurd. Yet, their correlation is about 0.95. Scholars have long observed that regressing one nonstationary time series on another can produce similarly misleading results. To avoid this problem while not discarding potential inferences about long-term relationships by differencing, scholars developed the concept of cointegration and the error correction model. Cointegration links the relationship between nonstationary processes and the concept of long-run relationships.

The remainder of this chapter proceeds as follows. First, we discuss the motivations and intuitions behind the cointegration methodology and error correction models. Second, we review two of the more common methods for estimating error correction models: the Engle-Granger and Johansen approaches. Next, we briefly discuss relaxing the underlying assumption of the cointegration method: that our variables are nonstationary. Finally, we conclude with an example of the Engle-Granger method using data on Indian and Pakistani military spending.

6.2 THE INTUITION BEHIND COINTEGRATION

Clive W. J. Granger introduced the idea of cointegration in 1981. The statistical analysis was further developed in seminal works by Robert F. Engle and Granger, Soren Johansen, and Peter C.B. Phillips 1991 (Granger, 1981; Granger and Weiss, 1983; Engle and Granger, 1987). The development of the concept of cointegration by Granger and of error correction models by Engle and Granger was rewarded with the Nobel Prize in Economics in 2003.

In economics, the central problem tackled by cointegration models is that several core economic models suggest that the relationship between some sets of variables should be stationary over time. For example, the demand for money should be shaped by interest rates, income, and prices. Should large shocks influence any of these variables, the demand for money should naturally adjust. This suggests that errors (shocks) do not accumulate over time; that is, a model of the demand for money should have a stationary error term. Otherwise, the market for money would be in disequilibrium over time (an outcome we do not witness in the real world). The problem is that all of the variables in the model are nonstationary. Normally, regressing nonstationary variables on other nonstationary variables creates nonstationary error terms. Thus, modeling cointegration is a way to model systems of variables whereby the equilibrium relationships (long-run responses to shocks) and the short-term deviations are simultaneously modeled.

In the social sciences generally, these models have become widely used. For example, Lin and Brannigan investigated the hypothesis of a cointegrating relationship between the crime rate and the rate of immigration. Substantively they tested whether the variables drift apart over the short run while not diverging over the longer term (Lin and Brannigan, 2003, 156). Durr (1992) studied changes in U.S. domestic policy sentiment as responses to shifting economic expectations and federal policy outcomes. Ward and Rajmaira (1992) investigated Cold War political-military behavior between the superpowers. Ostrom and Smith (1992) investigated presidential approval, inflation, and unemployment. Ermisch (1988) studied birth rate dynamics and economic measures, and Jacobs and Helms (1996) examined prison admission rates and political and economic factors.

The basis of error correction models is the random walk, which is a nonstationary series.[1] Recall our random walk equation:

$$Y_t = Y_{t-1} + \epsilon_t, \tag{6.1}$$

where the values of the data-generating process today are predicted entirely by the values generated yesterday, plus a random noise element. In the univariate world, we differenced Y_t to remove everything but the stochastic process to facilitate our ARIMA modeling approach.

In past time series research, even in the multivariate world (e.g., time series regression or VAR), we would difference our random walk/nonstationary series to facilitate modeling. In this way, we were sure to avoid the Granger and Newbold (1974) problem of spurious regression, in which estimates of relationships between nonstationary series or variables could give nonsensical results by showing statistically significant relationships when they did not really exist. This problem could be caused by bias in the standard errors and coefficients, as well as inflated R-squared statistics.

To show how this problem can arise and could have serious consequences, let us begin with a simple example of population and per capita GDP measured from 1950 to 1998 on a yearly basis:

$$POPULATION_t = \alpha_0 + \alpha_1 \ Per \ Capita \ GDP_t + \epsilon_t. \tag{6.2}$$

This simple model looks great at first glance because the results in Table 6.1 are highly statistically significant and there is a large R-squared statistic for the model. We should all be so lucky as to have these wonderful results to publish, right?

Yet, substantively, something seems amiss. Generally, it is believed that higher income should lead to a leveling off of the birth rate. Wealthier societies tend to have lower birth rates, which makes our finding of wealth leading to larger populations puzzling. Moreover, a quick analysis of the residuals shows there still is a lot of nonwhite noise. The highly significant Q statistic ($Q = 79.09$; $p < 0.000$) indicates that something is definitely misspecified with the model. Figure 6.1 shows the ACF and PACF plots of the regression

---

[1] In the penultimate section of this chapter, we discuss the view that even stationary series may be modeled using the error correction methodology.

TABLE 6.1. *Regression of Population on Per Capita GDP: 1950–1998*

Variable	Coefficient
intercept	101405
	(2847)
pcGDP	5.82
	(0.14)

Notes: Standard errors in parentheses. Number of observations = 49, F(1,47) = 1696.60, Prob > F = 0.00, R-squared = 0.97.

residuals, which visually confirm what our Q statistic told us: our errors are nonstationary.

Recall Chapter 2 where we began looking at our data by performing some simple correlograms. We can perform this ARIMA-like analysis on our two variables to make sure we have removed any of the systemic temporal components from the data before estimating our regression.

Looking at the ARIMA analysis, it is clear that both series are nonstationary due to the slowly decaying ACFs of both (see Figures 6.2 and 6.3). In addition,

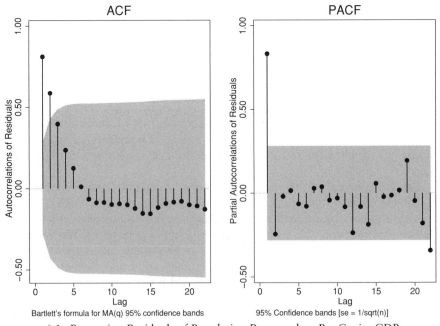

FIGURE 6.1. Regression Residuals of Population Regressed on Per Capita GDP.

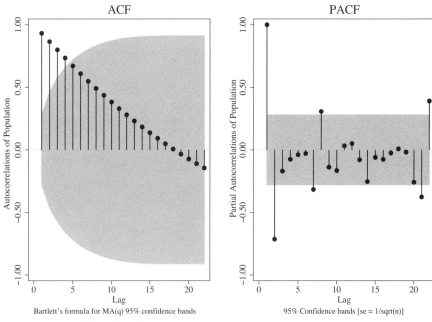

FIGURE 6.2. ACF/PACFs of Population.

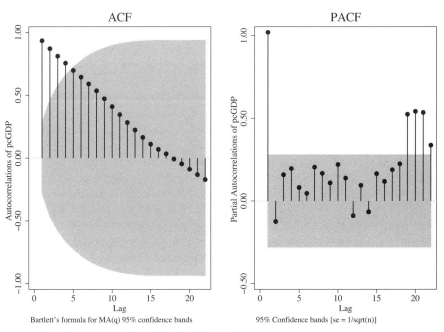

FIGURE 6.3. ACF/PACFs of Per Capita GDP.

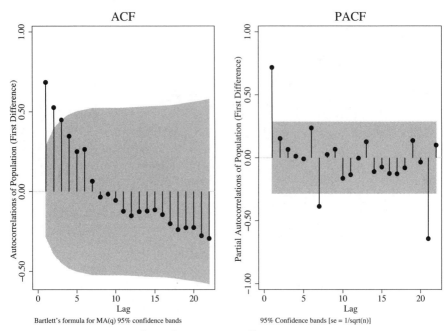

FIGURE 6.4. ACF/PACF of Population (First Difference).

an analysis of the differenced population series reveals the presence of an AR (1) process (see Figure 6.4).

Thus, following the advice of Chapter 2, we remove these systemic components of each variable so the series are filtered or "cleaned" to make each series stationary. We difference per capita GDP to remove the nonstationarity. We model population as shown in Table 6.2, as an ARIMA(1,1,0) process, saving the residuals from this model as the "cleaned" population time series.

Rerunning the regression on this transformed data provides a new (and very different) answer, shown in Table 6.3. Now larger changes in per capita GDP are associated with *lower* population growth rather than higher population growth. Note that this new estimate is also statistically significant. Moreover, as shown in Figure 6.5, the correlograms of the residuals from this regression show no sign of temporal dynamics. In addition, the Q statistic is not statistically significant ($Q = 15.76$, $p = 0.83$). By eliminating the systematic temporal components in the data, we have avoided making a spurious inference.

There is one major problem with this approach, however: it might throw the proverbial baby out with the bathwater. That is, there may be long-run relationships captured in multivariate models that would be washed away by the differencing. There may be real correlation among stochastic trends that suggests there is some equilibrium relationship between the variables and we do not want to discard this information. Essentially this approach provides a

TABLE 6.2. *ARIMA(1,1,0)*
Model of Population

Variable	Coefficient
Intercept	2617.90
	(167.24)
ϕ_1	0.72
	(0.20)
σ	319.73
	(43.14)

Note: Standard errors in parentheses.

statistical model based on differences that may be able to capture the short-run dynamics, but is not able to provide insight into the long-run covariation about the series.

We therefore want to account for the nonstationary nature of the data by allowing for the possibility of a long-run relationship, while also investigating whether short-term perturbations are related. Error correction models (ECMs) are designed to do exactly this. Note that the discussion currently only considers the knife-edged distinction of stationary ($I = 0$) versus nonstationary ($I = 1$), but this assumption is relaxed later in Chapter 7 when considering fractional cointegration.

Substantively, what is accomplished by adopting an ECM-type model? ECMs allow theory to play a central role. Theory may suggest that some set of variables are in equilibrium, yet, the variables are nonstationary. Normally this implies a nonstationary error term, but this makes little sense. If there is nonstationarity, then the errors are permanently integrated into the set of variables, which throws the system out of equilibrium or forces constant reequilibration. Instead, there must be some combination of these variables

TABLE 6.3. *Regression of Filtered*
Population on Differenced Per Capita
GDP

Variable	Coefficient
Intercept	92.406
	(60.580)
pcGDP	−0.236
	(0.098)

Notes: Number of observations = 48, $F(1,46)$ = 5.80, Prob > F = 0.020, R-squared = 0.11.

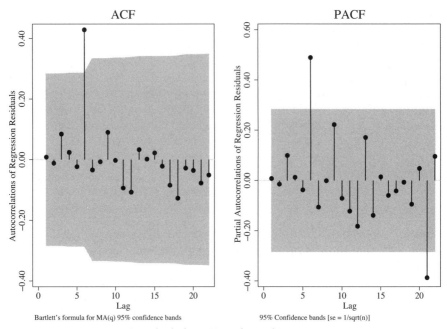

FIGURE 6.5. Regression Residuals from Transformed Data.

that yields an error term that is stationary, so that shocks are not permanent and the system holds its equilibrium. Lin and Brannigan (2003, 156) provide further substantive insight: "The concept of cointegration allows a researcher to examine the existence of the long term relationship among different time series that are individually nonstationary. For instance, if the argument that immigrants have a high tendency to commit crimes is valid, then the crime rate and the immigration rate should be cointegrated and should share a common trend over a long period. If cointegration is established, research can capture the magnitude of the equilibrium effect."

There are three major steps involved in cointegration analysis. First, determine whether the individual series are stationary or integrated. Second, if the series are integrated, find out if they are cointegrated (i.e., if a linear combination of the series is stationary). Third, fit a multivariate error correction model.

Formally, we first determine if X_t and Y_t are I(1). This is important because in the classical sense, for two variables to be cointegrated they must be integrated of the same order. We relax this assumption when discussing fractional cointegration in the next chapter, but we stick to the fundamentals here.

We begin with

$$Y_t = \beta X_t + \epsilon_t, \tag{6.3}$$

where ϵ_t is the error term. Therefore ϵ_t represents the variation in Y_t that cannot be explained by the model. The spurious regression problem of Yule and of Granger and Newbold arises if the random error term is nonstationary because a standard regression test may show that the coefficients for X_t are not zero even if the true value is zero. Unfortunately, this result holds even asymptotically – no amount of data can be mustered to obtain consistent coefficient estimates and accurate t-statistics if we regress one nonstationary series on another without either differencing the data or employing the techniques discussed in this chapter.

By rearranging the equation we have

$$\epsilon_t = Y_t - \beta X_t, \tag{6.4}$$

where β is the cointegrating vector that makes ϵ_t an I(0) variable. This equation says that the partial (or weighted) difference between the two series may be stable around a fixed mean; that is, the series are moving together in a long-run equilibrium. Recall that the data are still in levels. One way to think about the intuition behind this vector is to consider the cointegrating vector as a set of weights to relate X and Y such that the error term is stationary.

To express the same logic using a multiequation setup, take two series,

$$Y_t = \eta_{Y_t} + \epsilon_{Y_t} \tag{6.5}$$

$$Z_t = \eta_{Z_t} + \epsilon_{Z_t}, \tag{6.6}$$

where η are random walk components for each variable and ϵ are stationary noise components of the series. The presence of η in each series means that both Y and Z will be nonstationary. If they are cointegrated, however, adding Y and Z must yield a stationary component (i.e., the η must go away so the ϵ can remain).

To begin, multiply equations 6.5 and 6.6 by a constant (β) and then add each side of each equation, yielding

$$\beta_1 Y_t + \beta_2 Z_t = \beta_1 (\eta_{Y_t} + \epsilon_{Y_t}) + \beta_2 (\eta_{Z_t} + \epsilon_{Z_t}). \tag{6.7}$$

Now, multiply the betas through and regroup terms:

$$\beta_1 Y_t + \beta_2 Z_t = (\beta_1 \eta_{Y_t} + \beta_2 \eta_{Z_t}) + (\beta_1 \epsilon_{Y_t} + \beta_2 \epsilon_{Z_t}). \tag{6.8}$$

The first set of grouped terms must equal zero, so the second set (the stationary terms) can remain. The first set of grouped terms is then made equal to zero:

$$0 = \beta_1 \eta_{Y_t} + \beta_2 \eta_{Z_t}. \tag{6.9}$$

Solve for $\eta_{Y_t} = (-\beta_2 \eta_{Z_t})/\beta_1$.

Thus, up to some scalar $-\beta_2/\beta_1$, two I(1) processes must have the same stochastic trend. The only way that two series can be cointegrated is if they have a common trend. (Greene, 2003, 654) found that "a set of M series that are cointegrated can be written as a stationary component plus linear combinations of a smaller set of common trends. The effect of the cointegration is to purge these common trends from the resultant variables."

The logic is that X and Y are influenced not just by short-term shocks but also by how much they have moved apart. There is a reequilibrating process that pushes them back together; this notion of pushing a system out of equilibrium back toward equilibrium is the logic behind the cointegrating vector. Although we focus on ECMs with linear specifications for these long-run relationships in the data, there are also techniques for estimating and modeling error correction relationships that allow for nonlinear adjustments in long-run relationships. These techniques fall under the umbrella of smooth transition regression techniques and are covered in Kilic (2011) and Kapetanios, Shin, and Snell (2006), among others works.

In general, if there are M series or variables in the system, there could be up to M-1 linearly independent cointegrating vectors. We refer to the number of linearly independent cointegrating vectors that exist as the cointegrating rank of the system. Stock and Watson (1988) have developed two tests for the number of common stochastic trends (i.e., the order of cointegration).

There are also general criteria for cointegration and ECMs:

- There must be a linear combination of terms to yield a stationary series. In addition, the cointegrating vector is not unique (i.e., any set of weights that yields a stationary series could be multiplied by a constant and still work). Therefore, one of the weights, (a β), is usually fixed at 1.
- All variables must be integrated of the same order (e.g., I(1); I(2), etc). Most of the work in ECMs assumes the variables are I(1), but this assumption has loosened over time. In Chapter 7, in the fractional cointegration discussion we relax this to be within a standard deviation.
- When there are more than two variables, there can be multiple cointegrating vectors. This is referred to as the cointegrating rank of X_t where X is a matrix.

6.3 ESTIMATING AN ECM

There are two main approaches to cointegration analysis. The first is a regression or least-squares-based test on the residuals from the OLS estimates of the cointegrating equation. The basic idea of Engle and Granger (1987) is to assess whether single equation estimates of the equilibrium errors appear to be stationary. The second is based on the vector autoregressive model (VAR) and is sometimes referred to as the Johansen method: its logic is that, in an unrestricted VAR, a set of cointegrated variables could be detected via the implied restrictions.

6.3.1 Engle-Granger Regression-Based Approach

Tradtionally, the Engle-Granger regression approach has been the most commonly used methodology. The steps for a two-variable model are as follows:

(1) Pretest the variables for the order of integration. Use unit root tests such as the Dickey-Fuller, augmented Dickey-Fuller, KPSS, and the variance ratio test.[2]
(2) Find the cointegrating vector. In levels, regress

$$Y_t = \beta_0 + \beta_1 X_t + \epsilon_t \tag{6.10}$$

using OLS. The residuals from this regression, $\widehat{\epsilon}_t$, should be stationary if X and Y are cointegrated.
(3) Test the $\widehat{\epsilon}_t$ to see if they are indeed stationary. The test is based on the following regression:

$$\Delta\widehat{\epsilon}_t = \alpha_1\widehat{\epsilon}_{t-1} + Z_t. \tag{6.11}$$

We are interested in whether $\alpha_1 = 0$. If we can reject this hypothesis, then we can conclude the series is stationary and our variables are cointegrated. If we fail to reject this hypothesis, then while our variables are nonstationary, they do not appear to be cointegrated. We should then move to estimating a VAR in first differences because the assumption would be that there is no evidence of an equilibrium between the series.

However, it is important to realize that the test for $\alpha_1 = 0$ is not as straightforward as it may appear. Indeed, it is normally a Dickey-Fuller (or augmented Dickey-Fuller) test, but because we are using an estimate of an estimate, we need to utilize nonstandard, nonstandard tables (recall from Chapter 5 that the normal Dickey-Fuller test relies on a nonstandard distribution). Here, the rejection of the null hypothesis means that the residual series from the cointegrating regression is stationary, implying cointegration. That is, a regression of nonstationary variables has yielded a series that is stationary. Failure to reject the null hypothesis (indicating a unit root in the residual series) suggests that there is no cointegration among the variables and one can proceed to analyze the data as a VAR in first differences.

---

[2] Fractional integration tests (discussed in Chapter 7) for the value of d and the associated standard error are also recommended in practice due to the low power of the alternative tests (see Maddala and Kim, 1998). Fractional integration tests are particularly important when analysts find themselves rejecting the null hypothesis of both I(0) and I(1) data based on the results of the Dickey-Fuller, augmented Dickey-Fuller, KPSS, and variance ratio tests.

(4) Estimate your ECM. We are assuming two lags for each variable in this example.

$$\Delta X_t = \alpha_{10} + \alpha_{11}[X_{t-1} - \beta_1 Y_{t-1}] + \alpha_{12}\Delta X_{t-1} + \alpha_{13}\Delta X_{t-2}$$
$$+ \alpha_{14}\Delta Y_{t-1} + \alpha_{15}\Delta Y_{t-2} + \epsilon_{X_t}. \tag{6.12}$$

$$\Delta Y_t = \alpha_{20} + \alpha_{21}[X_{t-1} - \beta_1 Y_{t-1}] + \alpha_{22}\Delta X_{t-1} + \alpha_{23}\Delta X_{t-2}$$
$$+ \alpha_{24}\Delta Y_{t-1} + \alpha_{25}\Delta Y_{t-2} + \epsilon_{Y_t}. \tag{6.13}$$

The grouped term at the start of each equation is the error correction portion of the model. This term shows the response of each variable to movements out of equilibrium between the variables. In terms of interpretation, the equilibrium suggests that any random shock that separates the series will be short-lived. The series will return to equilibrium through error correction.

Other than the addition of this term, the rest of the model is a simple VAR in first differences. Each equation has identical right-hand-side variables and can therefore be estimated using OLS, as discussed in Chapter 3.

So, how is the ECM term estimated? It turns out that because $\widehat{\epsilon}_{t-1}$ is the size of the deviation from equilibrium between X and Y, it can be used as an instrument for the $[X_{t-1} - \beta_1 Y_{t-1}]$ term in equations 6.12 and 6.13. Thus, we can estimate the following regressions as a VAR in first differences with the error correction term as an exogenous variable in each equation.[3] To determine the appropriate lag length, one can use traditional likelihood ratio tests or information criteria, but it is important to remember to difference the variables before performing these tests. Moreover, in most statistical programs, one can specify exogenous variables to include in the tests. In this case, one would specify the error correction term as exogenous:

$$\Delta X_t = \alpha_{10} + \alpha_{11}\widehat{\epsilon}_{t-1} + \alpha_{12}\Delta X_{t-1} + \alpha_{13}\Delta X_{t-2} + \alpha_{14}\Delta Y_{t-1}$$
$$+ \alpha_{15}\Delta Y_{t-2} + \epsilon_{X_t}. \tag{6.14}$$

$$\Delta Y_t = \alpha_{20} + \alpha_{21}\widehat{\epsilon}_{t-1} + \alpha_{22}\Delta X_{t-1} + \alpha_{23}\Delta X_{t-2} + \alpha_{24}\Delta Y_{t-1}$$
$$+ \alpha_{25}\Delta Y_{t-2} + \epsilon_{Y_t}. \tag{6.15}$$

The α_{11} and α_{21} are important parameters of interest known as the *speed of adjustment parameters*. These estimates tell us how each dependent variable responds to deviations from the long-run equilibrium. There are two important points to keep in mind about these estimates. First, one or all of these terms should be statistically significant – otherwise, the ECM

---

[3] Here, exogenous implies that the error correction term will not appear on the left-hand side of the system of equations.

reduces to a VAR in first differences with no error correction process present. If none of the estimates are statistically significant, one should revert to a VAR in first differences because no cointegration is apparent in the data.

Second, the estimates of the adjustment parameters will take on opposite signs. Intuitively, if each variable responds to long-run disequilibrium in the same direction, the system would remain in disequilibrium. Thus, in our two-variable example, it should be the case that one $\alpha > 0$ and another $\alpha < 0$.

(5) Assess model adequacy.

As with traditional VAR models, various tests can be used to assess model adequacy. In particular, one should be concerned with serial correlation in the residuals. Nonwhite noise residuals are a sign that longer lag lengths are required in the error correction model. Lagrange multiplier tests (such as those discussed in Chapter 3) or traditional ARIMA techniques may be used to check for residual serial correlation after estimation.

A unique issue arising with ECM estimation is normalization; that is, because the cointegrating vector is not unique, we choose to normalize one β in the cointegrating equation to 1. Although in theory the choice of which coefficient to normalize is not important, in practice, it can be. To put it more plainly, when we estimate our cointegrating vector, does it matter whether X_t or Y_t is the dependent variable (and thus normalized to one)? Asymptotically, the answer is no, yet in finite samples, the answer is often yes. One should be careful to reestimate steps 2 and 3 while, alternating the normalization choice. If cointegration can only be accepted in one estimation, one should be wary of using the ECM approach. Results should not be sensitive to the typically arbitrary choice of which variable to normalize.

Finally, as with traditional VAR estimates, one can perform post-estimation simulations, including impulse response functions and variance decompositions. Again, recall that in the Engle-Granger methodology, our estimates are traditional VARs in first differences with one additional exogenous variable. Thus, the same approaches used in Chapter 4 can be used here. Out-of-sample forecasting can also be done following estimation of an ECM. Iqbal (2011) reviews the ECM forecasting literature – generally, improvements in forecasting gained by estimating an ECM instead of a VAR with no cointegration are only obtained in the long run if they are obtained at all; results are mixed on this point. Iqbal finds that the Johansen method produces better forecasts than the Engle-Granger method. Moreover, as pointed out by Enders (2004, 339), because all the variables in the ECM are I(0), the impulse responses should converge to zero. This is also a check on the theory, because the nondecaying responses indicative of I(1) variables are removed by the differencing and error correction mechanism.

6.3.2 Johansen's VAR Approach

The second approach to cointegration is estimated via maximum likelihood and based on the VAR model. It is also referred to as the Johansen method (1988). In macroeconomics, Johansen's method has become the most popular method of estimating ECMs (Ahking, 2002). Although its implementation is more complex, this method has several advantages over the Engle-Granger approach. First, because the Johansen method estimates the entire system of equations simultaneously, the test for cointegration does not rely on an arbitrary choice of specification for the cointegrating vector (the normalization issue discussed in the previous section). Second, in the case of three or more variables, this method more easily identifies the presence of multiple cointegrating vectors. Finally, it is not clear that traditional tests of statistical significance can be applied to the estimates of the speed of adjustment parameters in the Engle-Granger approach because they are based on estimated data in the two-step process. The Johansen method allows us to avoid some of these difficulties that arise with the Engle-Granger approach.

Recall from Chapter 5 our discussion of the Dickey-Fuller test:

$$Y_t = \rho_1 Y_{t-1} + \epsilon_t. \tag{6.16}$$

Subtracting Y_{t-1} from both sides, we obtain

$$\Delta Y_t = (\rho_1 - 1)Y_{t-1} + \epsilon_t. \tag{6.17}$$

We then need to test whether ($a_1 - 1 = 0$). Now, generalize this logic to n variables:

$$X_t = A_1 X_{t-1} + \epsilon_t, \tag{6.18}$$

again, subtracting X_{t-1} from both sides so that

$$\Delta X_t = A_1 X_{t-1} - X_{t-1} + \epsilon_t \tag{6.19}$$

$$= (A_1 - I)X_{t-1} + \epsilon_t \tag{6.20}$$

$$= \pi X_{t-1} + \epsilon_t, \tag{6.21}$$

where, $A_1 = n \times n$ matrix of parameters, $I = n \times n$ identity matrix, and $\pi = (A_1 - I)$. Note that this is identical to the Dickey-Fuller derivation (equation 6.16).

The rank of π equals the number of cointegrating vectors. Recall that the rank of a matrix is equal to the number of nonzero characteristic roots. For example, let $\pi = \lambda_1, \lambda_2, \ldots, \lambda_n$. If all $\lambda_n = 0$, then the rank of $\pi = 0$: all the variables contain unit roots. Thus, there is no linear combination of the variables that are stationary, implying no cointegration. If the rank of $\pi = 1$, then $0 < \lambda_1 < 1$, with the remaining $\lambda_i = 0$, and we can conclude there is one cointegrating vector in the system. It is possible that the rank of π will be greater than or equal to 0 and less than n, where n is the number of equations in the system.

To test for the number of roots in our π matrix, we compute two test statistics. The first is the λ_{TRACE} statistic:

$$\lambda_{TRACE}(r) = -T\,\Sigma_{i=r+1}^{n}\,ln(1 - \widehat{\lambda}_i). \tag{6.22}$$

The second, is the λ_{MAX} statistic, given by

$$\lambda_{MAX}(r, r+1) = -T\,(ln(1 - \widehat{\lambda}_{r+1}). \tag{6.23}$$

In these tests, $\widehat{\lambda}$ are estimates of characteristic roots (also known as eigenvalues) obtained from the π matrix, and T is the number of usable observations. For each variable in the system, an eigenvalue is computed (λ_1 through λ_n), resulting in n values of the λ_{TRACE} and λ_{MAX} statistics. One then compares the critical values for each test (which can also be found in the online appendix, www.politicalscience.osu.edu/faculty/jbox/tsass).[4]

The larger the value of the characteristic roots (that is, the farther the roots are from zero, which would be a pure unit root), the larger the λ_{TRACE} and λ_{MAX} statistics. The TRACE statistic tests the hypothesis that the number of cointegrating vectors is less than or equal to r. The MAX statistic tests that the number of cointegrating vectors is equal to r, rather than $r - 1$. Using these two tests, one can determine whether the system of variables has cointegrating vectors. Take the following example of these tests, based on simulated data in a three-variable system. Solving for the eigenvalues (estimating the λs), one generates the following test values:

λ	λ_{MAX}	λ_{TRACE}
0.32	38.51	2.52
0.13	14.10	16.62
0.03	2.52	55.13

Table 6.4 presents the critical values for the appropriate tests for each hypothesis. Using the TRACE test, given the value of the test statistic, we can reject the hypothesis that there are less than two cointegrating vectors in our data. Using the MAX statistic, we cannot reject the null hypothesis that $r = 2$. Thus, for our simulated data, there appears to be convergence on the possibility of two cointegrating vectors.

Two specification issues arise in the Johansen model. First, there is the issue of lag length. As with all of our time series techniques, the lag length for this methodology can be determined by information criteria or by choosing the shortest lag length that results in serially uncorrelated residuals. It should be noted that Stock and Watson (1993) find that Johansen's cointegration test is quite sensitive to the lag lengths chosen. And although researchers should be

---

[4] The values of the test are generated by Monte Carlo analysis. It is important to remember that the appropriate critical value is not only based on sample size but also on whether constants or drift are specified in the model.

TABLE 6.4. *The λ_{MAX} and λ_{TRACE} Tests*

Null Hypothesis	Alternative Hypothesis		95% Critical Value	90% Critical Value
λ_{TRACE} tests:		λ_{TRACE} value		
$r = 0$	$r > 0$	55.13	29.68	26.79
$r \leq 1$	$r > 1$	16.62	15.41	13.33
$r \leq 2$	$r > 2$	2.52	3.76	2.69
λ_{MAX} tests:		λ_{MAX} value		
$r = 0$	$r = 1$	38.51	20.97	18.60
$r = 1$	$r = 2$	14.10	14.07	12.07
$r = 2$	$r = 3$	2.52	3.76	2.69

particularly aware of how lag length choice affects the Johansen models, the same argument can be made about the model sensitivity of many time series techniques.

The second issue is the presence of a deterministic trend. Johansen (1995) and Hansen and Juselius (1995) both note that the asymptotic properties of the cointegration test statistics are particularly sensitive to the inclusion of a deterministic trend. Ahking (2002) shows that a set of empirical results using Johansen's method is also particularly sensitive to the presence of a deterministic trend in the model. Again, this presents significant similarities to the tests for cointegration in single-variable tests such as the DF and ADF models, where the presence or absence of a deterministic trend can yield significantly different results. In each of these cases, as we discussed in the beginning of Chapter 5, analysts must consider whether their time series possess an element of a deterministic component that is separate from the stochastic trend that may be present in the data-generating process.

6.3.3 Application: The Engle-Granger Methodology and the Indo-Pakistani Arms Race

Arms races have long been a central area of interest in the field of international relations. Beginning with the seminal work of weatherman-turned-political scientist Lewis Richardson, scholars have been interested in the dynamics of whether, when, and to what extent states match their rivals' spending on military weapons. The question was particularly important during the Cold War, when numerous scholars examined the dynamics of the U.S.-Soviet arms race. Although the arms race literature has faded in importance in the field of international relations with the end of the Cold War, there are still important rivalries around the world that maintain the competitive dynamics that could lead states to spend heavily on weapons to match their competitors.

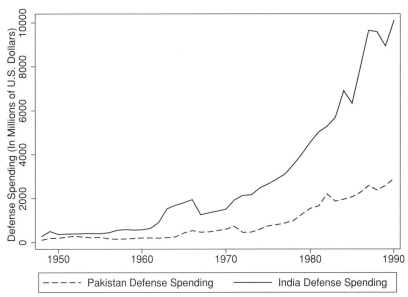

FIGURE 6.6. India and Pakistan Defense Spending: 1948–1990. Compiled by the authors from Correlates of War National Material Capabilities Data Set v4.0.

One intense non-superpower rivalry that has garnered some attention in the arms race literature is that between India and Pakistan.[5] Figure 6.6 shows both countries' defense spending over the 1948–1990 period, when the rivalry was at its most intense. What is important to consider when modeling defense spending data is that the series often contain unit roots. A Dickey-Fuller test of both the India and Pakistan series fails to reject the null hypothesis of nonstationarity. The DF test for the Pakistan series yields a test statistic of 1.786, whereas that for the India series yields a test statistic of 2.270. In both cases, the 5% critical value to reject nonstationarity is 2.952.[6]

Because we have confirmed nonstationarity in both series, the next step is to investigate the possibility of cointegration. Initially, we regress India's defense spending on Pakistan's, saving the residuals. The DF test of these regression residuals generates a test statistic of 3.51. Given the sample size, the 5% critical value for the nonstationarity of cointegrating residuals is 3.461; thus we can reject the null hypothesis of nonstationarity. By regressing one I(1) variable on another, we have created a stationary series, suggesting that over the long run, India and Pakistan defense spending are cointegrated.

We next turn to estimating our ECM. Armed with our residual series, which will serve as the cointegrating vector in our ECM, we difference each series and

---

[5] For other explorations of this and other developing-country arms races, see Freeman (1983), Majeksi (1985), and Ward (1984).

[6] The KPSS test yields identical substantive results.

TABLE 6.5. *Lag Length Tests*

lag	LL	LR	FPE	AIC	HQIC	SBIC
0	-1052.85		4.9×10^{21}	49.74	49.74†	49.74†
1	-1052.62	0.46	6.0×10^{21}	49.94	50.00	50.11
2	-1051.75	1.73	7.1×10^{21}	50.10	50.22	50.45
3	-1038.05	27.40†	4.3×10^{21}†	49.59†	49.77	50.11
4	-1034.10	7.90	4.4×10^{21}	49.59	49.84	50.28

Notes: LL = log likelihood; LR = likelihood ratio test; FPE = final prediction error; AIC = Akaike's information criteria; HQIC = Hannan and Quinn information criteria; SBIC = Schwarz's Bayesian information criteria. † = model favored by this criteria.

perform lag length tests for the optimal specification of our ECM. We generate several tests for lag length, shown in Table 6.5. Unfortunately, across the five statistics, there is not complete agreement as to the appropriate lag length. Both the zero-lag and three-lag model receive some support. We now proceed with both models to illustrate the ECM building process.

Initially, we estimate a model (using OLS) for each differenced series, where the only explanatory variable in the model is the error correction vector (the speed of adjustment parameter).[7] Table 6.6 presents these estimates. For the India model, the error correction term is positive and statistically significant (at the $p < .05$ level), suggesting that as India and Pakistan's military spending drift apart, India spends more to "catch up." Looking at the graph of the raw data, it is clear that India spends more than Pakistan over the entire period of analysis. Thus, the clearest inference to make from this model is that India attempts to keep a particular distance between it and Pakistan in terms of military spending. As Pakistan begins to close that gap, India increases its spending to return to this equilibrium gap.

Table 6.7 presents the estimates of the three-lag ECM. The first item to note is the statistical significance of the estimate of the error correction term in the India equation. As in the first ECM, India appears to respond to the disequilibrium in defense spending by increasing its own spending relative to Pakistan's. The estimate of the error correction component in the Pakistan model again does not achieve statistical significance. As previously discussed, the statistical significance of the error correction term in both models is a nice check on the finding of cointegration. Had none of the estimates of the term achieved statistical significance, we would have doubted our initial diagnosis of cointegration.

Second, although the coefficient estimates on the variables in both equations vary in their statistical significance, the Granger causality tests of statistical

---

[7] One could use SUR to estimate this model, but recall that with identical right-hand-side variables, SUR estimates are identical to OLS estimates.

TABLE 6.6. *Zero Lag ECM of India-Pakistan Defense Spending*

Model	Variable	Coefficient
India	Intercept	234129
		(70851)
	EC	0.96
		(0.42)
Pakistan	Intercept	66687
		(23405)
	EC	−0.19
		(0.14)

Notes: Standard errors in parentheses. N = 48. India: $R^2 = 0.11$, Prob > F = 0.03. Pakistan: $R^2 = 0.05$, Prob > F = 0.17.

significance of the block of estimates (which also incorporate the error correction component) are statistically significant in both cases. There appears to be a reciprocal relationship between Indian and Pakistani defense spending. Third, an analysis of the residuals from the three-lag ECM (using a Lagrange multiplier test) rejects that there is any autocorrelation left in the residuals, suggesting our model specification is appropriate, at least using this metric.

Finally, it is important to note that, had we not checked for the existence of cointegration, but simply differenced our data before specifying our VAR, our conclusions would have differed greatly in several ways. First, the lag length selection statistics are influenced by the presence of the exogenous cointegrating vector. Reestimating these statistics yields even more mixed evidence on the appropriate lag length, yet still suggesting zero lags as a strong possibility. Second, it is clear that, without the addition of the error correction term, the model would be misspecified (bringing all the traditional maladies associated with a misspecified model). In both the zero- and three-lag specification, at least one of the error correction terms was statistically significant. The most egregious error related to this possibility would be selecting the zero-lag case, in which a model without the error correction term would yield essentially no result, leading to a conclusion that no interaction dynamics existed between India and Pakistan.

6.4 ECMS FOR NON-INTEGRATED DATA?

This chapter has proceeded with the approach to ECMs consistent with that used by most time series econometrics books. That is, a key requirement of any ECM model is to find two nonstationary variables, integrated of the same order, and then test for the presence of cointegration. DeBoef and Keele (2008) note that, in their survey of 18 econometrics texts, only 5 discuss the idea of

TABLE 6.7. *Three Lag ECM of India-Pakistan Defense Spending*

Model	Variable	Coefficient
India	Intercept	182495
		(74649)
	India_{t-1}	0.41
		(0.16)
	India_{t-2}	−0.07
		(0.15)
	India_{t-3}	0.71
		(0.15)
	Pakistan_{t-1}	−0.49
		(0.52)
	Pakistan_{t-2}	−0.36
		(0.51)
	Pakistan_{t-3}	−2.0
		(0.48)
	EC	1.58
		(0.47)
Pakistan	Intercept	31854
		(28576)
	India_{t-1}	0.02
		(0.06)
	India_{t-2}	−0.03
		(0.06)
	India_{t-3}	0.18
		(0.06)
	Pakistan_{t-1}	−0.05
		(0.20)
	Pakistan_{t-2}	0.03
		(0.20)
	Pakistan_{t-3}	−0.07
		(0.19)
	EC	−0.15
		(0.18)

Granger Causality Results Independent Variable → Dependent Variable	χ^2	Prob > χ^2
India→Pakistan	18.29	0.00
Pakistan→India	12.10	0.01

Notes: Standard errors in parentheses. N = 39. India: $R^2 = 0.50$, $\chi^2 = 39.38$, Prob > $\chi^2 = 0.00$. Pakistan: $R^2 = 0.29$, $\chi^2 = 16.12$, Prob > $\chi^2 = 0.02$.

using ECMs with stationary data (as we do in Chapter 3 in discussing the Bardsen transformation). The implication of their survey is that ECMs are still thought about almost exclusively in terms of nonstationary data. Yet, there is a growing sentiment that ECMs may be justified solely on substantive (versus statistical) grounds.

Indeed, more than two decades ago in political science, Beck (1992) noted that ECMs may be appropriate even if the variables are not I(1); that is, if we have strong theory suggesting that there is an equilibrium, we may not care that our variables are not strictly I(1), which is a hard and fast rule. His argument was made on intuitive grounds and foresaw the relaxation of the assumption that the variables be I(1).

Of course, the underlying puzzle that drove the development of these models dealt with nonstationary data: how could two stationary series be in equilibrium to create a stationary series? Yet, as Beck, De Boef, and Keele have all argued, the underlying substantive idea behind ECMs need not be limited to cases of nonstationary data. An exogenous variable may have short-term and long-term impacts on a dependent variable of interest. Thus, we agree that ECMs can be substantively appropriate, even if they are not considered statistically appropriate. If the analyst believes two (or more) variables are in long-run equilibrium, the ECM methodology is appropriate, even when using stationary data.

6.5 CONCLUSION

In this chapter, we laid out the methodology of cointegration. We see this as an under-utilized time series methodology for analyzing potentially complex relationships between variables. We often use variables that have the potential for short- and long-term relationships. Yet, out of concern for nonstationarity, we difference our data, throwing out the long-term dynamics. ECMs provide a solution to this problem by allowing the modeling of both short-term and long-term dynamics. ECMs are an excellent analytical tool that offers a straight-forward approach that melds methodological and substantive understandings. And although the impetus behind these models was an effort to deal with nonstationary data, increasingly, scholars have turned to these models when they are justified substantively.

We have now discussed what we consider to be the core methodologies of time series analysis. In the next chapter, we turn to more advanced topics that are increasingly being used in the social sciences.

6.6 FOR FURTHER READING

Blaydes, Lisa and Mark A. Kayser. 2011. "Counting Calories: Democracy and Distribution in the Developing World." *International Studies Quarterly* 55 (4): 887–908.

Casillas, Christopher J., Peter K. Enns, and Patrick C. Wohlfarth. 2011. "How Public Opinion Constrains the U.S. Supreme Court." *American Journal of Political Science* 55 (1): 74–88.

Enns, Peter K. and G. E. McAvoy. 2012. "The Role of Partisanship in Aggregate Opinion." *Political Behavior* 34 (4): 627–651.

Fish, M. Steven and Omar Choudhry. 2007. "Democratization and Economic Liberalization in the Postcommunist World." *Comparative Political Studies* 40 (3): 254–282.

Haber, Stephen and Victor Menaldo. 2011. "Do Natural Resources Fuel Authoritarianism? A Reappraisal of the Resource Curse." *American Political Science Review* 105 (1): 1–26.

Keele, Luke. 2007. "Social Capital and the Dynamics of Trust in Government." *American Journal of Political Science* 51 (2): 241–254.

Kono, Daniel. 2008. "Democracy and Trade Discrimination." *Journal of Politics* 70: 942–955.

Kristal, Tali. 2010. "Good Times, Bad Times: Postwar Labor's Share of National Income in Capitalist Democracies." *American Sociological Review* 75 (5): 729–763.

Lebo, Matthew J., Adam J. McGlynn, and Gregory Koger. 2007. "Strategic Party Government: Party Influence in Congress, 1789–2000." *American Journal of Political Science* 51 (3): 464–481.

Lebo, Matthew and Will Moore. 2003. "Dynamic Foreign Policy Behavior." *Journal of Conflict Resolution* 47 (1): 13–32.

Ramirez, Mark D. 2009. "The Dynamics of Partisan Conflict on Congressional Approval." *American Journal of Political Science* 53 (3): 681–694.

Volscho, Thomas W. and Nathan J. Kelly. 2012. "The Rise of the Super-Rich." *American Sociological Review* 77 (5): 679–699.

7

Selections on Time Series Analysis

The analysis of time series data is a vast enterprise. With this fact in mind, the previous chapters introduced the core concepts and analytic tools that form a foundational understanding of time series analysis. This chapter presents four more advanced topics: fractional integration, heterogeneity, forecasting, and estimating and modeling with unknown structural breaks. Although by no means an exhaustive list, the topics presented in this chapter represent concerns of the contemporary literature: they extend some of the previously discussed concepts, provide additional means of evaluating time series models, and are a means through which time series analysis can inform policy.

Fractional integration is an extension of the preceding discussion of unit roots and of tests for unit roots. The first few chapters assumed that our time series data was stationary, but it was subsequently presented that this may not necessarily be the case; as a result, tests for unit roots or an integrated series were presented in detail in Chapter 5. However, as intuition may suggest, it may not always be the case in practice that every series can be appropriately characterized as either stationary or integrated, as shocks may enter the series, persist for a nontrivial amount of time, and eventually dissipate. In such a case, the series is neither stationary nor integrated, because the shocks do not rapidly exit the series, nor do they persist indefinitely. Fractional integration provides an alternative in which the value of d is not restricted to either 0 or 1. This is an important point, because it is likely that many of the series that we encounter in the social sciences exhibit this sort of behavior (Lebo, Walker, and Clarke, 2000) and if d is misdiagnosed, the inferences drawn may be incorrect. Therefore, with the techniques discussed later, it becomes possible to develop and test theories that seek to explicitly determine the duration of the effect that shocks have on a series.

Heterogeneity is another important concept in time series analysis. Although much of the focus of the preceding chapters has been on estimating the mean of a given series, it is also the case that the *variance* of a series may change over time. More specifically, a given series may experience a considerable amount of volatility in some periods and relatively little in others. As a result, it is incorrect to assume that the variance of the series is constant. Although recognizing that this fact is clearly important for statistical reasons, it is also important for substantive applications and drawing sound inferences from the data in question. By recognizing that the variance of a series may change over time, it is possible for researchers to develop and test new and interesting theories that seek to explain the source of this variation. For example, Gronke and Brehm (2002) show that volatility of presidential approval in the United States increases across presidential administrations and over time, primarily as a consequence of weakening partisan attachments. Volatility decreases during election and after presidential honeymoons, whereas relevant events vary in their effect on both the mean level and volatility of presidential approval.

Our next topic, forecasting, at its most basic level, has the stated goal of estimating the likelihood of future events conditioned on past events. Although forecasting is not without its controversies, as is discussed later, it is nevertheless an important tool for evaluating the performance of estimated time series models. More specifically, it can be used to critically evaluate competing hypotheses and models to determine which one performs best when compared to the empirical record. Moreover, forecasting can also play an important role in policy analysis, because it may be possible to use it to model the likely effects of policy decisions or even shocks, as well as outcomes of interest such as elections. Although forecasting has been used most prominently in economics – for instance, in economic projections of growth or unemployment rates – the discussion later in this chapter demonstrates the useful role that forecasting may play in other social sciences as well, such as providing an early warning of intra- and interstate conflict.

The final topic covered in this chapter is estimating and modeling time series that may be subject to unknown structural breaks. Increasingly, analysts are interested in determining whether a series of data, through some combination of unobserved or endogenous factors, undergoes a change (or several) in its underlying data-generating process at some point(s) in the data sample. Properly estimating the location of unknown and possibly endogenous structural breaks is a critical first step before analysts insert a dummy variable for an exogenous intervention into a time series model. If, for example, a time series was exposed to an exogenous intervention at time t, but in fact underwent an endogenous structural change at, say, time $t-5$, then the dummy variable for the exogenous intervention will likely return a significant result, even if the exogenous intervention had no effect on the series. Caporale and Grier (2005) present this critique as a warning to scholars working with time series data. We discuss how analysts can test for multiple, endogenous structural breaks in a time series, how to test hypotheses of no structural break versus the alternative of one or more breaks, and how to estimate the most likely locations of these breaks.

7.1 FRACTIONAL INTEGRATION

Fractional integration is part of an approach in time series analysis referred to as "long memory models," which address the degree of persistence in the data. Specifically, it allows for modeling the dynamics of a time series with fractional lag exponents, and not just $d = 0$ (stationary) or $d = 1$ (integrated). When d takes on fractional values, it allows the data to be mean reverting, yet still maintain its long memory.

Fractional integration enables scholars to relax the knife-edged assumption about the characterization of the series, which in turn allows important substantive interpretations of our data: "If data are stationary, external shocks can have a short-term impact, but little long-term effects, as the data revert to the mean of the series at an exponential rate. In contrast, integrated data do not decay, i.e., do not return to the previous mean after an external shock has been felt. By allowing d to take fractional values, we allow data to be mean reverting and to still have long memory in the process" (Box-Steffensmeier and Tomlinson, 2000, 64–65). In an ARFIMA model (to be described later), the autocorrelation function dies out very slowly, at a hyperbolic rate. So distant observations are highly correlated, or long memoried. When presented this way, ARIMA models can be seen as a particular case of the more general ARFIMA models.

Continuing with the substantive interpretation, fractionally integrated series are such that the persistence of shocks is long, yet not as long as when $d = 1$. Although theoretically any shock to an integrated series should remain in the system for the entire series, in practice, shocks may dissipate over long periods of time. As an empirical example of this phenomenon, consider the discussion of macropartisanship presented in Chapter 5, in which a number of unit root tests were conducted for three different series: presidential approval, consumer sentiment, and macropartisanship. A process of triangulation was discussed in which the results of each of the low-power unit root tests were interpreted in light of the other test results to produce a stronger assessment of whether the series in question were characterized by a unit root or not. However, these test results were not always consistent with one another, which made it difficult to conclude definitively that there was or was not a unit root present in any of the series. For example, recall that it was possible to reject the null hypothesis of a unit root for the presidential approval series using a DF test, but that the variance ratio test produced a contrary result: it was not possible to consistently reject the null hypothesis of a unit root. Moreover, the findings from the KPSS test indicated that the presidential approval series is not strong mixing. Combining these results, it was possible to conclude that the presidential approval series is neither integrated, nor stationary, which in turn suggests that it is in fact fractionally integrated, although the degree to which it is fractionally integrated is not particularly clear from these tests alone.

This observation is consistent with work by MacKuen, Erikson, and Stimson (1989), who find that macropartisanship is a complex mix of dynamic behaviors. The combination of long and medium term dynamics provides layers of stability to macropartisanship that are qualitatively different from the stable equilibrium and random walk models. In other words, their statistical models for stationary processes and integrated random walk processes fail to capture the dynamics of macropartisanship: neither stationary processes nor integrated processes fit this characterization. Such results suggest a fractional process.

In our earlier discussion of Box-Jenkins or ARMA modeling, we generally assumed that our variables were stationary. We then examined whether the series contained a unit root, introducing the "I" in ARIMA modeling. We now reexamine the "I," relaxing the assumption that d is equal to 0 or 1, thereby allowing d to be a fractional value. We now to this type of model as an autoregressive fractionally integrated moving average (ARFIMA) model. ARFIMA models often more appropriately characterize time series than do approaches that force the data to be characterized as either I(0) or I(1). ARFIMA models are generalizations of the ARMA and ARIMA models for a time series:

$$\Phi(B)(1 - B)^d x_t = \Theta(B)\epsilon_t, \tag{7.1}$$

where d is a non-negative integer; $\Phi(B)$ and $\Theta(B)$ are the stationary autoregressive (AR) and moving average (MA) components, respectively; and ϵ_t has an unconditional $N(0, \sigma^2)$ distribution. B is the backshift operator, discussed in Chapter 2. In contrast to an ARIMA process, an ARFIMA process allows d to take fractional values, thereby allowing a more flexible characterization of a time series. If $d > 0$, the process is referred to as a long memory process. A long memory process has an autocorrelation structure that slowly decays to zero (a hyperbolic rate), which suggests stronger dependence on past values of the time series (Dueker and Asea, 1997, 3). In contrast, an ARMA process, where $d = 0$, possesses short memory (an exponential decay rate). Both ARMA and ARFIMA models are mean reverting, unlike ARIMA models.

Table 7.1 characterizes different types of time series according to the type of memory each possesses. An ARFIMA model captures different kinds of shorts and long-term memory. Fractionally integrated processes, which are distinct both from stationary processes and from integrated, unit root series, are characterized by persistence and long memory, but the effects of a shock do not persist at full force in each period: the memory of a fractionally integrated series is long, but not infinite. Even though fractionally integrated series have long memory, eventually the effects of a shock will dissipate and the series returns to its mean level. The absolute value of d determines the persistence of the series. That is, the closer the absolute value of d is to 1, the longer the memory and the more persistent are the effects of shocks.

TABLE 7.1. *Typology of Memory*

Series Type	Near Integrated	ARMA Stationary	ARFIMA Fractionally Integrated		ARIMA Integrated
Values of (p,d,q),	$d = 0$, $p \neq 0$,	$d = 0$	$0 < d < 0.5$	$.5 < d < 1$	$d = 1$
and ρ	$q \geq 0$, $\rho = 1 - \epsilon$	$p, q \geq 0$	$p, q \geq 0$	$p, q \geq 0$	$p, q \geq 0$
Memory	intermediate	short	short and long		short and infinite
Mean reversion	yes	yes	yes		no
variance	finite, time dependent in sample	finite	finite	infinite	infinite

Table 7.1 also clarifies the relationship between fractional and near-integrated series, which we discuss in more detail later. Integrated series are more likely to be the exception, rather than the more nuanced fractional alternative in social science data. The most obvious distinction between the two series is that $d = 0$ for a near-integrated series, whereas $d > 0$ for a fractionally integrated series. For all series, the values of p and q must meet stationarity and invertibility requirements. For the special case where $p = q = 0$, the process exhibits no short-term memory.

It is critical to correctly identify the type of memory of your series and, more generally, the model to be estimated. An early approach for identifying the type of memory in a series used multiple standard unit root tests. As Baillie, Chung, and Tieslau (1996, 12) pointed out, by investigating the pattern of rejections that results from using tests for unit roots in conjunction with tests for strong mixing, analysts can obtain information about whether a time series is fractionally integrated with $0 < d < 1$. For instance, rejection of both the null of strong mixing and the null of a unit root is consistent with the hypothesis that the process under investigation is fractionally integrated. Thus, these diagnostic tests provide analysts with some information about whether a time series is "closer" to being stationary with $d = 0$ or integrated with $d = 1$. Although such a strategy can provide some information as to whether a series is fractionally integrated, it is nevertheless an imperfect approach. Our position is that direct estimators of d are superior diagnostic tools, especially given that some of those estimators explicitly test the hypotheses that $d = 0$ and $d = 1$.

Estimation of the long-range component within ARFIMA models may be classified into two general types: parametric or semi-parametric. To obtain estimates of d, either Sowell's exact MLE or Robinson's semi-parametric do well.[1] With correct specification – in other words, including the correct AR and MA components – parametric maximum likelihood estimators, such as Sowell's (1992), have superior asymptotic properties (Dahlhaus, 1989). However, such estimates are inconsistent if incorrectly specified. Thus the approach is generally

---

[1] Research is still ongoing with respect to the tradeoffs between Sowell's and Robinson's estimates.

to estimate all models up to a (3,d,3) model and then use an information criterion to choose among the MLE estimators. In contrast, the semi-parametric methods, such as the log-periodogram estimator of Geweke and Porter-Hudak (1983); (often referred to as GPH) and its extension by Robinson (1995), are popular because they do not require researchers to make strong assumptions about the short-term components of the model. Other types of semi-parametric estimators use a local whittle or average periodogram approach.

As is common in semi-parametric estimation, these estimators face a bias versus efficiency tradeoff in selecting an optimum bandwidth, and they generally require larger samples (Hurvich and Beltrao, 1993; Hurvich, Deo, and Brodsky, 1998). Of the two semi-parametric approaches, Robinson's modification is generally considered to perform better than the GPH in practice. Although the issue has still not been completely resolved, Robinson's estimator is generally used in the current literature.[2]

Of course, estimates from short series result in larger standard errors, so the typical cautions about shorter versus longer series apply. Lebo, Walker, and Clarke (2000) provide convincing evidence that most political science series are likely to be fractionally integrated. Mounting evidence shows the same for other series of interest to social scientists.

7.1.1 Fractional Cointegration

Fractional cointegration (FCI) is a generalization of cointegration where the original series are I(d) and the cointegrating errors have a lower level of integration, I(b) where $b < d$. When two variables are found to be fractionally integrated, the two variables are in equilibrium, but the error correction is long memoried. This means that the shocks that move the series apart dissipate slower than in the traditional cointegration case (Baillie and Bollerslev, 1994; Cheung and Lai, 1993; Dueker and Startz, 1998).

Robinson and Marinucci (1998) discuss the "I(1)/I(0) paradigm" where $d = 1$ and $b = 0$. Fractional cointegration departs from this paradigm by allowing b to be fractionally integrated and, more recently, d as well. This is a welcome breakthrough because cointegrating relationships are theoretically interesting and the empirical possibility of a long-run stable relationship exists even if the parent series are not unit root I(1) or the cointegrating errors are not necessarily short-memory I(0) processes.

Cheung and Lai (1993) relax the assumption that the residuals need to be I(0) and instead allow them to be I(d), where d can vary between 0 and 1. They point out that fractional cointegration is theoretically important because it allows a long-term equilibrium relationship between the two parent series.

---

[2] If the process contains a trend (drift), it must be accounted for by the inclusion of a constant when d is estimated from first differences, as is the case when the series is nonstationary in levels (see Baillie, 1996, and Beran, 1994).

The relationship responds to exogenous shocks, but then returns to equilibrium at a rate expressed by the value of d. So in the fractional cointegration case the equilibrium errors can respond more slowly to shocks, which results in highly persistent deviations from equilibrium.

The Engle and Granger (1987) regression approach from the last chapter is easily used for fractionally cointegrated data. One series is regressed on the other, and then d is estimated for the residual series. If d is not an integer, then the parent series are fractionally cointegrated. Dueker and Startz (1998) extend the work such that only a lower order of integration for the residuals compared to the parent series is required.

In applied work using the fractional cointegration methodology, Lebo, McGlynn, and Koger (2007) provide a clear melding of fractional integration and cointegration. They hypothesize "that parties will approximate each other's level of party unity over time by reducing past differences between the parties" (Lebo, McGlynn, and Koger, 2007, 16). In their study, they theorize that party unity scores (the rate at which members of political parties in Congress vote with the party) will be cointegrated. More specifically, because their variables are fractionally integrated, they posit that the variables will be fractionally cointegrated. This simply means that, as in cointegration, there will be an equilibrium relationship over time between the variables. The authors argue that their party-level variables will likely to be characterized as fractionally integrated because they are created by aggregating across a heterogeneous group of legislators. Further, "the behavior of each legislator evolves in its own way. The extent to which present party voting record or ideology is based on the past can vary across legislators. Likewise, each election relies to a varying extent on the previous election" (Lebo, McGlynn, and Koger, 2007, 15). Empirically, this expectation is borne out. That is, $d = 0.69$ and 0.78 for yearly Democratic and Republican unity series, with standard errors $= 0.06$ for each.

More generally, Lebo and Moore (2003) argue that fractional cointegration is particularly insightful for studying action-reaction processes where one actor responds with similar actions to either hostile or cooperative behavior from the other. They find evidence of fractional cointegration, and thus any widening of the gap between the parties is quickly counteracted by strategic party behavior (action-reaction). The fractional error correction model coefficient for the Senate is $d = 0.54$, which means that when the two parties' unity differs in the Senate, 54% of the unity gap is corrected in the first year.

7.1.2 Near and Fractional Integration

It is important to note the differences and similarities between fractionally and near-integrated data.[3] First, both fractionally integrated and near-integrated series are highly persistent and exhibit long memory, but differ from integrated

---

[3] See Table 7.1 for the pertinent features of near and fractionally integrated data.

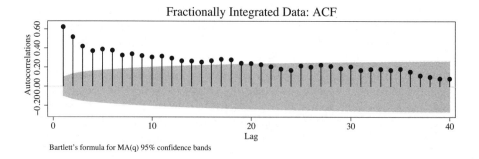

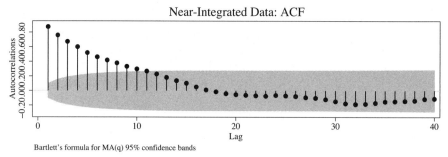

FIGURE 7.1. Comparison of Near-Integrated and Fractionally-Integrated Series.

series because they are both mean reverting. In the long run both types of series will exhibit an equilibrium outcome to which they should return. However, this tendency is difficult to estimate, especially within small samples, because tests such as the augmented Dickey-Fuller often fail to reject that either series is a unit root (Box-Steffensmeier and Smith, 1998; DeBoef and Granato, 1997).

Beyond these similarities in long memory and mean reversion there are important differences. First, near-integrated data should exhibit a consistent variance, whereas fractionally integrated data with d greater than .5 have infinite variance. This means that tests that are based on the variance of the series, such as the variance ratio test, are helpful in discriminating between the two processes. Second, fractionally integrated series and near-integrated series show noticeably different rates of decay within their autocorrelation functions. Near-integrated series exhibit an exponential rate of decline in their ACFs, whereas fractionally integrated series decay follows a hypergeometric rate. The former exhibits a consistent proportional reduction in ACF lag values, whereas the latter exhibits increasingly smaller reduction in lag values. For example, Figure 7.1 compares the ACFs for 400 simulated values of a near-integrated series ($\rho = .90$) to those of a fractionally integrated series ($d = .45$). Notice that in the near-integrated data, the larger ACF estimates consistently decay, whereas the top graph showing fractionally integrated data has initial rates of decay that get smaller for longer lags.

The estimation of d has little cost and a potentially important inferential payoff. As was seen in the macropartisanship example, a failure to directly estimate d resulted in conflicting empirical findings, which were based on knife-edged assumptions about whether d was equal to 1 or 0. By directly estimating d, it became possible to move away from such assumptions and to directly observe the duration of the effect of an exogenous shock on the series, thus more effectively adjudicating between the competing theories. Given the clear substantive implications of directly estimating d, as well as the minimal cost of doing so, it seems reasonable that the estimation of d should be one more standard diagnostic that time series analysts use.

7.2 INCORPORATING HETEROGENEITY

So far we have only discussed modeling the mean of the time series based on the assumption that the variance is constant. However, a class of models relaxes this assumption: autoregressive conditional heteroskedasticity (ARCH) models, which were first introduced by Engle (1982), model the variance of series as well. A series is called conditionally heteroskedastic if the unconditional (or long-run) variance is constant, but there are periods in which the variance changes, whether becoming higher or lower.

Thinking about ARCH models may help researchers step back and ask, before they begin analyzing the series, whether the series shows relatively tranquil periods followed by periods of volatility. They may also think, before even graphing the data, what might cause the series to react in such a way. Thus substantive or theoretical reasons may encourage analysts to take the possibility of heterogeneity seriously.

Bauwens, Laurent, and Rombouts's (2006, 79) literature survey on ARCH models concludes that "it is now widely accepted that financial volatilities move together over time across assets and markets. Recognizing this feature through a multivariate modelling framework leads to more relevant empirical models... [and] opens the door to better decision tools." It is easy to imagine political and other social science volatilities that move together across time as well, which leads to an application of Bauwens et al.'s conclusion to other social science domains as well. Does the volatility of one series lead to volatility in another series? Is the volatility of a series transmitted to another series directly (through its conditional variance) or indirectly (through its conditional covariances)? Does a shock increase the volatility of another series and, if so, by how much? Is the impact the same for negative and positive shocks of the same amplitude? Relatedly, are the correlations between series higher during periods of higher volatility (perhaps associated with crises)? Are the correlations between series increasing in the long run, perhaps due to globalization? Such issues can be studied directly by using a multivariate ARCH model and bringing to the forefront dynamic conditional correlation models. These models provide unique insights, but are not yet as widely applied in the social sciences.

Maestas and Preuhs (2000) provide clear motivation for modeling the variance of time series data as a way to explore and understand the dynamics of volatility associated with political phenomena. For example, an unpredictable event may cause a sharp decline in stock prices, so that investors quickly become sensitive to news related to the market. A minor bit of good news following a sharp decline can cause the market to soar, whereas that same good news on a typical day would have little impact. Or suppose that the expected mean of aggregate Democratic partisanship is constant over time so that it is only affected by random shocks. In other words, nothing systematically influences partisanship, but partisanship varies from quarter to quarter in response to random and unpredictable events. However, during the quadriennal presidential election season, voters pay more attention to events that might influence how they feel about the political parties. During such periods, partisanship would be more volatile because informational shocks would have a greater impact on party identification as people are more sensitive to political events or information. One might expect this volatility to show autoregressive characteristics because as public awareness of new events is heightened following significant political incidents and once volatility is sparked, it may not decay immediately.

A stochastic variable with a constant variance is called homoskedastic (in contrast to heteroskedastic). For a volatile series, the unconditional variance may be constant even though the variance during some periods is unusually large. Yet the short-run variance is conditioned on the past values of the error term. The size of the effect of each new event or shock on the series is determined in part by the conditional variance. Two identical shocks will have a different magnitude of effect depending on the value of the conditional variance, because that variance depends on how past events affected the series. A large shock in one period increases the magnitude of the effect of new shocks on the series in subsequent periods. Substantively, this seems to capture the dynamic of increased public attention to events that follow a significant and unexpected political or economic incident.

To see how this works in practice, consider a basic time series equation for the conditional mean of the series, which should be familiar to you:

$$y_t = b_0 + b_1 y_{t-1} + e_t, \tag{7.2}$$

where

$$e_t = v_t h_t^{1/2} \tag{7.3}$$

and v_t is a white noise process with mean $= 0$ and variance $= 1$, meaning that it is a random set of shocks that affect the conditional mean of the series. Given this, the conditional variance of the series, h_t is

$$h_t = \alpha_0 + \alpha_1 e_{t-1}^2. \tag{7.4}$$

Thus, it can be seen that the effect of a random shock on the series is determined, in part, by the conditional variance of the series, which in turn

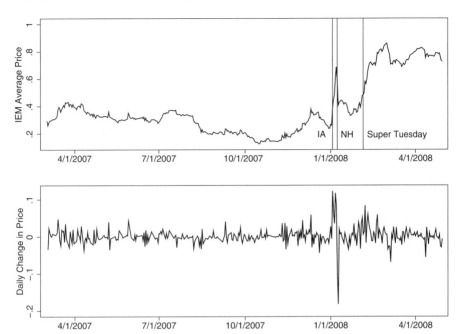

FIGURE 7.2. Probability of Obama's Winning the 2008 Democratic Party Nomination, 2007:1–2008:4. Compiled by the authors, with permission, from the Iowa Stock Market Historical Database.

depends on past shocks to the series. Therefore, to substantively understand what impact an exogenous shock will have on a series of interest, we must turn our attention to the conditional variance of the series.

Because the conditional variance only affects the magnitude of the shock and not its direction, this process does not affect the conditional mean of the series. Simply put, the conditional variance does not affect the conditional mean of the series because the variance, regardless of its magnitude, is still centered around the conditional mean of the series. However, this variance process creates a dynamic where large shocks tend to cluster together into identifiable patterns of volatility. So short-run volatility can be interpreted as an autoregressive process in the variance.

To see how these conditional heteroskedasticity dynamics appear in real data, consider the top panel of Figure 7.2, which presents each day's reported closing trading value, from March 2007 until April 2008, for a contract on Barack Obama's winning the Democratic presidential nomination in the Iowa Electronic Market, a market run by the University of Iowa (see www. biz.uiowa.edu/iem). In this market, shares speculating on the possibility of a future event are traded, and the shares pay off at $1 if the event (such as Obama's winning the nomination) occurs. People can then buy and sell contracts based on which candidates they feel have the best chance of winning.

Contracts are traded anywhere between 0 and 1 points, where point values represent the percent value of the cash payout and, intuitively, the probability of an event occurring. The bottom graph in Figure 7.2 shows the daily change in closing values. During the year 2007, the market gave Obama a fair chance of winning, as his contract traded in between 20 and 40 cents. The market also showed only incremental day-to-day changes in value. However, as the early nomination contests began to take place, one can see substantial changes in market trading values. Obama's contract value shoots up after his win in Iowa, drops considerably after his loss in New Hampshire, and then climbs back up after the Super Tuesday primaries on February 5, 2008. This creates noticeable heteroskedasticity in the series' daily changes.

The Lagrange multiplier (LM) Test for ARCH disturbances is typically used to identify an ARCH model and is what Maestas and Preuhs (2000) apply as well. This test proceeds in several steps. First, estimate the most appropriate model for your series with a linear regression or a Box-Jenkins approach and save the residuals. Second, produce the square of the fitted errors and regress the squared residuals on a constant and on the n lagged values of the squared residuals. If there are no ARCH effects, the estimated values of the coefficients for the squared residuals should be zero. This regression will have little explanatory power, and the coefficient of determination (R^2) will be very low. The final step in this process is to calculate the Lagrange multiplier, which is equal to $L = T R^2 \sim \chi_q^2$, where T is the total number of observations, R^2 is derived from the regression of the squared residuals in the preceding steps, and q is the order of the autoregressive process. Using this test statistic, it is then possible to evaluate the null hypothesis that there is no systematic variation in the variance of the series over time (i.e., that an ARCH model is unnecessary).

An extension of Engle's pioneering work by Bollerslev (1987) allows the conditional variance to be an ARMA process. This is a generalized ARCH, or GARCH, model that allows for both autoregressive and moving average components in the heteroskedastic variance. The residuals from a fitted model should show such a pattern. That is, if you fit a model of the series and it is appropriate, your residuals should be a white noise process, which your ACF and PACF will show, for example. However, if a GARCH model is more appropriate, the ACF of the squared residuals should help identify the process. The benefits of a GARCH model include that a higher order ARCH model may have a more parsimonious GARCH representation that is easier to identify and estimate. More parsimonious models contain less coefficient restrictions.

There are a variety of ARCH modifications, and it is still an active area of research. Some authors argue that long-run dependencies may be better characterized by a fractionally integrated ARCH (FIGARCH) model (e.g., Andersen and Bollerslev, 1997; Baillie, Chung, and Tieslau, 1996). ARCH models focus only on short-term volatility specification and forecasting. In contrast, FIGARCH models imply a finite persistence of volatility shocks, whereas there is no persistence in the GARCH framework; that is, it is characterized by long memory behavior and a slow rate of decay after a volatility shock. An

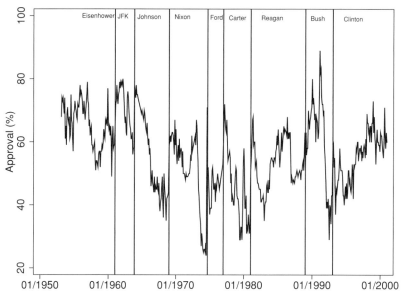

FIGURE 7.3. Volatility in U.S. Presidential Approval, 1953–2000. Compiled by the authors from Gallup Polls.

integrated GARCH (IGARCH) model implies complete persistence of a shock, but its use has seemed to quickly fall out of favor. Interestingly, the FIGARCH (1,d,1) nests a GARCH(1,1) with $d = 0$ and the IGARCH model for $d = 1$. Engle, Lilien, and Robins (1987) extend the basic ARCH framework to allow the mean of the series to depend on its own conditional variance.

In their work on presidential approval. Gronke and Brehm (2002) provide an excellent application that illustrates what might affect not only the mean of a series but also its volatility. Methodologically they want to go beyond identifying whether the series is conditionally heteroskedastic (they say that it is): they also want to explain what causes movement in the variance. Given the substantive importance of this question, the authors endeavor to identify and explicitly model the factors that may increase or decrease the volatility of presidential approval. They refer to this model as an ARCH-MH. The authors find that volatility has been increasing in a linear fashion since World War II as an increasing number of individuals self-identify as independents, meaning that support for a particular party has eroded over that period. This finding can be clearly seen in Figure 7.3, which is reproduced from Gronke and Brehm's model of volatility: it shows the variance of the series increasing steadily over time. Furthermore, the authors note that there are no discernible differences in the volatility of presidential approval between any of the different postwar administrations demarcated in the figure. Conversely, the authors find that volatility decreases during election years as partisan identifications become more salient and rigidly defined, but ultimately returns to higher levels following the election.

The broad class of models dealing with heterogeneity in time series data remains a rich area of research. For instance, Lebo and Box-Steffensmeier (2008) present applications of the dynamic conditional correlation (DCC) model, which derives from ARCH models. The DCC allows over-time variation in both the mean and variance of time series so one can study the evolution of relationships over time. To see how this process works, consider the likelihood of the DCC estimator:

$$L = -0.5 \sum_{t=1}^{T} (k \ log(2\pi) + 2log(|D_t|) + log(|R_t|) + \epsilon_t' R_t^{-1} \epsilon_t), \qquad (7.5)$$

where "R_t is a $k \times k$ time varying correlation matrix and D_t is a $k \times k$ diagonal matrix of conditional, i.e. time-varying, standardized residuals, ϵ_t, that are obtained from the univariate GARCH models" (Lebo and Box-Steffensmeier, 2008, 694). Estimation of this model proceeds in two steps, because there are two components in the likelihood function (equation 7.5) that can vary: the volatility component, D_t, and the correlation component, R_t. Thus, the first step maximizes D_t by replacing R_t with a $k \times k$ identity matrix. The second step then maximizes R_t by using the estimated values of D_t from the first step. The second step in the estimation procedure produces the DCC parameters, α and β, such that

$$R_t = (1 - \alpha - \beta)\overline{R} + \alpha \epsilon_{t-1} \epsilon_{t-1}' + \beta R_{t-1}. \qquad (7.6)$$

Using this model, Lebo and Box-Steffensmeier show how the importance of subjective evaluations of the economy as predictors of presidential approval is not constant, but varies considerably over time. Figure 7.4 depicts the raw series for national prospections and presidential approval. As the DCC estimates in Lebo and Box-Steffensmeier's work show, there is an extreme amount of variability in the correlation between the two series, ranging from a high of approximately 0.6 to a low of approximately -0.5. Substantively, this tells us that voters are not consistent in how their opinions about the economy affect their evaluations of the performance of political leaders. As a result, it is clear that exogenous circumstances play an important role in shaping how this process works, because at times there will be a positive relationship between the two series, but as the external political environment evolves, this relationship may become negative. Thus, the DCC model is quite valuable because it prevents researchers from making assumptions that the relationship between two series will remain constant over time.

DCC models also allow asymmetric effects. For example, they allow the impact of positive and negative media coverage on expected votes to be, as is theoretically expected, unequal. Context comes into time series models here because we can discover the circumstances, such as varying political, social, and economic environments, under which relationships change, when using time-varying parameters. Time-varying parameter models inform us about how effects differ across time. A dynamic conditional correlation approach increases

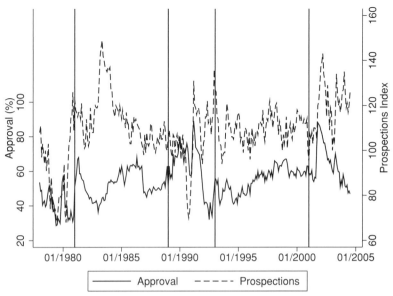

FIGURE 7.4. Presidential Approval and Consumer Expectations in the U.S., 1978–2004. Approval series compiled by authors from Gallup Polls. Consumer Expectations series compiled by authors, with permission, from Surveys of Consumers, University of Michigan.

modeling flexibility by dropping assumptions about constancy in the means and variances of variables and in the relationships among them. The DCC model does so by calculating a current correlation between variables of interest as a function of past realizations of both the volatility within the variables and the correlations between them.

The literature on ARCH modeling reflects the general concern in methodology with accounting for heterogeneity. Engle's (2002) piece on "New Frontiers for Arch Models" highlights promising avenues for continued work. In particular, we find the discussions about high-frequency volatility models, large-scale multivariate ARCH models, application to non-negative processes, and the use of Monte Carlo simulations to be particularly interesting. Bauwens, Laurent, and Rombouts (2006, 105) highlight promising areas of research in time series ARCH modeling: more flexible specifications for the dynamics of correlations, such as the DCC models; conditions for efficient two-step estimations in multivariate ARCH models; asymptotic properties of maximum likelihood estimators and when they hold; and further development of multivariate diagnostic tests.

7.3 FORECASTING

Forecasting serves as a test for model adequacy by discriminating between competing hypotheses and models. It is used for both model validation and for policy analysis. The origins of time series analysis are strongly connected to forecasting, and indeed Box and Jenkins' (1970) influential work has the word "forecasting" in the subtitle, *Time Series Analysis: Forecasting and Control*. However, the traditional emphasis in most social sciences on explanation has resulted in little attention being paid to forecasting outside of economics. We argue instead that forecasting should be used more in the social sciences. Fildes and Steklerm (2002) also call on researchers to devote resources to improving forecasting accuracy.

The prevailing notion appears to be that forecasting is not an important topic for most of the social sciences – again, with the notable exception of economics. However, even in economics, the forecasting literature's ability to predict trends has been strongly criticized. Fundamentals, in economics, such as growth and inflation in the U.S. economy, have not been forecasted as accurately as critics contend they need to be. Fildes and Steklerm (2002, 442) are dismayed that "errors occurred when the economy was subject to major perturbations, just the times when accurate forecasts were most needed. We feel there are few excuses to be made for the persistent, systematic errors we observe." Critics do acknowledge that shocks, such as a price change by the Organization of the Petroleum Exporting Countries (OPEC), cannot be forecasted while insisting that the prediction of their effect is vital. Similar criticisms could be made of other fields in social science. While, we may not be able to predict the occurrence of shocks such as scandals, but we should be able to predict their effects on various public opinion series.

Although this section serves only as a brief introduction and reference guide to forecasting there are now useful handbooks, such as *The Handbook of Economic Forecasting*, and an entire journal dedicated to the topic, the *International Journal of Forecasting*. No doubt this is partly the result of policy demands. Forecasting topics of interest to social scientists include work on early warning systems in international relations, election forecasting in political science (e.g., Sigelman, Batchelor, and Steklar's (1999) special issue in the *International Journal of Forecasting* and regular symposiums in *PS: Political Science and Politics*), and mortality in demography (e.g., Lee and Carter (1992) and rejoinders in the *Journal of the American Statistical Association*).

More interesting questions than why there has not been more attention to forecasting in the social sciences include the following. What is the current status of ARIMA methods in the area of forecasting? What alternative forecasting models exist? Which data situations and/or theories suggest which forecasting methods? How are the forecasts evaluated?

7.3.1 Purpose and Definitions

Following Fildes and Steklerm (2002), we argue that forecasts should provide information about the series' direction of movement, the timing of turning points, the magnitude of change, and the length of time over which a movement is expected to persist. Advances in forecasting allow researchers to do exactly this.

We begin by providing basic definitions that are useful in our discussion of the forecasting literature.

Forecasting: The likelihood of future events given current and past information

Point Forecast: Prediction of a single number

Interval Forecast: Prediction of the interval in which a number will lie

Ex Post Forecast: After the fact forecast; in this case, one knows all the values of the exogenous and endogenous variables with certainty, so accuracy can be evaluated exactly

Ex Ante Forecast: A prediction beyond the estimated period using explanatory variables with and without certainty

Additional definitions to consider include the following:

Unconditional Forecast: All explanatory variables are known with certainty. Thus all the ex post forecasts are unconditional. Some ex ante forecasts are also unconditional.

Conditional Forecast: Forecasts themselves are used to predict values. Values for one or more explanatory variables are unknown, so that forecasts must be used to produce the forecast on the dependent variable. Thus, explanatory variables need to be forecast as well.

To better understand these terms, consider this example. If $s(t)$ is linearly related to two variables, X_1 and X_2, but with lags of three and four months, respectively, then we can write

$$s(t) = a_0 + a_1 X_1(t-3) + a_2 X_2(t-4) + \epsilon_t. \tag{7.7}$$

If this equation is estimated, the results can be used to produce an unconditional forecast of $s(t)$ one, two, and three periods into the future. To get the three-month forecast of $s(t)$, we would use the current value of X_1 and last month's value of X_2, both of which are known. Thus, it is both an ex ante and unconditional forecast.

Starting with arguably the most straightforward case, we turn to an unconditional forecast for an AR(1) model.

Unconditional Forecast for AR(1)

$$(1 - \phi_1 B) y_t = a_t \tag{7.8}$$

$$y_t = (1 - \phi_1 B)^{-1} a_t,$$

where B is a backshift operator, ϕ is the coefficient estimate for the AR process, and a_t is the remaining white noise process or random shock. Recall that

$$(1 - B)^{-1} = 1 + B + B^2 + \cdots + B^k + \cdots \tag{7.9}$$

so that

$$\begin{aligned}
y_t &= (1 + \phi_1 B + \phi_1^2 B^2 + \cdots + \phi_1^n B^n + \cdots)a_t \\
&= a_t + \phi_1 a_{t-1} + \phi_1^2 a_{t-2} + \cdots + \phi_1^n a_{t-n} + \cdots
\end{aligned} \tag{7.10}$$

Since

$$y_t = y_t - \theta_0 \tag{7.11}$$

$$\Rightarrow y_t = y_t + \theta_0, \tag{7.12}$$

then

$$\begin{aligned}
E[y_t] &= E[y_t] + \theta_0 \\
&= 0 + \theta_0 \\
&= \theta_0 \quad \text{(Mean)}.
\end{aligned} \tag{7.13}$$

Taking expectations and distributing the expectation operator on the right side of the equation yields

$$\begin{aligned}
E[y_t] &= E[a_t] + \phi_1 E[a_{t-1}] + \phi_1^2 E[a_{t-2}] + \cdots + \phi_1^n E[a_{t-n}] + \cdots \\
&= 0 + \phi_1 \cdot 0 + \phi_1^2 \cdot 0 + \cdots + \phi_1^n \cdot 0 + \cdots \\
&= 0.
\end{aligned} \tag{7.14}$$

"Extrapolating" yields

$$y_t(1) = E[y_{t+1}] = 0$$

$$\vdots$$

$$y_t(n) = E[y_{t+n}] = 0. \tag{7.15}$$

This implies that an unconditional forecast will always have the same value: *the series mean.* This result is expected because the series is stationary.

Conditional Forecasts for AR(1)

Conditional forecasts depend on previous forecasts, in contrast to the unconditional forecast for AR(1). Consider a one-step-ahead expression for an

AR(1) model:

$$y_{t+1} = \phi_1 y_t + a_{t+1}$$
$$(1 - \phi_1 B) y_{t+1} = a_{t+1}$$
$$y_{t+1} = (1 - \phi_1 B)^{-1} a_{t+1}$$
$$= (1 + \phi_1 B + \phi_1^2 B^2 + \cdots) a_{t+1}$$
$$= a_{t+1} + \phi_1 a_t + \phi_1^2 a_{t-1} + \cdots \tag{7.16}$$

Taking expectations yields

$$E[y_{t+1}] = E[a_{t+1}] + \phi_1 a_t + \phi_1^2 a_{t-1} + \cdots + \phi_1^n a_{t-n}$$
$$= E[a_{t+1}] + \phi_1 y_t$$
$$= 0 + \phi_1 y_t$$
$$= \phi_1 y_t. \tag{7.17}$$

Thus, the conditional forecasts for an AR(1) point estimate are given by

$$y_t(1) = E[a_{t+1}] + \phi_1 y_t = \phi_1 y_t$$
$$y_t(2) = \phi_1^2 y_t$$
$$\vdots$$
$$y_t(n) = \phi_1^n y_t \tag{7.18}$$

The next step is to construct confidence intervals. We want to do this because the expected value of y_{t+n} is meaningless without some idea of how far the expected value is likely to be away from the real value. To construct confidence intervals, it is necessary to write the model in terms of an infinite weighted sum of shocks (i.e., in terms of ϕ weights):

$$y_t = a_t + \phi_1 a_{t-1} + \phi_2 a_{t-2} + \cdots + \phi_k a_{t-k} + \cdots \tag{7.19}$$

Consider an example where we have an AR(1) model with a fourth-order seasonal lag. This can be thought as the quarterly data for toy sales or ice cream, a political-business cycle, or the cyclical crime rate.

$$(1 - \phi_1 B)(1 - \phi_4 B^4) y_t = a_t$$
$$y_t = (1 - \phi_1 B)^{-1} (1 - \phi_4 B^4)^{-1} a_t$$
$$= (1 + \phi_1 B + \phi_1^2 B^2 + \cdots)(1 + \phi_4 B^4 + \phi_4^2 B^8 + \cdots) a_t$$
$$= a_t + \phi_1 a_{t-1} + \cdots + (\phi_1^4 + \phi_4) a_{t-4} + (\phi_1^5 + \phi_1 \phi_4) a_{t-5} + \cdots \tag{7.20}$$

The ϕ's can be considered weights (ψ). The interval forecasts can be calculated for these weights.

For y_{t+1} we have

$$y_{t+1} = a_{t+1} + \psi_1 a_t + \psi_2 a_{t-1} + \cdots + \psi_k a_{t-k+1} + \cdots \qquad (7.21)$$

Taking expectations yields

$$E[y_{t+1}] = E[a_{t+1}] + \psi_1 a_t + \psi_2 a_{t-1} + \cdots + \psi_k a_{t-k+1} + \cdots \qquad (7.22)$$
$$= 0 + \psi_1 a_t + \psi_2 a_{t-1} + \cdots + \psi_k a_{t-k+1} + \cdots$$
$$= \psi_1 a_t + \psi_2 a_{t-1} + \cdots + \psi_k a_{t-k+1} + \cdots$$

$E[a_{t+1}] = 0$ is used here because the value of the future random shock (a_{t+1}) is unknown.

Assuming that all the ψ weights and past shocks are known, we can use the conditional expectation as a forecast of y_{t+1}.

Therefore, the *error in forecasting* is given by

$$e_{t+1} = y_{t+1} - E[y_{t+1}] \qquad (7.23)$$
$$= y_{t+1} - y_t(1)$$
$$= a_{t+1}. \qquad (7.24)$$

The *forecast variance* is given by

$$Var(1) = E[e_{t+1}^2] = \sigma_a^2, \qquad (7.25)$$

which is simply the variance of the white noise process.

Therefore, the interval forecast at the 95% confidence level of y_{t+1} is given by

$$-1.96\sqrt{Var(1)} < y_t(1) < 1.96\sqrt{Var(1)} \qquad (7.26)$$

Similarly, it can be shown that

$$Var(2) = (1 + \psi_1^2)\sigma_a^2. \qquad (7.27)$$

If $\phi_1 \neq 0$, $Var(2)$ will have a larger error component, $(1 + \psi_1^2)$, than $Var(1)$. So,

$$-1.96\sqrt{Var(2)} < y_t(2) < 1.96\sqrt{Var(2)}. \qquad (7.28)$$

Moreover we can generalize,

$$Var(n) = (1 + \psi_1^2 + \psi_2^2 + \cdots + \psi_{n-1}^2)\sigma_a^2. \qquad (7.29)$$

So $Var(n)$ will be even larger if uncertainty exists, resulting from a poor fit of coefficient estimates.

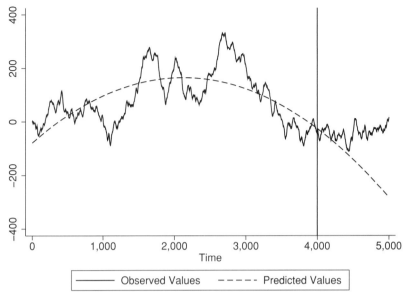

<small>FIGURE</small> 7.5. Forecasting via Curve Fitting.

7.3.2 Approaches to Forecasting

An easy way to begin to conceptualize forecasting is to think of curve fitting. That is, one uses a formula for a fitted curve where future time points are the input and the output is the forecast for future values of the series.

Here we simulate 5,000 observations of an ARIMA(1,1,1) series with coefficients of AR = 0.9 and MA = −0.4. We then regress the series on a quadratic function for just the first 4,000 observations. The resulting model has an R-squared of 0.44 and an F-statistic of 1536.31. When we compare the predicted and observed values for observations beyond 4,000 however, seen in Figure 7.5, it is easy to see the inaccuracy problem that arises.

As shown in Figure 7.5, the curve may fit quite accurately and a prediction from a fixed equation is easy to obtain. The problem is that a curve fit to observed values may pick up random variation while that curve is then set in the forecasting period. Thus, future values may diverge quickly.

Another intuitive and slightly more sophisticated approach would be to use exponential smoothing. In this case one would use a long, say 10 time points, moving average to smooth the curve and make a one-step-ahead forecast (see Yaffee and McGee, 2000, for an example). The improvement over curve fitting, which is a deterministic approach, is that adjustments can be made for trends in the data to improve the forecasts. Yet forecasts are still limited to one-step, two-step, etc., forecasts. In an effort to allow more flexibility and accuracy, forecasters have moved to a broader conception of modeling the data-generating process through ARIMA modeling.

Forecast Profiles

Over time, forecast profiles have been developed for ARIMA models. We follow McCleary and Hay (1980) in using the profiles to illustrate how the nature of the point forecasts and confidence intervals differ. These profiles vary with respect to the conditional nature of the forecasts and as interval forecasts due to different ψ weights. Here we consider six typical ARIMA profiles.

(1) An ARIMA(0,0,0) – White Noise

Here there are uniformly zero weights:

$$\psi_1 = \psi_2 = \psi_3 = \cdots = \psi_k = 0 \tag{7.30}$$

The point forecasts are

$$y_t(1) = E[a_{t+1}] = 0 \tag{7.31}$$

$$y_t(2) = E[a_{t+2}] = 0 \tag{7.32}$$

$$\vdots$$

$$y_t(n) = E[a_{t+n}] = 0. \tag{7.33}$$

Because the ψ weights are zero, the variance around these point estimate forecasts is constant for all lead times. Therefore,

$$Var(1) = \sigma_a^2 \tag{7.34}$$

$$Var(2) = \sigma_a^2 \tag{7.35}$$

$$\vdots$$

$$Var(n) = \sigma_a^2. \tag{7.36}$$

So for the white noise profile, the conditional and unconditional expectations are identical. The best forecast is the process mean. Moreover, knowing the history of the process results in no improvement to the prediction. This is expected because the history of a random shock does not provide additional information.

(2) An ARIMA(0,1,0) – Random Walk

For the random walk profile, the confidence intervals become so large after only two or three steps into the future as to make the interval forecasts meaningless. This is illustrated clearly in Figure 7.6. The figures for the forecast profiles were all created by simulating 400 observations with a standard error shock of .5 and then forecasting the next five time periods. A nonstationary process has no finite variance, so as lead time increases the variance goes to infinity.

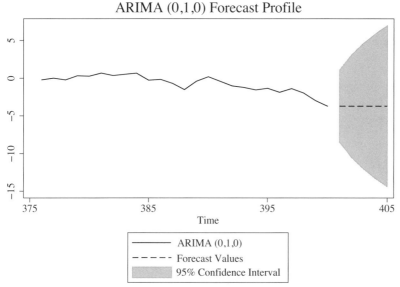

FIGURE 7.6. Forecast Profile for a Random Walk.

(3) An ARIMA(2,0,0) – Autoregressive
The series presented in Figure 7.7 is for an AR(2) with coefficients 0.6 and 0.3 and no constant. We see that, as the lead time increases, the forecast regresses to the process mean, and the confidence intervals at each point forecast increase with increases in lead time (with the confidence intervals increasing at a rate determined by ϕ_1).

(4) An ARIMA(0,0,1) – Moving Average
The series presented in Figure 7.8 is for an MA(1) with a coefficient of 0.7 and no constant. This typical moving average profile shows that for lead times (n) greater than one observation, $y_t(n)$ equals the process mean, while $Var(n)$ remains constant. So the forecast confidence intervals are the same for two periods ahead, three periods ahead, and so on.

(5) An ARIMA(1,1,0) – Mixed (Autoregressive and Integrated)
Figure 7.9 presents an ARIMA (1,1,0) with a coefficient of 0.7. The negative trend is predicted to continue in the future, but with smaller expected negative shocks.

(6) An ARIMA(0,1,1) – Mixed (Moving Average and Integrated)
Finally, an ARIMA(0,1,1) series where the coefficient is -0.6 is simulated in Figure 7.10 to illustrate the final forecast profile.

De Gooijer and Hyndman (2006) point out that the success of ARIMA forecasting is "founded on the fact that the various models can, between

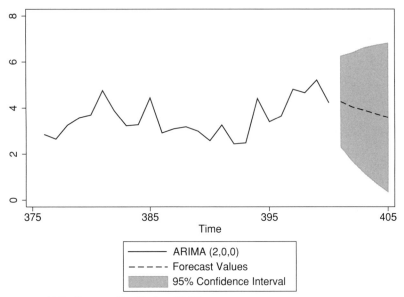

FIGURE 7.7. Forecast Profile for AR(2).

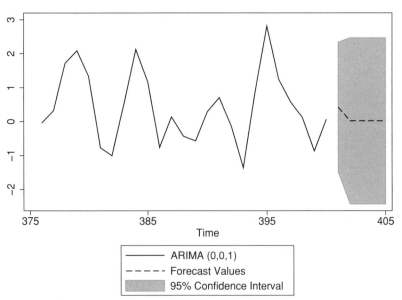

FIGURE 7.8. Forecast Profile for MA(1).

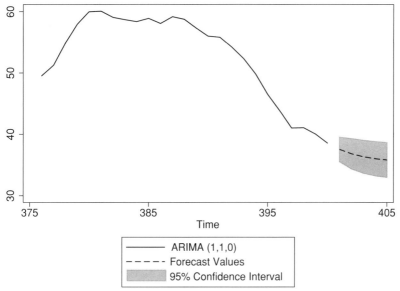

FIGURE 7.9. Forecast Profile for ARIMA(1,1,0).

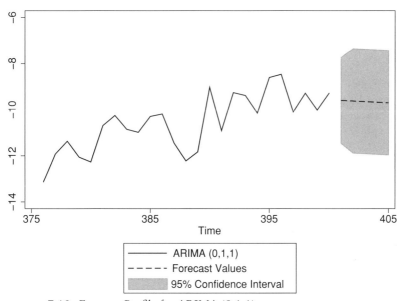

FIGURE 7.10. Forecast Profile for ARIMA (0,1,1).

them, mimic the behavior of diverse types of series – and do so adequately without usually requiring very many parameters to be estimated in the final choice of the model." Over time, testing of which model performs best has been subjected to additional mathematical rigor, such that we rely on criterion such as Akaike's or Bayes information criteria. For a summary of forecasting developments for ARIMA models and other approaches, see De Gooijer and Hyndman's (2006) 25-year review.

Forecasting Extensions and Models

Forecasting methods have evolved to become ever more complex as researchers strive to become increasingly accurate. Many authors stress the value of ARIMA models for *short-run* forecasting purposes. This is because $MA(q)$ processes have a memory of only q periods, while only the most recent observations have much impact on the $AR(p)$ forecast because exponential weights and invertibility will wipe out the effect of long memory (seasonality is something of an exception here). Also, for most ARIMA models the last observation often has the most impact. If the last observation is an extreme value, its presence can be problematic. To address the short-run versus long-run forecasting value of ARIMA approaches, scholars have turned to comparisons with ARFIMA models, which are specifically designed to capture long-run dynamics. The literature remains mixed on whether ARFIMA models predict better in the short run (e.g., Cheung, 1993; Franses and Ooms, 1997; Ray, 1993), although there is mounting evidence that there is substantial improvement over longer time frames (e.g., Barkoulas and Baum, 1997, 2006).

Extensions for ARIMA forecasting include not only ARFIMA characterizations but also ARCH variations and are generally straightforward and promising for forecasting. Franses and van Dijk (2005) strongly advocate use of more elaborate models, arguing that they clearly yield more accurate long-run forecasts.

More sophisticated forecasting approaches routinely use multivariate VAR and ECMs. Lien and Tse (1999) provide such a sophisticated example. They find that a fractionally integrated error correction model (FIECM) with a generalized autoregressive conditional heteroskedasticity (GARCH) structure provides the most accurate forecast when using mean squared error and mean absolute percentage error. They argue that it is particularly accurate for long forecast horizons because the FIECM accounts for the long memory of the cointegration relationship. An ECM will be misspecified due to omitted variables if fractional cointegration exists, whereas an ECM is nested in the FIECM and is thus a "safer" model to estimate because less restrictions are imposed by the model being estimated.[4]

---

[4] For further advanced reading on forecasting, see, Box, Jenkins, and Reinsel (2008); Bowerman, O'Connell, and Koehler (2004); and Brockwell and Davis (2003), which are all book-length treatments of the subject.

7.3.3 Criteria for Determining Optimum Forecast

Mean square forecast error (MSFE) is a commonly used measure for assessing how well a forecast performs. The MSFE compares point estimates y_t, $y_t + 1$, $y_t + 2$, etc., with observed values at time t, $t + 1$, $t + 2$, etc. Using MSFE, one can then compare two or more time series forecasting models:

$$MSFE = \frac{1}{n}\sqrt{\sum_{i=1}^{n}(y_{t+i} - y_{t^i})^2}, \tag{7.37}$$

where, y_{t^i} is the forecast from time t, out i steps. More recently, the predictive distribution, rather than the mean squared error, has been used to assess how well a forecast performs.

Fildes and Steklerm (2002) advocate for predictive forecasts to be compared to benchmark series. The basic idea is that a benchmark series is chosen and all forecasts are compared to it. A benchmark that is typically used is one of pure chance, which is a naive random walk: it says that the best forecast of a series at t is the value of the series at $t - 1$, plus some noise. By calculating Theil's U coefficient (e.g., Theil, 1966), one can then compare the errors of the forecast and the naive model. The numerator is the mean square error of the forecast, and the denominator is the mean square forecasting error of the naive forecast. So if Theil's U is less than 1, the forecast has smaller errors than the naive model. When U = 1, the forecast and the naive forecast are equally good, whereas values greater than 1 indicate that the forecast is not useful. Theil's U can be used when a series can experience both positive and negative changes, such as a presidential or congressional approval rating. In contrast, it is an inappropriate test for series that generally only change in the positive direction, such as the percent of college educated in the United States. However, even for series that have both positive and negative changes and when Theil's U is less than 1, its use has been criticized because the result does not guarantee that the forecast is statistically significantly better than the naive model.

There is a large literature on forecasting competitions run in an effort to find the "best" forecasting method. Makridakis et al. (1984), Makridakis et al. (1993), and Makridakis and Hibon (2000) are known as the M, M-2, and M-3 competitions, respectively. The M and M-3 studies used only automatic forecasting procedures and looked at 24 methods on 1,001 series and 3,003 series, respectively, a huge undertaking. The M-2 study looked at 29 series using nonautomatic forecasting procedures. Given the wide-ranging methods and datasets used, few consistent conclusions about a particular method always being best have been drawn, a fact that harkens back to Reid (1972), who was one of the first to say that the accuracy of forecasting methods varies according to the properties of the series. Meade (2000, 516) provides two useful conclusions about the selection of forecasting methods: the characteristics of the data series are an important factor in determining relative performance, and statistically complex methods do not necessarily produce more accurate forecasts. Both De Gooijer and Hyndman (2006) and Hendry (2003) provide summaries, suggestions, and provocative conclusions about forecasting accuracy and research.

There is growing consensus in the literature supporting the need for a test for statistically significant differences between the two sets of errors generated from the forecast and benchmark series. Diebold and Mariano (1995) persuasively make this case and provide guidance. Importantly, Harvey, Leybourne, and Newbold (1997) and Ashley (1998) use bootstrapping to extend this work to small samples.

Franses and van Dijk (2005) argue that no matter which model is used for forecasting a time series, it is always relevant to examine how the model performs out of sample. This examination should be done across different forecast horizons too. That is, one model may provide a better six-month forecast and still another a better six-year forecast. Depending on the substantive question, either may be preferred.

The concept of a forecast combination, which is a simple unweighted average of forecasts from all individual models, may be useful as well. Franses and van Dijk (2005, 101) leave us with a challenge, which is for scholars to develop more "elaborate models, which allow for a better understanding of the data in terms of changes in seasonal patterns and of business cycle asymmetry, that also yield better long-run forecasts."

7.3.4 Illustration: Forecasts of the U.S. Uniform Crime Reports Homicide Data, 1975–1993

The Uniform Crime Reports Homicide Series (see Figure 7.11) is an important and popularly analyzed dataset in criminology[5] used by many scholars to test a variety of hypotheses, ranging from the efficacy of deterrence theory (Bailey, 1974) to the relationship between gun laws and homicides (Olson and Maltz, 2001). Rather than use aggregate homicide data, most of these studies disaggregate the Uniform Crime Reports data by age, type of crime, or victim-offender relationship and assess these disaggregated trends across time. For example, Olson and Maltz (2001) disaggregate the homicide data by weapon type, victim-offender relationship, and victim characteristics. In so doing, they show that right-to-carry concealed weapons laws do not necessarily reduce the incidence of violent crime. Studies have also used the Uniform Crime Reports data to assess juvenile crime. One shows that the rate of juvenile violent crime has increased at a significantly faster rate than both adult violent crime and total juvenile criminal offenses between 1982 and 1991 (Ruttenberg, 1994). Another study shows that juvenile gun crimes have climbed at a higher rate than

---

[5] As noted in Chapters 1 and 2, disaggregated monthly data in the Uniform Crime Reports are less reliable than the annualized data. As such, although we present monthly data here for pedagogical purposes, we recommend that scholars use only the annualized Uniform Crime Reports data for publishable analysis.

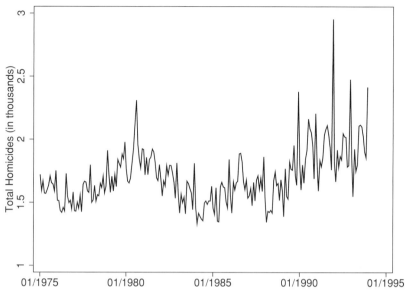

FIGURE 7.11. Homicides in the U.S., 1975–1993. Compiled by authors from FBI Uniform Crime Reports.

juvenile non-gun crimes since the mid-1980s (Zimring, 1996). To analyze the deterrent effects of capital punishment, Bailey (1974) uses the Uniform Crime Reports data to compare the number of first-degree murders, second-degree murders, total murders, and homicides in abolitionist versus capital punishment states. Contrary to what deterrent theory predicts, the capital punishment states have higher rates of murder and homicide than abolitionist states.[6] As a final example, Zimring, Mukherjee, and Van Winkle (1983) show that although total homicides increased in number from 1962 to 1980, the number of spousal and relative homicides remained stable during this period. They attribute the increase in total homicides during this period to male-to-male killings.

Building on the analysis in Chapter 2, we can present classical forecasting, based on the best fitting seasonal ARIMA model shown in Section 2.5. We begin with an in-sample forecast that is one step ahead. The forecast error plotted at the bottom of Figure 7.12 is simply the observed value of homicides in time $t + 1$ minus the forecasted value for homicides in time $t + 1$ (McCleary and Hay, 1980, 211). The 95% confidence interval is obtained by multiplying $+/-1.96$ by the square root of the mean square error.

Analysts can also use these techniques to predict future values of series out-of-sample. Figure 7.13 shows homicide forecasts beyond the range of our data. Out-of-sample comparisons can also be made with a constrained sample, in which the predicted versus observed evaluation can be achieved by cutting off

---

[6] See Land, Teske, and Zheng (2009) for an update on these findings.

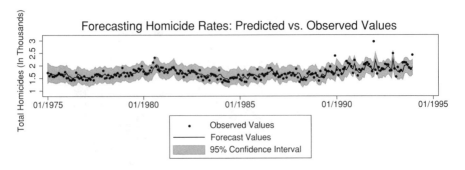

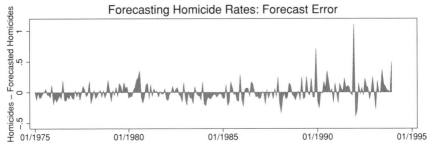

FIGURE 7.12. Classical Forecasting: Observed versus Predicted Values for Homicide Rates.

the last two years of data. We make the comparison between one-step-ahead and dynamic forecasting using this technique in Figure 7.14.

7.3.5 Forecasting Discussion

High-frequency data are becoming more and more common in time series. They help address the concern of having too little data for time series analysis, but do raise the issue of how to effectively manage so much data and whether the density of observations fits the natural time unit for the theoretical problem at hand. Automated content coding of websites and newspapers is just one way in which high-frequency data are becoming a reality. For example, Schrodt's (1994) work, beginning with the KEDS (Kansas Event Data Project), uses automated coding schemes that use news reports from wire services to code interaction among countries (see also Schrodt and Gerner 1997). Typically, in such techniques daily datasets are produced, though even more fine-grained interactions may be studied. The Visible Primary of 2008 Project of Christenson and Smidt (2008) is another exciting high-frequency data collection effort that has been using daily automated content coding of candidate and newspaper websites since the summer of 2007 to capture dynamic mechanisms of presidential primary campaigns. Kinlay (2005, 4) contends that "the use of

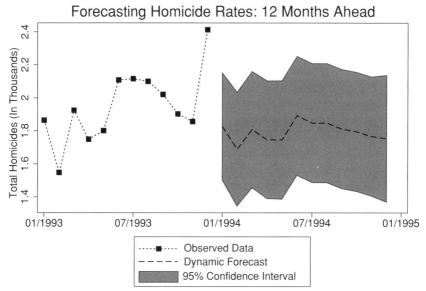

FIGURE 7.13. 12-Step Out-of-Sample Forecasts.

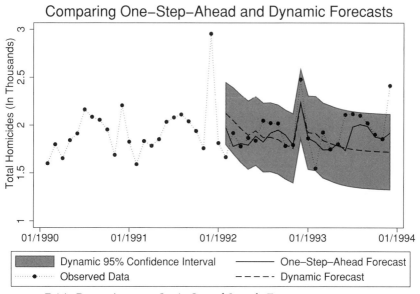

FIGURE 7.14. Dynamic versus Static Out-of-Sample Forecasts.

high frequency data has led to a dramatic improvement in both measuring and forecasting volatility."

Polling data have been a consistent source of data for forecasting elections, used by both political scientists and the public. "The history of polling in the United States goes back to 1824, when two newspapers, the Harrisburg *Pennsylvanian* and the *Raleigh Star*, organized 'show votes' to determine the political preferences of voters prior to the presidential election of that year" (*Columbia Encyclopedia*, N.d.). Under debate is whether the use of electoral markets should be preferred because of their accurate predictive track record. Participants buy candidate shares that pay out much like a stock market does. In vote share markets, the candidate's price is a forecast of how well he or she is expected to do in the popular vote. Since 2001, the commercial venture, Intrade: The Prediction Market (see www.intrade.com), has allowed buyers to invest in elections, current events, and almost anything else. The argument about why markets are better than polls is an efficiency argument (e.g., Kou and Sobel, 2004), and such markets may offer a rich, new source of data for time series analysts.

In contrast to high-frequency data, which tend to have very long series but offer challenges in data management and summary, short series have always been a perplexing problem for time series analysis. However, even for short series there are exciting advances. As mentioned previously, bootstrapping methods have found an important niche in time series analysis. In the forecasting literature, Harvey et al. (1997) and Ashley (1998), use bootstrapping to extend their forecasting work to small samples.

The greater availability of time series data, coupled with the growing interest in macro system models, has led to a growth in the area of forecasting with many predictors. There are three primary approaches in the literature: forecast combination, dynamic factor models, and Bayesian model averaging. Stock and Watson (2007) provide a helpful guide to these three competing approaches and outline future directions for forecasting with many predictors. Forecast combination is essentially the pooling of many forecasts to produce a single forecast. In contrast, dynamic factor models assume that the comovement among series is a result of a small number of unobserved factors, so estimates of the factors are used to forecast individual series. Importantly, the estimates of the factors become more precise as the number of series increases. Finally, Bayesian model averaging works by averaging based on the posterior probability assigned to each model. Fildes and Steklerm (2002) advocate a Bayesian approach to time series forecasting and highlight its potential as a very promising route for future research. They call for more effective use of expertise by examining the role of judgment and how to best incorporate additional information sources into the model's framework. Stock and Watson's (2006) example uses all three of the approaches and is a fascinating study forecasting the growth rate of the U.S. index of industrial production by using 130 predictor series. Even with substantially smaller models, these three approaches have a lot to offer forecasting scholars.

Although most of the forecasting literature focuses on linear forecasts, Franses and van Dijk (2005) push the field forward in their consideration of linear and nonlinear time series models in forecasting. Their comparative work looks at industrial production in 18 countries belonging to the Organization for Economic Cooperation and Development (OECD). They conclude that, in general, linear models with fairly simple descriptions of seasonality outperform nonlinear models at short forecast horizons, whereas nonlinear models with more elaborate seasonal components dominate at longer horizons. Montgomery et al. (1998) argue that nonlinear time series are particularly promising in forecasting. Thus the concern with long- and short-term forecasts again comes into consideration when choosing forecasting methods.

7.4 ESTIMATING AND MODELING WITH UNKNOWN STRUCTURAL BREAKS

Of growing interest to scholars who work with time series data is estimating the location of unknown structural breaks. A structural break occurs when an entire series is no longer characterized by the same underlying process, and instead, there are two (or more) distinct subsamples of the observations, each of which is characterized by a unique underlying process. Such breaks may either be the result of an observed event or of an unobserved combination of factors. These breaks are not equivalent to the intervention models discussed in Chapter 2; rather than estimating the effect of an exogenous intervention on one process, structural break tests attempt to identify the point(s) at which the entire underlying data-generating process of a series changes. To clarify, an intervention model is best suited to situations such as the applied example we discussed in Section 2.7.1. Did the Oslo Accords of 1993 (an obvious, clear intervention point in a series) significantly affect U.S. cooperation with Israel?

Conversely, consider the example of global terrorist events from 1970–2003, drawn from Enders and Sandler (2005). Can we characterize the complex process by which different terrorist organizations plan and carry out their attacks with the same structural pattern for that entire period? The world has changed a great deal since 1970, but is there one singular exogenous moment that one could pinpoint to test using an intervention model? In Chapter 2, Section 2.7.2, we discussed how analysts can use a Chow test to test for structural breaks if the analyst can specify a priori when such a break might have occurred. We could test, for instance, whether 9/11 represents a structural change in global terrorism with such a method. But the 9/11 terror attack is not an intervention similar to the Oslo Accords, but rather a data point in the series itself; testing its "effect" on the series with an intervention model clearly invites a host of undesirable concerns about endogeneity. Further, although we could specify that

September 2001 is a possible point of a structural break and apply the Chow test, what if the true process of global terrorism experienced a structural break several months or years before and the attack of 9/11 is just a manifestation of an already changed process? Caporale and Grier (2005) point out that such a strategy has a nontrivial potential for type 1 error (falsely concluding that 9/11 represented a significant structural break in this example). The point is that structural changes may result not from one obvious abrupt point, but rather from a partially or wholly endogenous combination of factors that manifest more slowly, meaning that specifying a break point a priori to test may be difficult or impossible. In applied work, analysts have also sought to identify multiple structural breaks in monetary policy in the United States and United Kingdom (Caporale and Grier 2005), and the opinion-writing behavior of U.S. Supreme Court justices (Smyth and Narayan 2006).

This diversity of applications shows that for some problems it may be better to let the data speak for itself and to identify which point or points are statistically most likely to represent a break in the underlying process. Perhaps there is no structural break. Perhaps there are several. Questions such as these are best addressed with the methods we discuss in this section. We begin with a discussion of estimating the location of a single unknown break based on the technique of Bai (1994), because its exposition is simpler than the multiple break model. We continue with a presentation of the Bai and Perron (1998) technique for multiple breaks, which relies on similar logic to the Bai (1994) single break model.

7.4.1 Identifying a Single Unknown Structural Break

Consider the following simple model, following the notation of Bai (1994):

$$Y_t = \mu(t) + X_t, \quad t = 0, 1, 2, \ldots, T. \tag{7.38}$$

Here, $\mu(t)$ is a nonstochastic function in time and X_t is a linear stochastic process (i.e., the error structure), with $X_t = \sum_{j=0}^{\infty} a_j \epsilon_{t-j}$. We assume that ϵ_t are either *i.i.d.* with mean 0 and variance σ^2 or, alternately that ϵ_t are martingale differences such that the expectation of ϵ_t is 0, with variance converging in probability to σ^2 conditional on the stochastic process of the errors up until time t.

X_t is just a representation of time dependency in the error structure; assuming that ϵ_t are *i.i.d.* posits no time dependency, whereas the alternate assumption merely means that we can turn the errors into white noise through some function of past realizations of the errors. This function can be an ARMA process, for example, whose order and coefficients can be estimated along with the unknown structural break. We focus here on the estimation of the structural break point.

To estimate the location of a single structural break, let $\mu(t)$ take on a value μ_1 before time $t = k_0$, and a different value μ_2 after $t = k_0$. Our problem then is to estimate three unknown parameters: μ_1, μ_2, and the break point k_0.

We can estimate the most probable location of the break point $\hat{k}$ as follows:

$$\hat{k} = argmin_k \left[min_{\mu_1, \mu_2} \left\{ \sum_{t=0}^{k}(Y_t - \mu_1)^2 + \sum_{t=k+1}^{T}(Y_t - \mu_2)^2 \right\} \right]. \tag{7.39}$$

Bai's estimator minimizes the sum of squares of the residuals among all possible sample splits. Denote the mean of all observations for $t = 0, \ldots, k$ as $\overline{Y}_k$, and the mean of all observations for $t = k + 1, \ldots, T$ as $\overline{Y}_k^*$. If a point k is the shift point, then $\overline{Y}_k$ and $\overline{Y}_k^*$ are the usual least squares estimators of μ_1 and μ_2, respectively. For shift point k, the sum of squares of residuals is defined as

$$S_k^2 = \sum_{t=0}^{k}(Y_t - \overline{Y}_k)^2 + \sum_{t=k+1}^{T}(Y_t - \overline{Y}_k^*)^2. \tag{7.40}$$

Our best estimate of the break point, $\hat{k}$, therefore, is whichever point solves $\hat{k} = argmin_k(S_k^2)$, and least squares is used to estimate μ_1 and μ_2 as $\overline{Y}_k$ and $\overline{Y}_k^*$. In a nutshell, Bai (1994) creates a framework for identifying an unknown structural break: we test all possible break points in a series, allowing the mean of the series to change at each break point, and then choose whichever point minimizes the sum of squared residuals.

Bai (1994) derives further results for this estimator, along with a procedure for testing the null hypothesis of no structural break against the alternative hypothesis of one structural break. Because the more common procedure of Bai and Perron (1998) involves similar tests, readers are referred to the original paper of Bai (1994) for further details on this estimator. The procedure we discuss next for the detection of multiple structural breaks can be used to determine the location of a single structural break as well.

7.4.2 Identifying Multiple Unknown Structural Breaks

Bai and Perron (1998) extend the general intuition of the single break method to the estimation of multiple breaks. We focus here on the simplest case of the multiple structural break estimator: a model that includes only an intercept. This technique can be extended to time series regression models that contain exogenous covariates. Coefficients on exogenous covariates can themselves be subject to structural breaks (a pure structural break model with all parameters subject to breaks), or these coefficients may be held constant while the mean of the series is subject to structural breaks (a partial structural break model), per the choice of the analyst.

Consider a time series, ranging from points $t = 0, \ldots, T$, with dependent variable Y_t. Y_t experiences a certain number, m, of break points, meaning that there are a total of $m + 1$ regimes in the series. We can represent this series, modeled with constants that may vary by regime, as follows:

$$Y_t = \beta_1 Z_{t1} + E_t; \qquad t = 0, 1, \ldots, T_1$$
$$Y_t = \beta_2 Z_{t2} + E_t; \qquad t = T_1 + 1, \ldots, T_2$$

$$\vdots$$

$$Y_t = \beta_{j-1} Z_{tm} + E_t; \quad t = T_{m-1} + 1 \ldots T_m$$
$$Y_t = \beta_j Z_{tm+1} + E_t; \quad t = T_m + 1, \ldots, T. \tag{7.41}$$

Here, the Z_t variables are simply columns of ones, the β_j are the constants in the $j = 1, 2, \ldots, m + 1$ regimes, and E_t is the error term. The assumptions about the error term needed for this model are complex and are omitted here for clarity. Interested readers are referred to Bai and Perron (1998, 50–51), (particularly assumptions A4(i) for models without a lagged dependent variable and A4(ii) for models with a lagged dependent variable). The relevant information for our purposes here is that the errors are allowed to be serially correlated – Bai and Perron suggest the correction of Andrews (1991) for serially correlated errors.

The break points in the series $(T_1, \ldots, T_m)$ are treated as unknown. We therefore must estimate the vector of break points, as well as the unknown regression coefficients. In practice, the true number of regimes $(m + 1)$ is unknown. In the following presentation, we first treat the number of breaks m as known/assumed. Analysts can and should test for the true number of regimes; we cover these tests after presenting the method for estimating unknown break points for a given number of breaks m.

The estimation of the unknown break points in a series, $(T_1, \ldots, T_m)$, proceeds as follows: for a specified number of breaks m, for each partition $(T_1, \ldots, T_m)$, our estimated parameters β_j are those that minimize the sum of the squared residuals:

$$\sum_{i=1}^{m+1} \sum_{T_{i-1}+1}^{T_i} (Y_t - Z_T' \beta_j)^2. \tag{7.42}$$

From there, we have an estimated set of $\hat{\beta}_j(T_1, \ldots, T_m)$ coefficients that are associated with specified m partition $(T_1, \ldots, T_m)$. We then substitute these estimated coefficients back into equation 7.42, and estimate the location of the break points in the series with

$$(\hat{T}_1, \ldots, \hat{T}_m) = min_{T_1, \ldots, T_m} S_T (T_1, \ldots, T_m). \tag{7.43}$$

In equation 7.43, $S_T(T_1, \ldots, T_m)$ is the sum of the squared residuals. Thus, our estimated locations of the break points in the series are the global minimizers of the sum of squared residuals. Alert readers might note the similarity of this process to Bai's (1994) process for estimating the location of a single unknown structural break. The global minimization of this function for all possible locations of break points has the potential to be computationally complex for any specified number of breaks greater than two, but Bai and Perron (2003) present an efficient algorithm for this procedure, which Zeileis et al. (2003) implement for practical use. Once we have the estimated locations of the break points, we substitute these estimated break points $\hat{T}_1 \ldots, \hat{T}_m$ back into our objective function (equation 7.42) to obtain our final estimates of the parameters given these estimated break points, $\hat{\beta}_j(\hat{T}_1, \ldots, \hat{T}_m)$. Along with parameter estimation, Bai and Perron (1998, 2003) derive asymptotic results for the construction of confidence intervals around the estimated break points; statistical software can report these as well (Zeileis et al. 2003).

In practice, analysts must also specify a "trimming" parameter h to control the distance allowed between estimated break points; that is, $\frac{T_i - T_{i-1}}{T} \geq h$ (recall that T is the total length of our series). If, for instance, $h = 0.05$, and our series is 100 points long, each regime must be at least 5 time points long. Bai and Perron (2003) recommend trimming parameters as small as 0.05 when errors are homogeneous and do not exhibit serial correlation, advising a higher trimming parameter otherwise. For T of 125, Bai and Perron (2003) recommend $h = 0.15$ in the presence of heterogeneity, and $h = 0.20$ in the presence of serial correlation. Standard values of trimming parameters are 0.05, 0.10, 0.15, 0.20, and 0.25; 0.15 is a common default.

7.4.3 Hypothesis Tests for Multiple Structural Breaks

Estimating the location of structural breaks for some arbitrary amount m of breaks is clearly only half the battle. Analysts are almost always interested in knowing whether a structural break occurred at all and, if so, how many breaks occurred. Bai and Perron (1998) suggest several tests for two important null hypotheses: first, that no structural break occurred against the alternative hypothesis that the true number of breaks $m = l$, (where $l > 0$), and second, the null that the true number of breaks $m = l$ against the alternative hypothesis that $m = l + 1$ breaks.

Bai and Perron present two types of tests for these null hypotheses. The first test, known as a $SupF_t(l)$ test, is used to test either null hypothesis; that the true number of breaks $m = 0$ versus the alternative that $m = l$, or that the true number of breaks $m = 1$ versus the alternative that $m = l + 1$.

In the first instance – no structural break versus the alternative of l breaks – the null can be equivalently stated as $\beta_1 = \beta_2 = \cdots = \beta_{m+1}$ in the model of equation 7.41. The $SupF_t(l)$ searches over all possible break dates (contingent on the trimming parameter h discussed earlier) for l breaks, maximizing the difference between the restricted and unrestricted models. The *Sup* in the name of the test refers to the fact that we take the highest value, or supremum, of the F-statistics from the tests between the restricted and unrestricted versions of the model. That is, we consider the highest possible F-statistic obtained by comparing a model with l breaks to a model with 0 breaks. Bai and Perron (1998) provide critical values for this test: if the greatest F-statistic exceeds this critical value, then we reject the null hypothesis of 0 breaks and fail to reject the alternative hypothesis of l breaks.

To continue probing the null hypothesis of zero structural breaks, Bai and Perron further recommend that analysts conduct what they term a "double maximum" test. This test are not used to determine precisely how many structural breaks exist in the series, but rather they strengthen inferences about whether at least one (but possibly more) structural breaks occurs as opposed to none. The first component of the double maximum test is a UDmax test; the test statistic here is simply the greatest value of the $Sup F_t(l)$ for a sequence of $Sup F_t(l)$ tests for $(1, \ldots, l)$ possible breaks. Bai and Perron (1998) provide critical values for this test: if the test statistic exceeds the critical value, we reject the null of no structural break at the specified level of confidence.

The second maximum of the double maximum tests is the WDmax test. One potential issue with the UDmax test noted by Bai and Perron (2003, 59) is that, for a time series of fixed length (T in equation 7.41), as we posit more and more possible breaks (l), the F-statistics generated become less and less informative. Why? The F-statistic for a model with l breaks can be viewed as a sum of l dependent chi-squared variables, each divided by l. Thus, if we hold the number of parameters in the model otherwise fixed, larger values of l have lower critical values for the $Sup F_t(l)$ test than iterations of the $Sup F_t(l)$ for fewer possible breaks. The upshot is that if we choose a high value of l, the resulting test may have lower power because the UDmax test will include these lower critical values when the number of possible breaks is large. The WDmax test addresses this problem by weighting the F-statistics from the sequence of $Sup F_t(l)$ tests such that the marginal *p*-value for each possible number of breaks is the same. If the results of both double maximum tests are statistically significant, then analysts may reject the null hypothesis of no structural break in the data with the specified level of confidence.

Once an analyst rejects the null of no structural break, determining how many breaks to include in the model, l, can be done with a series of $Sup F_t(l)$ tests. We begin with the null hypothesis that there is 1 break ($l = 1$), and test that against the alternate hypothesis of $l + 1$ breaks. The $Sup F_t(l)$ test here will maximize the F-statistic for the difference between a model with two as opposed to one structural break. If this test is statistically significant, we then test a model with three structural breaks against a model with two, proceeding with successive tests of l vs. $l + 1$ breaks until the $Sup F_t(l)$ tests are no longer significant. When the test of l vs. $l + 1$ is not significant, analysts should then proceed to estimating the locations of l breaks in their series with the method described earlier. An alternative approach to using sequential $SupF_t(l)$ tests for determining the optimal number of structural breaks is using whichever number of breaks minimizes the BIC. Although this option is available in statistical packages (Zeileis et al. 2003), Bai and Perron (2003) show that the sequential method is preferable, because it can handle heterogeneity across segments while the BIC method cannot; further, the BIC performs poorly for a null hypothesis of no break, especially in the presence of serial correlation. Thus, we advocate that analysts use the sequential method for determining the optimal number of breaks to estimate.

In practical applications, analysts are often interested not only in the endogenous structural change in a series but also in how external factors might influence the series, above and beyond endogenous change. Caporale and Grier (2005) provide a good set of instructions for analysts who seek to model data that might be subject to structural breaks, specifically, to test the hypothesis that a certain moment is associated with a structural break in a series. First, determine the extent of structural change in the model using the technique discussed earlier. Second, model breaks appropriately, using the sequential method. If the hypothesized moment falls within the confidence interval for the break, then reject the null that this moment does not represent a significant change in the series. If the hypothesized moment is not within the confidence interval of the identified structural break, then reestimate the model with the appropriate break points, and include a dummy variable for the hypothesized moment of change. If the coefficient is significant, then conclude that the hypothesized moment does have additional explanatory power for the dynamics of the series.

7.5 CONCLUSION

This chapter provided a brief overview of four topics – fractional integration, heterogeneity, forecasting, and modeling and estimating with unknown structural breaks – as well as pointers to relevant reference works. Fractional integration may provide a more accurate characterization of the series through the direct estimation of d. Thus, it may prove useful in modeling by allowing more nuance in both statistical and substantive terms: it enables researchers to move away from knife-edged assumptions about whether shocks persist in a series indefinitely or vanish almost immediately. For example, its use allows the reexamination of hypotheses about the rate of decay of a shock to a series. One need only consider the previous discussion of macropartisanship in the U.S. political context to understand how relying on the assumption that d is equal to either 1 or 0 can prove quite limiting, as well as how the direct estimation of d can help settle such debates by alleviating the need to make restrictive assumptions about the series in question.

The chapter also discussed how to incorporate heterogeneity into time series analysis. An important and growing component of time series analysis, it allows researchers to move beyond a straightforward consideration of the series mean and instead consider other forms of variation that may be occurring, specifically periods of relatively high and low volatility. ARCH models, among numerous others, allow for this volatility to be explicitly modeled, opening up new lines of inquiry that are simply missed if our only consideration is the mean of the series. Thus, by taking heterogeneity into account, it is possible not only to consider whether the volatility of the series varies systematically over time but also to develop and test hypotheses that seek to explain this volatility.

Forecasting was discussed as a relatively new advance in the social sciences; it is our expectation that forecasting will continue to increase in usage in those disciplines. This will occur not only because considerable technical advances allow researchers to better tailor their forecasts depending on the series in question and to provide more accurate estimates of the uncertainty surrounding such predictions but also because of the substantive importance of such developments. Simply put, forecasting allows researchers to evaluate the merits of competing models by comparing how each model performs in out-of-sample predictions, which in turn provides a straightforward metric to evaluate the models. Moreover, being able to forecast effects is also an extremely valuable goal in terms of policy analysis because it is extremely important to be able to understand the likely effects that policies or exogenous shocks will have on outcomes of interest.

Finally, we discussed techniques for estimating the existence and location of multiple unknown structural breaks in time series data. Many social processes are complex, and their underlying data-generating processes may shift endogenously in ways that are difficult to pinpoint a priori. The techniques discussed for estimating whether a break occurred in a series at all, along with the amount and location of breaks, allow for exciting new opportunities for rigorous inference. Given that most social processes are the complex product of numerous endogenous and exogenous factors, structural break analysis allows analysts to control for the endogenous change in some social variable's underlying data-generating process *before* testing for the effect of exogenous interventions. If, after controlling for endogenous structural change, an exogenous intervention variable remains significant, then analysts can proceed with considerably greater confidence that the intervention truly affected the series.

7.6 FOR FURTHER READING

Brandt, Patrick T., John R. Freeman, and Philip A. Schrodt. 2011. "Real Time, Time Series Forecasting of Inter-and Intra-State Political Conflict." *Conflict Management and Peace Science* 28 (1): 41–64.

Box-Steffensmeier, Janet M., David Darmofal, and Christian A. Farrell. 2009. "The Aggregate Dynamics of Campaigns." *Journal of Politics* 71 (1): 309–323.

Clarke, Harold D. and Matthew Lebo. 2003. "Fractional (Co)integration and Governing Party Support in Britain." *British Journal of Political Science* 33 (2): 283–301.

DeBoef, Suzanna and Jim Granato. 1997. "Near-Integrated Data and the Analysis of Political Relationships." *American Journal of Political Science* 41 (2): 619–640.

Dickinson, Matthew J. and Matthew Lebo. 2007. "Reexamining the Growth of the Institutional Presidency, 1940–2000." *Journal of Politics* 69 (1): 206–219.

Enders, Walter and Todd Sandler. 2005. "After 9/11: Is It All Different Now?" *Journal of Conflict Resolution* 49 (2): 259–277.

Freeman, John, Jude C. Hays, and Helmut Stix. 2000. "Democracy and Markets: The Case of Exchange Rates." *American Journal of Political Science* 44 (3): 449–468.

Kriner, Douglas and Liam Schwartz. 2009. "Partisan Dynamics and the Volatility of Presidential Approval." *British Journal of Political Science* 39 (3): 609–631.

Leblang, David. 2004. "Presidential Elections and the Stock Market: Comparing Markov-Switching and Fractionally Integrated GARCH Models of Volatility." *Political Analysis* 12 (3): 296–322.

Leblang, David and William Bernhard. 2006. "Parliamentary Politics and Foreign Exchange Markets: The World According to GARCH." *International Studies Quarterly* 50 (1): 69–92.

Park, Jong Hee. 2010. "Structural Change in the U.S. Presidents' Use of Force Abroad." *American Journal of Political Science* 54 (3): 766–782.

8

Concluding Thoughts for the Time Series Analyst

We began this book by suggesting that scholars in the social sciences are often interested in how processes – whether political, economic, or social – change over time. Throughout, we have emphasized that although many of our theories discuss that change, often our empirical models do not give the concept of change the same pride of place. Time series elements in data are often treated as a nuisance – something to cleanse from otherwise meaningful information – rather than part and parcel of the data-generating process that we attempt to describe with our theories.

We hope this book is an antidote to this thinking. Social dynamics are crucial to all of the social sciences. We have tried to provide some tools to model and therefore understand some of these social dynamics. Rather than treat temporal dynamics as a nuisance or a problem to be ameliorated, we have emphasized that the diagnosis, modeling, and analysis of those dynamics are key to the substance of the social sciences. Knowing a unit root exists in a series tell us something about the data-generating process: shocks to the series permanently shift the series, integrating into it. Graphing the autocorrelation functions of a series can tell us whether there are significant dynamics at one lag (i.e., AR(1)) or for more lags (e.g., an AR(3)). Again, this tells us something about the underlying nature of the data: how long does an event hold influence?

The substance of these temporal dynamics is even more important when thinking about the relationships between variables. Most social scientists write down statistical models (what we refer to as "structural models") based on loosely specified theory that pertains to two to four variables of interest (even though our models end up with far more variables than this on the right-hand side). These models are then tweaked to account for the possibility that the dependent variable might be sticky over time (i.e., contain autocorrelation), which means our tried-and-true OLS estimation could run into trouble.

Worse, social scientists may believe their dependent variable may be trending over time, either up or down, but rather than subjecting this belief to empirical investigation, they stick a deterministic counter variable in the model as an independent variable and assume that doing so takes care of the problem. Yet, we rarely check whether this is the case.

As you have now learned, however, there are other ways to conceive of multivariate dynamic processes over time. VAR methods and cointegration techniques allow us to specify these temporal elements in a more dynamic fashion rather than assume they are deterministic. Tests for cointegration help us ensure that the relationships we find between variables are not spurious, but substantively meaningful.

Sometimes, we hear critics of time series analysis used the dreaded "I" word: inductive. Time series analysts, they argue, allow for too much induction. Induction certainly has its dangers, but so do assumptive restrictions in models. Are our theories really specific enough to tell us that our dependent variable is only a first-order autoregressive process? Did our theory suggest we only needed one lag of that independent variable in the model? Is our theory certain that our explanatory variables are strictly exogenous?

The point here is not to berate those who engage in structural equation modeling. That approach, like many others, has value when used wisely. Nor is the point to defend methodological inductivism. Rather, it is to suggest that all methods and approaches have tradeoffs. For some questions (or researchers), induction will be a powerful tool to understand social dynamics. For other questions, induction may be less helpful. But we would suggest that if one is not nervous about making strongly restrictive assumptions in regression models, then one should not be too nervous about induction. Moreover, we are adamant that time series properties in data should be taken seriously.

Time series analysis is not a question of methodological necessity: it is a matter of substantive interpretation and understanding. That is our core message to those who want to perform time series analysis: the methods discussed in this book have substantive motivations and will assist in the interpretation of data.

The remainder of this chapter reviews the methods we have discussed and looks forward to the future of time series analysis.

8.1 A REVIEW

Chapter 1 introduced the idea of time series analysis and the concept of social dynamics. We then discussed three basic issues in the construction of time series data: systematic sampling, temporal aggregation, and data vintaging. The first two techniques – sampling and aggregation – are often done by social scientists without consideration of their implications. Usually, to cope with too much data or to merge data gathered at disparate time intervals, analysis will sample or aggregate data. Yet the choice to do so, as we show, has substantive implications.

Chapter 2 began our exploration of univariate ARMA time series models through the use of the Box-Jenkins methodology. This approach builds models of a single time series by using a number of diagnostic tests and plots and then matching the results of those diagnostics against well-known properties of existing models. The process is inductive, yet allows a modeler to thoroughly investigate the temporal dynamics of a series using over- and under-modeling. Any preconceived notions about the nature of the data-generating process must be thrown out to facilitate diagnosis. We then built univariate models of American homicide rates, as well as political-military interactions in the Middle East, to demonstrate the use of the methodology. Finally, the chapter reviewed a useful but often under-utilized method: intervention models. These models allow one to test for breaks in the data, which indicate changes in the underlying data-generating process that the analyst posits before examining the series. This method allows a researcher to test hypotheses about events that could change the series.

Chapter 3 reviewed models that may be more commonly known to students of typical social science methods: the time series regression model. We focused initially on what we labeled the "workhorse model" of time series regression: the regression model with a lagged endogenous variable and potentially including lags of other explanatory variables. We reviewed the circumstances under which these models would be appropriate and strategies to obtain estimates for them. We illustrated this methodology with the example of voting intentions in the United Kingdom. Finally, we briefly examined dynamic regression models with multiple lags of independent variables, including autoregressive distributed lag models.

Chapter 4 began with a brief review of dynamic regression models from Chapter 3, adding a new example of British monetary policy. This review set the stage for the introduction of vector autoregressive (VAR) models that more fully specify potential relationships among all variables in a system. VAR models contain few restrictions, which is both their advantage and disadvantage. On the positive side, VAR models' lack of restrictions allows the discovery of many possible relationships between variables with no assumptions about exogeneity. The challenge, of course, is that VAR models can then contain numerous coefficient estimates, the interpretation of which is conditional on many other coefficients. To that end, we introduced concepts such as the analysis of Granger causality and innovation accounting to evaluate VAR systems. We concluded the chapter with a reanalysis of British monetary policy to illustrate the differences between structural equation models and VAR models.

Chapter 5 returned to the world of univariate ARMA models, but how relaxing the assumption of stationarity in our data. Nonstationary data (and the diagnosis thereof) bring new challenges to the time series analyst. The chapter focused on the diagnosis of the presence of nonstationarity. Using the example of macropartisanship in American politics, we walked through the diagnosis of a nonstationary series, discussed why this diagnosis was important substantively, and built a univariate ARIMA model, showing the differences between this model and its equivalent assuming stationarity.

Chapter 6 took our newly gained knowledge about nonstationarity and returned to the world of multivariate time series models. Error correction models have emerged as a well-used methodology in the social sciences in the past five years. In this chapter, we reviewed two approaches to the diagnosis and estimation of cointegrated data and the corresponding error correction models. After reviewing the Engle-Granger and Johansen approaches, we turned to an example of the Indo-Pakistani arms race to show how a shock to the underlying equilibrium in arms spending by both sides would dissipate, returning arms spending to that previous equilibrium after a period of time.

Finally, Chapter 7 examined advances in four areas in time series methodology that we believe will be increasingly important (if not already so) to the social sciences. We reviewed fractional integration, autoregressive conditionally heteroskedastic (ARCH) models, forecasting, and estimating structural breaks. Fractional integration deals with series that have a long but not infinite (e.g., $d = 1$) memory. ARCH models are designed to model the volatility inherent in time series, whereas our review of forecasting suggested that social scientists could more fruitfully use time series methods to create predictions from their models. Finally, our discussion of structural breaks was substantively related to intervention models (Chapter 2), but these newer methods allow the estimate of shifts in the data without the analyst specifying them a priori.

8.2 LOOKING AHEAD

The field of time series analysis, as with all fields of methodology, is constantly changing and evolving. And although Chapter 7 reviewed what we view as four of the most promising developments in the field of time series, other advances also loom large. An increasing turn to Bayesian time series methods has emerged in the past five years (e.g., Brandt and Freeman, 2006). New methodologies in the area of VAR are allowing estimation with even fewer specification of lag lengths (Tahk et al., 2013). Yet, almost no matter what new advances emerge in the field, you will now be able to understand the starting point for these advances based on this material presented here.

Perhaps more important than advances in techniques is that the number of rich, high-frequency (i.e., large T) time series is increasing dramatically. Due in part to the Big Data movement and also driven by the capture of social media streams, data availability is exploding. Whether from hourly RSS news feeds, Twitter feeds, or high-frequency financial data, we are now seemingly awash in data that begs for time series analysis. From a social science perspective, the question will be whether there are enough other variables that can be captured at this low level of aggregation and high frequency to conduct extensive multivariate analysis. Yet, what we have emphasized here is that even a univariate analysis of time series data can provide substantive information. Discovering the temporal dynamics of these new series can help us understand the nature of the memory process, the transitory nature (or not) of exogenous shocks, and allow the exploration of shifts in the underlying data-generating process.

Of course, new techniques and new data do not guarantee excellent analysis. That requires careful exploration of data using the appropriate tools. Those tools begin with a simple examination of the data. Recall Chatfield's (2003, 13) insight from Chapter 2: "The first, and most important, step in any time-series analysis is to plot the observations against time." No estimator, no matter how complex, will behave well in the presence of outliers, missing data, or simply noisy data. That requires looking at and understanding the context of the data.

You are now armed with a host of additional tools: correlograms, Box-Ljung tests, tests for stationarity, ARIMA models, tests for fractional integration, VAR methods, cointegration models, ARCH models, Granger causality tests, and of course, renewed knowledge of the workhorse time series regression model. We hope you now have a better understanding of time series analysis. We wish you the best as you embark on implementing these techniques to explore your own questions involving social dynamics.

Appendix

Time Series Models as Difference Equations

A.1 INTRODUCTION

The material in this appendix is aimed at readers interested in the mathematical underpinnings of time series models. As with any statistical method, one can estimate time series models without such foundational knowledge. But the material here is critical for any reader who is interested in going beyond applying existing "off the shelf" models and conducting research in time series methodology.

Many social theories are formulated in terms of changes in time. We conceptualize social processes as mixes of time functions. In so doing, we use terms such as trend and cycle. A trend usually is a function of the form $\alpha \times t$ where α is a constant and t is a time counter, a series of natural numbers that represents successive time points. When α is positive (negative), the trend is steadily increasing (decreasing). The time function $\sin \alpha t$ could be used to represent a social cycle, as could a positive constant times a negative integer raised to the time counter: $\alpha(-1)^t$. In addition, we argue that social processes experience sequences of random shocks and make assumptions about the distributions from which these shocks are drawn. For instance, we often assume that processes repeatedly experience a shock, ϵ_t, drawn independently across time from a normal distribution with mean zero and unit variance.

Social processes presumably are a combination of these trends, cycles, and shocks. Our goal is to decompose time series into these parts and to understand what they imply individually and collectively about processes' out-of and in-equilibrium behaviors. With this knowledge we can explain (forecast) why processes (will) behave as they do (in the future).[1] For example, reconsider

---

[1] Temporal decomposition is at the heart of time series analysis. For instance, see Enders (2010, 1–3).

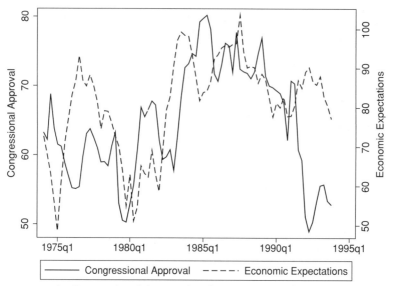

FIGURE A.1. Congressional Approval and Economic Expectations in the U.S., 1974q1–1993q4. Compiled by the authors from replication data on website of Christina Wolbrecht (Durr, Gilmour, and Wolbrecht, 1997).

the pattern of congressional approval and economic expectations in the United States (Figure A.1). In the 1970s and early 1980s public approval of Congress increased. Congressional approval remained relatively high until the early 1990s when it dropped precipitously. At the same time, approval of Congress displays both cyclical behavior and momentary surges and declines. The surges and declines such as those that occurred in the late 1980s presumably are caused, in part, by political shocks of various kinds (Erikson, MacKuen, and Stimson 2002). Congressional approval thus is conceived as a *mix* of trends, cycles, and a random element.

Although we conceptualize social processes in terms of a mix of time functions, we *model* them as equations. As explained in Chapter 1, because of the way we measure our variables, these equations usually are expressed in discrete rather than continuous time.[2] Illustrative of the univariate equations we use are

$$A_t = \alpha A_{t-1} + \epsilon_t \qquad\qquad (A.1)$$

---

[2] We think that processes such as international conflict and cooperation, crime, and popular evaluation of the president are continuously ongoing. But we only (systematically) sample these processes at discrete times and almost always at regular intervals. Continuous time models are used occasionally. In this case, scholars model social processes in terms of deterministic or stochastic differential equations. But, again, these are exceptions. As regards the translation from verbal concepts to mathematical equations, graph algebra can be used for this purpose. Cortes, Przeworski, and Sprague (1974) explain this algebra and show how it can be applied to the study of conflict dynamics and other social problems. This algebra is not widely used in the social sciences, however.

and

$$A_t = \alpha_0 + \alpha_1 A_{t-1} + \alpha_2 A_{t-2} + \beta t + \epsilon_t, \tag{A.2}$$

where A_t is the level of congressional approval in month t, each α is a constant coefficient, β also is a constant coefficient, t once more is the time counter, and ϵ_t, is an independent, normally distributed shock at time t. Equations such as equation A.1 and equation A.2 often are the statistical models we use in social sciences. They are used to represent such processes as habit formation and, in other contexts, bureaucratic inertia and incrementalism. The idea is that because of the workings of the respective social processes the level of a variable at time t is directly related to its levels at times $t - 1, t - 2, \ldots$ Put another way, if A_t is a single time function, the values of this time function at time t are directly related to its values at previous times; if A_t is a *mix* of time functions, as we believe congressional approval to be, then the current value of this mix of time functions at time t is directly related to the past values of the mix of time functions that constitutes congressional approval.

Of course, there are many other univariate equations that we might use to model social processes, including

$$A_t = t A_{t-1} + \epsilon_t \tag{A.3}$$

$$A_{t+2} = (t + 2) A_{t+1} - t A_t + t + \epsilon_t, \tag{A.4}$$

as well as equations of the form

$$A_t = \alpha_0 (A_{t-1})^2 + \alpha_1 A_{t-2} + \epsilon_t. \tag{A.5}$$

$$A_{t+1} = -t A_{t+1} A_t + A_t + \epsilon_t. \tag{A.6}$$

But, usually, we employ statistical models that resemble equations A.1 and A.2.

Social scientists often say that our equations describe social processes. For instance, we put a lag of our dependent variable on the right side of our equations and say it represents bureaucratic incrementalism or some kind of habitual behavior. But the corresponding equations also are mathematical statements. For example, equation A.1 says that there is a time function or mix of time functions, A_t, such that, at all points in time, its current values are equal to its values in the last period times a constant (α) plus a random variable (ϵ_t). Equation A.3 says that there is a time function or mix of time functions such that its current values at all time points equal its previous values multiplied by the time counter plus the same random variable.

What we will learn in this appendix is that all these expressions can be analyzed as difference equations. Put simply, a difference equation is an expression that relates the value of a function or the value of a mix of time functions at one point in time to its values at other points in time.[3]

---

[3] Another way to write the difference equations in equations A.1–A.6 is to rewrite them in terms of $A(t + 2)$, $A(t + 1)$, $A(t)$ and $A(t - 1)$ where $A()$ is a function of time. We use this form sometimes later in this appendix.

Several terms are used to characterize difference equations. The first concerns the nature of the coefficients on the functions on the right-hand side. They can be constants or, as we have just seen, functions of time. Equations A.2 and A.3 illustrate this distinction. Equation A.2 has constant coefficients; the coefficient in equation A.3 is a time function, t. Second, in addition to the variables of interest, difference equations often contain other functions and variables: deterministic time functions or random variables. The additional time functions on the right-hand side of the equation sometimes are called the forcing process (Enders, 2010, 8). In social science these often are called the exogenous variables.[4] Equations A.2 and A.4 have such variables on their right-hand sides in the form of the deterministic time functions βt and t respectively. Expressions containing random exogenous variables are called stochastic difference equations. Each of the six equations – A.1–A.6 – is a stochastic difference equation because each contains the random variable ϵ_t.[5] If the expression is written solely in terms of the variable of interest and if the equation has no such additional functions in it, we say the difference equation is "homogeneous." Otherwise, we say it is "nonhomogeneous." An example is of a homogeneous equation is

$$A_t = \theta_1 A_{t-1}. \tag{A.7}$$

where θ is a fixed parameter. Note that this equation also can be written as

$$A_t - \theta_1 A_{t-1} = 0. \tag{A.8}$$

Now, if we add a constant and a deterministic time function $\theta_2 t$ to the right-hand side of equation A.7, we have the nonhomogeneous equation

$$A_t = \theta_0 + \theta_1 A_{t-1} + \theta_2 t. \tag{A.9}$$

This expression can be rewritten as

$$A_t - \theta_1 A_{t-1} = \theta_0 + \theta_2 t. \tag{A.10}$$

The order of a difference equation is just the number of points in the function's past values that are related to its value in the present or, equivalently, the number of future values of the function that are related to its present values. So, for instance, both equations A.2 and A.4 are second-order difference equations. According to these equations, there are mixes of time functions such that the current value is related to the values one and two periods in the past and the values two periods ahead depend on the values one period ahead and the

---

[4] Hamilton (1994, 36–37) calls the univariate model the "equation of motion" and the other right-hand-side functions "driving variables."

[5] Equations A.1–A.6 are all discrete, stochastic difference equations. A similar continuous time model is the stochastic differential equation $\frac{dA_t}{dt} = \alpha A_t + \epsilon_t$. On the connection between deterministic differential and deterministic difference equations see such works as Cull, Flahive, and Robson (2005, section 3.1.1) and Goldberg (1986, section 1.7).

current value, respectively. Finally, a difference equation is linear if it can be written as a weighted sum of the values of the function at different points in time where the weights are not themselves values of the function. Equation A.4 therefore is linear because its coefficients are deterministic functions of time, whereas equation A.6 is nonlinear because in it A_{t+1} multiplies A_t.[6]

Putting these terms together, we say, for example, that equation A.3 is a first-order, nonhomogeneous linear stochastic difference equation with time-varying coefficients. Equation A.5, in contrast, is a second-order, nonhomogeneous, nonlinear stochastic difference equation with constant coefficients. An example of a linear, homogeneous difference equation with a constant coefficient is equation A.7.[7]

The challenge is to figure out what models like these imply about the composition of social processes. Put another way, we want to know the (mix) of time function(s) that is implied when we write down equations such as A.1–A.7: we want to know the (mix of) time function(s) that makes the equation true. What we will learn in this appendix is how to find these solutions to the difference equations. And once we know these solutions (a single time function or a mix of time functions), we can discover nonintuitive properties of social processes – the ways they equilibrate, for instance – and also forecast their behavior.

The same logic applies in multivariate analysis.[8] When we theorize about relationships such as that between congressional approval and economic expectations, we think in terms of the impact of one trending (cyclical) variable on another or in terms of the trends and cycles common to both variables. When we model such relationships we write down equations like the following:

$$A_t = \alpha_0 + \alpha_1 A_{t-1} + \beta_1 X_{t-1} + \epsilon_t, \qquad (A.11)$$

where α, β, and ϵ_t are defined as before and X_{t-1} is the level of economic expectations at month $t-1$. To capture common trends we use slightly more complex equations like

$$A_t - A_{t-1} = X_{t-1} - X_{t-2} - \lambda(A_{t-1} - X_{t-1} - C) + \epsilon_t \qquad (A.12)$$

[6] A difference equation over a set S is *linear* if it can be written in the form

$$f_0(t)y_{t+k} + f_1(t)y_{t+k-1} + \cdots + f_n(t)y_t = g(t)$$

where $f_0, f_1, \ldots, f_n$ and g are each functions of t but not of y_t and each function is defined over S. S is the set of numbers over which the difference equation is defined. Usually S is (an) the (in)finite set of successive integers. See, for instance, Goldberg (1986, section 2.1).

[7] There are still other types of models such as random coefficient and partial difference equations. For instance, to distinguish them from partial difference equations the difference equations in the text sometimes are called "ordinary." See, for instance, Kelley and Peterson (2001, Chapter 10).

[8] In this book we define "multivariate" models as those that include two or more *theoretically defined or "regular"* variables in the forcing function. Models composed of one regular variable and a forcing function that consists of a time counter and(or) "irregular" variable, ϵ_t are called univariate.

where λ and C are constants. Note that, in both equations, we assume economic expectations cause the level (changes) of (in) congressional approval. Implicit here is the idea that economic expectations are governed by a separate equation in which congressional approval does not appear; economic expectations is a univariate process. In other words, implicit in both models in equation A.11 and equation A.12 is a system of equations where the equation for X_t is a function of itself alone. For example, equation A.11 could be a system such as

$$A_t = \alpha_0 + \alpha_1 A_{t-1} + \beta_1 X_{t-1} + \epsilon_{1t}. \tag{A.13}$$

$$X_t = \gamma_0 + \gamma_3 X_{t-3} + \epsilon_{2t}.$$

The system of equations in A.13 says there are two (mixes of) time functions in a social system. The value of the (mix of) time function(s) for congressional approval is such that its present values are equal to the sum of a constant plus another constant times its previous values plus still another constant times the previous values of economic expectations plus a random variable. And, at the same time, there is a (mix of) time function(s) for economic expectations such that its current values are equal to a constant plus a different constant times the previous values of economic expectations plus a distinct random variable. In other words, the value of the (mix of) time function(s) for congressional approval depends on its (their) own immediate past value and the immediate past value of economic expectations. But, once more, the values of the economic expectations (mix of) time function(s) do not depend on the values of the congressional approval (mix of) time functions.

When we think causation runs in both directions, we make the system of relationships explicit. Recall the example of U.S.-Chinese relations discussed in the context of temporal aggregation in Chapter 1. Denote U.S. behavior toward China at time t by UC_t and Chinese behavior toward the U.S. at time t by CU_t. Then we might write the system governing their relations as

$$UC_t = \alpha_0 + \alpha_1 UC_{t-1} + \alpha_2 CU_{t-1} + \epsilon_{1t}. \tag{A.14}$$

$$CU_t = \beta_0 + \beta_1 CU_{t-1} + \beta_2 UC_{t-1} + \epsilon_{2t}.$$

Or, we might model this same system with time-varying coefficients and non-linear relationships between the two behaviors:

$$UC_{t+1} = \alpha_0 t UC_t + \alpha_1 CU_t + \epsilon_{1t}. \tag{A.15}$$

$$CU_{t+1} = \beta (UC_t)^2 + \epsilon_{2t}.$$

The second system is much more complex than the first insofar as it says that the weight of incremental policy behavior of the United States toward China (UC) becomes greater over time and at the same time that Chinese behavior toward the United States varies exponentially with U.S. behavior toward China.

The same terminology applies. Equations A.13 and A.14 are systems of linear, nonhomogeneous stochastic difference equations with constant coefficients. Equation A.15 is a system of nonlinear, nonhomogeneous stochastic difference equations with time-varying coefficients.[9]

Once more, the challenge is to discover the mix of time functions that solve these multivariate (multiequation) models and then to learn from these functions the implications for social equilibration and forecasts. In this way, these more complex models also have implications for social dynamics.

Table A.1 summarizes some of the difference equation models that we might use to analyze social processes.[10] We focus in this Appendix on categories I and II; elsewhere in this book we study particular models of these types. For example, equation A.12, a multivariate linear stochastic difference equation, is known as an error correction model that is studied in detail in Chapter 6.

There are several reasons why we focus on linear difference equations with constant coefficients. These types are the most simple models; parsimony always is a virtue. Second, mastering linear models with constant coefficients is the first step toward learning more advanced models. Last, models in categories I and II currently are the most widely used in the social sciences and are the bases for most of the time series regression models we use. For this reason alone, it is important that social scientists learn their dynamical implications. But there are social processes that, by all indications, are governed by the other kinds of models.[11]

The rest of this appendix is divided into two parts. The first explains the nature of difference equations and their solutions. In it, we introduce the concept of a linear operator and show how it can be used to express difference equations. We then explain what it means exactly to say that a time function solves a difference equation. How to find these time functions (solutions) is the

---

[9] There is a famous model in international relations called the Richardson equations that resembles the equation system in equation A.14. It explains the ways nation-states build arms as a function of their own military-industrial inertia and in response to the arms buildup of their adversary. See Sandler and Hartley (1995); Isard et al. (1989); and Dunne and Smith (2007).

[10] No distinction is drawn in the table between deterministic and stochastic difference equations. Analytically, we follow convention in studying the former before the latter. Also the multivariate cases subsume the ideas of implicit and explicit systems of difference equations. Some types of equations are omitted from the table such as partial difference equations.

[11] Technically, cases III and IV are studied under the rubric of regression models with time-varying coefficients. There also are a few applications of deterministic nonlinear difference equations in the social sciences. Illustrative is Huckfeldt, Kohfeld, and Likens (1982). They study political mobilization as represented by the equation $M_t - M_{t-1} = g(L - M_t) + sM_t[(L - M_t) - g(L - M_t)] - fM_t$ where g, s, f, and L are constants and M_t is the level of mobilization at time t. For mathematical treatments of deterministic cases III and IV see Kelley and Peterson (2001, section 3.5). For studies of nonlinear difference equations, cases V–VIII, see Kelley and Peterson (2001, sections 3.6, 4.5, chapter 9); Cull, Flahive, and Robson (2005, chapter 10), and Spiegel (1971, chapter 5). Collections of works that employ nonlinear models in political analysis are Richards (1993, 2000).

TABLE A.1. *Some Types of Difference Equation Models*

	Coefficients	Univariate	Multivariate (Multiequation)
Linear	Constant	I	II
	Time Varying	III	IV
Nonlinear	Constant	V	VI
	Time Varying	VII	VIII

subject of the second part. We begin by showing how to solve the most simple cases: first-order deterministic and stochastic difference equations. Various methods to solve second-order difference equations and systems of difference equations are explained next. The main point of the analysis is to show the contrasting kinds of dynamics that are implied by (systems of) difference equations and their solutions. These dynamics hold the key to discovering how (if) social systems equilibrate and to forecasting their behavior.

A.2 THE NATURE OF DIFFERENCE EQUATION MODELS

In reading the introduction you may have wondered how the word "difference" applies to the equations. More important, the idea that a time function solves an equation might be new to you. To understand the nature of difference equations, we need to introduce some special mathematical operators and to explain how time functions solve those equations. Grasping the dynamical implications of these solutions is the next step. Each solution implies a particular kind of qualitative behavior; for example, whether our social process gravitates toward a fixed (moving) equilibrium or not and(or) whether the process has a deterministic or stochastic trend. These are the topics of this section.

A.2.1 Expressing Difference Equations

Anyone who has studied mathematics has encountered the idea of an operator. Operators transform variables and functions. A simple example is the operator of squaring. Denote this operator by S. If x is a variable, $S(x) = x^2$. Consider the function $f(x) = 2x$. Then $S(f(x)) = (2x)^2 = 4x^2$. Readers who have studied calculus are familiar with the derivative and integral operators. For instance, the former sometimes is written as D to mean $\frac{d}{dx}$. So, for our function, $f(x)$, we have $D(f(x)) = D(2x) = \frac{d}{dx}(2x) = 2$. An algebra of operators has been developed by mathematicians. For instance, operators such as D can be applied to sums. That is, if $f(x)$ and $g(x)$ are differentiable functions, $D(f + g) = D(f(x)) + D(g(x))$.

Among the operators that are used in time series analysis, three are especially important. The first is the backshift operator, B, also known as a lag operator. This operator simply takes the previous value of a time function or, for a time function, $y(t)$, $B(y(t)) = y(t-1)$. Say, $y(t)$ is $.5^t$. Then $B(y(t)) = B(.5^t) = .5^{t-1}$. If the function is a constant, its lag stays the same (because y always has the same value in the past and future). Backshift operators also apply to sums. Here is an example that illustrates these two properties of this first operator: $B(.4t + .1) = B(.4t) + B(.1) = .4(t-1) + .1 = .4t - .3$. When B is raised to a power, such as B^i where i is a natural number, it means take the ith lag of a time function. So $B^i(y(t))$ is equal to $y(t-i)$. An important property of the backshift operator that we use repeatedly in this book is the following: for a constant α such that $|\alpha| < 1$, the infinite sum $(1 + \alpha B + \alpha^2 B^2 + \cdots)y(t) = \frac{y(t)}{(1-\alpha B)}$.[12]

The second operator, the difference operator, can be written in terms of the backshift operator. The difference operator, Δ, is simply $(1 - B)$. We write $\Delta y(t)$ to mean $(1-B)y(t) = y(t) - y(t-1)$. Returning to our earlier examples, $\Delta(.5^t) = .5^t - .5^{t-1}$, and $\Delta(.4t + .1) = (.4t + .1) - (.4(t-1) + .1) = .4$.[13] The difference operator also can be raised to a power. Its relation to the backshift operator helps interpret powers of Δ. Consider the square of the difference operator:

$$\Delta^2 y(t) = (1-B)^2 y(t) = (1 - 2B + B^2)y(t) = y(t) - 2y(t-1) + y(t-2).$$

(A.16)

So, if $y(t)$ again is $.5^t$, we have

$$\Delta^2(.5^t) = .5^t - 2(.5^{t-1}) + .5^{t-2} = .5^t.$$

(A.17)

The third is called the "expectations" or "lead" operator. It is denoted either as E or as the inverse lag operator, B^{-1}. Simply put, $Ey(t) = y(t+1)$. For our second example, $E(.4t + .1) = B^{-1}y(t) = .4(t+1) + .1 = .4t + .5$. For a time function, $y(t)$, we can combine all three operators together in the following way:

$$E\Delta y(t) = E(1-B)y(t) = B^{-1}(1-B)y(t) = (B^{-1} - 1)y(t) = y(t+1) - y(t).$$

(A.18)

---

[12] This fact is based on the properties of geometric series. A simple proof can be found in Enders (2010, section 9). In this section, Enders lists the properties of the backshift operator we discussed in the text plus a few additional ones.

[13] Once more, we defined the function of interest in terms of time, t, and our focus is on the "difference interval" equal to one. The more general treatment of difference equations considers functions of any variable and alternative sampling intervals. In this treatment the difference equation is written in a form like $\Delta y(x) = y(x+h) - y(x)$ where h is this difference interval. See Goldberg (1986, chapter 1). A still more general treatment of these equations conceptualizes them in terms of linear recurrences. See Cull, Flahive, and Robson (2005).

In other words the lead of the difference between $y(t)$ and $y(t-1)$ is equal to the difference between $y(t+1)$ and $y(t)$.[14]

Now, a difference *equation* is a claim about how the application of these operators to an unknown time function produces a particular equality. Let us again call this unknown time function $y(t)$. A difference equation for $y(t)$ might be

$$\Delta y(t) = .25^t + .3. \tag{A.19}$$

Equation A.19 says that the difference in our unknown function at all points in time is always equal to .25 to the t power plus .3. Here is another example of a difference equation:

$$\Delta^2 y(t) = .1t + .05 + \epsilon(t). \tag{A.20}$$

Here the claim is that the unknown time function is such that, at each instant, its second difference always equals .1 multiplied by the value t plus the constant .05 plus the random variable $\epsilon(t)$.

Mathematically then, a difference equation relates the values of a function $y(t)$ and one or more of its differences, $\Delta y(t)$, $\Delta^2 y(t)$, ... for each t-value of the natural numbers (for which each of these functions is defined).[15]

Who makes claims of these kinds? *We do!* Every time we formulate a model such as those described in the introduction to this Appendix, we are writing (an expansion) of a difference equation. We are making a claim about the nature of an unknown time function. Put another way, the equations we write down when modeling social processes are simply expansions of underlying difference equations. To see this, recall that we learned that the square of the difference operator can be written in terms of the lag operator (equation A.16). So, replacing Δ^2 with its equivalent expression, we can rewrite A.20 as

$$y(t) - 2y(t-1) + y(t-2) = .1t + .05 + \epsilon(t) \tag{A.21}$$

---

[14] Some mathematicians develop difference equations in terms of the E operator rather than the B operator. They define Δ as $E-1$ rather than $1-B$. We use both conventions here, but emphasize the latter.

[15] This definition is paraphrased from Goldberg (1986, 50) and written in a fashion that is useful for conventional time series analysis. The more general definition is "an equation relating the values of a function y and one or more of its differences $\Delta y, \Delta^2 y, \ldots$ for each x-value of some set of numbers S (for which each of the functions is defined)" Spiegel's (1971, 150–151) definition is expressed as an analogy to that of differential equations. He lets $y = f(x)$ and then defines a difference equation as a relationship of the form $F(x, y, \frac{\Delta y}{\Delta x}, \frac{\Delta^2}{\Delta x^2}, \ldots, \frac{\Delta^n y}{\Delta x^n}) = 0$. Since $\Delta x = h$, the difference interval, the items in his brackets can be written x, $f(x)$, $f(x+h)$, $f(x+2h), \ldots, f(x+nh)$. A difference equation therefore can be written as a relationship of the form $G(x, f(x), f(x+h), f(x+2h), \ldots, f(x+nh)) = 0$ where, once more, $f(x) = y$ is the unknown function.

Moving the lagged values of $y(t)$ to the right-hand side we have an equation that looks just like equation A.2 in the introduction to this Appendix:

$$y(t) = 2y(t-1) - y(t-2) + .1t + .05 + \epsilon(t). \qquad (A.22)$$

In this way, we often formulate statistical models that are, in effect, difference equations. However, we usually do not study the dynamical implications of those models: the time functions implied by our functional forms (coefficient estimates) and what those functions say about the movement of our social processes through time. The study of difference equations helps us understand the dynamics that are implicit in our equations.[16]

A.2.2 The Solutions of Difference Equations

Most of us are familiar with equations that have scalars (numbers) as their solutions. For instance, suppose you are asked to solve the equation $2z - 10 = 0$. Your knowledge of algebra teaches you that the solution for z is 5; $z = 5$ makes the equation true. Similarly, if asked to solve the quadratic equation $z^2 - 4 = 0$, you would answer $z = 2$ and -2; both $z = 2$ and $z = -2$ make this second equation true. The logic for difference equations is the same, only now the solution is a time function or a mix of time functions. This (mix of) time functions makes the difference equation true for the initial time point $(t = 0)$, and for all other time points $t = 1, 2, \ldots$.

In what follows we give examples of solutions to difference equations of types I and II. We assume that the initial conditions of the social process are known. To establish these conditions we need a theory about or test for when a particular social system came into existence. We also need a measure of $y(t = 0)$ and also, for higher order difference equations, of $y(t = 1)$ and maybe $y(t = 2)$. For example, we might hypothesize that social systems begin anew after a major war, a political realignment, or a landmark policy reform. Operationally, this kind of "diachronic change" usually is associated with permanent change in the values of the coefficients of our difference equations.[17] Again, the first step is to show that the solution – a particular (mix of) time function(s) – produces the initial (condition). The second step is to show that if we substitute the solution into the difference equation, we obtain a true statement or, again, that the solution makes the difference equation true for all time points (other than the initial condition(s)). After we understand the nature of a solution to a difference equation, we will learn how to find them.

---

[16] In Chapter 3 we go into greater detail about how difference equations are employed in regression analysis. In this context, we show how scholars often add lags of variables on the right-hand-side of their equations in order to eliminate serial correlation; more specifically, they conceive of social dynamics as a statistical "nuisance."

[17] On the idea of "diachronic change," see the epilogue of Cortes, Przeworski, and Sprague (1974).

Example A.1: A First-Order Deterministic Difference Equation

Consider the following equation:

$$y_t = 2y_{t-1} + 1 \qquad y_0 = 5 \qquad\qquad (A.23)$$

Equation A.23 says that a time function, y_t, is always equal to two times its previous value plus one. This could represent a high degree of habitual behavior or bureaucratic inertia, for example.

We claim that the solution has the following form:

$$y_t = 6 \times 2^t - 1. \qquad\qquad (A.24)$$

First, consider the initial condition. For $t = 0$,

$$y_t = 6 \times 2^0 - 1 \qquad\qquad (A.25)$$
$$= 6 - 1$$
$$= 5.$$

So the initial condition is satisfied. For all other t, we want to establish that the time function $y_t = 6 \times 2^t - 1$ makes the difference equation in equation A.23 true. To do this we put our solution on the left side of the equation and on the right side of the equation. But on the right side, we write the version of the time function indicated by equation A.23; we write the solution with t replaced by $t - 1$.

To following equations show how this is done. They use the laws of exponents to show how the solution makes the difference equation in A.23 true:

$$6 \times 2^t - 1 = 2[6 \times 2^{t-1} - 1] + 1 \qquad\qquad (A.26)$$
$$= 2 \times 6 \times 2^{t-1} - 2 + 1$$
$$= 6 \times 2^1 \times 2^{-1} \times 2^t - 1$$
$$= 6 \times 2^t - 1.$$

In this way we have shown that the time function in equation A.24 is a solution to the difference equation in equation A.23. Finally, note that this solution can be depicted as a steadily increasing function of time (Figure A.2). For $t = 0, 1, 2, \ldots$ this time function is the sequence of numbers $\{5, 11, 23, 47, 95, \ldots\}$.[18]

Example A.2: Another First-Order Deterministic Difference Equation

Suppose we change the coefficient from 2 to -2 in equation A.23 and make the initial condition $y_0 = 0$. Then the new difference equation is

$$y_t = -2y_{t-1} + 1 \qquad y_0 = 0 \qquad\qquad (A.27)$$

---

[18] To better see the qualitative nature of the time function that constitutes the solution to equation A.23, we connect the time points in the sequence in this and the figures that follow.

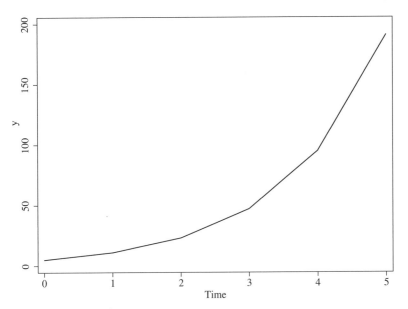

The new solution is

$$y_t = .33 - .33(-2)^t. \tag{A.28}$$

The qualitative behavior of this time function is very different from that which we studied in Example A.1. First, we establish that it is a solution to equation A.27. As regards the initial condition, we have

$$y_t = .33 - .33(-2)^0 = 0. \tag{A.29}$$

Second, when we put the solution on the left side of the equality, and with t replaced by $t - 1$ also on the right side, we have

$$.33 - .33(-2)^t = -2[.33 - .33(-2)^{t-1}] + 1 \tag{A.30}$$
$$= -.66 + .66(-2)^{t-1} + 1$$
$$= -.66 + 1 + .66(-2)^{-1}(-2)^t$$
$$= .33 - .33(-2)^t.$$

Thus the time function in equation A.28 solves the first-order deterministic difference equation in equation A.27, as shown in Figure A.3. Notice how it differs from the time function that solves Example A.1. This second time function *oscillates* without bound. It implies a sequence of values $\{0, .99, -.99, 2.97, -4.95, 10.89, \ldots\}$. It might represent a war–peace cycle or an economic cycle of some kind.

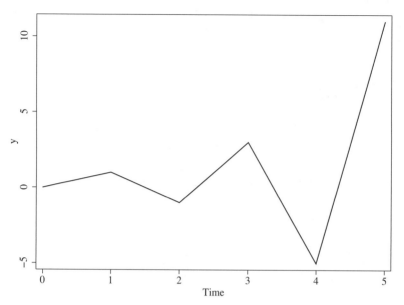

FIGURE A.3. Example A.2.

Example A.3: A Second-Order Deterministic Difference Equation

We often argue that habit, human organization, and other factors produce social processes that depend on more than one previous level of a variable. Examples might be civil conflict in which the memory of past conflict carries over for two months, or because of the social process in criminal organizations, the amount of robberies in one period depends on the amount in the past two periods. Second-order difference equations capture this more complicated relationship between current and past levels of variables. For instance, suppose we have a model like the following:

$$y_t = 3y_{t-1} - 2y_{t-2} - 1 \tag{A.31}$$

Suppose further that the observed values of y at times 0 and 1 are -3 and 5, respectively.

The solution for the second-order difference equation is

$$y_t = -10 + 7 \times 2^t + t. \tag{A.32}$$

Looking first at the initial conditions ($t = 0, 1$) we have

$$y_0 = -10 + 7 \times 2^0 + 0 \tag{A.33}$$

$$= -10 + 7$$

$$= -3$$

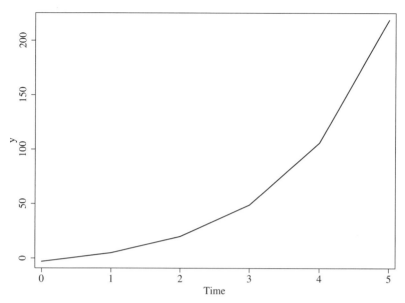

FIGURE A.4. Example A.3.

and

$$y_1 = -10 + 7 \times 2^1 + 1 \qquad (A.34)$$
$$= -10 + 14 + 1$$
$$= 5.$$

Thus the initial conditions are satisfied. The second step is to establish that the equality in equation A.31 holds for this solution. To do this we insert the solution on the right-hand side of equation A.31, but now change the t to $t-1$ in the first term and to $t-2$ in the second term:

$$-10 + 7 \times 2^t + t = 3[-10 + 7 \times 2^{t-1} + (t-1)] - 2[-10 + 7 \times 2^{t-2}$$
$$+ (t-2)] - 1 \qquad (A.35)$$
$$= -30 + 21 \times 2^{t-1} + 3t - 3 + 20 - 14 \times 2^{t-2} - 2t + 4 - 1$$
$$= -10 + 21 \times 2^{t-1} + t - 14 \times 2^{t-2}$$
$$= -10 + 21 \times 2^{t-1} + t - 14 \times 2^{-1} \times 2^{t-1}$$
$$= -10 + 14 \times 2^{t-1} + t$$
$$= -10 + 7 \times 2^t + t.$$

Like its counterpart in Example A.1, this solution increases without bound (Figure A.4). It is the sequence of numbers $\{-3, 5, 20, 49, \ldots\}$ for $t = \{0, 1, 2, 3, \ldots\}$.

Example A.4: Still Another First-Order Deterministic Different Equation
Consider another simple difference equation:

$$y_t = \frac{1}{10} y_{t-1}. \tag{A.36}$$

This difference equation also can be expressed as

$$y_t - \frac{1}{10} y_{t-1} = 0 \tag{A.37}$$

Its solution is of the form,

$$y_t = C \left(\frac{1}{10} \right)^t. \tag{A.38}$$

This time function solves the difference equation for an unspecified constant, C. To show this, note that for any C we have

$$C \left(\frac{1}{10} \right)^t - \frac{1}{10} \left[C \left(\frac{1}{10} \right)^{t-1} \right] = 0 \tag{A.39}$$

$$C \left(\frac{1}{10} \right)^t - C \left(\frac{1}{10} \right)^1 \left(\frac{1}{10} \right)^{t-1} = 0$$

$$C \left(\frac{1}{10} \right)^t - C \left(\frac{1}{10} \right)^t = 0.$$

This highlights the basic idea of having a general solution to the equation, but *not* having one unique solution – instead, many different functions solve the equation. That is, with C assuming many different values we have many different solutions to the original equation. For example,

If $y_0 = 0$, then $C = 0$ and

$$y_t = 0 \left(\frac{1}{10} \right)^0 = 0. \tag{A.40}$$

If $y_0 = 1$, then $C = 1$ and

$$y_t = 1 \left(\frac{1}{10} \right)^0 = 1. \tag{A.41}$$

If $y_0 = 100$, then $C = 100$ and

$$y_t = 100 \left(\frac{1}{10} \right)^0 = 100. \tag{A.42}$$

These are solutions deriving from the initial condition or from the value of y_t when $t = 0$. When we change the value of $y_t = 0$, we obtain different solutions, but qualitatively they all behave like the case depicted in Figure A.5. From the

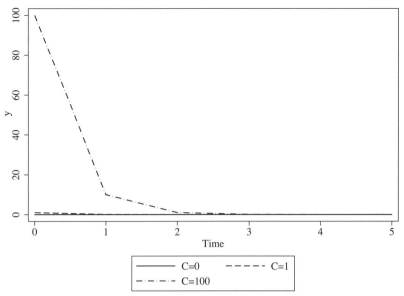

FIGURE A.5. Example A.4.

initial conditions (C), the time functions decrease to the value of zero. This is because as t grows in size, $\frac{1}{10}$ is raised to a higher and higher exponent. As a consequence the value of y_t decreases. The sequence of numbers representing the function is $\{C \times \frac{1}{10}, C \times \frac{1}{100}, C \times \frac{1}{1000}, \ldots\}$.

Example A.5: A First-Order Stochastic Difference Equation

When we work with data we always assume there is a stochastic element to social processes. Normally, we associate this element with the "error term." Example A.5 is a first-order stochastic difference equation:

$$y_t = y_{t-1} + \epsilon_t. \tag{A.43}$$

This says simply that, for all t, a variable y_t is equal to its previous value plus a random shock at t. The idea that in the United States macropartisanship is a "running tally" of politically relevant shocks produces an equation of this kind (Erikson, MacKuen, and Stimson, 1998). We assume that we know the initial value of the variable, y_0. The solution of this difference equation turns out to be

$$y_t = y_0 + \sum_{i=1}^{t} \epsilon_i. \tag{A.44}$$

To show that the expression in equation A.44 is a solution of equation A.43, we rewrite equation A.43, but on the right side we take the sum up to $t - 1$

instead of t and add ϵ_t:

$$y_0 + \sum_{i=1}^{t} \epsilon_i = [y_0 + \epsilon_1 + \epsilon_2 + \cdots + \epsilon_{t-1}] + \epsilon_t \tag{A.45}$$

$$= y_0 + \sum_{i=1}^{t} \epsilon_i.$$

Thus the expression in equation A.44 solves this simple, first-order stochastic difference equation.

Notice what this solution says about the social process. First, past shocks are not forgotten: each past shock is remembered in full at each time t. Second, the time series has what is called a stochastic trend. Its movement is a combination of its initial value and the *sum* of all the past shocks the process has experienced. Because these shocks are drawn from a probability distribution, a single series can appear to have the kind of upward trend we saw for Examples A.1 and A.3 or the cyclical pattern displayed by the time function in Example A.2. Moreover, each series is *one realization* of what could be many different time paths. Figure A.6 depicts two such realizations of the model with the initial condition $y_0 = 1$; each time path is from the same initial conditions, but with different sets of draws from a normal distribution with mean zero and unit variance. Notice how in many respects these series appear quite different, despite the fact that they were generated by the same model.[19]

This simple stochastic difference equation is called a random walk. Econo–mists argued for many years that efficient financial markets generate prices that are best described by a random walk process. Once more, the idea of a "running tally of political shocks" producing such a model for macropartisanship is well established in political science. We discuss this model in Chapter 5.

Example A.6: A Second-Order Stochastic Difference Equation

Second-order models such as that in Example A.3 also can have stochastic elements. Let us return to the robberies illustration. The observed frequency of robberies is likely to mirror such processes as cycles in the supply of drugs and/or the intensity of law enforcement. This frequency also is likely to reflect strictly random factors such as gang wars, weather, or the like. Suppose that these two kinds of factors are represented in the form of a second-order

---

[19] To clarify, in each of the two cases, we drew 50 values of *epsilon* from a normal distribution with mean zero and unit variance, keeping track of the order in which we drew each value. We formed the y_t in the expression in equation A.44 by sequentially adding them to the initial condition of $y_0 = 1$. We did this twice to show how the same model can produce two series depending on the collection (order) of 50 draws one obtains. R was used for this purpose. We used a different seed value for the second set of draws.

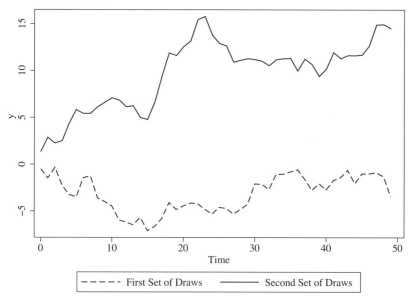

FIGURE A.6. Example A.5.

autoregressive structure plus a stochastic variable. Suppose further that we estimate such a model and obtain the following coefficients[20]:

$$y_t = 3 + .9y_{t-1} - .2y_{t-2} + \epsilon_t, \tag{A.46}$$

where ϵ_t has the same properties as in Example A.5.[21] Now, to make things a bit simpler, we assume that $y_0 = 0$ and $y_1 = 2$ and also that $\epsilon_0 = \epsilon_1 = 0$. Then the solution to this difference equation is

$$y_t = 10 + 30(.4)^t - 40(.5)^t + \sum_{i=0}^{t-2} \alpha_i \epsilon_{t-i}, \tag{A.47}$$

where $\alpha_0 = 1, \alpha_1 = .9$, and the remaining α's are defined by the formulas (recursion) $\alpha_i = .9\alpha_{i-1} - .2\alpha_{i-2}$.

To establish that the initial conditions are satisfied by the solution, let us focus on the first three terms in equation A.47. For $t = 0$, the solution becomes

$$y_0 = 10 + 30 \times 1 - 40 \times 1 = 0. \tag{A.48}$$

For $t = 1$, we have

$$y_1 = 10 + 30 \times .4 - 40 \times .5 = 2. \tag{A.49}$$

Thus these two initial conditions are met.

---

[20] In Chapter 2 we explain how such an equation and its coefficients might be estimated from robbery data for a given place and time period.

[21] This example is taken from Enders (2010, 38–39).

To establish that the time function in equation A.47 solves equation A.46 is more difficult. Let us begin with the *nonstochastic* part of the solution. If the expression in equation A.47 solves equation A.46, we must have

$$10 + 30(.4)^t - 40(.5)^t = 3 + .9[10 + 30(.4)^{t-1} - 40(.5)^{t-1}] \qquad (A.50)$$

$$- .2[10 + 30(.4)^{t-2} - 40(.5)^{t-2}]$$

$$= 3 + 9 + 27(.4)^{-1}(.4)^t - 36(.5)^{-1}(.5)^t - 2$$

$$- 6(.4)^{-2}(.4)^t - 8(.5)^{-2}(.5)^t$$

$$= 10 + 67.5(.4)^t - 72(.5)^t - 37.5(.4)^t + 32(.5)^t$$

$$= 10 + 30(.4)^t - 40(.5)^t.$$

Turning to the *stochastic* part of the solution to this difference equation, recall that the weights on the shocks have numerical values; these are the α's defined earlier. On the right side of equation A.47 we have the weighted sum of shocks in the solution:

$$\sum_{i=0}^{t-2} \epsilon_t = \epsilon_t + .9\epsilon_{t-1} + .61\epsilon_{t-2} + .369\epsilon_{t-3} + \cdots \qquad (A.51)$$

When we insert the same summation on the right side of equation A.46, lag all the shocks either one or two times, and put in the values for the first several values of alpha, we obtain the term

$$.9[\epsilon_{t-1} + .9\epsilon_{t-2} + .61\epsilon_{t-3} + \cdots] \qquad (A.52)$$

$$- .2[\epsilon_{t-2} + .9\epsilon_{t-3} + .61\epsilon_{t-4} + \cdots] + \epsilon_t$$

$$= .9\epsilon_{t-1} + (.81 - .2)\epsilon_{t-2} + (.549 - .18)\epsilon_{t-3} + \cdots + \epsilon_t$$

$$= \epsilon_t + .9\epsilon_{t-1} + .61\epsilon_{t-2} + .369\epsilon_{t-3} + \cdots$$

The equality for the rest of the coefficients follows. Thus, this stochastic part of the solution holds as well.

We study the stochastic second-order difference equation in equation A.46 in more detail when we discuss solving stochastic difference equations. We will graph some of its solutions there. For now, note that, if the variance of ϵ_t is small relative to the size of the deterministic terms, the latter will dominate the solution's early behavior. But then, as these deterministic terms decay, the stochastic trend will dominate the behavior of the solution.

We have seen that the solutions to difference equation models can imply distinctive dynamics. The solutions in Examples A.1 and A.3 were time functions that diverged or increased without bound over time. The solution in Example A.2 also diverged, but in an oscillatory fashion. Convergence to a fixed equilibrium was implied by the solution in Example A.4. And the models in Examples A.5 and A.6 implied that the solutions were composed of stochastic trends. These six examples thus show how simple models can have very different dynamic implications and, in the case of the stochastic trends, produce patterns of social behavior that can easily be misinterpreted. Studying difference equations helps us understand what is implicit in our models at the same time that it illuminates potentially useful ideas like that of a stochastic trend. Learning to solve difference equations therefore can be of much value. The solutions illuminate the deeper nature of social processes, a nature that is not immediately clear from the difference equation itself.

Example A.7: A System of Deterministic Difference Equations
All the equations we studied thus far assume that a variable evolves according to an endogenous process such as bureaucratic inertia and/or by an exogenous forcing function. But as we noted in the introduction to this Appendix, many social processes are characterized by mutual causation and feedback. International relations and societal conflict processes are illustrative. Nation-states reciprocate each others' actions, and societal conflict is an outgrowth of the two-way causation between rebellion and repression.

Consider the following system of deterministic difference equations:

$$US_{t+1} = .9US_t + C_t + t. \tag{A.53}$$
$$C_{t+1} = .9C_t + .1US_t.$$

We might think of this system as a model of naval arms spending between the United States and China. U.S. spending at time $t + 1$ is a function of its immediate past spending (with allowance for dismantling of some obsolete navel armaments), Chinese spending, and a time trend (to represent cost inflation and, perhaps, a desire on the part of the United States to become hegemonic in Asia). The Chinese military might not emphasize naval operations, but China still may continue 90% of its past spending and also try to match 10% of U.S. spending. Finally, say that at the start of this rivalry the United States and China spent 50 and 20 billion dollars, respectively, on naval armaments.[22]

The time functions that solve both equations *simultaneously* and, at the same time, preserve the initial conditions are

$$US_t = 67.3168(1.2162)^t - 3.738(.5838)^t - 1.1112t - 13.58 \tag{A.54}$$

and

$$C_t = 21.287(1.2162)^t + 1.182(.5838)^t - 1.1112t - 2.469. \tag{A.55}$$

---

[22] So, in terms of the scaling used in the equations, each year, 1 additional billion of nominal U.S. dollars is committed to U.S. naval expenditure as embodied in t.

As regards the initial conditions, set $t = 0$ in both these equations. This yields

$$US_t = 67.3168(1) - 3.738(1) - 1.1112(0) - 13.58 = 50. \qquad (A.56)$$

$$C_t = 21.287(1) + 1.1820 - 1.1112(0) - 2.4689 = 20.$$

Hence we know this pair of time functions satisfy the conditions $US_0 = 50$ and $C_0 = 20$.

Next consider the second equation in the system. The expression of the left side of the equality is the time function for C_t evaluated at $t + 1$; that is,

$$C_{t+1} = 21.287(1.2162)^{t+1} + 1.182(.5838)^{t+1} - 1.1112(t + 1) - 2.4689$$

$$= 21.387(1.2162)(1.2162)^t + 1.182(.5838)(.5838)^t$$

$$- 1.1112(1) - 1.1112t - 2.4689$$

$$= 25.8898(1.2162)^t + .69(.5838)^t - 1.1112t - 3.580. \qquad (A.57)$$

Now, on the right side of the second equation in equation A.53, we have a weighted sum of the two solutions:

$$.9C_t + .10US_t = 19.1583(1.2162)^t + 1.0638(.5838)^t - 1.0008t - 2.222$$

$$+ 6.7317(1.2162)^t - .3738(.5838)^t - .1112t - 1.358$$

$$= 25.8898(1.2162)^t + .69(.5838)^t - 1.1112t - .3580. \qquad (A.58)$$

But this is exactly equal to C_{t+1}. We leave it to the readers to convince themselves that when the two solutions are substituted into the first equation in the system, an equality also is established. Figure A.7 depicts the behavior of this rivalry system. Notice that as time increases the second term in the solutions disappears, and the depressing effect of the trend term in the solution also dissipates. Naval arms spending by both countries eventually rises exponentially, although the level of U.S. spending far exceeds that of China.

A.3 FINDING THE SOLUTIONS OF DIFFERENCE EQUATION MODELS

Much has been written in mathematics and other fields about how to solve difference equations. Here we review some of the most parsimonious results and methods. The idea is to give readers a sense of the explanatory power of existing solutions to certain kinds of difference equations and also of what is involved in solving more complex difference equations.

A.3.1 Solving the Most Simple First-Order Difference Equations

Examples A.1, A.2, and A.4 illustrated solutions of one of the most simple models: the first-order, linear deterministic difference equation with constant coefficients and either a constant or stochastic variable (forcing function) on

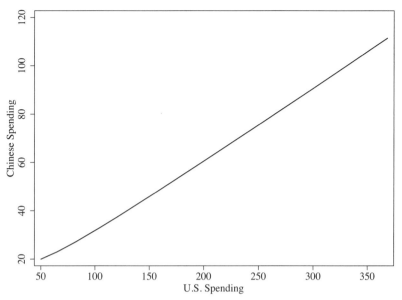

FIGURE A.7. Example A.7.

the right-hand side. This simple model has been used to explain a number of important social processes such as the changing level of party control over seats in the U.S. House of Representatives (Gilmour and Rothstein, 1993; Sprague, 1981) and fluctuations in the partisan makeup of the American electorate (Erikson, MacKuen, and Stimson 2002). Let us write this equation in the general form

$$y_{t+1} = Ay_t + B \tag{A.59}$$

where A and B are constant coefficients and the initial condition for y_t is known to be a constant denoted by C.[23]
    We now illustrate the method of iteration or of recursive substitution. Suppose we know the initial value of the time series, y_0. Then, if the difference equation is true, at $t = 1$ we know

$$y_1 = Ay_0 + B. \tag{A.60}$$

---

[23] This form of the model can be obtained from those in the examples by applying the E operator to both sides of the equations. Take the model in Example A.1. We have

$$E[y_t] = E[2y_{t-1} + 1]$$
$$y_{t+1} = 2y_{t-1+1} + 1$$
$$= 2y_t + 1.$$

Also at $t = 2$ it must be true that

$$y_2 = Ay_1 + B. \tag{A.61}$$

But we know the value of y_1, so we can substitute it in the equation for y_2:

$$y_2 = A[Ay_0 + B] + B = A^2 y_0 + AB + B = A^2 y_0 + B(1 + A). \tag{A.62}$$

By the same logic, we have for $t = 3$

$$y_3 = A[A^2 y_0 + B(1 + A)] + B = A^3 y_0 + B(1 + A + A^2). \tag{A.63}$$

In this way we can show that at t,

$$y_t = A^t y_0 + B(1 + A + A^2 + \cdots + A^{t-1}). \tag{A.64}$$

When A is not equal to 1, the factor on the right that multiplies B is a geometric series. Hence we know its sum is $\frac{1-A^t}{1-A}$.[24] When $A = 1$ the quantity in this same factor amounts to adding the value of 1 t times. So it adds to t. Thus we have found the solution of a first-order deterministic difference equation with constant coefficients with a known initial value of y_0:

$$y_t = \begin{cases} y_0 A^t + B\left(\frac{1-A^t}{1-A}\right) & \text{if} \quad A \neq 1 \\ y_0 + Bt & \text{if} \quad A = 1 \end{cases} . \tag{A.65}$$

This result is easy to apply. Consider Example A.1. In this case we have $A = 2$, $B = 1$, $y_0 = 5$. So the solution is

$$y_t = 5 \times 2^t + 1\left(\frac{1-2^t}{1-2}\right) \tag{A.66}$$

$$y_t = 6 \times 2^t - 1.$$

This is the time function we analyzed earlier. Example A.2 also is a first-order deterministic difference equation with constant coefficients. For this equation we have $A = -2$, $B = 1$, and $y_0 = 0$. Applying the solution in equation A.66 we obtain

$$y_t = 0(-2)^t + 1\left[\frac{1-(-2)^t}{1-2}\right] \tag{A.67}$$

$$y_t = .33 - .33(-2)^t.$$

It turns out that if we know the values of the time function at any point(s) in time, then, using this information, we can obtain a *unique* solution to the difference equation. Return to Example A.3. We derived a general solution to this time function in terms of an unknown constant, C. There are many solutions to the difference equations depending on the value of C we prescribed. But once we set the value of C, there is one and only one solution of the

---

[24] See footnote 11.

respective, first-order, deterministic difference equation. This result generalizes to higher order difference equations of this type.[25]

It is possible to characterize fully the dynamics implied by this difference equation. Consider the case where $A \neq 1$ and note that the solution of this difference equation can be rewritten as

$$y_t = A^t y_0 + \frac{B}{1-A} - \frac{B}{1-A} A^t \tag{A.68}$$

$$= A^t (y_0 - \frac{B}{1-A}) + \frac{B}{1-A}.$$

Let $y^* = \frac{B}{1-A}$. Then we have a new expression for our solution:

$$y_t = A^t (y_0 - y^*) + y^* \tag{A.69}$$

Using this new variable, $y^* = \frac{B}{1-A}$, we can categorize all the different conditions we might encounter for this difference equation, as well as the dynamics of the respective solutions. Table A.2 summarizes this information.[26]

Consider Example A.1. In this case $A > 1, y^* = \frac{1}{1-2} = -1$, and $y_0 = 5$. So row two in Table A.2 applies. We obtained a time function that increased without bound. In Example A.2, $A < -1, y^* = \frac{1}{1-2} = .33$ and $y_0 = 0$. So, in this case, row eight applies; we obtained a time function that oscillates without bound. Students of the U.S. Congress argue that models in rows four and five best describe party competition and retirement propensities. They fit the difference equation to data for the U.S. Congress and then derive values for y^*, values that connote the long-term party seat balance toward which the House of Representatives gravitates in particular periods of American political history.

The same method can be used to solve first-order stochastic difference equations. Take Example A.5. Say we know at $t = 0$ that $y_t = y_0$. Then starting again at $t = 1$ we have

$$y_1 = y_0 + \epsilon_1 \tag{A.70}$$

$$y_2 = y_1 + \epsilon_2 = (y_0 + \epsilon_1) + \epsilon_2 \tag{A.71}$$

$$y_3 = y_2 + \epsilon_3 = (y_0 + \epsilon_1 + \epsilon_2) + \epsilon_3. \tag{A.72}$$

---

[25] Here is the theorem from Goldberg (1986, section 2.3): The linear difference equation of order n $f_0 y_t + n + \cdots + f_n y_t = g(t)$ over a set S of consecutive integer values of t has one and only one solution y_t for which values at n consecutive t-values are arbitrarily prescribed. By prescribed we usually mean known or given values. These values need not be the initial value and the set S need not begin at $t = 0$.

[26] For a development of the same results in terms of the concept of a linear recurrence, see Cull, Flahive, and Robson (2005, 34–36) and Elaydi (1999, chapter 1).

TABLE A.2. *The Solution to the First Order Deterministic Difference Equations with Constant Coefficients A and B and initial condition y_0. Reprinted with permission by Dover Publications, Inc. from Goldberg (1986:84). In Goldberg's analysis the equation is defined for a set of k values; in time series analysis k is an ordered time unit, t.*

	Hypotheses				Conclusions
Row	A	B	y_0	For $t = 1, 2, 3 \ldots$	The sequence $\{y_t\}$ is
(a)	$A \neq 1$		$y_0 = y^*$	$y_t = y^*$	constant
(b)	$A > 1$		$y_0 > y^*$	$y_t > y^*$	monotone increasing; diverges to $+\infty$
(c)	$A > 1$		$y_0 < y^*$	$y_t < y^*$	monotone decreasing; diverges to $-\infty$
(d)	$0 < A < 1$		$y_0 > y^*$	$y_t > y^*$	monotone decreasing; converges to y^*
(e)	$0 < A < 1$		$y_0 < y^*$	$y_t < y^*$	monotone increasing; converges to limit y^*
(f)	$-1 < A < 0$		$y_0 \neq y^*$		dampened oscillatory; converges to limit y^*
(g)	$A = -1$		$y_0 \neq y^*$		divergent; oscillates finitely
(h)	$A < -1$		$y_0 \neq y^*$		divergent; oscillates infinitely
(i)	$A = 1$	$B = 0$		$y_t = y_0$	constant
(j)	$A = 1$	$B > 0$		$y_t > y_0$	monotone increasing; diverges to $+\infty$
(k)	$A = 1$	$B < 0$		$y_t < y_0$	monotone decreasing; diverges to $-\infty$

If we continue with the recursive substitution we eventually obtain

$$y_t = y_0 + \epsilon_1 + \cdots + \epsilon_t = y_0 + \sum_{i=1}^{t} \epsilon_i. \tag{A.73}$$

This is the solution we obtained earlier. It implies that, at any point in time, the solution is a sum of the initial value and the (unweighted) sequence of shocks the process has experienced. Is it a "unique" solution? Note in the sense that there is one and only one time function that solves it for a given initial condition. This is because the stochastic trend term will be different for each set of draws of ϵ_i. Some students of American politics argue that macropartisanship is just such a "running tally" of various kinds of shocks.[27]

---

[27] See the debate between Green et al. and Erikson et al. about the nature of macropartisanship in the 1998 issue of the *American Political Science Review*, 92(4): 883–900 and 901–912, respectively.

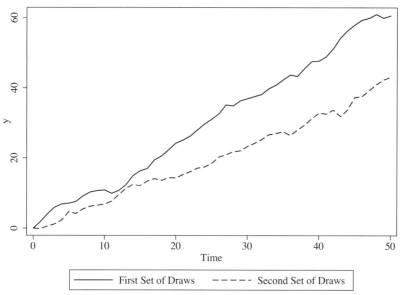

FIGURE A.8. First Order Stochastic Difference Equation With a Deterministic Trend.

Suppose we had included a constant in the equation in Example A.5. Say this constant is 1 so that the first-order stochastic difference equation now is

$$y_t = 1 + y_{t-1} + \epsilon_t. \tag{A.74}$$

The solution to equation A.74 is

$$y_t = y_0 + t + \sum_{i=1}^{t} \epsilon_i. \tag{A.75}$$

And now we have two trends: one deterministic and the other stochastic. At any point in time the series is the sum of the initial value, t incremental increases of one unit each, and (all) the (unweighted) sum of the shocks it has experienced. Figure A.8 depicts this time function for the case in which $y_0 = 0$. Notice how the sequences steadily increase at the same time that they wander about the time counter. How they wander depends on the sequence (sums) of shocks they experience in each of the two cases.

The general form of the first order stochastic difference equation is

$$y_t = b + a y_{t-1} + \epsilon_t. \tag{A.76}$$

For a known initial condition, y_0, this equation has the solution

$$y_t = b \sum_{i=0}^{t-1} a^i + a^t y_0 + \sum_{i=0}^{t-1} a^i \epsilon_{t-i}. \tag{A.77}$$

If you look closely you can see the parts that derive from the deterministic part of the equation in the first and second terms on the right side of equation A.76. The stochastic element results in the weighted sum of shocks that is the third term of the solution. That is, if we dropped the ϵ_t from the general expression in equation A.76, we would have the deterministic case. In addition, we could apply the formulas for the sum of a geometric series to the first sum on the right side of the solution. For example, assume $|a| < 1$. Then it follows that as t goes to infinity

$$\lim y_t = \frac{b}{1-a} + \sum_{i=0}^{\infty} a^i \epsilon_{t-i}. \tag{A.78}$$

Under the assumption that $|a| < 1$, a^i will get smaller and smaller; hence, the initial condition eventually will disappear from the solution and distant shocks will produce less and less influence on the current value of y_t. Finally, note that because the numerator of the quotient is on the right side of equation A.78, the constant in the original equation, b, helps define the long-term value toward which y_t moves.[28]

A.3.2 Solving More Complicated Difference Equations

All of the equations studied thus far are first order in nature. They also have a constant or a simple stochastic term on their right-hand sides. But when modeling social processes, scholars often put a time counter in their equations to control for such elements as economic and demographic trends. Many times they also include multiple lags of their endogenous variable to capture such processes as bureaucratic inertia and social memory. As we will see, such equations imply richer dynamics than those we have studied so far.

To solve more complex equations of these kinds, a multistep procedure normally is used. This procedure breaks the difference equation into parts, finds the solutions associated with each part, adds these solutions together, and then reconciles the initial conditions.[29]

The Deterministic Case
Recall the distinction between the homogeneous and nonhomogeneous type of difference equation. The former is written only in terms of the variable(s) of

---

[28] A good exposition of this model can be found in Enders (2010, 10–11, also 54–55). Note that Enders labels the coefficients in the model a_0 and a_1, whereas we use a and b to underscore the connection between the first-order deterministic and stochastic cases.

[29] The mathematical basis for this approach is developed by Goldberg (1986, sections 3.1 and 3.2). See also Cull, Flahive, and Robson (2005, section 3.2).

interest; the latter contains additional time functions and variables. An example of a first-order, nonhomogeneous deterministic equation is

$$y_{t+1} + Ay_t = R_t \tag{A.79}$$

where R_t is some unspecified time function. The second-order, nonhomogeneous deterministic case can be written as

$$y_{t+2} + A_1 y_{t+1} + A_2 y_t = R_t \tag{A.80}$$

where R_t again is an unspecified time function.

To solve nonhomogeneous deterministic difference equations such as these, we proceed as follows:

1. Find the solutions of the homogeneous part of the equation.
2. Find a particular solution for the nonhomogeneous form of the equation.
3. Add these solutions together to form what we will call the total solution.
4. Find the values of the coefficients in this total solution that make the initial conditions true.
5. Analyze the limiting behavior of this final, total solution.[30]

The procedure is relatively easy to illustrate for the first-order and second-order cases. These cases employ mathematical tools that should be familiar to most readers.

Example A.8

Consider a first-order deterministic difference equation with constant coefficients for which R_t includes the time counter, t. Such counters are frequently used in macro social science research to represent long-term factors or deterministic trends in in a variable; for instance, the cumulative effects of technological innovation on economic variables. An equation of this form is

$$y_{t+1} = .2y_t + t + 1. \tag{A.81}$$

We can rewrite this equation as

$$y_{t+1} - .2y_t = t + 1. \tag{A.82}$$

---

[30] Goldberg (1986, 122ff) explains why the sum of solutions of a difference equation is itself a solution. He also explains why the sum of the general solution(s) of the homogeneous version of the equation and the particular solution of the complete version includes *all* the solutions of the equation. (What is confusing in Goldberg's explanation is that he uses the term "particular" both to describe the solutions of the homogeneous and complete equation [e.g., on page 140–141]). Finally, to ensure that unique solutions can be found for the initial conditions, a condition regarding the initial values of the solutions must hold. In the case of the second-order determinisitic equation with solutions $y^1(t)$, $y^2(t)$ condition this is $y_0^{(1)} y_1^{(2)} - y_0^{(2)} y_1^{(1)} \neq 0$ where $y_i^{(j)}$, $i, j = 1, 2$ are the solutions of the homogeneous equation evaluated at $t = 0, 1$. See also Elaydi (1999, chapter 2).

Its homogeneous form is

$$y_{t+1} - .2y_t = 0. \tag{A.83}$$

We then study the corresponding characteristic equation. It is simply a polynomial of the same order and with the same coefficients as those of the homogeneous equation. In the present example, we are working with a first-order equation. So the characteristic equation is

$$r - .2 = 0. \tag{A.84}$$

The "root" of this characteristic equation is .2; $r = .2$ makes the expression above true. The general solution, what we will call Y_t, then is $C(.2)^t$ where C is an unknown constant. If you substitute this time function back into the homogeneous equation, you will see that, just as in Example A.4, this Y_t solves it.[31]

Denote the particular solution by y^*. Finding y^* for the complete equation is a bit more challenging. The method of undetermined coefficients often is used for this purpose. These rules have been developed to aid in the process: (a) the trial time function for the particular solution should be of the same functional form as the right-hand time function R_t unless (b) there is a relationship between the roots of the characteristic function and this trial solution. More specifically, if the initial trial solution has the same root(s) as the characteristic equation, the trial function should be multiplied by t. For instance, if R_t is a constant, then the trial solution is also a constant. If R_t is a time counter, t, then the trial solution is $A_0 + A_1 t + A_2 t^2 + + \cdots + A_n t^n$.[32]

Return to the present example. In this case, $R_t = t + 1$ and the root of the characteristic equation is, as we found, .2. So we try a trial particular solution of $A_0 + A_1 t$. Substitute this into the complete equation, A.82, and collect terms:

$$[A_0 + A_1(t + 1)] - .2[A_0 + A_1 t] = t + 1 \tag{A.85}$$

$$(A_1 - .2A_1)t + (A_1 + A_0 - .2A_0) = t + 1$$

$$(.8A_1)t + (A_1 + .8A_0) = t + 1.$$

Note that in this R_t the coefficient on t is 1 and the constant also is 1. Therefore, if we equate these coefficients, we know that $.8A_1 = 1$ and $(A_1 + .8A_0) = 1$. The first equality implies that $A_1 = 1.25$. Using this fact, we find that $(1.25 + .8A_0) = 1$ or A_0 must be $-.3125$. From this result, it follows that the particular solution is $y^* = 1.25t - .3125$.

---

[31] For instance, for a general second-order homogeneous difference equation of the form $ay_{t+2} + by_{t+1} + cy_t$ where a, b, and c are constants, the characteristic equation would be $ar^2 + br + c$.

[32] If R_t is a constant, c, raised to the t power, c^t, then the initial trial solution is Ac^t. For other trial solutions for other R_t's see Goldberg (1986, section 3.4). An example of the need to adjust the trial solution is when R_t is 2^t and 2 is a root of the homogeneous equation. Then the trial solution is $At2^t$.

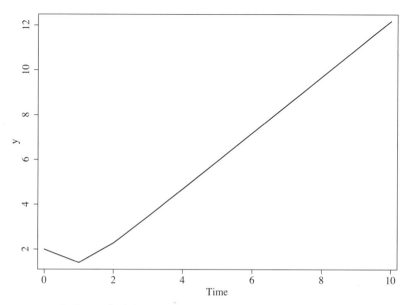

FIGURE A.9. Example A.8.

Finally, we add Y_t and y^* to obtain the total solution to equation A.81: $y_t = C(.2)^t + 1.25t - 3.125$. Say that the initial value of the time function is known to be 2. Then it is easy to solve for C:

$$2 = C(.2)^0 + 1.25(0) - .3125 \tag{A.86}$$

$$2 = C - .3125$$

$$2.3125 = C$$

Thus the solution to the complete equation with the indicated initial condition is $y_t = 2.3125(.2)^t + 1.25t - .3125$. As time increases the first term decays because $(.2)^t$ decays to zero; the time function is dominated by the time counter, which increases without bound as shown in Figure A.9.

Again, social scientists often use equations with more than one lag of their endogenous variables, and they often use difference equations of a higher order. The second-order case illustrates what is involved in unlocking the dynamics of these more complex equations. The characteristic equations for them are second-order polynomials. In fact, they are the familiar quadratic equations. As such, we can use the quadratic formula to find their roots. There are three possibilities: the roots are unequal, equal, or imaginary. The general solution for the homogeneous equation for second-order difference equations varies depending on which one of these three possibilities arises. To be specific, if the roots are real and not equal,

$$Y_t = C_1(r_1)^t + C_2(r_2)^t; \tag{A.87}$$

if the roots are real and equal,

$$Y_t = C_1(r_1)^t + C_2 t(r_2)^t; \tag{A.88}$$

and if the roots are imaginary,

$$Y_t = Am^t \cos(t\theta + B), \tag{A.89}$$

where r_1, r_2 are the two roots of the second-order polynomial corresponding to the characteristic equation of the second-order difference equation in equation A.80; C_1, C_2, A, and B are unknown constants; and m is the modulus and θ the angle from the imaginary roots in their polar form.[33]
The next few examples illustrate each of these possibilities.

Example A.3 Revisited
Using the E operator we can rewrite equation A.31 as

$$y_{t+2} - 3y_{t+1} + 2y_t = -1 \tag{A.90}$$

The homogeneous equation implies the following characteristic equation:

$$r^2 - 3r + 2 = (r - 1)(r - 2) = 0 \tag{A.91}$$

So the two, real unequal roots are 1 and 2. Hence the general solution for this equation is $Y_t = C_1(1)^t + C_2(2)^t$ or, more simply, $Y_t = C_1 + C_2(2)^t$. The special rule about the trial solution applies here because the root is 1 and $R_t = 1$. Hence, for the particular solution, we try $t \times 1 = t$. Substituting this function into the complete equation we have

$$(t + 2) - 3(t + 1) + 2t = -1 \tag{A.92}$$
$$t + 2 - 3t - 3 + 2t = -1.$$

Thus we have shown that $y^* = t$. The total solution is $y_t = C_1 + C_2(2)^t + t$. Example A.3 prescribed initial conditions of $y_0 = -3$ and $y_1 = 5$. These conditions imply certain values for C_1 and C_2. To find these values, we evaluate the total solution at $t = 0, 1$. For $t = 0$ we have

$$y_0 = -3 = C_1 + C_2(2)^0 + 0 = C_1 + C_2. \tag{A.93}$$

For $t = 1$, we have

$$y_1 = 5 = C_1 + 2C_2(2)^1 + 1 = C_1 + 2C_2 + 1 \tag{A.94}$$

Thus, we obtain two equations and two unknowns. The solution to this system of equations is $C_1 = -10$ and $C_2 = 7$. In this way we have found the unique time function that solves our equation: it is unique in the sense that it alone produces the prescribed initial conditions. This time function is:

---

[33] Recall that if a polynomial has the conjugate, imaginary roots a±bi, these roots can be written as $m(\cos\theta + i\sin\theta)$ where m = $\sqrt{a^2 + b^2}$ and $\cos\theta = \frac{a}{m}, \sin\theta = \frac{b}{m}$, and $-\pi \leq \theta \leq \pi$.

$y_t = -10 + 7(2)^t + t$. In fact, we verified this in Example A.3. Again, we have a time function that increases without bound (see Figure A.4).

Example A.9

An illustration of a second-order deterministic difference equation of the first type that implies convergent, stable behavior is the following:

$$y_{t+2} = -.6y_{t+1} + .07y_t + 1.53. \tag{A.95}$$

The homogeneous equation in this case is

$$y_{t+2} + .6y_{t+1} - .07y_t = 0 \tag{A.96}$$

So the characteristic equation is

$$r^2 + .6r - .07 = (r - .1)(r + .7). \tag{A.97}$$

The general solution therefore is of the form $C_1(.1)^t + C_2(-.7)^t$. Because here R_t is a constant and it is neither $.10$ nor $-.7$, we try a constant as a trial, particular solution and find that $y^* = 1$.[34] So the total solution is simply $C_1(.1)^t + C_2(-.7)^t + 1$. Suppose that $y_0 = 0$ and $y_1 = 2$. Then, we again have two equations and two unknowns:

$$y_0 = 0 = C_1(.1)^0 + C_2(-.7)^0 + 1 = C_1 + C_2 + 1. \tag{A.98}$$

$$y_1 = 2 = C_1(.1)^1 + C_2(-.7)^1 + 1 = .1C_1 - .7C_2 + 1. \tag{A.99}$$

The solution to this system of equation is $C_1 = .375, C_2 = -1.375$. For these prescribed initial conditions then, the time function $y_t = .375(.1)^t - 1.375(-.7)^t + 1$ solves the complete equation. As Figure A.10 shows, the behavior of this time function is quite different from the one that solves Example A.3. Rather than increasing without bound, the solution here converges to 1 in a nonmonotonic (oscillatory) fashion.

Example A.10

To illustrate the case of a second-order deterministic difference equation with repeated real roots, consider the following expression:

$$y_{t+2} = .8y_{t+1} - .16y_t + 2t. \tag{A.100}$$

To begin, note that this equation can be rewritten as

$$y_{t+2} - .8y_{t+1} + .16y_t = 2t. \tag{A.101}$$

Its homogeneous form implies the characteristic equation

$$r^2 - .8r + .16r = (r - .4)(r - .4) = 0. \tag{A.102}$$

Hence the general solution is $Y_t = C_1(.4)^t + C_2t(.4)^t = (C_1 + C_2t)(.4)^t$. Because the time function on the right side of equation A.101 is a simple

---

[34] This is easy to verify. Putting 1 into the complete equation we have $1 + .6 - .07 = 1.53$.

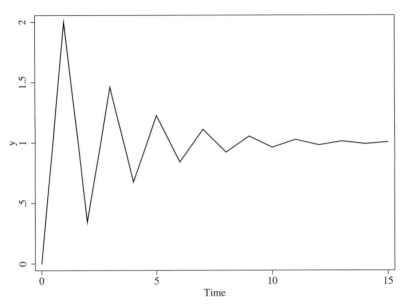

FIGURE A.10. Example A.9.

time counter or first-order polynomial in t, we use the trial particular solution of $A_0 + A_1 t$. Substituting this trial solution into the complete equation yields

$$[A_0 + A_1(t + 2)] - .8[A_0 + A_1(t + 1)] + .16[A_0 + A_1 t] = 2t$$
$$(A_1 - .8A_1 + .16A_1)t + (A_0 + 2A_1 - .8A_0 - .8A_1 + .16A_0) = 2t$$
$$(.36A_1)t + (.36A_0 + 1.2A_1) = 2t. \quad \text{(A.103)}$$

Now equate the coefficients on each side of the above equality. The coefficient on t on the right is 2, so A_1 must be 5.55. The constant on the right side is zero. This means, that if A_1 is 5.55, A_0 must be -18.52. The total solution for this example therefore is $y_t = (C_1 + C_2 t)(.4)^t + 5.55t - 18.25$. Say that we know $y_0 = 0$ and $y_1 = 1$. Then $0 = C_1 - 18.25$ so C_1 is 18.52. Using this value of C_1, we know $1 = (C_1 + C_2)(.4) + 5.55 - 18.52 = (18.52 + C_2)(.4) - 12.97$. It follows that C_2 must equal 16.405. So, for these initial conditions, we have $y_t = (18.52 + 16.405t)(.4)^t + 5.55t - 18.52$. Once again we have a time function in which the first term gradually decays, but the second term increases without bound as we show in Figure A.11.[35]

---

[35] As regards the term $16.405(.4)^t$, it can be shown that the function $t^n n^t \to 0$ for any positive integer t if the absolute value of n is less than 1. Goldberg (1986) cites Hardy (1949) for a demonstration.

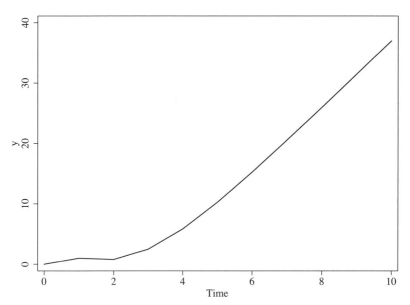

FIGURE A.11. Example A.10.

Example A.11

Finally, suppose the characteristic function for our second-order deterministic homogeneous equation has imaginary roots. This final example illustrates this case. Consider the equation

$$y_{t+2} = -y_t + t. \tag{A.104}$$

The homogeneous equation then is

$$y_{t+2} + y_t = 0. \tag{A.105}$$

And the characteristic equation is

$$r^2 + 1 = (r - i)(r + i) = 0, \tag{A.106}$$

where $i = \sqrt{-1}$. This means that the polar coordinates are zero and 1. The modulus is $\sqrt{0^2 + 1^2} = 1$. We also know that $\cos\theta = \frac{0}{1} = 0$ and $\sin\theta = \frac{1}{1} = 1$. So, $\theta = \frac{\pi}{2}$. The general solution therefore has the form $Y_t = A(1)\cos(\frac{\pi t}{2} + B)$. Because we have t on the right side of the complete equation in A.104, we again use as our trial solution, $A_0 + A_1 t$. This yields

$$[A_0 + A_1(t + 2)] + [A_0 + A_1 t] = t \tag{A.107}$$

$$2A_1 t + (2A_0 + 2A_1) = t.$$

Equating the coefficients so that t is multiplied by 1 and the constant is zero on the left side of the equality, we find that $A_0 = -.5$ and $A_1 = .5$. So the

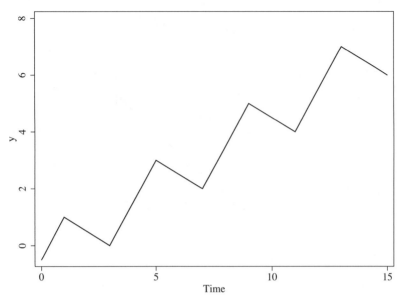

FIGURE A.12. Example A.11.

particular solution in this case is $y^* = -.5 + .5t$. The total solution therefore is

$$y_t = A\cos\left(\frac{\pi t}{2} + B\right) + .5t - .5 \qquad (A.108)$$

Say that we know $y_0 = -.5$ and $y_1 = 1$. Then it follows that

$$-.5 = A\cos(B) - .5 \qquad (A.109)$$
$$0 = A\cos(B).$$

Hence $B = \frac{\pi}{2}$. Turning to the second initial condition for which $t = 1$, we have

$$1 = A\cos\left(\frac{\pi}{2} + \frac{\pi}{2}\right) + .5 - .5 = A\cos(\pi) = -A \qquad (A.110)$$

This implies that $A = -1$. So, under the prescribed initial conditions the total solution is $y_t = -\cos(\frac{\pi t}{2} + \frac{\pi}{2}) + .5t - .5$. But $\cos(\theta + \frac{\pi}{2}) = -\sin\theta$. So we can rewrite the final solution as $y_t = \sin(\frac{\pi t}{2}) + .5t - .5$. Interestingly this is a time function that oscillates around an increasing trend; see Figure A.12.[36]

---

[36] To show that this time function solves the respective complete equation, use the facts that $\cos(\theta + \pi) = -\cos(\theta)$, $\sin(\theta + \pi) = -\sin\theta$, and $\cos(\alpha + \beta) = \cos(\alpha)\cos(\beta) - \sin(\alpha)\sin(\beta)$ and $\cos(\frac{t}{2} + \pi) = -\cos(\frac{t}{2})$ and $\sin(\frac{t}{2} + \pi) = -\sin(\frac{t}{2})$.

In theory, higher order deterministic difference equations are solved in the same way. Consider an equation of order n:

$$y_{t+n} + a_1 y_{t+n-1} + \cdots + a_n y_t = R_t \tag{A.111}$$

The homogeneous form of this equation produces a characteristic equation of the form:

$$r^n + a_1 r^{n-1} + \cdots + a_n = 0 \tag{A.112}$$

This equation has n roots. They all could be real and equal. Some of them could be real and repeated. There could be one or more pairs of imaginary roots. For instance, say that all the roots are real and that one of of them is repeated p times; the n-p remaining roots are real and distinct. Denote the repeated root by r_1 and the others by $r_2, \ldots, r_{n-p+1}$. Then the general solution will have a component of the form $A_1 r_1^t + A_2 t r_1^t + A_2 t^2 r_1^t + \cdots + A_p t^{p-1} r_1^t$. Otherwise the general solution will be composed of terms for each of the other (real, unequal) roots raised to the power of t. If, in the complete equation, R_t is a constant, the particular solution will be a constant. If R_t contains a time trend, an expression like bt, the total solution will include an additional trend.[37]

Practically speaking, solving such equations is tedious. The multiple roots of the homogeneous equation must be found. Methods such as undetermined coefficients require a great deal of algebra. Whether alternative approaches such as transform methods are preferable depends on the problem at hand.[38]

As regards the qualitative behavior of the solutions of higher order systems, there are some results for the homogeneous and special complete equations. If the roots are real and distinct, for instance, the general solution of the homogeneous equation will converge to a constant value (regardless of the initial conditions), if the roots are all less than 1 in absolute value. A sufficient condition for stability of this kind is that the sum of the absolute values of the coefficients of the homogeneous equation be less than one. But, once more, when there is a time trend on the right-hand-side of the complete equation, as there often is in social science models, the total solution will have a time trend. *The important point is that when one writes down a deterministic difference equation of a high order, one is allowing for a solution composed of one or more kinds of time functions, some of which could exhibit qualitatively*

---

[37] See Enders (2010, section 7) for a discussion of the higher order deterministic case when R_t is a constant or a time trend. Goldberg (1986, 163–165) solves some illustrative third- and fourth-order cases. He also derives the conditions on the initial values of the total solution so that it is possible to satisfy the initial conditions of the solution. A theorem about the form of the solutions for the general case in which R_t is a polynomial in t is proved by Cull, Flahive, and Robson (2005, section 3.3). See also Elaydi (1999, chapter 2).

[38] These methods transform the difference equation from its time domain to a form in which the domain is the complex plane, solves the equation in the complex plane, and then transforms the solution back into the time domain. See, for instance, Muth (1977, esp. chapters 4–6) and Elaydi (1999, chapter 5).

distinct kinds of behavior. Exactly what combination of dynamics is implied, as we have seen, depends on the coefficients in the equation and the assumed form of the forcing function, R_t.[39]

The Stochastic Case

Recall that these equations have a stochastic term in R_t. They also can be solved with the method of undetermined coefficients. The trial solution for the particular solution must include a stochastic trend term; more specifically, a term that represents a weighted sum of past realizations of the random variable. The interpretation of and solution for the initial conditions are more complex than for deterministic difference equations. Technically, the initial condition is itself the sum of previous values of the time function and of realizations of the stochastic variable for $t < 0$. For example, in equation A.74, we have

$$y_0 = 1 + y_{-1} + \epsilon_0. \tag{A.113}$$

Enders (2010, chapter 1) shows how, if there is no knowledge about the value of the initial condition, the method of backward iteration can produce a particular solution for y_t that includes a sum of realizations an infinite number of steps back into time, including time before $t = 0$. He then shows how to reconcile this solution for y_t with a known initial condition. In so doing, it is possible to produce a unique total solution to the stochastic difference equation for the respective initial condition, a solution that includes a stochastic trend that is the sum of realizations from the order of the difference equation plus one forward to t.

To illustrate how one solves such equations, reconsider Example A.6.[40] The equation of interest is

$$y_t = 3 + .9y_{t-1} - .2y_{t-2} + \epsilon_t. \tag{A.114}$$

For instance, equation A.114 might be a model of government spending, y_t, in billions of U.S. dollars; it says that spending at time t is always equal to a fixed amount, 3 billion, plus .9 time the previous level of spending, minus .2 times the level of spending two periods prior to the present, plus a shock due to such factors as good or bad weather (the presence or absence of natural

---

[39] Goldberg (1986, sections 3.5 and 4.1) derives some stability conditions for second-order deterministic homogeneous difference equations. Technically, his theorem about the conditions under which solution of the homogeneous equation always converges to a fixed value is framed in terms of the size of the root with the largest absolute value (that this root's absolute value be less than one). Enders (2010, chapter 1) provides a geometric interpretation of this second-order case. He also summarizes some conditions that apply to the coefficients in the general deterministic homogeneous difference equation that are necessary and sufficient to ensure stability in the sense of convergence to a fixed value. In this context he introduces the idea of representing the roots on the unit circle. Cull, Flahive, and Robson (2005, appendix D) summarize and illustrate Marden's method for finding the number of roots for any polynomials that are in the unit circle.

[40] Recall that this example is taken from Enders (2010, 38–39).

disasters that require government to spend unexpectedly more or less to help citizens in a given time period). Equation A.114 can be rewritten as

$$y_t - .9y_{t-1} + .2y_{t-2} = 3 + \epsilon_t. \tag{A.115}$$

So the homogeneous equation is

$$r^2 - .9r + .2r = (r - .4)(r - .5). \tag{A.116}$$

Hence the general solution is $Y_t = C_1(.4)^t + C_2(.5)^t$. The forcing function in this example is composed of a constant and a stochastic term. Let us solve for the former first. Because 3 is not a root of the homogeneous equation, we try as a particular solution a constant, A. Substituting A into the complete equation and ignoring, for the moment, the stochastic term, we have

$$A - .9A + .2A = 1.2A - .9A = .3A = 3. \tag{A.117}$$

So A must equal 10. Now, for the stochastic term in the forcing function on the right-hand side of the complete equation, we try the trial solution $y_t = \sum_{i=1}^{\infty} \alpha_i \epsilon_{t-i}$. We then substitute this trial solution into the complete equation, this time ignoring the constant. To clarify how the lag in t is incorporated in the summation of the stochastic variable, we will write the full expansion of ϵ_t that appears when the solution for y_t is inserted in the original equation.[41] The left-hand side of equation A.114 will have the term

$$\epsilon_0 + \alpha_1 \epsilon_{t-1} + \alpha_2 \epsilon_{t-2} + \alpha_3 \epsilon_{t-3} \cdots \tag{A.118}$$

The summation of the stochastic term is lagged and multiplied by the respective coefficients on the right side of the complete equation. This yields

$$.9[\alpha_0 \epsilon_{t-1} + \alpha_1 \epsilon_{t-2} + \cdots] - .2[\alpha_0 \epsilon_{t-2} + \alpha_1 \epsilon_{t-3} + \cdots] + \epsilon_t. \tag{A.119}$$

If both sides are equal, the coefficient on each ϵ_{t-i} must be equal. This means the following set of restrictions must hold:

$$\alpha_0 = 1 \tag{A.120}$$

$$\alpha_1 = .9\alpha_0 \tag{A.121}$$

$$\alpha_2 = .9\alpha_1 - .2\alpha_0 \tag{A.122}$$

$$\alpha_3 = .9\alpha_2 - .2\alpha_1. \tag{A.123}$$

Notice that the first and second conditions in the list imply that $\alpha_1 = .9$. The third and fourth illuminate a recursive formula by which all the other α's can be found; namely, $\alpha_i = .9\alpha_{i-1} - .2\alpha_{i-2}$. With this formula, it easy to show that $\alpha_2 = .610, \alpha_3 = .369, \alpha_4 = .210$, etc. Thus, the total solution of this

---

[41] The equality for this stochastic trial solution is not affected by the constant. The constant is preserved by the trial solution we just found, $A = 10$.

second-order stochastic difference equation in equation A.114 is of the general form

$$y_t = 10 + C_1(.5)^t + C_2(.4)^t + \sum_{i=0}^{\infty} \alpha_i \epsilon_{t-i}, \tag{A.124}$$

where, again, the weights on the past history of realizations of ϵ_t are defined as $\alpha_0 = 1, \alpha_1 = .9$, and $\alpha_i = .9\alpha_{i-1} - .2\alpha_{i-2}$.[42]

As regards the initial conditions for this equation, say we know the values of y_0 and y_1. Technically, each value is, in part, the result of realizations of ϵ at times $t \le 0$. Formally, we have

$$y_0 = 10 + C_1 + C_2 + \sum_{i=0}^{\infty} \alpha_i \epsilon_{-i}. \tag{A.125}$$

$$y_1 = 10 + C_1(.5) + C_2(.4) + \sum_{i=0}^{\infty} \alpha_i \epsilon_{1-i}. \tag{A.126}$$

These equations can be rewritten and substituted into equation A.124. This will eliminate the C_1 and C_2, leaving a solution expressed solely in terms of y_0 and y_1.[43] Enders reports that this solution is

$$y_t = 10 + (.4)^t[5y_0 - 10y_1 + 50] + (.5)^t[10y_1 - 4y_0 - 60] + \sum_{i=0}^{t-2} \alpha_i \epsilon_{t-i}, \tag{A.127}$$

where the α_i weights are defined as before. Notice that this sum of realizations of the random variable extends back to $\epsilon_{t-(t-2)} = 2$ because this is a second-order equation.[44] Finally, with this fact, it is easy to show that the time function in equation A.127 preserves the initial conditions. For instance, if at $t = 0$ we have

$$y_0 = 10 + [5y_0 - 10y_1 + 50] + [10y_1 - 4y_0 - 60] \tag{A.128}$$

$$y_0 = 10 + 50 - 60 + 5y_0 - 4y_0 - 10y_1 + 10y_1$$

$$y_0 = y_0$$

We leave it as an exercise to demonstrate that the time function also preserves the value of y_1.

---

[42] Compare equations A.124 and A.47.

[43] For instance, we can use the equation for y_0 to solve for C_1, yielding the identity: $C_1 = y_0 - 10 - C_2 - \sum_{i=0}^{\infty} \alpha_i \epsilon_{-i}$.

[44] Again, note that we assume that the shocks are zero for all time points less than 2.

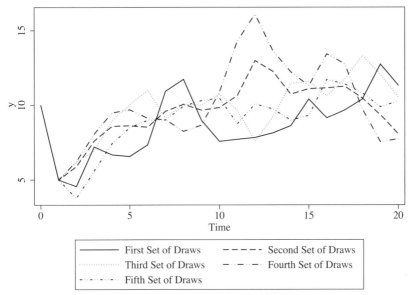

Illustrative Solutions to Equation A.114.

Figure A.13 depicts the solutions to equation A.114 for the initial conditions $y_0 = 10, y_1 = 5$, and several collections of realizations of the same random variable we used before in this Appendix; more specifically, five collections of draws of ϵ_t where ϵ_t is i.i.d. with mean zero and variance 1.[45] The deterministic elements always die out, and the series becomes a stochastic trend. Once more, the characteristics of the stochastic trend differ slightly depending on the collection of values of ϵ_t that are realized in each case. But, in our illustration, these trends always remain in narrow bands.[46]

A.3.3 Solving Systems of Difference Equations

Higher order difference equations can be written as systems of lower order difference equations. And, as we pointed out in the introduction to this Appendix and illustrated in Example A.7, some social processes are characterized by mutual causation and feedback. Just as for single equations, there are numerous methods for solving systems of difference equations. For instance, Goldberg (1986, section 4.5) shows how the method of iteration yields a solution expressed in terms of t-th power of the matrix of the coefficients in the system. He then explains how this matrix can be expressed in the form of the

---

[45] We thank Patrick Brandt for help in constructing this figure. As regards the initial conditions, to better illustrate the influence of the deterministic and stochastic parts of the solution, y_0 and y_1 are different from those used by Enders (2010, 38–39).

[46] If we increased the variance in ϵ_t these bands would be wider.

solutions we studied earlier; this requires application of the concept of similarity for matrices or of the Cayley-Hamilton theorem. Transform methods also can be used to solve systems of difference equations.[47]

To demonstrate how a system of this kind can be solved, we employ a very simple method. Recall that the linear operater E is defined as the lead of a time series; $E(y_t) = y_{t+1}$. Rewrite the system of equations in equation A.53 with this operator:

$$EUS_t = .9US_t + C_t + t. \tag{A.129}$$

$$EC_t = .9C_t + .1US_t.$$

Now collect terms so that the two endogenous variables are on the left hand sides of the equations:

$$EUS_t - .9US_t - C_t = t. \tag{A.130}$$

$$-.1US_t + EC_t - .9C_t = 0.$$

This form of the system can be rewritten as

$$(E - .9)US_t - C_t = t. \tag{A.131}$$

$$-.1US_t + (E - .9)C_t = 0.$$

Multiply the first equation on both sides by (E-.9) and then add the resulting equation to the bottom equation in equation A.130. This yields

$$(E - .9)(E - .9)US_t - .1US_t = (E^2 - 1.8E + .71)US_t = .1t + 1. \tag{A.132}$$

But this is a familiar second-order difference equation similar to the equations we studied in subsection A.3.2. We therefore can use the same methods we illustrated there to find:[48]

$$US_t = C_1(1.2162)^t + C_2(.5838)^t - 1.111t - 13.58. \tag{A.133}$$

Then we can use the first equation in the original system to solve for C_t. According to this equality,

$$C_t = US_{t+1} - .9US_t - t. \tag{A.134}$$

---

[47] For an explanation of how a single higher order difference equation can be written as a systems of lesser order difference equations see Goldberg (1986, example 4, 233); see also Hamilton (1994, chapter 1). Goldberg's development of matrix methods is based on the analysis of two-dimensional Markov chain models. Cull, Flahive, and Robson (2005, chapter 7) is a more recent presentation of matrix methods, a presentation based on the concept of a collection of related, linear recurrences; see also Elaydi (1999, chapters 3 and 4).

[48] For instance, equation A.132 indicates that the characteristic equation for US_t is a second-order polynomial. We therefore can use the quadratic formula to find the roots of 1.2162 and .5838. And because the forcing function is t, for our particular solution, we can try the trial solution $A_0 + A_1 t$. This yields $A_0 = -13.58$ and $A_1 = -1.111$.

All we need to do is evaluate our solution for US_t at $t + 1$, subtract $.9 \times US_t$, and subtract t. This gives us the solution we seek for Chinese naval spending:

$$C_t = .3162C_1(1.2162)^t - .3162C_2(.5838)^t - 1.1112t - 2.4689 \quad \text{(A.135)}$$

To solve for the values of $C_{1,2}$, we set $t = 0$ in both solutions. This produces another system of two equations and two unknowns:

$$C_1 + C_2 - 13.58 = 50. \quad \text{(A.136)}$$

$$.3162C_1 - .3162C_2 - 2.4689 = 20.$$

The solutions are $C_1 = 67.3168, C_2 = -3.738$. Substituting these values into the total solutions for US_t, C_t, we obtain the final solutions reported in Example A.7:

$$US_t = 67.3168(1.2162)^t - 3.738(.5838)^t - 1.1112t - 13.58. \quad \text{(A.137)}$$

$$C_t = 21.287(1.2162)^t + 1.1820(.5838)^t - 1.1112t - 2.4689.$$

Earlier in the Appendix, we graphed this solution in Figure A.7. This figure showed how the solution predicts an eventual monotonic increase in naval spending for both the United States and China. But as you understand by now, if the system was structured differently or the coefficients had different values, the arms race could have looked quite different. If the roots of the respective homogeneous equation(s) had been imaginary, cyclical spending patterns could have been predicted, for instance.

A.4 BRING ON THE DATA

The Appendix shows how to induce the functional forms of our difference equations from data and how to evaluate the empirical power of the functional forms we posit on the basis of our theoretical understanding of social processes. The difference equations we induce or posit imply particular (mixes of) time paths for our variables. Each functional form implies exponential, trigonometric, and/or stochastic functions, the combination of which produces qualitatively different paths. Hence the functional forms have different implications for how (if) a social process equilibrates.

Bibliography

Abramson, Paul R. and Charles W. Jr. Ostrom. 1991. "Macropartisanship: An Empirical Reassessment." *American Political Science Review* 85(1):181–192.

Achen, Christopher H. 2000. "Why Lagged Dependent Variables Can Suppress the Explanatory Power of Other Independent Variables." Paper presented at the Annual Meeting of Political Methodology, Los Angeles.

Ahking, Francis. 2002. "Model Mis-specification and Johansen's Cointegration Analysis: An Application to the U.S. Money Demand." *Journal of Macroeconomics* 24(1):51–66.

Andersen, Torben G. and Tim Bollerslev. 1997. "Intraday Periodicity and Volatility Persistence in Financial Markets." *Journal of Empirical Finance* 4(2-3):115–158.

Andersen, T. G., T. Bollerslev, F. X. Diebold, and H. Ebens. 2001. "The Distribution of Realized Stock Return Volatility." *Journal of Financial Economics* 61(1):43–76.

Andrews, Donald W. K. 1991. "Heteroscedasticity and Autocorrelation Consistent Covariance Matrix Estimation." *Econometrica* 59(3):817–858.

Andrews, Donald W. K. 1993. "Tests for Parameter Instability and Structural Change with Unknown Change Point." *Econometrica* 61(4):821–856.

Ashley, Richard. 1998. "A New Technique for Postsample Model Selection and Validation." *Journal of Economic Dynamics and Control* 22(5):647–665.

Bai, Jushan. 1994. "Least Squares Estimation of a Shift in Linear Processes." *Journal of Time Series Analysis* 15(5):453–472.

Bai, Jushan and Pierre Perron. 1998. "Estimating and Testing Linear Models with Multiple Structural Changes." *Econometrica* 66(1):47–78.

Bai, Jushan and Pierre Perron. 2003. "Computation and Analysis of Multiple Structural Change Models." *Journal of Applied Econometrics* 18(1):1–22.

Bailey, W. C. 1974. "Murder and the Death Penalty." *Journal of Criminal Law and Criminology* 65(3):416–423.

Baillie, Richard T. 1996. "Long Memory Processes and Fractional Integration in Econometrics." *Journal of Econometrics* 73(1):5–59.

Baillie, Richard T. and Tim Bollerslev. 1989. "Common Stochastic Trends in a System of Exchange Rates." *Journal of Finance* 44(1):167–181.

Baillie, Richard T. and Tim Bollerslev. 1994. "Cointegration, Fractional Cointegration, and Exchange Rate Dynamics." *Journal of Finance* 49(2):737–745.

Baillie, Richard T., Ching-Fan Chung, and Margie A. Tieslau. 1996. "Analyzing Inflation Integration in Econometrics." *Journal of Econometrics* 70:5–59.

Banerjee, Anindya, Juan Dolado, J. W. Galbraith, and David Hendry. 1993. *Co-Integration, Error Correction, and the Econometric Analysis of Non-stationary Data.* Oxford: Oxford University Press.

Barkoulas, John, Christopher F. Baum, and Mustafa Caglayan. 1997. "Fractional Monetary Dynamics." Working Paper. Boston: Boston College.

Barkoulas, John and Christopher F. Baum. 2006. "Long-Memory Forecasting of US Monetary Indices." *Journal of Forecasting* 25(4):291–302.

Bartlett, Maurice S. 1955. *An Introduction to Stochastic Process.* Cambridge: Cambridge University Press.

Baumer, Eric P., Steven F. Messner, and Richard Rosenfeld. 2003. "Explaining Spatial Variation in Support for Capital Punishment: A Multilevel Analysis." *American Journal of Sociology* 108(4):844–875.

Bauwens, Luc, Sébastien Laurent, and Jeroen V. K. Rombouts. 2006. "Multivariate GARCH Models: A Survey." *Journal of Applied Econometrics* 21(1):79–109.

Beck, Nathaniel. 1991. "The Illusion of Cycles in International Relations." *International Studies Quarterly* 35(4):455–476.

Beck, Nathaniel. 1992. "The Methodology of Cointegration." *Political Analysis* 4:237–247.

Beck, Nathaniel. 2012. "Sweeping Fewer Things under the Rug: Tis Often (Usually?) Better to Model than Be Robust." Paper Presented at the Annual Meeting of the Society for Political Methodology, University of North Carolina, Chapel Hill.

Beck, Nathaniel and Jonathan N. Katz. 1996. "Nuisance vs. Substance: Specifying and Estimating Time-Series-Cross-Section Models." *Political Analysis* 6(1):1–36.

Beck, Nathaniel and Jonathan N. Katz. 2011. "Modeling Dynamics in Time-Series-Cross-Section Political Economy Data." *Annual Review of Political Science* 14:331–352.

Beran, Jan. 1994. *Statistics for Long-Memory Processes.* Boca Raton, FL: CRC Press.

Bollerslev, Tim. 1987. "A Conditionally Heteroskedastic Time Series Model for Speculative Prices and Rates of Return." *Review of Economics and Statistics* 69(3):542–547.

Bowerman, Bruce L., Richard O'Connell, and Anne B. Koehler. 2004. *Forecasting, Time Series, and Regression.* 4th ed. Belmont, CA: Thomson-Brooks/Cole.

Box, George E. P. and G. Jenkins. 1970. *Time-Series Analysis: Forecasting and Control.* San Francisco: Holden Day.

Box, George E. P. and G. Jenkins. 1976. *Time Series Analysis: Forecasting and Control.* 2nd ed. San Francisco: Holden-Day.

Box, George E. P., Gwilym M. Jenkins, and Gregory C. Reinsel. 2008. *Time Series Analysis: Forecasting and Control.* 4th ed. New York: John Wiley and Sons.

Box, George E. P. and David A. Pierce. 1970. "Distribution of Residual Autocorrelations in Autoregressive-Integrated Moving Average Time Series Models." *Journal of the American Statistical Association* 65(332):1509–1526.

Box, George E. P. and G. C. Tiao. 1975. "Intervention Analysis with Applications to Economic and Environmental Problems." *Journal of the American Statistical Association* 70(349):70–79.

Box-Steffensmeier, Janet M. and Bradford S. Jones. 2004. *Event History Modeling: A Guide for Social Scientists.* New York: Cambridge University Press.

Box-Steffensmeier, Janet M. and Tse-Min Lin. 1995. "A Dynamic Model of Campaign Spending in Congressional Elections." *Political Analysis* 6(1):37–66.

Box-Steffensmeier, Janet M. and Renee M. Smith. 1996. "The Dynamics of Aggregate Partisanship." *American Political Science Review* 90(3):567–580.

Box-Steffensmeier, Janet M. and Renee M. Smith. 1998. "Investigating Political Dynamics Using Fractional Integration Methods." *American Journal of Political Science* 42(2):661–689.

Box-Steffensmeier, Janet M. and Andrew R. Tomlinson. 2000. "Fractional Integration Methods in Political Science." *Electoral Studies* 19(1):63–76.

Brandt, Patrick T. and John R. Freeman. 2006. "Advances in Bayesian Time Series Modeling and the Study of Politics: Theory Testing, Forecasting, and Policy Analysis." *Political Analysis* 14(1):1–36.

Brandt, Patrick T. and John R. Freeman. 2009. "Modeling Macro-Political Dynamics." *Political Analysis* 17(2):113–142.

Brandt, Patrick T., John R. Freeman, and Philip A. Schrodt. 2011. "Real Time, Time Series Forecasting of Inter-and Intra-State Political Conflict." *Conflict Management and Peace Science* 28(1):41–64.

Brandt, Patrick T. and John T. Williams. 2007. *Modeling Multiple Time Series.* Thousand Oaks, CA: Sage Publications.

Brockwell, P. J. and R. A. Davis. 2003. *Introduction to Time Series and Forecasting.* New York: Springer Verlag.

Bueno de Mesquita, Bruce. 1997. "A Decision Making Model: Its Structure and Form." *International Interactions* 23(2):235–266.

Campbell, Angus, Philip E. Converse, Warren E. Miller, and Donald E. Stokes. 1968. *The American Voter.* Chicago: University of Chicago Press.

Campbell, D. T. and H. L. Ross. 1968. "The Connecticut Crackdown on Speeding: Time-Series Data in Quasi-Experimental Analysis." *Law and Society Review* 3(1):33–53.

Cantor, David and Kenneth C. Land. 2001. "Unemployment and Crime Rate Fluctuations: A Comment on Greenberg." *Journal of Quantitative Criminology* 17(4):329–342.

Caporale, Tony and Kevin Grier. 2005. "How Smart Is My Dummy? Time Series Tests for the Influence of Politics." *Political Analysis* 13(1):77–94.

Caporaso, James A. and Alan L. Pelowski. 1971. "Economic and Political Integration in Europe: A Time-Series Quasi-Experimental Analysis." *American Political Science Review* 65(2):418–433.

Chamlin, Mitchell B. 1988. "Crime and Arrests: An Autoregressive Integrated Moving Average (ARIMA) Approach." *Journal of Quantitative Criminology* 4(3):247–258.

Chatfield, Chris. 2003. *The Analysis of Time Series: An Introduction.* 6th ed. London: Chapman and Hall/CRC.

Cheung, Yin-Wong. 1993. "Long Memory in Foreign-Exchange Rates." *Journal of Business and Economic Statistics* 11(1):93–101.

Cheung, Yin-Wong and Kon S. Lai. 1993. "A Fractional Cointegration Analysis of Purchasing Power Parity." *Journal of Business and Economic Statistics* 11(1):103–112.

Choudhry, Taufiq. 1997. "Stock Return Volatility and World War II: Evidence from GARCH and GARCH-X Models." *International Journal of Finance and Economics* 2(1):17–28.

Christenson, Dino P. and Corwin Smidt. 2008. "The Visible Primary." http://visibleprimary.com. Last accessed April 28, 2014.

Clarke, Harold D., Marianne C. Stewart, and Paul F. Whiteley. 1998. "New Models for New Labour: The Political Economy of Labour Party Support, January 1992–April 1997." *American Political Science Review* 92(3):559–575.

Cochrane, John H. 1988. "How Big Is the Random Walk in GNP?" *Journal of Political Economy* 96(5):893–920.

Columbia Encyclopedia. (N.d.). New York: Columbia University Press.

Cooley, Thomas F. and Stephen F. Leroy. 1985. "Atheoretical Macroeconometrics: A Critique." *Journal of Monetary Economics* 16(3):283–308.

Cortes, Fernando, Adam Przeworski, and John Sprague. 1974. *Systems Analysis for Social Scientists.* New York: John Wiley and Sons.

Cox, Gary W. and Jonathan Katz. 1996. "Why Did the Incumbancy Advantage Grow?" *American Journal of Political Science* 40(2):478–497.

Cromwell, J., W. C. Labys, and E. Kouassi. 2000. "What Color Are Commodity Prices? A Fractal Analysis." *Empirical Economics* 25(4):563–580.

Cull, Paul, Mary Flahive, and Robby Robson. 2005. *Difference Equations: From Rabbits to Chaos.* New York: Springer.

Dagum, Estela Bee, Guy Huot, and Marietta Morry. 1988. "A New Look at an Old Problem: Finding Temporal Patterns in Homicide Series: The Canadian Case." *Canadian Journal of Statistics* 16(4):1749–1766.

Dahlhaus, Rainer. 1989. "Efficient Parameter Estimation for Self-Similar Processes." *Annals of Statistics* 17(4):1749–1766.

D'Alessio, Stewart J. and Lisa Stolzenberg. 1995. "The Impact of Sentencing Guidelines on Jail Incarceration in Minnesota." *Criminology* 33(2):283–302.

Davenport, Christian. 1996. "The Weight of the Past: Exploring Lagged Determinants of Political Repression." *Political Research Quarterly* 49(2):377–403.

Davidson, Russell and James G. MacKinnon. 1993. *Estimation and Inference in Econometrics.* New York: Oxford University Press.

DeBoef, Suzanna and Jim Granato. 1997. "Near-Integrated Data and the Analysis of Political Relationships." *American Journal of Political Science* 41(2):619–640.

DeBoef, Suzanna L. and Luke J. Keele. 2008. "Taking Time Seriously: Dynamic Regression." *American Journal of Political Science* 52(1):184–200.

DeFronzo, James. 1984. "Climate and Crime." *Environment and Behavior* 16(2):185–210.

De Gooijer, Jan G. and Rob J. Hyndman. 2006. "25 Years of Time Series Forecasting." *International Journal of Forecasting* 22(3):443–473.

Dejong, David N. and C. Dave. 2007. *Structural Macroeconometrics.* Princeton, NJ: Princeton University Press.

Dickey, David and Wayne A. Fuller. 1979. "Distribution of the Estimates for Autoregressive Time Series with a Unit Root." *Journal of the American Statistical Association* 74(366):427–431.

Dickey, David A., and Wayne A. Fuller. 1981. "Likelihood Ratio Statistics for Autoregressive Time Series with a Unit Root." *Econometrica* 49(4):1057–1072.

Dickinson, Matthew and Matthew Lebo. 2007. "Reexamining the Growth of the Institutional Presidency, 1940–2000." *Journal of Politics* 69(1):206–219.

Diebold, Francis X. 1989. "Random Walks vs. Fractional Integration: Power Comparisons of Scalar and Joint Tests of the Variance-Time Function." *Advances in Econometrics and Modeling* (15):29–45.

Diebold, Francis X. and Roberto S. Mariano. 1995. "Comparing Predictive Accuracy." *Journal of Business and Economic Statistics* 13(3):253–263.

Dolado, Juan J., Jesus Gonzalo, and Laura Maryoral. 2002. "A Fractional Dickey-Fuller Test for Unit Roots." *Econometrica* 70(5):1963–2006.

Dueker, Michael and Patrick K. Asea. 1997. "Working Paper 1995–003a: Non-Monotonic Long Memory Dynamics in Black-Market Exchange Rates." Federal Reserve Bank of St. Lans.

Dueker, Michael and Richard Startz. 1998. "Maximum-Likelihood Estimation of Fractional Cointegration with an Application to U.S. and Canadian Bond Rates." *Review of Economics and Statistics* 80(3):420–426.

Dunne, J. P. and R. Smith. 2007. *The Econometrics of Military Arms Races*. Cambridge, MA: Elsevier Science and Technology Books.

Durr, Robert H. 1992. "An Essay on Cointegration and Error Correction Models." *Political Analysis* (4):185–228.

Elaydi, Saber. 1999. *An Introduction to Difference Equations*. New York: Springer.

Enders, Walter. 2004. *Applied Econometric Time Series*. 2nd ed. Hoboken, NJ: John Wiley and Sons.

Enders, Walter. 2010. *Applied Econometric Time-Series*. 3rd ed. New York: John Wiley and Sons.

Enders, Walter and Todd Sandler. 2005. "After 9/11: Is It All Different Now?" *Journal of Conflict Resolution* 49(2):259–277.

Engle, Robert F. 1982. "Autoregressive Conditional Heteroscedasticity with Estimates of the Variance of United Kingdom Inflation." *Econometrica* 50(4):987–1007.

Engle, Robert F. 2002. "New Frontiers for ARCH Models." *Journal of Applied Econometrics* 17(5):425–446.

Engle, Robert F. and C. W. J. Granger. 1987. "Co-Integration and Error Correction: Representation, Estimation, and Testing." *Econometrica* 55(2):251–276.

Engle, Robert F., David Lilien, and Russell Robins. 1987. "Estimating Time Varying Risk Premia in the Term Structure: The ARCH-M Model." *Econometrica* 55(2):251–276.

Erikson, Robert S., Michael B. MacKuen, and James A. Stimson. 1998. "What Moves Macropartisanship? A Reply to Green, Palmquist and Schickler." *American Political Science Review* 92(4):901–912.

Erikson, Robert S., Michael B. MacKuen, and James A. Stimson. 2002. *The Macro Polity*. Cambridge: Cambridge University Press.

Ermisch, John. 1988. "Econometric Analysis of Birth Rate Dynamics in Britain." *Journal of Human Resources* 23(4):563–576.

Fair, Ray C. 1970. "The Estimation of Simultaneous Equation Models with Lagged Endogenous Variables and First Order Serially Correlated Errors." *Econometrica* 38(3):507–516.

Ferdere, J. Peter. 1996. "Oil Price Volatility and the Macroeconomy." *Journal of Macroeconomics* 18(1):1–26.

Fildes, Robert and Herman Steklerm. 2002. "The State of Macroeconomic Forecasting." *Journal of Macroeconomics* 24(4):435–468.

Franses, Philip Hans and Dick van Dijk. 2005. "The Forecasting Performance of Various Models for Seasonality and Nonlinearity for Quarterly Industrial Production." *International Journal of Forecasting* 21(1):87–102.

Franses, Philip Hans and Marius Ooms. 1997. "A Periodic Long-Memory Model for Quarterly UK Inflation." *International Journal of Forecasting* 13(1):117–126.

Freeman, John R. 1983. "Granger Causality and the Time Series Analysis of Political Relationships." *American Journal of Political Science* 27(2):327–358.

Freeman, John R. 1989. "Systematic Sampling, Temporal Aggregation, and the Study of Political Relationships." *Political Analysis* 1(1):61–98.

Freeman, John R., Jude C. Hays, and Helmut Stix. 2000. "Democracy and Markets: The Case of Exchange Rates." *American Journal of Political Science* 44(3):449–468.

Freeman, John R. and Daniel Houser. 1998. "A Computable Equilibrium Model for the Study of Political Economy." *American Journal of Political Science* 42(2):628–660.

Freeman, John R. and Daniel Houser. 2001. "Economic Consequences of Political Approval Management in Comparative Perspective." *Journal of Comparative Economics* 29(4):692–721.

Freeman, John R. and Duncan Snidal. 1983. "DeGustibus Non Est Disputandum? (There is no arguing about tastes?)." *Canadian Journal of Political Science* 16(1):155–160.

Freeman, John R., John T. Williams, and Tse-Min Lin. 1989. "Vector Autoregression and the Study of Politics." *American Journal of Political Science* 33(4):842–877.

Frühwirth-Schnatter, Sylvia. 2006. *Finite Mixture and Markov Switching Models*. New York: Springer.

Garratt, Anthony and Shaun P. Vahey. 2006. "UK Real-Time Macro Data Characteristics." *Economic Journal* 116(509):F119–F135.

Gelman, Andrew and Gary King. 1990. "Estimating Incumbency Advantage without Bias." *American Journal of Political Science* 34(4):1142–1164.

Geweke, John and Susan Porter-Hudak. 1983. "The Estimation and Application of Long Memory Time Series Models." *Journal of Time Series Analysis* 4:221–238.

Gilmour, John B. and Paul Rothstein. 1993. "Early Republican Retirement: A Cause of Democratic Dominance in the House of Representatives." *Legislative Studies Quarterly* 18(3):345–365.

Goldberg, Samuel. 1986. *Introduction to Difference Equations: With Illustrative Examples from Economics, Psychology, and Sociology*. New York: Dover Publications.

Golder, Matt. N.d. "Time Series Models." Available at https://files.nyu.edu/mrg217/public/timeseries.pdf.

Goldstein, Joshua S. 1988. *Long Cycles: Prosperity and War in the Modern Age*. New Haven, CT: Yale University Press.

Granato, Jim and Renee Smith. 1994a. "Exogeneity, Inference, and Granger Causality: Part I, The Stationary Case." *The Political Methodologist* 5(2):24–28.

Granato, Jim and Renee Smith. 1994b. "Exogeneity, Inference, and Granger Causality: Part II, The Case of Integrated Regressors." *The Political Methodologist* 6(1):23–26.

Granger, Clive W. 1981. "Some Properties of Time Series Data and Their Use in Econometric Model Specification." *Journal of Econometrics* 16(1):121–130.

Granger, Clive and Paul Newbold. 1974. "Spurious Regressions in Econometrics." *Journal of Econometrics* 2(2):111–120.

Granger, Clive W. and A. A. Weiss. 1983. "Time Series Analysis of Error-Correction Models." in Studies in Econometrics, Time Series, and Multivariate Statistics. New York: Academic Press, pp. 255–278.

Green, Donald P. and Bradley Palmquist. 1990. "Of Artifacts and Partisan Instability." *American Journal of Political Science* 34(3):872–902.

Green, Donald P., Bradley Palmquist, and Eric Schickler. 1998. "Macropartisanship: A Replication and Critique." *American Political Science Review* 92(4):883–899.

Greenberg, David F. 2001. "Time Series Analysis of Crime Rates." *Journal of Quantitative Criminology* 17(4):291–327.

Greene, William H. 2003. *Econometric Analysis.* 5th ed. Upper Saddle River, NJ: Prentice Hall.

Gronke, Paul and John Brehm. 2002. "History, Heterogeneity, and Presidential Approval: A Modified ARCH Approach." *Electoral Studies* 21(3):425–452.

Hamilton, J. D. 1994. *Time Series Analysis.* Princeton, NJ: Princeton University Press.

Hansen, H. and K. Juselius. 1995. *CATS in RATS. Manual to Cointegration Analysis of Time Series.* Evanston, IL: Estima.

Hardy, G. H. 1949. *A Course of Pure Mathematics.* New York: MacMillan.

Harvey, David, S. Leybourne, and P. Newbold. 1997. "Testing the Equality of Prediction Mean Squared Errors." *International Journal of Forecasting* 13(2):281–291.

Hatanaka, Michio. 1974. "An Efficient Two-Step Estimator for the Dynamic Adjustment Model with Autoregressive Errors." *Journal of Econometrics* 2(3):199–220.

Hays, Jude C., John R. Freeman, and Hans Nesseth. 2003. "Exchange Rate Volatility and Democratization in Emerging Market Countries." *International Studies Quarterly* 47(2):203–228.

Hendry, David F. 2003. "Forecasting Pitfalls." *Bulletin of EU and US Inflation and Macroeconomic Analysis* 100:65–82.

Heo, Uk. 1996. "The Political Economy of Defense Spending in South Korea." *Journal of Peace Research* 33(4):483–490.

Hetherington, Marc J. and Thomas J. Rudolph. 2008. "Priming, Performance, and the Dynamics of Political Trust." *Journal of Politics* 70(2):498–512.

Hibbs, Douglas A. Jr. 1973–1974. "Problems of Statistical Estimation and Causal Inference in Time-Series Regression Models." *Sociological Methodology* 5:252–308.

Hibbs, Douglas. 1982. "More on Economic Performance and Political Support in Britain." *American Political Science Review* 76(2):282–284.

Hooker, R. H. 1905. "On the Correlation of Successive Observations." *Journal of the Royal Statistical Society* 68(4):696–703.

Huckfeldt, R. Robert, Carol W. Kohfeld, and Thomas W. Likens. 1982. *Dynamic Modeling: An Introduction.* Beverly Hills, CA: Sage Publications.

Hurvich, Clifford M. and Kaizo I. Beltrao. 1993. "Asymptotics for the Low-Frequency Ordinates of the Periodogram of a Long-Memory Time Series." *Journal of Time Series Analysis* 14(5):455–472.

Hurvich, Clifford M., Rohit Deo, and Julia Brodsky. 1998. "The Mean Squared Error of Geweke and Porter-Hudak's Estimator of the Memory Parameter of a Long-Memory Time Series." *Journal of Time Series Analysis* 19(1):19–46.

Ingram, Beth F. and Charles H. Whiteman. 1994. "Supplanting the 'Minnesota' Prior: Forecasting Macroeconomic Time Series Using Real Business Cycle Model Priors." *Journal of Monetary Economics* 34(3):496–510.

Isard, Walter, Christine Smith, Charles Anderton. 1989. *Arms Races, Arms Control, and Conflict Analysis: Contributions from Peace Science and Peace Economics.* Cambridge, UK: Cambridge University Press.

Iqbal, Javed. 2011. "Forecasting Performance of Alternative Error Correction Models." MPRA Paper, University Library of Munich, Germany. Available at http://EconPapers.repec.org/RePEc:pra:mprapa:29826.

Jacobs, David and Jason T. Carmichael. 2002. "The Political Sociology of the Death Penalty: A Pooled Time-Series Analysis." *American Sociological Review* 67(1):109–131.

Jacobs, David and Ronald E. Helms. 1996. "Toward a Political Model of Incarceration: A Time-Series Examination of Multiple Explanations for Prison Admission Rates." *American Journal of Sociology* 102(2):323–357.

Johansen, Soren. 1988. "Statistical Analysis of Cointegration Vectors." *Journal of Economic Dynamics and Control* 12(2-3):231–254.

Johansen, Soren. 1995. *Likelihood-Based Inference in Cointegrated Vector Autoregressive Models.* Oxford: Oxford University Press.

Kapetanios, George, Yongcheol Shin, and Andy Snell. 2006. "Testing for Cointegration in Nonlinear Smooth Transition Error Correction Models." *Econometric Theory* 22(2):279–303.

Keele, Luke J. and Nathan J. Kelly. 2006. "Dynamic Models for Dynamic Theories: The Ins and Outs of Lagged Dependent Variables." *Political Analysis* 14(2):186.

Kelley, Walter G. and Allan C. Peterson. 2001. *Difference Equations: An Introduction with Applications.* San Dieto, CA: Harcourt Academic Press.

Kennedy, Peter. 2008. *A Guide to Econometrics.* 6th ed. Cambridge, MA: MIT Press.

Kilic, Rehim. 2011. "Testing for Co-Integration and Nonlinear Adjustment in a Smooth Transition Error Correction Model." *Journal of Time Series Analysis* 32(6):647–660.

Kim, Chang-Jin and Charles R. Nelson. 1999. "Has the U.S. Economy Become More Stable? A Bayesian Approach Based on a Markov-Switching Model of the Business Cycle." *Review of Economics and Statistics* 81(4):608–616.

King, Anthony and Robert J. Wybrow. 2001. *British Public Opinion: 1937–2000, The Gallup Polls.* London: Politico's Publishing.

Kinlay, Jonathan. 2005. "Forecasting and Trading Volatility in the S&P 500 Index: An Empirical Test of Options Market Efficiency." Available at http://www.investmentanalytics.com.

Knopf, Jeffrey W. 1998. "How Rational Is the Rational Public? Evidence from US Public Opinion on Military Spending." *Journal of Conflict Resolution* 42(5):544–571.

Kou, S. G. and Michael E. Sobel. 2004. "Forecasting the Vote: A Theoretical Comparison of Election Markets and Public Opinion Polls." *Political Analysis* 12(3):277–295.

Krolzig, Hans-Martin. 1997. *Markov Switching Vector Autoregressions. Modelling, Statistical Inference and Application to Business Cycle Analysis.* Berlin: Springer.

Kwiatkowski, Denis, Peter C. B. Phillips, Peter Schmidt, and Yongcheol Shin. 1992. "Testing the Null Hypothesis of Stationarity against the Alternative of a Unit

Root: How Sure Are We That Economic Time Series Have a Unit Root?" *Journal of Econometrics* 54(1):159–178.

Kydland, Finn E. and Edward C. Prescott. 1991. "The Econometrics of the General Equilibrium Approach to Business Cycles." *Scandinavian Journal of Economics* 93(2):161–178.

Land, Kenneth C., Raymond H. C. Teske Jr., and Hui Zheng. 2009. "The Short-Term Effects of Executions on Homicides: Deterrence, Displacement, or Both?" *Criminology* 47(4):1009–1043.

Lebo, Matthew and Janet M. Box-Steffensmeier. 2008. "Dynamic Conditional Correlations in Political Science." *American Journal of Political Science* 52(3):688–704.

Lebo, Matthew, Adam J. McGlynn, and Gregory Koger. 2007. "Strategic Party Government: Party Influence in Congress, 1789–2000." *American Journal of Political Science* 51(3):464–481.

Lebo, Matthew and WIll Moore. 2003. "Dynamic Foreign Policy Behavior." *Journal of Conflict Resolution* 47(1):13–32.

Lebo, M., R. W. Walker, and Harold D. Clarke. 2000. "You Must Remember This: Dealing with Long Memory in Political Analyses." *Electoral Studies* 19(2):31–48.

Levitt, Steven D. 2001. "Alternative Strategies for Identifying the Link between Unemployment and Crime." *Journal of Quantitative Criminology* 17(4):377–390.

Lewis-Beck, Michael S. 1979. "Some Economic Effects of Revolution: Models, Measurement, and the Cuban Evidence." *American Journal of Sociology* 84(5):1127–1149.

Lien, Donald and Yiu Kuen Tse. 1999. "Fractional Cointegration and Futures Hedging." *Journal of Futures Markets* 19(4):457–474.

Lin, Zhiqiu and Augustine Brannigan. 2003. "Advances in the Analysis of Non-Stationary Time Series: An Illustration of Cointegration and Error Correction Methods in Research on Crime and Immigration." *Quality and Quantity* 37(2):151–168.

Liu, C. Y. and He J. 1991. "A Variance Ratio Test of Random Walks in Foreign Exchange Rates." *Journal of Finance* 46(2):773–785.

Ljung, G. M. and G. E. P. Box. 1978. "On a Measure of Lack of Fit in Time Series Models." *Biometrika* 65(2):297–303.

Ljungqvist, Lars and Thomas J. Sargent. 2000. *Recursive Macroeconomic Theory*. Cambridge, MA: MIT Press.

Lo, Andrew. 1991. "Long-Term Memory in Stock Market Prices." *Econometrica* 59(5):1279–1313.

Lo, Andrew and Craig MacKinlay. 1988. "Stock Market Prices Do Not Follow Random Walks: Evidence from a Simple Specification Test." *Review of Financial Studies* 1(1):41–66.

Lucas, Robert Jr., Nancy Stokey, and Edward C. Prescott. 1989. *Recursive Methods in Economic Dynamics*. Cambridge, MA: Harvard University Press.

Lütkepohl, Helmut. 2005. *New Introduction to Multiple Time Series Analysis*. Berlin: Springer-Verlag.

MacKuen, Michael B., Robert S. Erikson, and James A. Stimson. 1989. "Macropartisanship." *American Political Science Review* 83(4):1125–1142.

MacKuen, Michael B., Robert S. Erikson, and James A. Stimson. 1992. "Peasants or Bankers? The American Electorate and the U.S. Economy." *American Political Science Review* 86(3):597–611.

Maddala, G. S. and In-Moo Kim. 1998. *Unit Roots, Cointegration, and Structural Change*. New York: Cambridge University Press.

Maestas, Cherie and Robert R. Preuhs. 2000. "Modeling Volatility in Political Time Series." *Electoral Studies* 19(1):95–110.

Majeksi, Stephen J. 1985. "Expectations and Arms Races." *American Journal of Political Science* 29(2):217–245.

Makridakis, Spyros, A. Anderson, R. Carbone, R. Fildes, M. Hibon, R. Lewandowski, J. Newton, E. Parzen, and R. Winkler. 1984. *The Accuracy of Time Series Methods*. New York: John Wiley and Sons.

Makridakis, S., C. Chatfield, M. Hibon, M. Lawrence, T. Mills, K. Ord, and L. F. Simmons. 1993. "The M2-Competition: A Real-Time Judgmentally Based Forecasting Study." *International Journal of Forecasting* 9(1):5–22.

Makridakis, Spyros and M. Hibon. 2000. "The M3-Competition: Results, Conclusions and Implications." *International Journal of Forecasting* 16(4):451–476.

Marinucci, D., & Robinson, P. M. 2001. Semiparametric fractional cointegration analysis. *Journal of Econometrics* 105(1):225–247.

McCleary, Richard and Richard A. Hay. 1980. *Applied Time Series for the Social Sciences*. Beverly Hills: Sage Publications.

McDowall, David. 2002. "Tests of Nonlinear Dynamics in U.S. Homicide Time Series, and Their Implications." *Criminology* 40(3):711–736.

McDowall, David and Colin Loftin. 2005. "Are U.S. Crime Rate Trends Historically Contingent?" *Journal of Research in Crime and Deliquency* 42(4):359–383.

McDowall, David, Colin Loftin, and Matthew Pate. 2012. "Seasonal Cycles in Crime, and Their Variability." *Journal of Quantitative Criminology* 28(3):389–410.

McDowall, David, Richard McCleary, Errol Meidinger, and Richard A. Hay. 1980. *Interrupted Time Series Analysis*. Beverly Hills, CA: Sage Publications.

McDowell, Allen. 2004. "From the Help Desk: Polynomial Distributed Lag Models." *Stata Journal* 4:180–189.

McLeary, R. and R. A. Hay. 1980. *Applied Time Series Analysis for the Social Sciences*. Beverly Hills, CA: Sage Publications.

McLeod, A. Ian, Ian B. MacNeill, and Jahnabimala D. Bhattacharyya. 1985. "Seasonal Effects in Canadian Murders." *Canadian Journal of Statistics* 13(4):269–275.

Meade, Nigel. 2000. "Evidence for the Selection of Forecasting Methods." *Journal of Forecasting* 19(6):515–535.

Mebane, Walter R. Jr. 2000. "Coordination, Moderation, and Institutional Balancing in American Presidential and House Elections." *American Political Science Review* 94(1):37–57.

Mebane, Walter R. 2005. "Partisan Messages, Unconditional Strategies, and Coordination in American Elections." Revised version of a paper originally presented at the Annual Meeting of the Political Metholodolgy Society, Stanford University.

Merritt, Richard, Robert G. Muncaster, and Dina A. Zinnes. 1993. *International Event Data Developments: DDIR Phase II*. Ann Arbor: University of Michigan Press.

Miller, Michael P. 1994. "A Drunk and Her Dog: An Illustration of Cointegration and Error Correction." *The American Statistician* 48(1):37–39.

Monroe, Burt L. and Philip A. Schrodt. 2008. "Introduction to the Special Issue: The Statistical Analysis of Political Text." *Political Analysis* 16(4):351–355.

Monroe, Kristen R. 1978. "Economic Influences on Presidential Popularity." *Public Opinion Quarterly* 42(3):360–369.

Monroe, Kristen R. 1979. "'God of Vengeance and of Reward?': The Economy and Presidential Popularity." *Political Behavior* 1(4):301–329.

Montgomery, Alan L., Victor Zarnowitz, Ruey S. Tsay, and George C. Tiao. 1998. "Forecasting the U.S. Unemployment Rate." *Journal of the American Statistical Association* 93(442):478–493.

Muth, Eginhard J. 1977. *Transform Methods with Applications to Engineering and Operations Research*. Englewood Cliffs, NJ: Prentice Hall.

Neill, Christine, and Andrew Leigh. 2008. "Do Gun Buy-Backs Save Lives-Evidence from Time Series Variation." *Current Issues in Criminal Justice* 20(2):145–162.

Neill, Christine and Andrew Leigh. 2010. "Do Gun Buybacks Save Lives? Endux from Panel Data." American Law and Economics Review 12(2):509–557.

Newey, W. K. and K. D. West. 1987. "A Simple, Positive Semi-Definite, Heteroskedasticity and Autocorrelation Consistent Covariance Matrix." *Econometrica* 55(3):702–708.

Newton, H. Joseph. 1988. *Timeslab: A Time Series Analysis Laboratory*. Belmont, CA: Wadsworth Publishing.

Norpoth, Helmut and Thom Yantek. 1983. "Macroeconomic Conditions and Fluctuations of Presidential Popularity: The Question of Lagged Effects." *American Journal of Political Science* 27(4):785–807.

O'Brien, Robert M. and Jean Stockard. 2006. "A Common Explanation for the Changing Age Distributions of Suicide and Homicide in the United States, 1930 to 2000." *Social Forces* 84(3):1539–1557.

Olson, David E. and Michael D. Maltz. 2001. "Right-to-Carry Concealed Weapon Laws and Homicide in Large U.S. Counties: The Effect on Weapon Types, Victim Characteristics, and Victim-Offender Relationships." *Journal of Law and Economics* 44(S2):747–770.

Organski, A. F. K. 2000. *The Outcome of the Negotiations over the Status of Jerusalem: A Forecast*. Ann Arbor: University of Michigan Press, pp. 343–59.

Ostrom, Charles W. Jr. and Renee M. Smith. 1992. "Error Correction, Attitude Persistence, and Executive Rewards and Punishments: A Behavioral Theory of Presidential Approval." *Political Analysis* 4(1):127–183.

Pevehouse, Jon C. and Jason Brozek. 2010. "Time–Series Analysis." in *Oxford Handbook of Political Methodology*. Oxford: Oxford University Press, pp. 456–474.

Phillips, P. C. B. and P. Perron. 1988. "Testing for a Unit Root in Time Series." *Biometrika* 75(2):335–346.

Pierce, David A. 1977. "Relationships – and Lack Thereof – Between Economic Time Series, with Special Reference to Money and Interest Rates." *Journal of the American Statistical Association* 72(357):11–22.

Pindyck, Robert S. and Daniel L. Rubinfeld. 1998. *Microeconomics*. 4th ed. Upper Saddle River, NJ: Prentice Hall.

Powell, G. Bingham Jr. and Guy D. Whitten. 1993. "A Cross-National Analysis of Economic Voting: Taking Account of the Political Context." *American Journal of Political Science* 37(2):391–414.

Ray, B. K. 1993. "Modeling Long-Memory Processes for Optimal Long-Range Prediction." *Journal of Time Series Analysis* 14(5):511–525.

Reid, D. J. 1972. "A Comparison of Forecasting Techniques on Economic Time Series." In *Forecasting in Action*, Bramson, M. J., Helps, I. G. & Watson-Gandy, J. A. C. C., eds. Birmingham, U.K.: Operational Research Society.

Richards, Diana. 1993. "A Chaotic Model of Power Concentration in the International System." *International Studies Quarterly* 37(1):55–72.

Richards, Diana, ed. 2000. *Political Complexity: Nonlinear Models of Politics*. Ann Arbor: University of Michigan Press.

Robert H. Durr, John B. Gilmour, and Christina Wolbrecht. 1997. "Explaining Congressional Approval." *American Journal of Political Science* 41(1):175–207.

Robertson, John C. and Ellis W. Tallman. 1998. "Data Vintages and Measuring Forecast Model Performance." *Federal Reserve Bank of Atlanta Economic Review* (4):4–20.

Robinson, P. M. 1995. "Log-Periodogram Regression of Time Series with Long Range Dependence." *Annals of Statistics* 23(3):1048–1072.

Ruttenberg, Hattie. 1994. "The Limited Promise of Public Health Methodologies to Prevent Youth Violence." *Yale Law Journal* 103(7):1885–1912.

Sabasteanski, Anna. 2005. "Chronology of Significant Terrorist Incidents 1961–2005." *Patterns of Global Terrorism*, pp. 728–868.

Sabasteanski, Anna, ed. 2005. *Patterns of Global Terrorism 1985–2005: U.S. Department of State Reports with Supplementary Documents and Statistics*. Great Barrington, MA: Berkshire Publishing Group.

Samuelson, Larry. 1997. *Evolutionary Games and Equilibrium Selection*. Cambridge, MA: MIT Press.

Sanders, David, David Marsh, and Hugh Ward. 1993. "The Electoral Impact of Press Coverage of the British Economy, 1979–87." *British Journal of Political Science* 23(2):175–210.

Sandler, Todd and Keith Hartley. 1995. *The Economics of Defense*. Cambridge, UK: Cambridge University Press.

Sandler, Todd and Walter Enders. 2004. "An Economic Perspective on Transnational Terrorism." *European Journal of Political Economy* 20(2):301–316.

Sattler, Thomas, Patrick T. Brandt, and John R. Freeman. 2010. "Democratic Accountability in Open Economies." *Quarterly Journal of Political Science* 5(1):71–97.

Sattler, Thomas, John R. Freeman, and Patrick T. Brandt. 2008. "Political Accountability and the Room to Maneuver: A Search for a Causal Chain." *Comparative Political Studies* 41(9):1212–1239.

Schmidt, P. and P. C. B. Phillips. 1992. "LM Test for a Unit Root in the Presence of Deterministic Trend." *Oxford Bulletin of Economics and Statistics* 54(3):257–287.

Schrodt, Philip A. 1994. "The Statistical Characteristics of Event Data." *International Interactions* 20(1-2):35–53.

Schrodt, Philip A. and Deborah J. Gerner. 1997. "Empirical Indicators of Crisis Phase in the Middle East, 1979–1995." *Journal of Conflict Resolution* 41(4):529–552.

Shor, Boris, Joseph Bafumi, Luke Keele, and David Park. 2007. "A Bayesian Multilevel Modeling Approach to Time-Series Cross-Sectional Data." *Political Analysis* 15(2):165–181.

Sims, Christopher. 1980. "Macroeconomics and Reality." *Econometrica* 48(1):1–49.

Sims, Christopher A., James H. Stock, and Mark W. Watson. 1990. "Inference in Linear Time Series Models with Some Unit Roots." *Econometrica* 58(1):113–144.

Sims, Christopher A. and Tao Zha. 1998. "Bayesian Methods for Dynamic Multivariate Models." *International Economic Review* 39(4):949–968.

Sims, Christopher A. and Tao Zha. 1999. "Error Bands for Impulse Responses." *Econometrica* 67(5):1113–1156.

Smyth, Russell and Paresh Narayan. 2006. "Multiple Regime Shifts in Concurring and Dissenting Opinions on the U.S. Supreme Court." *Journal of Empirical Legal Studies* 3(1):79–98.

Sowell, Fallaw. 1992. "Maximum Likelihood Estimation of Stationary Univariate Fractionally Integrated Time Series Models." *Journal of Econometrics* 53(1):165–188.

Spiegel, Murray R. 1971. *Schaum's Outline of Theory and Problems of Calculus of Finite Differences and Difference Equations.* New York: McGraw-Hill.

Sprague, John. 1981. "One-Party Dominance in Legislatures." *Legislative Studies Quarterly* 6(2):259–285.

Steffensmeier, Darrell, Ben Feldmeyer, Casey T. Harris, and Jeffery T. Ulmer. 2011. "Reassessing Trends in Black Violent Crime, 1980–2008: Sorting Out the "Hispanic Effect" in Uniform Crime Reports Arrests, National Crime Victimization Survey Offender Estimates, and US Prisoner Counts." *Criminology* 49(1):197–251.

Stock, James and Mark Watson. 1988. "Testing for Common Trends." *Journal of the American Statistical Association* 83(404):1097–1107.

Stock, James H. and Mark W. Watson. 1993. "A Simple Estimator of Cointegrating Vectors in Higher Order Integrated Systems." *Econometrica* 61(4):783–820.

Stock, James H. and Mark W. Watson. 2006. "Forecasting with Many Predictors." *Handbook of Economic Forecasting.* New York: Elsevier, pp. 515–554.

Stock, James H. and Mark W. Watson. 2007. *Introduction to Econometrics.* 2nd ed. Boston: Addison, Wesley, Longman.

Strazicich, Mark C., J. Lee, and E. Day. 2004. "Are Incomes Converging among OECD Countries? Time Series Evidence with Two Structural Breaks." *Journal of Macroeconomics* 26:131–145.

Tahk, Alex, Jon A. Krosnick, Dean Lacy, and Laura Lowe. 2013. "Do the News Media Shape How Americans Think about Politics? New Statistical Procedures Cast New Light on an Old Hypothesis." Working Paper, University of Wisconsin.

Tennenbaum, Abraham N. and Edward L. Fink. 1994. "Temporal Regularities in Homicide: Cycles, Seasons, and Autoregression." *Journal of Quantitative Criminology* 10(2):317–342.

Theil, Henri. 1966. *Applied Economic Forecasting.* Amsterdam: North-Holland Publishing Company.

Tsay, Ruey S. 2002. *Analysis of Financial Time Series.* New York: John Wiley and Sons.

Wallis, Kenneth F. 1967. "Lagged Dependent Variables and Serially Correlated Errors: A Reappraisal of Three-Pass Least Squares." *Review of Economics and Statistics* 49(4):555–567.

Ward, Michael D. 1984. "Differential Paths to Parity: A Study of the Contemporary Arms Race." *American Political Science Review* 78(2):297–317.

Ward, Michael D. and Sheen Rajmaira. 1992. "Reciprocity and Norms in U.S.-Soviet Foreign Policy." *Journal of Conflict Resolution* 36(2):342–368.

Wawro, Gregory J. 2002. "Estimating Dynamic Panel Models in Political Science." *Political Analysis* 10(1):25–48.

Weisberg, Herbert F. and David Kimball. 1995. *Attitudinal Correlates of the 1992 Presidential Vote: Party Identification and Beyond.* Chatham, NJ: Chatham House.

Weisberg, Herbert F. and Charles E. Smith, Jr. 1991. "The Influence of the Economy on Party Identification in the Reagan Years." *Journal of Politics* 53(4):1077–1092.

Whiteley, Paul F. 1988. "The Causal Relationships between Issues, Candidate Evaluations, Party Identification, and Vote Choice – the View from 'Rolling Thunder.'" *Journal of Politics* 50(4):961–984.

Wood, Dan B. 2000. "Weak Theories and Parameter Instability: Using Flexible Least Squares to Take Time Varying Relationships Seriously." *American Journal of Political Science* 44(3):603–618.

Wray, Matt, Cynthia Colen, and Bernice Pescosolido. 2011. "The Sociology of Suicide." *Annual Review of Sociology* 37:505–528.

Yaffee, Robert A. and Monnie McGee. 2000. *An Introduction to Time Series Analysis and Forecasting: With Applications of SAS and SPSS.* Cambridge, MA: Elsevier Science and Technology.

Young, H. Peyton. 1993. "An Evolutionary Model of Bargaining." *Journal of Economic Theory* 59(1):145–168.

Yule, G. Udny. 1921. "On the Time-Correlation Problem, with Especial Reference to the Variate-Difference Correlation Method." *Journal of the Royal Statistical Society* 84(4):497–537.

Yule, G. Udny. 1926. "Why Do We Sometimes Get Nonsense-Correlations between Time-Series? A Study in Sampling and the Nature of Time-Series." *Journal of the Royal Statistical Society* 89(1):1–63.

Zeitzoff, Thomas. 2011. "Using Social Media to Measure Conflict Dynamics: An Application to the 2008–2009 Gaza Conflict." *Journal of Conflict Resolution* 55(6):938–969.

Zeileis, Achim, Christian Kleiber, Walter Kramer, and Kurt Hornik. 2003. "Testing and Dating of Structural Changes in Practice." *Computational Statistics and Data Analysis* 44(1):109–123.

Zimring, Franklin E. 1996. "Kids, Guns, and Homicide: Policy Notes on an Age-Specific Epidemic." *Law and Contemporary Problems* 59(1):25–37.

Zimring, Franklin E., Satyanshu K. Mukherjee, and Barrik Van Winkle. 1983. "Intimate Violence: A Study of Intersexual Homicide in Chicago." *University of Chicago Law Review* 50:910.

Zinnes, Dina A. and Robert G. Muncaster. 1984. "The Dynamics of Hostile Activity and the Prediction of War." *Journal of Conflict Resolution* 28(2):187–229.

Index